Frescobaldi Studies

Sources of Music and Their Interpretation
Duke Studies in Music

_____

GENERAL EDITOR   Peter Williams
ADVISORY EDITORS   Tilman Seebass,
Alexander Silbiger, R. Larry Todd

FRESCOBALDI STUDIES

Edited by Alexander Silbiger

DUKE UNIVERSITY PRESS   DURHAM 1987

© 1987 Duke University Press

All rights reserved

Printed in the United States of America on

acid-free paper ∞

Library of Congress Cataloging-in-Publication Data

Frescobaldi studies.

Collection of papers based on the Quadricentennial Frescobaldi
Conference, Madison, Wis., 1983.

Bibliography: p.

Includes index.

1. Frescobaldi, Girolamo, 1583–1643—Congresses.

I. Silbiger, Alexander, 1935–   . II. Quadricentennial
Frescobaldi Conference (1983 : Madison, Wis.)

ML410.F85F7   1987   786.5'092'4   86-32862

ISBN 0-8223-0711-1

IN MEMORIAM James H. Moore

Contents

On *Artificioso* Compositions at the Time of Frescobaldi

The Influence and Tradition of Frescobaldi's Works in the
Transalpine Countries

FRESCOBALDI'S INSTRUMENTAL MUSIC:
COMPOSITIONAL PROCEDURES AND RHETORIC   233

The Origins of Frescobaldi's Variation Canzonas Reappraised

Frescobaldi's Reworked Ensemble Canzonas

The Rhetorical Aspect of Frescobaldi's Musical Language

PERFORMANCE PRACTICES AND ORIGINAL
PERFORMANCE CONDITIONS   299

Tempo Relationships in Frescobaldi's *Primo Libro di Capricci*

Pier Francesco Valentini on Tactus and Proportion

The Liturgical Use of the Organ in Seventeenth-Century Italy:
New Documents, New Hypotheses

Preface

IN APRIL 1983 a group of scholars and musicians gathered on the Madison campus of the University of Wisconsin for an international conference on the Italian composer Girolamo Frescobaldi (1583–1643). The conference was the first of a number of events organized during that year to celebrate the 400th anniversary of the composer's birth.[1] For Frescobaldi scholarship, the Madison conference was, however, of special significance. It provided the first occasion in modern times for scholars from all over the world, who for many years had been working on this composer, to come together and discuss their common interests. On those present, the conference had an extraordinary impact, for reasons that—in retrospect—are not difficult to understand.

Intensive scholarly work on Frescobaldi commenced only some twenty years ago. To be sure, two basic studies on the composer, those by F. X. Haberl and by Alberto Cametti, date back much further.[2] By the beginning of this century, these two authors had established the basic outlines of our knowledge of the composer's life and had provided brief, largely descriptive surveys of his oeuvre. But during the following half-century, no scholar seems to have concentrated his research efforts on Frescobaldi. There was a scattering of archival contributions touching on the composer, a few biographies based almost entirely on the earlier studies by Haberl and Cametti, and some editions of his music.[3] Yet even the most comprehensive of these editions had made only a fraction of his works accessible.

Then, during the late 1960s and early '70s, a number of young American and European scholars, quite independently, turned their full attention to various aspects of Frescobaldi's life and works, and to related questions regarding early seventeenth-century music. A major stimulus to this renewed interest was undoubtedly provided by artists such as Gustav Leonhardt and Luigi Fernando Tagliavini, who, by their eloquent and stylistically informed performances on appropriate historical instruments, revealed, perhaps for the first time in centuries, the beauties and richness of Frescobaldi's keyboard music. An additional impetus was provided by the projected publication of a complete critical edition of his work, under the auspices of the Società italiana di musicologia.[4]

At first, most of these scholars worked by themselves and were barely aware of each other's efforts. They had no tradition to build upon, and each had to do his own groundwork, such as untangling the complex publication histories of the sources, about which no accurate information was available in the literature.[5] As time went on, more communication was established, and a remarkable spirit of cooperation evolved. Still, since most lived at great distance from one another, opportunities for a personal, intensive exchange of ideas were rare. Neither did the work of these scholars, in spite of its significance, succeed in penetrating far into the consciousness of the musical public at large, since most of it appeared in doctoral dissertations and in a few articles scattered over specialized European and American journals. The most comprehensive of these projects, Frederick Hammond's full-scale study on the composer's life and works, did not appear in book form until late in 1983.[6]

In light of this history, it should be clear why the gathering of many of these scholars in Madison to devote a few days exclusively to the discussion of this composer and his works was such a significant occasion. Out of the conference emerged a host of new insights on Frescobaldi, his music, and his times. The meeting also marked the beginning of a dialogue on unresolved issues, a discussion which was continued at subsequent meetings during the anniversary year in Boston, Ferrara, and elsewhere.[7]

An urgent need was felt at the Madison conference to disseminate its results to a wider public. We hope to accomplish this with the present publication, which brings together a set of articles that the authors have based on their presentations at the conference and the ensuing discussions. To provide a background for these papers, I have contributed "An Introduction to Frescobaldi," which presents a brief review of Frescobaldi's compositional development with emphasis on the composer's unprecedented explorations of instrumental styles and genres. The introduction also notes contributions to Frescobaldi scholarship since the Madison conference, and hence serves to update Frederick Hammond and Anthony Newcomb's bibliographies.[8]

The papers have been grouped under four general topics, corresponding roughly to the conference sessions at which they were originally presented. A few papers pertain to more than one of these topics, and hence their placement was somewhat arbitrary; for example, James Ladewig's study of the variation canzonas covers both the contributions of Frescobaldi's predecessors and the composer's own procedures. Each section is preceded by a brief summary of the papers it includes, with observations on their significance.

Most papers make frequent reference to the original seventeenth-century editions of Frescobaldi's works; these are cited in the form of short titles, for which a key is provided in the bibliography on p. 385, along with other pertinent information. All other citations are given in full at their first appearance in each paper, and in short form at subsequent appearances within the paper.

We wish to thank the many individuals and institutions who made the conference and the publication of this volume possible. Invaluable assistance for the conference was provided by many members of the administration, staff, and faculty of the University of Wisconsin–Madison, as well as by numerous graduate students; we wish in particular to acknowledge the enthusiastic support of Dean E. David Cronon of the College of Arts and Sciences and Dr. Eunice Boardman Meske, Director of the School of Music. The conference was aided by grants from the National Endowment for the Humanities, the University of Wisconsin Institute for Research in the Humanities, the University Lectures Committee, the Elvehjem Museum of Art, the Brittingham Fund, Inc., the Humanistic Foundation, the Knapp Bequest, the University of Wisconsin Consortium of the Arts, the William F. Vilas Trust Estate, and the Madison Chapter of the American Guild of Organists. We are indebted to Kenneth Kreitner, research assistant in the Department of Music of Duke University, and to Anne and Stephen Keyl of the Duke University Press for their careful editorial work on the manuscript. Finally, we wish to express our deep gratitude to Kathy Silbiger for her advice and assistance during many phases of the preparation of this book.

The essay by James Moore that concludes this volume is his last published work; this brilliant young scholar passed away during a research trip in Venice not long after the conference. His tragic death is mourned by all his friends and colleagues.

Alexander Silbiger
Durham, North Carolina
June 1986

Notes

1. Other events of scholarly significance included the Frescobaldi Symposium in Boston, Massachusetts (26 May), organized in conjunction with the Boston Early Music Festival; the Convegno internazionale di studi "Frescobaldi e il suo tempo" in Ferrara (9–14 September); and a session devoted largely to Frescobaldi topics at the Forty-Ninth Annual Meeting of the American Musicological Society in Louisville, Kentucky (27–30 October).

2. Franz Xaver Haberl, "Hieronymus Frescobaldi: Darstellung seines Lebensganges und Schaffens auf Grund archivalischer und bibliographischer Documente," *Kirchenmusikalisches Jahrbuch* 2 (1887): 67–82; and Alberto Cametti, "Girolamo Frescobaldi in Roma: 1604–1643," *Rivista musicale italiana* 15 (1908): 701–40.

3. See Frederick Hammond, *Girolamo Frescobaldi* (Cambridge, Mass.: Harvard University Press, 1983) and Anthony Newcomb, "Girolamo Frescobaldi," in *The New Grove Italian Baroque Masters* (New York: Norton, 1984), 83–133, for bibliographies of earlier studies and editions.

4. Frescobaldi, *Opere complete* (Milan: Suvini Zerboni, 1977–).

5. Comprehensive and accurate information on the publications has now been provided by Hammond and Mischiati; see the "Bibliography of Frescobaldi's Printed Collections, with Key to Short Titles," this volume.

6. Hammond, *Frescobaldi*.

7. See n. 1, above.

8. See n. 3, above. I wish to add here two recent significant contributions to Frescobaldi scholarship: Claudio Annibaldi, "La didattica del solco tracciato: Il codice chigiano Q.IV.29; da *Klavierbüchlein* d'ignoti a prima fonte frescobaldiana autografo," *Rivista italiana di musicologia* 20 (1985): 44–97; and Anthony Newcomb, "Frescobaldi's Toccatas and Their Stylistic Ancestry," *Proceedings of the Royal Musical Association* 111 (1984–85): 28–44.

An Introduction to Frescobaldi

ALEXANDER SILBIGER

F RESCOBALDI WAS A native of Ferrara, a city which during the fifteenth century had emerged as one of the foremost musical trend-setters in Europe—a position it maintained until 1598, when it lost its privileged status as seat of the Este court.[1] Through the years, the patronage of the art-loving Este family had brought many leading European composers to the city, among them Josquin, Obrecht, Willaert, and Rore. During Frescobaldi's youth there were extended visits by Wert and Gesualdo. The two musicians who probably exerted the most direct influence on the young composer were both Ferrarese: his teacher Luzzasco Luzzaschi and his older colleague Ercole Pasquini. Recently, new evidence has come to light concerning the impact of the Franco-Netherlandish-Italian contrapuntal tradition that flourished in Ferrara on Frescobaldi's compositional technique, a legacy that Frescobaldi in turn would pass on to later generations.[2]

The musical establishment at Ferrara collapsed in 1598 with the annexation of the city by the papacy; and when Frescobaldi's career as a publishing composer commenced in 1608, he had long since departed from the city. In his first publication, a collection of well-crafted but otherwise unremarkable madrigals, published during a sojourn in Brussels, the composer demonstrated his mastery over this fashionable medium of the time.[3] But in his next publication, issued only a few months later, he turned his back on contemporary fashions and embarked upon a road that eventually would lead to new styles for the world to emulate.

In the musical culture of Frescobaldi's time the literary text reigned supreme; to forward-looking composers, music's highest mission was to serve the word. Instrumental music, when needed, could be produced by "uneducated" musical technicians; it did not deserve the attention of great artists, and held little interest for composers such as Frescobaldi's great contemporary, Monteverdi. Yet Frescobaldi now turned his full attention to the exploration of this wordless sound, to the play of line against line, chord against chord, and he brought to this abstract world a range of emotional expression unsurpassed in the finest vocal music of his time.

The *Fantasie* of 1608 are complex works, exhaustive realizations of the potentials of seemingly simple musical subjects. The subtle spun-out fabric of overlapping voices, stretched to the limit by the avoidance of cadential closures, is more reminiscent of the Renaissance ricercars of Willaert and Giaches Brumel than of the instrumental polyphony of contemporaries such as Giovanni Gabrieli.[4]

During the early 1600s Frescobaldi had settled in Rome, and in 1608 he was appointed organist at St. Peter's, a post he held until his death. Although he was to enjoy the patronage of several important personages of his time, acknowledged in the dedications of his publications, he never listed any position in these publications but that of "organista di S. Pietro in Roma" (except in the *Arie musicali*, published in Florence while he was in the service of the Grand Duke of Tuscany [1628–34]).

In 1615, Frescobaldi issued two new publications of keyboard music, the *Recercari, et canzoni* and the *Toccate e partite d'intavolatura di cimbalo*. On the surface, these two collections appear to be a compendium of the varieties of genre in the keyboard music of the time. In truth, he redefined these genres, and introduced new norms that would be observed by many future generations. Each genre is represented in its purest form, as if to clarify its identity, and each is exemplified by a series of pieces that exhibit a wide range of possible realizations.

The distinction between the two volumes can be seen as a larger stylistic categorization, analogous to Monteverdi's *prima* and *seconda prattica* (although, of course, the relation to the text—the principal basis of Monteverdi's division—plays no role here), or to Christoph Bernhard's *stylus gravis* and *stylus luxurians*. The *Recercari, et canzoni* were published in four-part score and no instrument is mentioned in their title. Although they were no doubt conceived primarily for keyboard, they are, first of all, abstract works of musical counterpoint which could be realized by a harpsichordist, organist, or even by an instrumental ensemble. The *Toccate*, notated in two-stave keyboard score, were, on the other hand, medium-bound, as is indicated by their title and confirmed by their style.

Within each volume there are further subdivisions of this stylistic hierarchy. The ricercars in the *Recercari, et canzoni* represent the "old style" in a deliberately archaic manner and are models of sobriety. Unlike earlier ricercars and fantasias (including the composer's own *Fantasie*), no figurations in fast note values or sections in lighthearted triple meter are allowed to detract from their purity of style. The introduction of accidentals is severely restrained, resulting in a somewhat artificial modal idiom (in fact, closer to the modern than to the Renaissance conception of modality), and each ricercar represents a different mode, ordered according to a traditional scheme. Within that limited idiom, however, a different combination of contrapuntal artifices is displayed in each ricercar, thus illustrating the subclasses of the genre.[5]

The canzonas in this collection, although in a relatively conservative idiom, have less restrictive compositional premises than the ricercars and allow for a greater variety of metric organizations and rhythmic patterns. Their central device, the transformation of a subject through a series of clearly articulated sections, is also rooted in Ferrarese traditions; it was to be further developed in his later works in this genre.[6]

The joining of the ricercars and the canzonas in a single volume is appropriate, since the two genres, differentiated by contrasting character-istics within a shared stylistic tradition, evidently formed an especially fascinating duality in the minds of the composer and his contemporaries. Such dualities existed on different levels of the genre hierarchy, from the overall dichotomy of the old and new style to the romanesca/ruggiero and the ciaccona/passacaglia pairs; and the composer was to explore these dualities in several subsequent compositions.

Compared with the ricercars, the toccatas in the 1615 *Toccate e partite* stand at the other end of the stylistic spectrum. With these works Frescobaldi laid the foundation of the expressive keyboard style; they are the instrumental equivalents of the *seconda prattica* madrigals, which sacrifice the traditional rules of composition for the sake of the expres-sion of *affetti*. But, as with the ricercars, no two works are alike in charac-ter and structure. And as with the ricercars, the toccatas are kept stylistically "pure." Unlike many toccatas by earlier composers, no traditionally organized imitative segment is permitted to interrupt the free play of sound.[7]

A third style, which one could call the popular style, makes its appearance in this volume. It is represented by the *partite*, variations on traditional songs, and by a set of *correnti*. Actually, the *correnti* did not appear until the second edition of the volume, issued only months after the first version; they represent the "popular style" in its purest form. Although settings of dances and popular songs had formed part of the Italian keyboard repertory almost since its recorded beginnings, most earlier examples tend to be simple melody/bass settings, reinforced by triadic chords that follow each other with little regard for smooth voice leading. Frescobaldi introduced a more subtle and varied style in his dance and song settings, enlivened by a continual interplay of entering voices which vanish before they have a chance to burden the texture. The apparent simplicity of these charming dance tunes represents a side of Frescobaldi's art far removed from that of his works in the learned and expressive styles; but they must have found appreciative audiences in households all across Europe, since they made their way into the unpretentious dance manuscripts of many countries. Some of the *partite*, especially those on the romanesca and the ruggiero, contain a blend of the popular and expressive styles—the earliest examples of Frescobaldi's efforts to enrich keyboard music by the synthesis of different styles.

The publications of 1615 formed the first part of a canon of works that Frescobaldi would continue to revise, refine, and extend until his last years. Evidently he regarded the earlier publications of 1608 as youthful works that did not form part of this canon, since he never prepared revisions or reprints of these volumes.

The years 1624–28 produced a second wave of publications, which were no longer confined to keyboard music. In the *Capricci* of 1624, Frescobaldi explores a new genre. In spite of a few models, such as Giovanni de Macque's "Capriccio sopra re fa mi sol," the capriccio is very much Frescobaldi's creation, and demonstrates his compositional ingenuity and imagination at its highest level. A distinct idea, whether in the form of a musical theme or a compositional device, underlies each capriccio. Although for the most part the style is rigorously contrapuntal, the capriccios, unlike the ricercars and the canzonas, do not follow a circumscribed genre tradition, and each work treats its basic idea with an almost infinite diversity of techniques.[8]

In 1626 Frescobaldi prepared an edition which combined the *Recercari, et canzoni* and the *Capricci* in a single volume—an appropriate combination, since they shared the four-voiced contrapuntal texture and the open-score notation. The following year saw the publication of the *Secondo libro di toccate*. Although this volume includes some of the same genres as the first book, the conception of most of these genres is considerably broadened. This broadening is achieved in part by transgressions of the boundaries between these genres, so clearly defined in the 1615 collections. The toccatas cover a wider variety of types and styles, including the occasional insertion of canzona-like segments. Passages in various triple meters, absent in the first book, introduce a further element of variety. In addition, four toccatas are specifically designated for the organ; two are pedal toccatas and two are of the "per l'Elevatione" type.[9] The mixture of organ and harpsichord pieces, not found in the first book, is carried further by the inclusion of a group of liturgical plainchant variations, as well as by more dances and *partite*. Finally, another set of canzonas considerably extends the stylistic boundaries of this genre, in part by the admixture of toccata elements.

Of special interest among the *partite* are sets on the ciaccona and on the passacaglia. Frescobaldi appears to have been among the first composers to introduce these genres into the art music repertory, and may have been the first to juxtapose the two types. His sophisticated conceptions of these two genres were to serve as models for some time to come, but he appears not to have been happy with the particular guises in which they appeared here, because he omitted these settings in his subsequent revisions of the volume. The *partite* on the passacaglia is in fact atypical of his subsequent settings, in that it has a three-measure rather than a four-measure cursus.[10]

All of Frescobaldi's known published collections since the 1608 *Madrigali* had been devoted to keyboard music, but in the next four publications he temporarily turned his back on this medium and presented collections of sacred vocal, instrumental, and secular vocal ensemble music. There are indications that some of these volumes include works composed during earlier years, and probably all volumes gathered together ensemble pieces written over an extended period.[11] Nevertheless, as is the case with the keyboard publications (which, similarly, may have gathered earlier works), each volume presents a carefully planned and logically arranged series of pieces, demonstrating various types of possible compositions within a given framework.

The 1627 collection of thirty sacred works and the 1628 collection of forty ensemble canzonas are in many ways counterparts of one another. Each volume presents a series of pieces for one to four parts, in various combinations of high and low voices. Compared to the 1627 *Secondo libro di toccate*, both are written in a relatively conservative, restrained idiom that would make them suitable for liturgical use, although, unlike the keyboard ricercars, they are not written in a deliberately purified old style, and include numerous expressive *affetti*.[12] The two volumes of *Arie musicali* were published in 1630, when Frescobaldi served at the Medici court in Florence, but probably were written during earlier years in Rome.[13] Like the sacred concertos and the ensemble canzonas, the *Arie musicali* explore different combinations of high and low voices, but in addition they present a diversity of vocal genres, designated by the composer as canto in stile recitativo, aria, sonetto, madrigale, canzona, etc. Among these works are two genre pairs that Frescobaldi had coupled previously in keyboard settings: the romanesca/ruggiero and the ciaccona/passacaglia. Hence, in the *Arie musicali* one again sees the composer's ambition of providing compendia of different genres and styles within a particular compositional category.

Frescobaldi returned to Rome in 1634, and in the following year brought out another publication of keyboard music, the *Fiori musicali*. This is his only collection containing exclusively service music for the church, specifically for the celebration of the Mass, and it was to be his last publication devoted entirely to new works. The volume is organized not by genre, but according to the order of the Mass, and presents three cycles, for the Sunday Mass, the Mass of the Apostles, and the Mass of the Virgin.[14]

The *Fiori* cuts across several styles and genres, the only constraint being appropriateness to the dignity of the service. Virtually all genres found in his earlier works are represented here, except those in the popular style; his last contributions to the popular style would find a place in the supplement to his first book of toccatas, to appear a couple of years later.

Through the years, Frescobaldi continued to prepare new editions of some of his earlier collections. Probably the most thoroughly revised collection is that of the ensemble canzonas of 1634;[15] of the forty pieces, ten were entirely replaced, another sixteen were subject to various degrees of revision—further evidence, if any were needed, of Frescobaldi's concern not only for the text of individual works, but also for the contents of his collections as a whole. The added pieces include yet another ruggiero/romanesca pair.

In 1637 Frescobaldi brought out revisions of both books of toccatas. The first book includes a substantial supplement of new pieces in the popular style, entitled the "Aggiunta." Recently it has been shown that this supplement had been in preparation for some time and underwent considerable revision before its final publication; furthermore, Frescobaldi originally intended it to be added to his second rather than to his first book.[16]

The added works show that during his last years the composer became interested in the creation of extended compositions out of a succession of individual pieces. In some cases transitional passages provide musical continuity between the component pieces. Apparently a considerable amount of experimentation preceded the final products, which include several two-movement and three-movement sequences, as well as the lengthy *Cento partite sopra passacaglie*.

The composer seems to have had a special interest in refining his conception of the ciaccona/passacaglia pair. An example of one of these concludes all but one of the dance cycles, and their opposition (with a brief excursion to the *corrente*) forms the main subject of the *Cento partite*.

This last work, one of Frescobaldi's most impressive compositions, combines several pieces that originally were conceived as independent compositions. The final version is a masterful essay on the interplay between the passacaglia and ciaccona genres. The two genres are conceived dynamically rather than statically; they gradually change character, mode, and tempo, and become transformed into each other. To effect the transformations of rhythm and tempo, the composer introduces a number of notational devices which for years had puzzled scholars and performers but which were recently clarified by Etienne Darbellay.[17] A further extension of Frescobaldi's musical language in the "Aggiunta" is his use of nontraditional keys; in particular, several works are effectively in E minor (with the use of D-sharps).

Except for a new edition of the *Capricci* with only minor revisions, the 1637 volumes represent Frescobaldi's last publications. It has been suggested that some works surviving only in manuscript are compositions from his last years. A persuasive case could be made for the last three toccatas in Biblioteca Vaticana, Chigi Q.IV.25.[18] These works incorporate several new features that recur in the toccatas of Johann Jacob Froberger and Michelangelo Rossi, especially the inclusion of extended and sometimes motivically related canzona segments, and the exploration of unusual key areas. If these works are indeed authentic, they may represent the beginning of a third toccata cycle, left unfinished when the composer died in 1643.

Frescobaldi was the first of the great composers of the ancient Franco-Netherlandish-Italian tradition who chose to place the weight of his creative activity in instrumental music.[19] He systematically set out to give the medium a complex of styles worthy of this tradition, and to make the results available to the musical world by the publication of a comprehensive canon of his works. Such an undertaking was truly unprecedented and was to have profound long-range consequences; the contents of these publications were widely circulated and continued to provide compositional models to many later generations. The concentration on the abstract medium of instrumental music made these works independent of a particular language and, to some extent, of a particular culture and function. They provided valuable instructive examples to any composer concerned with the manipulation of tonal materials. His exhaustive explorations of the structural and expressive possibilities of the language of pure sound were to have a lasting impact on musical history. His works in the "learned style" assumed a role in the study of instrumental counterpoint comparable to that of Palestrina's works for vocal counterpoint. Indeed, recent studies have suggested that the instrumental polyphony of Frescobaldi rather than the vocal polyphony of Palestrina provided the models for the codification of counterpoint in Johann Joseph Fux's *Gradus ad Parnassum*, the textbook that has served as the basis for the teaching of this art to the present day.[20] And with regard to the long-lasting traditions of baroque keyboard composition, there is hardly a style, whether it be the fantastic style of the toccatas and preludes, the learned style of the fugues and canzonas, or the popular style of the dance suites and variations, that did not have its foundations in Frescobaldi's canon.[21]

But apart from his historical role, Frescobaldi continues to be a living reality in today's musical world. The unbridled passion and mystical ecstasy of his toccatas; the profundity and playfulness of his ricercars, canzonas, and capriccios; and the charm and grace of his dances and variations, whether in pure "historical" performances or in the most outlandish anachronistic arrangements, still excite and delight music lovers all over the world.

Notes

1. For detailed biographical information, see Frederick Hammond, *Girolamo Frescobaldi* (Cambridge, Mass.: Harvard University Press, 1983); recent additions to Frescobaldi's biography are presented in Hammond, Annibaldi, and Parisi, this volume, and in Dinko Fabris, "Risultati provvisori della ricerca presso l'Archivio Bentivoglio," in Sergio Durante and Dinko Fabris, eds., *Girolamo Frescobaldi: Nel quarto centenario della nascita,* Quaderni della Rivista italiana di musicologia 10 (Florence: Olschki, in press). Hammond's monograph and its bibliography serve also as reference for the subsequent discussion of Frescobaldi's works; in general, only publications that appeared too late to be included in his bibliography or that are still in press will be cited.

2. See Newcomb, this volume; on Ercole Pasquini, see Shindle, this volume.

3. The publication of a book of madrigals was a traditional means for a young composer to show that he had mastered his craft; in 1611 Heinrich Schütz concluded his apprenticeship under Giovanni Gabrieli with a similar *opus primum*.

4. See Newcomb, this volume.

5. See Durante, this volume, for a new approach to the intellectual background of this style.

6. See Ladewig, this volume.

7. For further discussion on Frescobaldi's toccatas, see Fadini, this volume; Anthony Newcomb, "Guardare ed ascoltare le *Toccate*," in Durante and Fabris, *Frescobaldi*; and Francesco Tasini, "'Vocalità' strumentale della toccata frescobaldiana: un linguaggio tradito," *Musica/Realtà* 4 (1983): 143–62.

8. On the *Capricci,* see Darbellay, this volume.

9. See Alexander Silbiger, *Italian Manuscript Sources of Seventeenth-Century Italian Keyboard Music* (Ann Arbor: UMI Research Press, 1980), 32–34.

10. See Thomas Walker, "Ciaccona and Passacaglia: Remarks on Their Origin and Early History," *Journal of the American Musicological Society* 21 (1968): 300–320.

11. The title of the 1627 volume of sacred concertos, *Liber secundus diversarum modulationum,* suggests that it was not Frescobaldi's first publication of this type. Furthermore, four individual concertos appeared in anthologies of works by various composers published in

1616, 1618, 1621, and 1625 (see Hammond, *Frescobaldi*, 317–18). Since the *Liber secundus* includes a concerto first published in the 1625 anthology, one can speculate that a *Liber primus* appeared between 1621 and 1624—a period that produced no other publications by the composer except for the *Capricci*.

12. On the sacred concertos, see Durante and Fabris, *Frescobaldi*; Jerome Roche, "I mottetti di Frescobaldi e la scelta dei testi nel primo Seicento"; G. Morche, "Freiheit und Zwang des Komponisten: zum *Liber secundus diversarum modulationum 1627* von Girolamo Frescobaldi"; Francesco Luisi, "Il *Liber secundus diversarum modulationum 1627*: Proposte di realizzazione della parte mancante"; and Christopher Stembridge, "Questioni di stile nella musica vocale di Frescobaldi." On the ensemble canzonas, see Harper and Ladewig, this volume, and Niels Martin Jensen, "La revisione delle *Canzoni* ed il suo significato per la comprensione del linguaggio frescobaldiano," in Durante and Fabris, *Frescobaldi*.

13. See Hill, this volume.

14. On the possible connections of this volume with Venice, see Moore, this volume.

15. See Harper, this volume.

16. See Etienne Darbellay, "New Light on the Chigi Manuscripts through an Investigation of the 'Aggiunta' (1637) to the First Book of Toccatas by Girolamo Frescobaldi" (paper delivered at the annual meeting of the American Musicological Society, Denver, 1981).

17. See Etienne Darbellay, "Les *Cento Partite* de Frescobaldi: Mètre, tempo et processus de composition: 1627–1637," in Durante and Fabris, *Frescobaldi*.

18. This case was first presented in Willi Apel, "Die handschriftliche Überlieferung der Klavierwerke Frescobaldis," in *Festschrift Karl Gustav Fellerer*, ed. Heinrich Hüschen (Regensburg: Bosse, 1962); see also Silbiger, *Italian Manuscript Sources*, 161–67. Support for a close connection of this manuscript with the composer was recently presented in Claudio Annibaldi, "Ancora sulle messe attribuite a Frescobaldi: Proposta di un profittevole scambio," in Durante and Fabris, *Frescobaldi*.

19. See Newcomb, this volume, on the connection of the composer with this tradition.

20. See Riedel, this volume.

21. Ibid.

Frescobaldi and His Patrons

T HE first three essays focus on a topic that increasingly is regarded as crucial for the understanding of the work of most early musicians: the relation between composer and patron. The close connection between the musical tastes and preferences of Frescobaldi's patrons and the direction of his compositional activity is a recurrent theme throughout Frederick Hammond's summary of newly discovered biographical information. Hammond fills in much interesting detail regarding Frescobaldi's relationship with his prominent protectors—the Bentivoglio, the Aldobrandini, the Medici, and the Barberini—and draws attention to some lesser-known patrons who nevertheless may have provided significant stimuli to his works. In addition some documents are presented related to other figures in Frescobaldi's circle—musicians, writers, and publishers—which offer revealing glimpses of the composer's personal life and character.

Claudio Annibaldi, taking as point of departure a legal battle between Frescobaldi and one of his patrons, examines the larger issue of patronage as a reflection of social attitudes of the time. He demythologizes idealized notions of the bond between benefactor and artist, showing that it was a highly paternalistic relationship, an "exchange of submission for protection" characteristic of the hierarchical structure of the society. His example points to the danger of interpreting biographical data by "common sense"—that is, by our own social experience—and thus, to the need for the biographer to become a historian as well.

Annibaldi's point is well illustrated by Susan Parisi's analysis of another, more significant event in Frescobaldi's life which had puzzled earlier biographers: his appointment in Mantua at one of Italy's most brilliant musical courts, and his abrupt resignation after only a few months' service. Drawing upon a large number of documents in the Mantuan archives—many presented here for the first time—Parisi examines this event in the light of the convoluted musical politics at the Gonzaga court, which in turn were the product of larger political events as well as of the musical interests and complex character of Duke Ferdinando. Her discussion of the musical and political machinations at the court extends well beyond Frescobaldi's brief presence and sheds light on the roles played by many other prominent musicians of the time, among them Frescobaldi's predecessor in Mantua, Claudio Monteverdi.

Girolamo Frescobaldi: New Biographical Information

FREDERICK HAMMOND

THE present essay comprises a summary of the new biographical material included in my *Girolamo Frescobaldi*,[1] a more extended examination of some of these points, and an updating with material that has appeared since then.

Ferrara

From Libanori's *Ferrara d'oro imbrunito* (1665–74) on, writers have referred to a relationship between Girolamo Frescobaldi of Ferrara and the homonymous noble family of Florence—a tradition still current among the Florentine Frescobaldi.[2] Such a relationship might be documented through the coat of arms of the Ferrarese Frescobaldi, but Libanori gave two differing descriptions of this: one identical with the arms of the Florentine Frescobaldi, the other bearing no relationship to it.[3] The famous letters concerning Girolamo Frescobaldi's possible employment at the Mantuan court are preserved in the Archivio di Stato of Mantua, their seals still attached and in some cases completely intact. These correspond not to the Florentine arms, but to the second seal described by Libanori: a gold and black chessboard, surmounted by three black pawns in a triangle on a gold field.[4] This therefore tends to lessen the probability of any close relationship with the Frescobaldi of Florence, but the very presence of a coat of arms confirms the respectable social position of the Ferrarese Frescobaldi.[5]

The question of the young Girolamo's musical training is one of considerable importance and interest. The sources, although still sparse and incomplete, have been augmented recently by two important documents:

a manuscript copy of Luzzascho Luzzaschi's second book of ricercars, the unique survivor of his volumes of keyboard music; and a letter stating that in 1607 Frescobaldi possessed a volume of ricercars by Adrian Willaert (perhaps the *Fantasie recercari et contrapunti a tre voci Di Adriano & de altri Autori* [Venice: Gardano, 1551, repr. 1559, 1593]).[6] The eventual examination of these two sources, and the investigation of other aspects of Ferrarese instrumental music ought to lead to a clearer understanding of the background of Frescobaldi's keyboard style and lessen still further its attribution to unlikely outside influences.[7]

Rome (to 1628)

Without doubt the most important study of Frescobaldi's relations with the Bentivoglio family, his first known patrons, in Rome is Anthony Newcomb's fascinating article in the *Gedenkschrift* for Mme. de Chambure.[8] To this material, as the result of my own researches in the Bentivoglio archive, I have been able to add a number of unpublished letters concerning Frescobaldi.[9] All of this material confirms the importance of the Bentivoglio in the career of the young musician, and especially the role of the head of the family, Enzo, rather than the better-known Guido. For example, the letters in the Bentivoglio archive document the decisive role played by Enzo in securing Girolamo's election as organist of the Cappella Giulia in 1608. The Ferrarese noble Monsignor Estense Tassoni, a cleric of St. Peter's, wrote to Enzo in August of 1608, "I am so much the more pleased in having favored Girolamo Frescobaldi for the place of organist here in St. Peter's, since I see that I have done a thing pleasing to Your Most Illustrious Lordship."[10] Frescobaldi's reluctance to travel to Rome in time for Enzo's arrival as Ferrarese ambassador to the Holy See is already known. Anthony Newcomb published an account of Girolamo's arrival in Rome and his first performances for the Cappella Giulia, contained in a letter from the Bentivoglio archive written by a certain Bernardo Bizzoni—an account quite different from that of Libanori, with the famous audience of thirty thousand.[11]

But the identity of the author of that letter is no less interesting than its contents. The writer can be identified with the "Bernardo Bizoni Romano" who wrote a manuscript account of the artistic journey made by the Marchese Vincenzo Giustiniani two years earlier, in 1606.[12] Accord-ing to the title page of this aesthetic odyssey, Bizzoni "accompanied the Marchese on the trip as companion, old friend, and confidant."[13] Other members of the Marchese's suite included the painter Pomarancio and, as courier and *maniscalco*, "Giuseppe Facconi from Mantua," probably a relative of the singer Paolo Facconi, who negotiated Frescobaldi's brief employment in Mantua. In March of 1606 Giustiniani stopped at Jesi, staying with Cardinal Gallo, uncle of the future dedicatee of Frescobaldi's *Toccate II*. In April Giustiniani and his suite arrived at Ferrara, where "the Marchese went to visit the Marchesa Bentivoglio, mother of Signor Guido, his great friend."[14] (Rather oddly, Isabella Bendidio devoted this inter-view to extorting from the forty-two-year-old Giustiniani a promise to stay away from Venetian prostitutes.)

Thus, the identification of Bizzoni shows that (contrary to the assertion of Giovanni Battista Doni, for example) Frescobaldi was hardly a stranger to the high culture of his time. Instead, as a new arrival he was already welcome in the circle of Giustiniani—the most rarefied cultural circle in Rome, full of names that were to recur in Girolamo's own career: Facconi, Gallo, Bentivoglio, and later the engraver Claude Mellan.

These unpublished letters from the Bentivoglio archive also add some piquant touches to the story of the disintegrating rapport between Frescobaldi and Enzo Bentivoglio in the matter of Girolamo's proposed marriage with the famous "Angiola" and subsequent events. In August 1609 a member of Enzo's household wrote him, "Girolamo of the spinet is saying that he does not want to marry Anzolla because his father has written him that he will give them both his curse. . . . We will have great trouble with this fool because we are in Rome and I cannot take him by force to make him marry her."[15] Frescobaldi eventually left the Bentivoglio, apparently returning only in 1612. His relations with his first patrons reached their nadir in 1613: "Signor Girollimo . . . has given lessons only a few times because he is taking a purge"; "Girollimo never comes here; and when he comes he shows [the pupil] two chords and goes off without caring"; "he always promises me that he will do better, but the poor man is half crazy as it seems to me."[16] However, even after his break with Enzo Bentivoglio and his entry into the service of Cardinal Pietro Aldobrandini, in 1615 Frescobaldi undertook the musical education of a young singer for Enzo's *musica*, working with Giovanni Bernardino Nanino, the Cavalier Marotta, and Marotta's wife, the celebrated singer Ippolita.[17]

Frescobaldi's trip to Mantua in 1615 is described in a series of letters published by Cametti and corrected and amplified by Susan Parisi.[18] The end of the story, however, was somewhat less unhappy than has been believed. In an unpublished letter to Duke Ferdinando Gonzaga, Frescobaldi thanked him for the gift of 300 scudi, in addition to the disappointing 143 1/2 scudi with which the Duke had rewarded the dedication of *Toccate I*.[19]

The present state of the Aldobrandini archive, damaged by a fire in Cardinal Pietro's *guardaroba* in 1617 and dispersed as a result of the Aldobrandini *fedecommesso*, furnishes little information on Frescobaldi's service with the cardinal: an inventory of musical instruments and an occasional reference in the cardinal's *libri mastro generale* to Frescobaldi's service for the music performed during the cardinal's banquets at the Villa Belvedere in Frascati (on one occasion for the melomane Cardinal Maurizio of Savoy, the patron of Michelangelo Rossi and Sigismondo d'India).[20] These references show that the performers were singers, accompanied probably by Frescobaldi on the harpsichord. From the *diari* of the Cappella Sistina it appears that the most frequent singers for Cardinal Pietro were Jeronimo Rossini and Ruggero Giovannelli.[21]

The most interesting aspect of the relationship between Frescobaldi and Cardinal Pietro was recently elucidated by Claudio Annibaldi: the history of the forced sale of the Frescobaldi house on Piazza Colonna (Orsola del Pino's dowry) to the cardinal. From the notary acts preserved in the Archivio di Stato in Rome it appears that the Frescobaldis contested the valuation of the house and brought suit against the cardinal. They won a revaluation of the property, but it was granted in shares and not in real estate—a Pyrrhic victory.[22]

The end of Frescobaldi's first Roman period is illuminated by a series of letters written from Rome between October 1623 and July 1625 by Francesco Toscani to his brother-in-law, the musician Francesco Nigetti, in Florence.[23] They regularly discuss an unidentified volume of music by Frescobaldi which was in the course of publication. Chronologically, the work in question is probably the 1624 edition of the *Capricci*, and Etienne Darbellay has shown that this identification is confirmed to a remarkable degree by the internal evidence of the volume itself.[24]

The *Capricci* (1624) were dedicated by Frescobaldi to Don Alfonso d'Este, Prince of Modena, and a previously unnoticed dedicatory letter in the Archivio di Stato of Modena recalls Girolamo's debt to Luzzaschi and to the house of Este.[25] (Three months earlier, Monteverdi had written that the Prince of Modena was "beginning to take pleasure in music,"[26] and these evidences of musical activity at the court of Modena are confirmed by the dedication of Sigismondo d'India's eighth book of madrigals [1624], works born "in the house of Este" and destined for a group of "the best singers that Europe can hear today.")[27]

The original print of the *Capricci* shows drastic *pentimenti* and insertions of material, and such a complex gestation and reworking is mirrored in Toscani's letters. On 21 October 1623 he wrote to Nigetti, "As to Frescobaldi, he has not published anything new except four madrigals to sing with the organ, without playing [probably the four secular pieces published 1621–22 in anthologies], which he says is not a good thing to send abroad. But nevertheless he is putting in order the book to send to Venice to print, since these printers here abide by a fixed price. Enough; when there is something new I will let you know." From then until 1625 the main theme of the letters is the same: the book is not finished. But along the way Toscani affords some glimpses of Frescobaldi from the life. On 24 February 1624: "This week I have spoken again to Frescobaldi about the book. He says that it will be in order in ten days, and I will send it to you." On 2 March: "As to the book of Frescobaldi, it is still not finished being printed, and I asked him the price of the aforesaid book: he told me we will be agreed. As to friendship, I have no knowledge that one can dispose it. *Basta*; he told me we will be agreed. I will see to it that as soon as it is in order I will send it to you." On 16 March: "The printing of the book is still not finished and I am grieved to the heart that it is not finished, which indeed distresses me. As soon as it will be finished, I will send it to you so that you may make use of it." On 27 April: "I forgot to tell you that the book is still not finished, but it is at the last folio, and Frescobaldi has told me all week that it will be completed, and I will send it to you immediately." On 14 June 1625 Toscani wrote, "As to the book of Frescobaldi, I went to find him and he told me that he has finished it, but at present he could not give it to me." On 28 June 1625: "I promised you to send you the book of Frescobaldi, but it was not possible, since he is a man so long drawn-out in his affairs as you could not believe, and this week I have been there every day. Finally he gave it to me. I had to stay at his house two full hours to wait while he corrected it, as you see, since the printer made some errors, but they are corrected."[28] (In fact, the first edition of the *Capricci* does contain a considerable number of printer's errors and doubtful readings.)

The terms in which Frescobaldi dedicated his next production, *Toccate II* (1627) to Luigi Gallo, Bishop of Ancona, Nuncio to Savoy, and nephew of the Dean of the College of Cardinals, who had traveled to Ferrara with Clement VIII, suggest a long and intimate rapport—"the long-standing service [*antica servitù*] that I have with you, since the time of the Most Illustrious Sig. Cardinal your Uncle." The praise of Gallo's prowess as a performer on the *Grauecembalo* suggests that he was a pupil of Frescobaldi.[29] Inasmuch as Gallo is the only contemporary keyboardist even mentioned—let alone praised—by Frescobaldi, he acquires a certain interest for the musicologist. (Although they make no reference to his musical abilities, the dispatches of the Venetian ambassador at Rome document Gallo's diplomatic failure as Nuncio of Savoy during these same years.)[30]

Florence (1628–34)

The details of Frescobaldi's Florentine period, almost six years, are the sparsest of all his mature life. It has been known that Frescobaldi was hired by the young Grand Duke of Tuscany, Ferdinando II, to whom he dedicated the *Canzoni* (Robletti, 1628). In 1629, Frescobaldi shared with Marco da Gagliano, the court maestro di cappella, the task of providing music for the canonization festivities of St. Andrea Corsini. Frescobaldi is mentioned only once in the voluminous court diaries of Tinghi, as performing in 1630 with two singers in the chamber of the grand duke's mother, the Archduchess Maria Maddalena of Austria, in the presence of Béthune, the French ambassador to Rome. In the same year Girolamo issued his two volumes of *Arie musicali* (through Galileo's printer Landini), the first book dedicated to the grand duke and the second to his Master of the Horse, Marchese Roberto Obizzi. Strangely, neither Girolamo nor any of his family appears in a detailed manuscript census of Florence taken in 1632.[31]

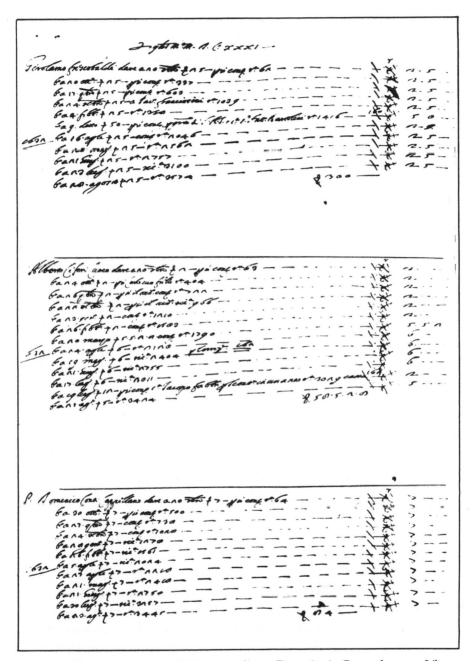

Plate 1. Florence, Archivio di Stato, mediceo, Depositeria Generale 1524, *Libro dei Salariati da S. A. S.*, September 1631–August 1632, c. 21.

It is possible to supplement this with new information. A book of *salariati* of the Tuscan court shows that Frescobaldi was paid twenty-five scudi a month (see plate 1)—more than any other court musician and a sum equal to the salary of the court sculptor, Pietro Tacca. Despite Libanori, there is no evidence that Frescobaldi was organist at San Lorenzo or at Santa Croce. However, in October 1630 he became organist of the Baptistery for a year.[32] In the same year he went with other court musicians (including Marco da Gagliano) for the dedication of the new cathedral of Colle Val d'Elsa.[33] Also in 1630 he made a visit to Venice, returning with a mosaic portrait for the grand duke.[34]

Some biographical details and an unusual testimony to Frescobaldi's reputation among Florentine musicians can be gathered from a Latin poem by Don Gregorio Rasi (1585–1658). Rasi was a Florentine priest and musician, teacher of the tenor, organist, and composer Don Onorato Maggi, who was one of the two singers named by Tinghi as performing with Frescobaldi. Gregorio Rasi was professed as a Vallombrosan monk in 1602 and was abbot of Vallombrosa from 1638 to 1642. The poem is addressed by its author to his nephew Giulio (1633–77), professed a Vallombrosan under the name of Francesco in 1648. This name was chosen in honor of another uncle, the famous singer Francesco Rasi, a Florentine who also served at the Mantuan court and in the retinue of Don Carlo Gesualdo at Ferrara (1594, 1595) and who created the roles of Aminta in Peri's *L'Euridice* and Apollo in Marco da Gagliano's *La Dafne*.[35]

> Girolamo Frescobaldi, of the choir of delights, the second Apollo of our age. Who, as he expressed the glory of all musicians not by unworthy imitation, so by the highest excellence of art he surpassed envy with his lyre. Whose penetrating talent and sweetness of genius declare that his soul is composed according to harmonic doctrine and is born for melody. Whom the City heard when he had barely attained the seventeenth year of his age playing instruments with wondrous skill, more by the heart [*corde*] than by the string [*chorda*], and was astonished. And who would not be astonished? With musical instruments he depicted human emotions, and measured the tones [*voces*] in them. Why should Italy envy Amphion of Thebes or their Orpheus of Thrace? This very Frescobaldi rendered all those of discernment, or men of raised eyebrows, who were enticed by number and sounding concord, motionless and almost stones. To the

player the Graces and the Muses thus seemed eagerly to arm his fingers, to give sweetness and to instill harmony in his fingers, so that where it was more compressed than all numbers this numbered sound, more perfect than all numbers, might everywhere flow. He is to be consecrated to the immortality of Fame by everlasting trumpets.

Well, nephew of his Francesco Rasi, lift up your soul. And propose to yourself for imitation this one man, whom all admire as the most distinguished of all the rest, like the sun among the stars. For thus [did] that most celebrated Francesco Rasi, your paternal uncle, whose name has not without reason been bestowed upon you, whom, when he was the leader of the art of music under the Most Serene Dukes of Mantua, not only Italy but even all Europe venerated. You follow virtue and glory; therefore dare to know; begin, and let delight, sweetness, but most of all holiness adorn your measures and harmonious sounds.

Don Gregorio Rasi, Abbot of Vallombrosa, once well-deserving of music, and although advanced in age, nonetheless he does not deign to be the disciple of such a man; [he], your uncle, dedicates this to his most sweet nephew.

This evidence of Frescobaldi's impact on cultivated Florentine musicians also poses a question. Rasi confirms Libanori's account of Girolamo's musical precocity and his musical travels in Italy. However, he does not identify the city that "heard, and was astonished." If it refers to Florence (and the Florentines did call their city simply "la Città"), it is of less interest. But if the classicizing Latin of Rasi employs *Urbs* in its traditional meaning, it implies that Frescobaldi was already present in Rome around 1600—perhaps with his teacher Luzzaschi in the suite of Cardinal Aldobrandini, or even with Cardinal Gallo.

This poem stresses the classical doctrine of music as harmony and sounding number (cf. the much-discussed "Discordia concors" block in the *Arie musicali*) in the context of Girolamo's work. This theme recurs in Girolamo's own prefaces and in the dedicatory letter of the *Capricci* (1624) to Alfonso d'Este, in which "the diversity of many sounds with ordered confusion is united to form a graceful harmony" as "magnanimity, goodness, valor, and other fine gifts" form the "virtuous harmony" of the prince's soul. It is significant that Rasi, an experienced professional musician closely related—in both senses of the word—to the tradition of Florentine music, connects Frescobaldi's instrumental music with the depiction of human emotion. Girolamo made the same connection in his own employment of the concept of *affetto*, which Caccini defined as "the force of various notes and various accents, tempering loud and soft; an expression of the words and of the concept, that are taken to be sung, fit to move emotion in the listener."[36]

John Hill's research has demonstrated the influence of the musical circle around Cardinal Montalto on the two volumes of *Arie musicali* that Frescobaldi published in Florence.[37] I would like to suggest a further reassessment of Girolamo's Florentine sojourn. Although he was nominally in the service of the grand duke, it is possible that Frescobaldi was more closely involved with the household of the Archduchess Maria Maddalena. The grand duke reached his majority in 1628, but liberated himself only gradually from the authority of his mother and grandmother. In 1631 Maria Maddalena died; in 1634 Ferdinando was betrothed to Vittoria della Rovere; in 1636 Christine of Lorraine died; and in 1637 Ferdinando's marriage was solemnized (an event symbolized by Pietro da Cortona's splendid cycle of frescoes in the Palazzo Pitti).[38]

The prevalence of religious texts (including a sonnet, "Maddalena al pie della Croce") in the *Arie* seems to mirror the piety of the two regents. (Maria Maddalena actually had herself painted as the repentant Magdalen.) Of the two dedicatees of the *Arie*, the grand duke disliked music, and Roberto Obizzi was more attuned to the clash of arms, as in the tourney that he presented in Ferrara in 1638. Certainly the lack of information about Frescobaldi's activities in Florence after 1630 is largely owing to the terrible plague of those years, but perhaps also to the death of the archduchess in 1631. Frescobaldi's presence at the Tuscan court after that date was perhaps not entirely voluntary: in April 1631 the Venetian ambassador wrote from Rome, "All those who leave this City to go in the places where the *malaria* has been, may not return except with the complete health of all Italy."[39]

Rome (1634–43)

The study of the Barberini archive has enlarged greatly our knowledge of Frescobaldi's last years. It was formerly believed that Girolamo entered the service of Cardinal Antonio Barberini, youngest of Urban VIII's three nephews.[40] In fact, he spent his last years in the immediate service of the oldest and most powerful nephew, Cardinal Francesco. Francesco apparently recalled Frescobaldi from Florence, since he paid 100 scudi for the trip.[41] He paid a monthly salary of 3 scudi 60 baiocchi and an additional 60 scudi a year for the rent of Frescobaldi's house. As Archpriest of St. Peter's, the cardinal augmented Girolamo's salary as organist of the Cappella Giulia from 72 to 96 scudi a year. The perfect patron, the cardinal even provided Frescobaldi with music paper.[42]

The documents of the Barberini archive reveal two types of musical activity in the Barberini family. The brilliant series of operas by Giulio Cesare Rospigliosi, set by Landi, Virgilio Mazzocchi, and others, is well known.[43] The extensive documentation of these performances makes no mention of Frescobaldi as performer, although they employed other Ferrarese artists under the patronage of Enzo and Guido Bentivoglio.[44]

Frescobaldi's contribution was presumably in the other area of Barberini music, the vocal and instrumental chamber music of the Barberini *accademie*.[45] Without question, the greatest artist in the employ of the family at this period was Gian-Lorenzo Bernini. The stark white oval hall of the Palazzo Barberini, in which the *accademie* may have been held, was probably designed by Bernini.[46] The discovery of an autograph receipt for the scene of the Fair of Farfa in the 1639 production of *Chi soffre speri* shows Bernini's involvement in the theatrical performances as well.[47] Some contact between Bernini and Frescobaldi is suggested by a caricature that strongly resembles Mellan's portrait of Girolamo.[48]

In these last years Frescobaldi found a new forum for public performance, the Oratorio of the Crocifisso. The description of its Lenten musical performances given by the French viol player André Maugars in his *Response* is confirmed by the archive of the Oratorio, full of detailed expenses for such items as the transport of instruments, tuning (their tuner was Giovanni Battista Boni da Cortona, also tuner and technician for the Barberini), down to wine and a urinal for the preachers.[49] A list of musicians for 1640 names Frescobaldi along with Loreto Vittori and Marc'Antonio Pasqualini, the two most famous castrati of the period (see plate 2).

A few surviving personal accounts of Frescobaldi date from this period, transmitted by the waspish Giovanni Battista Doni, a member of Cardinal Francesco's household.[50] In general, these have been accepted

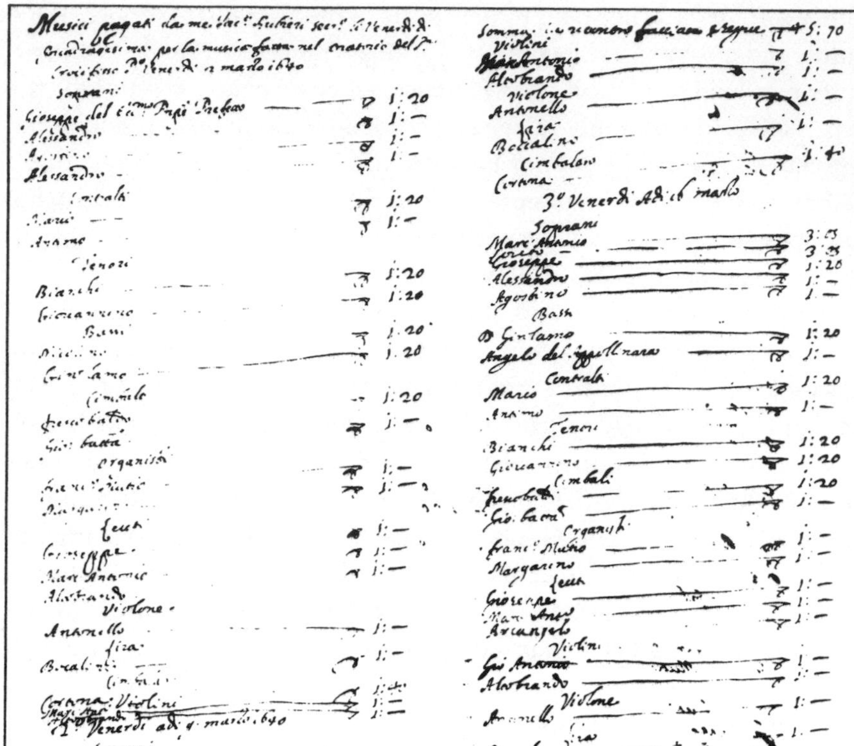

Plate 2.   Rome, Biblioteca Apostolica Vaticana, Archivio Segreto Vaticano, San Marcello, Arciconfraternita del Santissimo Crocifisso, F XIX 26.

Somma l'Arcivescovado ascende — 897.25
   Pifari
Mare' Antonio —————————— 1. —
Giuseppe —————————————— 1. —
Arcangelo —————————————— 1. —
   Viola
Gio: Antonio —————————— 1. —
Hilebrando —————————————— 1. —
   Violone
Antonelli ———————————————— 1. —
   Lira
Boccalino ———————————————— 1. —
   Cimbalo
Corona —————————————————— 1. 40

    S° Venerdì adi 30 marso

   Soprani
Giuseppe ———————————————— 1. 20
Honofrio ———————————————— 1. —
Aless.° ———————————————— 1. —
Agostino ———————————————— 1. —
   Contralti
Marco ——————————————————— 1. 20
Antimo ——————————————————— 1. —
   Tenori
Bianchi ———————————————— 1. 20
Giovannino ———————————————— 1. 20
   Bassi
Nicolino ———————————————— 1. 20
Girolamo ———————————————— 1. 20
   Cimbal.
frescobaldi ———————————————— 1. 20
Gio: battista ———————————————— 1. —
   organisti
francesco Mutio ———————————— 1. —
Margarino ———————————————— 1. —
   Pifari
Giuseppe ———————————————— 1. —
Marc' Anto° ———————————————— 1. —
Arcangelo ———————————————— 1. —
   Violini
Gio: Ant.° ———————————————— 2. —
Hilebrando ———————————————— 2. —
   Violone
Antonello ———————————————— 1. —
   Lira
Boccalino ———————————————— 1. —
   Cimbalo
Cortona —————————————————— 1. 40
                129.45

Restano in mano al maestro di Cappella
doble tre che con l'agio ————————— 9. 15
              1 n°

Più resta al maestro di Cappella
oltre le sopra.ª dette ——————————
Al organista per prestatura del org°
et accordatura delli organi ——————— 13. —
              167. 60

   B3. S° a ciascuno

at face value—Girolamo's exiguous literary culture, his lack of expertise in vocal composition, his heresies in the tuning of keyboard instruments. But Doni himself cannot be judged an impartial witness, from the evidence of two letters in the Archivio di Stato of Florence. In the first (Rome, 4 May 1630) Doni complains about a debt owed him by a young man, a certain Francesco Useppi, in whose good treatment "in the judgment of all, not only was I not lacking but rather overabundant." Useppi's undated answering letter, while recognizing the debt, continued, "but it is also most true that it will never be judged fitting that I have done many things for him and for Cardinal Barberini, for which he has had the praise, without any reward," and noted also "the rather immoderate character of Signor Doni."[51]

In denying the literary culture of Frescobaldi, Doni ignored the *Fiori musicali* of 1635, Girolamo's last complete new publication. There he added to the "Recercar con obligo di Cantare la Quinta parte senza Toccarla" the words "Intendomi chi può che m'intend'io [Understand me who can for I understand myself]" in playful reference to the fact that the entrances of the fifth part are not marked in the score.[52] In the original of this phrase (Canzone 105 of Petrarch, also quoted in *La regola del contraponto* . . . , 1622), the line is preceded by words that Frescobaldi might have applied to himself: "I' die' in guarda a san Pietro; or non più, no [I glanced at St. Peter's; now no more, no]." A glance at the poem as a whole confirms Frescobaldi's poetic sensibility. The canzone is filled with images of music (often music that is insufficiently appreciated), of renunciation, and of death—in one case, actually in the Po of Frescobaldi's native Ferrara.

Finally, it is possible that, as he was not insensitive to the powers of Italian poetry, Frescobaldi in turn may have inspired some lines by an English contemporary who visited Rome and frequented the Barberini in 1639:

> . . . whence the sound
> Of instruments that made melodious chime
> Was heard, of harp and organ; and who moved
> Their stops and chords was seen: his volant touch
> Instinct through all proportions, low and high
> Fled and pursued transverse the resonant fugue.
> (*Paradise Lost*, XI, 558–63)[53]

Notes

1. Frederick Hammond, *Girolamo Frescobaldi* (Cambridge, Mass.: Harvard University Press, 1983).

2. Personal communication from Marchese Ferdinando de' Frescobaldi.

3. Hammond, *Frescobaldi*, 326–27.

4. For example, Mantua, Archivio di Stato, Archivio Gonzaga E. XXV. 3, busta 1010, 245.

5. Hammond, *Frescobaldi*, 327.

6. Luzzasco Luzzaschi, *Il secondo libro di ricercari a quattro voci*, ed. Michelangelo Pascale (Rome: Pro Musica Studium, 1981); on the letter concerning the Willaert volume, see the contribution by Dinko Fabris in Sergio Durante and Dinko Fabris, eds., *Girolamo Frescobaldi: Nel quarto centenario della nascita*, Quaderni della Rivista italiana di musicologia 10 (Florence: Olschki, in press).

7. See Hammond, *Frescobaldi*, 117–25 and notes.

8. Anthony Newcomb, "Girolamo Frescobaldi, 1608–1615," *Annales musicologiques* 7 (1964–77): 111–58.

9. Hammond, *Frescobaldi*, 338, 339, 341, 342, 343.

10. Ibid., 33 and n. 4.

11. Newcomb, "Frescobaldi, 1608–1615," 118–19. The letter described by Newcomb and by the editors of the catalogue of the exhibition *Frescobaldi e il suo tempo nel quarto centenario della nascita* (Venice: Marsilio, 1983), 29 as lost is now in the Mary Flagler Cary Music Collection of the Morgan Library in New York City.

12. Ed. Anna Banti, *Europa mille seicentosei: Diario di viaggio di Bernardo Bizoni* (Milan and Rome: Il sofà delle muse, 1942).

13. Ibid., 27.

14. Ibid., 29, 35–36, 45.

15. Hammond, *Frescobaldi*, 41, 342.

16. Ibid., 44–45, 344–45.

17. Ibid., 39, 341–42. Both had a certain reputation as teachers; according to Giustiniani, G. B. Nanino and Giovannelli "made students of great success" (Angelo Solerti, *Le origini del melodramina* [Turin: Fratelli Bocca, 1903], 111).

18. See Parisi, this volume.

19. Hammond, *Frescobaldi*, 52, 347–48. The text of the letter has now been published by Paola Besutti, "Una lettera inedita di Girolamo Frescobaldi," *Rivista italiana di musicologia* 18 (1982): 207–11.

20. Frederick Hammond, "Cardinal Pietro Aldobrandini, Patron of Music," *Studi musicali* 12 (1983): 53–66; Alexander Silbiger, "The Roman Frescobaldi Tradition: c. 1640–1670," *Journal of the American Musicological Society* 33 (1980): 42–87; Glenn Watkins, preface to Sigismondo d'India, *Ottavo libro dei madrigali a cinque voci*, Musiche rinascimentali siciliane X (Florence: Olschki, 1980).

21. Information kindly furnished by Jonathan Couchman; see the addendum to Frederick Hammond, "Cardinal Pietro Aldobrandini, Patron of Music," *Studi musicali* 12 (1983): 53–66.

22. Annibaldi, this volume.

23. Hammond, *Frescobaldi*, 68–69, 352–53.

24. Darbellay, this volume.

25. Hammond, *Frescobaldi*, 67, 352; facsimile of the letter in the catalogue *Frescobaldi e il suo tempo*, 25.

26. Hammond, *Frescobaldi*, 67, 352.

27. Facsimile in Watkins, *ed. cit.*, plate 3.

28. Hammond, *Frescobaldi*, 68–69, 352–53.

29. The text of the dedication can be found in the catalogue of *Frescobaldi e il suo tempo*, 50.

30. Venice, Archivio di Stato, Senato III, dispacci degli ambasciatori, Rome, filza 96 (1627), fol. 167v; filza 100 (1629), fol. 319: "la continua*tio*ne de mali ufficij di quel mons.r Nuncio Gallo."

31. Hammond, *Frescobaldi*, 355 n. 12.

32. Hammond, *Frescobaldi*, 73, 355–56.

33. See Durante and Fabris, eds., *Frescobaldi*.

34. Hammond, *Frescobaldi*, 73, 355.

35. Original Latin text in Hammond, *Frescobaldi*, 329; on Francesco Rasi see Solerti, *Le origini*, 79, 110.

36. *Nuova maniera*, quoted by Solerti, *Le origini*, 74.

37. See Hill, this volume.

38. See Malcolm Campbell, *Pietro da Cortona at the Pitti Palace* (Princeton: Princeton University Press, 1977), 12–15.

39. Venice, Archivio di Stato, Senato III, dispacci, filza 104, fol. 152 (26 April 1631).

40. Henry Prunières, "Les musiciens du cardinal Antonio Barberini," *Mélanges de musicologie offerts à M. Lionel de la Laurencie* (Paris: Société française de musicologie, 1933), 117–22.

41. Hammond, *Frescobaldi*, 81, 357.

42. Frederick Hammond, "Girolamo Frescobaldi and a Decade of Music in Casa Barberini," *Analecta musicologica* 19 (1979): 109. The Venetian ambassador in Rome noted that the Arcipresbiteratto di S. Pietro "non arriua à mille scudi di rendita; mà molto stimato, per il modo che hà di benefficar molti seruitori, et adherenti di quel Capitolo" (Venice, Archivio di Stato, Senato III, dispacci, filza 108 [1633], fol. 133v).

43. See Hammond, "Decade of Music," and Margaret Murata, *Operas for the Papal Court 1631–1668* (Ann Arbor: UMI Research Press, 1981).

44. Venice, Archivio di Stato, Senato III, dispacci, filza 106, fol. 198v (22 January 1633): "Quel tal Ingegnero Guiti uenuto dà Ferrara se ne stà tutto il giorno con il Card.l Barberino, e con il D. Taddeo, l'humore de' quali hà egli assai captiuato nella constructione d'un Teatro, che con diuerse mutationi di scene deue seruire questo Carneuale per rappresentare l'historia di Tancredi del Tasso in musica; Nella quale opera questi signori spendono cinquemila scudi; et il Card.l Francesco n'e inamoratissimo, rubando ai negotij, et à suoi proprij commodi tutto quel più di tempo, che può assistere a detta constructione."

45. Cf. Hammond, "Decade of Music," 107–11.

46. Giuseppina Magnanimi, *Palazzo Barberini* (Rome: Editalia, 1983), 21, 29.

47. Hammond, "Decade of Music," 119.

48. In Hammond, *Frescobaldi*, 59.

49. Ibid., 89–92, 359–61.

50. See the entry "Doni, Giovanni Battista" in *The New Grove Dictionary of Music and Musicians* (London: Macmillan, 1980).

51. Florence, Archivio di stato, mediceo 1431, fols. 207–209.

52. See also Durante, this volume.

53. I am greatly indebted to John Hollander for drawing my attention to this passage.

A *Ritratto* of Frescobaldi:
Some Problems of Biographical Methodology

CLAUDIO ANNIBALDI

T HE title of this paper incorporates a pun on two meanings of *ritratto*—one current and familiar, the other obsolete, and both derived from the Latin root *re-trahere* (to draw or withdraw). The familiar meaning is that of "portrait"; however, in seventeenth-century Roman legal documents the term was also used to signify "dispossession" (e.g., of property).[1] I shall deal here chiefly with a number of archival documents concerning a legal process conducted in Rome between 1617 and 1618 that in fact terminated in the dispossession of a house owned by Girolamo Frescobaldi and his wife.[2]

Documents like these seem far less attractive than those dealing with Frescobaldi's musical activities. Moreover, Frederick Hammond came across some of these documents before I did, and both of us were preceded by Renato Lefevre, the author of several writings on the Palazzo Chigi of Rome, who repeatedly quoted from them and even published an abstract of one of them without realizing that it concerned one of the greatest musicians of the seventeenth century.[3]

Nevertheless, I think such documents are exceptionally interesting from a methodological point of view, because they point to a basic need for Frescobaldi's biographers as well as for every other biographer interested in the past: the need to go beyond superficial "common sense" interpretations at every level of research, and to discover the actual meaning of the documents at their disposal, whether they interpret a single word (such as *ritratto*), reconstruct biographical episodes (such as the legal process mentioned above), or try to explain the social relationships that were at the heart of artistic patronage in seventeenth-century Rome.

The documents I have studied present an excellent illustration of this methodological need, since they display all these problems like a set of Chinese boxes arranged one inside the other, so that we are confronted with them gradually. With the word *ritratto* and its peculiar meaning we have already considered the inner box of our imaginary set. Now let us pass to the bigger one, or to a more comprehensive problem: the *ritratto* as a legal action.

To be sure, it is a story without great biographical import. But it is very instructive, since it displays a divergence of interests that are normally expected to be convergent: on the one hand, the interest of an artist such as Girolamo Frescobaldi, and on the other, the interest of his patron—in this case, Cardinal Pietro Aldobrandini, to whom the musician dedicated his *Recercari*, published only a year prior to our story.

We begin in 1616, when Cardinal Aldobrandini bought a building near the corner of the right-hand side of Piazza Colonna and Via del Corso in Rome, at the exact location where today stands the Palazzo Chigi.[4] He wanted to transform the building into a monumental palace, so he claimed the use of the Constitutio gregoriana—a special law intended to promote the architectural embellishment of Rome by enabling owners who wished to enlarge a building to dispossess their neighbors.[5]

At the Cardinal's request, the Mastri di strada (Magistrates of the Streets) delivered five *monitori* (summonses) to the owners of five houses located where the front of the Palazzo Chigi is today.[6] This front now faces Piazza Colonna; at the time, however, those houses faced a little street running from the square to Montecitorio, since they were separated from the square by the so-called Isola di Colonna, a block torn down thirty years later.

Among the people to be summoned by the Mastri di strada were Frescobaldi and his wife Orsola del Pino, who owned—without living in it[7]—a little house with a courtyard in that street. Unfortunately, it is impossible to reconstruct the outward aspect of this house, in spite of the details given by our documents on its roofs, walls, windows, etc.[8] Similarly, it is impossible to locate it with the exactness suggested by the writings on Palazzo Chigi quoted above, according to which Frescobaldi owned the fourth house that a person walking toward Montecitorio would have seen on the right after having turned around the corner of Via del Corso and Piazza Colonna.[9] We can only say that it was, beyond any doubt, the house in which a parish register first studied by Alberto Cametti records the presence of the Del Pino family since 1610, and that of Girolamo in 1613 (the year of his marriage).[10]

The point now, however, is the judicial machine put in motion by the summonses delivered to the musician and his wife on 24 November and 8 December 1617. It was a machine precisely defined in seventeenth-century Rome as a *ritratto coattivo* or "forced dispossession," since it left the summoned owners no option.[11] They had to sell their house. The only thing they could hope was to sell it at a higher price than that proposed by the buyer. In fact, both parties of a *ritratto coattivo* were expected to present a special valuation of the building in dispute, and any divergence between the valuations involved the arbitration of the court of the Mastri di strada.[12]

Only two of the five owners valued their houses in disagreement with Cardinal Aldobrandini's expert; Frescobaldi was one of them.[13] The result was that on 3 April 1618 the musician and his wife were ordered to sell their house to the cardinal at a price fixed by the court of 689 Roman scudi and 27 baiocchi[14]—an amount that was nearly 65 scudi more than the price proposed by the cardinal's expert, but also nearly 150 scudi lower than the price proposed by their own expert.[15]

The Frescobaldis did not appeal the verdict. But less than a month later they too claimed the observance of the Constitutio gregoriana, which in the period between the valuation of a house and its sale regarded the new owner as a tenant of the old one and obliged him to pay rent.[16] Evidently, the musician himself made this claim to the notary of the Mastri di strada;[17] but in the surviving records of Cardinal Aldobrandini's bookkeepers there is only one payment concerning Girolamo and Orsola—a *mandato* signed by the cardinal on 11 May 1618 in his magnificent villa at Frascati near Rome—and it shows only the sum fixed by the court.[18]

The story of the *ritratto* ends with the contract signed on 22 May by Giovanni Battista Ciofano (the cardinal's attorney), Girolamo Frescobaldi, and Giovanni Del Pino, the musician's father-in-law, whose presence suggests that the house was part of Orsola's dowry.[19] The Latin text of the document, entirely standard in form, is of no interest, except for the fact that it concerns a patron and his protégé. I refer in particular to the clause that prevented the Frescobaldis from receiving the price of their house in cash and obliged them to accept it in *luoghi di monte non vacabili* (perpetual government bonds).[20]

This clause represented merely the application of a legal device pre-scribed by Constitutio gregoriana regarding the sale of real estate. It provided for the Mastri di strada to direct the seller to invest the money received for the sale into perpetual government bonds, unless the seller was in a position to provide other guaranties, such as the possession of other houses. This provision served to guarantee the buyer of the prop-erty (in this case, the cardinal and his heirs) the full restitution of the purchase price if he were to be subsequently evicted as the result of a court action by a third party, whose claims as true legal owner of the property resulted in the invalidation of the original purchase contract.[21]

The inclusion of this clause in the contract implies that Girolamo and Orsola did not possess any real property other than the house that they were forced to sell by the *ritratto*. It highlights the unfairness of this contract and of the law under which it was drawn up. The purchase allowed the cardinal to improve both his economic and social status: he acquired the house in order to tear it down and build a magnificent palace in its place. At the same time the sale represented to the Frescobaldi family both the economic loss of the only house they possessed and the resulting loss of their social status as property owners.

At this point our story leads us to a bigger box in our imaginary set. The conclusion of the *ritratto* contradicts the current notion of patronage as a relationship that was, if not idyllic, at least favorable to great artists. Consequently, in the relationship of Cardinal Aldobrandini and Fresco-baldi we are confronted with the problem of reconciling the musician's acknowledgment of the many benefits received from the cardinal with the lack of any document supporting his statements, and with the con-siderable evidence contradicting them.[22] But it is clear that we cannot resolve this apparent contradiction simply by dismissing seventeenth-century dedications as courtly exercises, or by explaining it in terms of Cardinal Aldobrandini's personality (he was a notorious miser).[23] Nor can we arrive at a satisfactory resolution by dramatizing the fact that Girolamo and Orsola never again lived in a house of their own,[24] and conclude that the *ritratto* story reveals in an almost symbolic manner how deeply the lives of seventeenth-century musicians were affected by the caprices of their masters.

Now, the main lesson of the *ritratto* documents is that any speculation based on sparse details must be rejected not only intuitively, but also on methodological grounds. To be sure, we cannot neglect any detail, and from a biographical point of view, we have to give as much attention to the personality of the patron as to that of the protégé. But no detail can explain another detail. A detail can be explained only through its systematic reference to the more comprehensive situation from which it always derives its true meaning. In short, the key to the *ritratto* is surely to be found in the relationship between Frescobaldi and Cardinal Aldobrandini. But first we have to clarify this relationship itself, and, for that purpose, examine the social premises of any relationship of patronage in seventeenth-century Rome.

What compels us to realize this need and to move to the outer box of our set of Chinese boxes is a detail of the sentence of the court of the Mastri di strada—that is, the signatures of the judges who ordered Orsola Del Pino and Girolamo Frescobaldi to sell their house to Cardinal Aldobrandini. The first of these may be translated as follows: "This verdict was made by me, Ercole Vaccari, in place of my lord, the most illustrious Cardinal Aldobrandini."[25]

We are confronted here with a detail which is far more enlightening than any speculation about the psychology of the cardinal, the financial position of Frescobaldi, or the dismal essence of their age. This detail reveals that in the story of the *ritratto*, Cardinal Aldobrandini was not only Girolamo's patron and his adversary during the process; he was also the Chamberlain of the Holy Roman Church and therefore the chief of the court that made the verdict in his own favor.[26]

Thus we get a glimpse of what formed the basis of the relationship between Frescobaldi and the cardinal: the social power of the latter. This power was no longer what it had been during the pontificate of his uncle Clement VIII, but it was still of formidable consequence, witness the three roles he played in the story of the *ritratto* (that of the rich owner, the prestigious patron, and the almighty Cardinal Chamberlain) and his ability to play all three roles simultaneously.

The relationship between Frescobaldi and his patron, or, for that matter, any relationship of patronage in seventeenth-century Rome, was in essence one of paternalism, that peculiar exchange of submission for protection between people of different ranks and classes that pervades many hierarchical societies, binds all their levels, and involves even the descendants of a person or the pupils of an artist.[27]

Indeed, Frescobaldi's own history suggests that his tenure in the household of Cardinal Aldobrandini was underlaid by a paternalistic relationship. It is no coincidence that the musician also served the heirs of the cardinal,[28] and that he had previously served two Ferrarese patrons, Guido and Enzo Bentivoglio.[29] Cardinal Aldobrandini, during the pontificate of his uncle, had in fact been the leader of the expedition that restored Ferrara to the Papacy—a success that, significantly, attracted many musicians of the late Duke Alfonso II to his services, including the Piccinini brothers and Luzzasco Luzzaschi, Frescobaldi's teacher.[30]

The well-known passage in the dedication of the *Recercari*, in which Frescobaldi states that he owes forever his possessions, person, and mind to Cardinal Aldobrandini, recalls word-for-word what beneficiaries would say in order to express their devotion to their patrons.[31] However, there is even more eloquent evidence of the paternalistic qualities of the relationship between Frescobaldi and the cardinal in the musician's negotiations with the Cardinal-Duke Gonzaga during the years 1614–15. In fact, the only occasion (insofar as I know) during which Frescobaldi tried to leave Cardinal Aldobrandini's service coincided exactly with a sudden fading of the political and economic power of his patron, that is, with a deterioration, even if temporary, of the very basis of paternalism.

It has been known that Gonzaga's agent, Paolo Facconi, began to write to Mantua on Frescobaldi's account on 1 November 1614. But it has remained thus far unnoticed that this letter followed shortly upon the beginning (two weeks earlier) of legal proceedings against two nephews of Cardinal Aldobrandini, which threatened to wreck the cardinal's countless efforts to recover his ancient power. His nephews were accused of having sheltered some bandits in the castle of Meldola, and Pope Paul V, by encouraging the proceedings against them, showed that he was still hostile toward their family[32] (now headed by Cardinal Pietro).[33] Moreover, the penalty for such a crime was death and confiscation, and the elder of the cardinal's nephews had become the legal owner of all the properties of the Primogenitura Aldobrandina, the imposing patrimony gathered in 1611.[34]

But there is another coincidence to be noted. In February 1615 Frescobaldi left Rome for Mantua; this happened two days after Cardinal

Aldobrandini's departure for Naples (where he remained as guest of the Spanish viceroy until 7 May).[35] Thus Frescobaldi's direct effort to look for a new patron coincided with the climax in the crisis of the Aldobrandini family. With the departure of the cardinal, all its members were away from Rome, and letters written to Cardinal Pietro by his sister Olimpia, by the aforementioned Ercole Vaccari, and by other members of his *famiglia* vividly hint at the anguish of the cardinal's relatives and at the anxious mobilization of his clients (above all, the so-called *creature*, the cardinals created by Clement VIII Aldobrandini).[36]

It is not surprising, at this point, to discover a third coincidence—that of the recovery of the cardinal's prestige with the end of Frescobaldi's negotiations with Mantua. In fact, the musician's letter of 16 May 1615, announcing his abandonment of plans to move to Mantua with his family, is dated two days after Cardinal Aldobrandini's return to Rome[37]—the eve of a predictable display of the cardinal's diplomatic gifts, for in July he succeeded in obtaining the pope's pardon for his two nephews.[38]

It goes without saying that the story of the *ritratto* now becomes quite compatible with the benefits that Frescobaldi admits having received from the cardinal. The power of the latter was always displayed either by benefitting his protégé or by robbing him in a more or less legal way.[39] To put oneself under the protection of such a power involved its acknowledgment—a confidence in it, supported by the presumption that the advantages would outweigh the drawbacks.

That such a presumption was reasonable even in the case of Frescobaldi may be demonstrated by one final coincidence. The year of the conclusion of the *ritratto*, 1618, also saw the publication of a reprint edition of the *Recercari*. The presence of Cardinal Aldobrandini's coat of arms on the title page of this volume surely had contributed to its success, for this coat of arms would have recommended the book to the reader's eye and formed, therefore, a guarantee of quality in the musical market of the time.[40]

Thus the phenomenon of paternalism proves actually to be the outer one of our Chinese boxes. On the one hand it contains the artistic patronage itself, and on the other it is contained in other problems, but these are no longer biographical since they concern the social and economic structures supporting the phenomenon in question. This potential transition from biography to history best summarizes the methodological relevance of the *ritratto* documents. Thus far its immediate ramifications have supplied us with an antidote to a superficial interpretation of evidence; now it suggests the possibility of redefining the scope and the methods of a biographical study according to its object.

I wish to avoid having this essay seem, in its turn, like a box contained in larger ones. For the sake of completeness, however, let me hint here at the peculiar terms of such a redefinition. Through the ramifications of the *ritratto* documents we have grasped the inner dynamic any biographical detail derives from being a part of a totality as complex as the existence of a human being. We can thus assume that to expose this dynamic is the main task for the biographer who concerns himself with a life history like Frescobaldi's, the anthropological context of which (that is, the totality from which Frescobaldi's music derived its authentic meaning) is deeply alien to him. Now, this assumption has both theoretical and practical implications. It implies, in fact, the need to discover again and again the formal devices most suitable to uncover the inner dynamic of the available evidence. But it also implies the need to reach a position from which the relationship of a biographical detail to the socio-cultural background remains beyond question, regardless of the interpretation suggested by this detail itself. Since the metaphor of the Chinese boxes has allowed us to correlate the *ritratto* of Frescobaldi with the all-pervading phenomenon of paternalism, the point of the story does not depend on whether, for instance, Cardinal Aldobrandini arrogantly played his many roles at his own protégé's expense, or whether he remained quite unaware of the outcomes of a lawsuit entirely entrusted to his experts, attorneys, and *uditori*.

In summary, the ultimate implications of the *ritratto* documents do not merely lead Frescobaldi's biographers to the boundary between biography and history, but compel them to become historians.

Appendix: Documents

DOCUMENT 1[41]

14 December 1617: valuation of Frescobaldi's house (AA, tomo 4: *Fabbricati. Palazzo Chigi in Piazza Colonna*, interno 1, fols. 6v–7v)[42]

1a. Stima della casa della signora Orsola del Pino posta nel Rione di Colonna nella strada che va da piazza Colonna verso Monte Citorio, quale s'affitta che confina da una banda con le Case dell'Illustrissimo signor Cardinal' Aldobrandino, e dall'altra banda, e per di dietro la Casa di Santo Gironimo della Carità, e dinanzi la via publica delle suddette strade, ò altri suoi piu veri confini etc La qual Casa vuole comprare il sopradetto Illustrissimo signor Cardinale Aldobrandino in virtù della Bolla Gregoriana de Iure Congrui misurata, e stimata da me sottoscritto con suoi Cimenti, sito, e suoi [sic] pertinenze, quale si trova essere della misura prezzo, e valore infrascritto come segue e[:]

Prima Muri di detta casa liberi e communi insieme canne 79 palmi 41 li quali considerati esser muri vecchi à giulij 18 la canna montano scudi 142.93. Colle canne 74 palmi 09 a baiocchi 20 la canna montano scudi 14.81. Amattonati in piano ordinarij canne 10 palmi 69 à giulij dieci la canna montano scudi 10.69. Tetti impianellati canne nove palmi 95 a giulij 32 la canna montano scudi 31.84. Solari di castagno politi senza regoli canne 3 palmi 96 a giuli 22 la canna montano scudi 8.71. Sito di detta casa pro indiviso con la suddetta Casa di Santo Geronimo fa quanto per la portione spettante à detta casa quad.^{to} [?] canne 5 palmi 41 à scudi 12 la canna presupponendolo libero di qualunque canone montano scudi 64.92. Partite de Cimenti diversi come fusti di porte, e finestre, conci, ferramenti agetti, et altre diverse cose di stime insieme montano scudi 77.40. Sommano insieme le sopradette partite dell [sic] valor de Cimenti, e sito della sopradetta Casa montano scudi trecento cinquant'uno e baiocchi 30 dico scudi 351.30. Il frutto della peggione di scudi 44 l'anno che se dice paga al presente detta Casa valutati à ragione di scudi 5 1/2 per cento monta detto frutto scudi 800. Che sommano insieme il valor de Cimenti e sito con il valor del frutto della peggione sudetta sono scudi mille cento cinquant'uno e baiocchi 30 scudi 1151.30. Li quali divisi per metà conforme lo stile sono scudi cinquecento settantacinque e baiocchi settantacinque di moneta e tanto essere [sic] il valore e prezzo di detta casa presupponendola libera di qualunque peso scudi 575.65. Per l'augumento che da la bolla suddetta à ragione della 12.ª del prezzo della somma di detta stima monta scudi 47.97. Somma in tutto e per tutto compreso l'augumento scudi seicento vinti tre e baiocchi settanta doi di moneta de giulij dieci per scudo dico scudi 623.62. Io Gio.Antonio Pomis eletto per parte dell'Illustrissimo signor Cardinal Aldobrandino mano propria[;]

1b. Misura e stima della Casa della signora Orsola figliola di messer Giovanni del Pino posta nella strada che va da piazza Colonna alla piazzetta di monte Citorio contigoua [sic] con il Palazzo dell'Illustrissimo et Reverendissimo Cardinal Aldobrandino qual casa compra Sua Signoria Illustrissima in virtu della Bolla Gregoriana come costa per l'atti delli ss.^{ri} [signori] Mastri di strada à quali s'habbia relatione mesurata e stimata da noi periti cioè dal signor Gio.Antonio de Pomis per parte di Sua Signoria Illustrissima da me Antonio Foglietta per parte di detta signora Orsola e prima sommano tutti li muri canne 85 palmi 55 à giulij 22 la canna monta scudi 188.21. Sommano tutte le case [recte: colle] canne 74 palmi 09 a baiocchi 25 la canna monta scudi 18.72. Sommano tutti li Mattonati canne 10 e palmi 69 à giulij 11 la canna monta scudi 11.75. Sommano tutti li tetti canne 9 palmi 95 à giulij 35 la canna monta scudi 34.82. Sommano tutti li solari canne 4 palmi 45 à giulij 20 la canna monta scudi 8.90 somma il sito canne 4 palmi 41 à scudi 15 la canna monta scudi 81.15. Somano tutte le partite messe à denari scudi 94.51. Sommano insieme le sopradette partite scudi 438.06. Soma la pegione à ragione di scudi 4 per cento scudi mille cento e dieci scudi 1110.

Somano insieme pegione e cimenti scudi 1548.06 partite per metà viene scudi 774 baiocchi 03. Per l'agomento della bolla à case che non habita il Padrone scudi 64 baiocchi 50. Somano insieme scudi 838.53. Somano tutte le suddette partite Cimenti, e sito quanto havendo hauto risguardo alla pegione e compresoci l'augumento della bolla scudi ottocento trent'otto baiocchi 53 di moneta scudi 838.53. Antonio Foglietta mano propria.

DOCUMENT 2

23 January 1618: note of the notary of the Mastri di strada (AS, Tribunale delle Acque e Strade, vol. 66. *Droliardus anni 1618*, fol. 100v)[42]

Pro DD [Dominis] Hieronimo Francisco Bagno [sic] et Ursola del Pino coniugibus contra Illustrissimum et Reverendissimum Dominum Cardinalem Aldobrandinum

In officio mei etc Dominus Antonius Foglietta peritus pro parte dd [dictorum] DD [Dominorum] Coniugum ut alteruter electus et medio Iuramento tactis etc retulit prout In folio tenoris etc.

DOCUMENT 3

25 January 1618: note of the notary of the Mastri di strada (ibid., fol. 116r)

Pro Illustrissimo et Reverendissimo Domino Petro Sanctae Romanae Ecclesiae Cardinali Aldobrandino contra Dominam Ursolam del Pino

In officio etc Dominus Ioannes Antonius de Pomis peritus electus et medio Iuramento tactis scripturis dedit relationem pro ut in folio tenoris etc protestans non aperiri nisi prius in actis exhibita alia relatione partis adversae omni etc.

DOCUMENT 4

1 February 1618: note of the notary of the Mastri di strada (ibid., fols. 146v–147r)

Pro Illustrissimo et Reverendissimo Domino Petro Cardinali Aldobrandino contra Dominum Hieronimum friscusbaldum [sic] ferrariensem organistam Ecclesiae Sancti Petri, et Dominam Ursulam de Pinis coniuges

Franciscus Sala Curiae Capitolij mandatarius retulit in scriptis se die 24. Novembris 1617 personaliter dictum Dominum Hieronimum, et Die 8.ª Decembris 1617 personaliter dictam Dominam Ursolam, et dimissa domi copia dictum Dominum Hieronimum monuisse prout in monitorio quod sic exequutum facto Dominus Joannes Baptista Ciofanus reportavit pro ut in folio tenoris etc.

DOCUMENT 5

3 April 1618: sentence of the *Tribunale dei Mastri di strada* (AS, Tribunale delle Acque e Strade, pacco 338: *Sententiae 1616 ad 1630*, interno 2: *Off.° Strade. Camerlengo, e Maestri di Strade. Sentenze orig.ⁱ 1618 e 1619*.[44]

Christi Nomine Invocato Pro tribunali Sedentes et solum Deum prae oculis habentes Per hanc nostram deffinitivam [sic] Sententiam q[uam de Jurispe]ritorum consilio et nos

Magistri Viarum de voto Domini Assessoris nostri ferimus in his scriptis in causa et causis quae coram nobis in prima seu alia [veriori versae fue]runt et vertuntur Instantia Inter Illustrissimum et Reverendissimum Dominum Petrum tituli Sanctae Mariae in Transtiberim Cardinalem Aldobrandinum acto[rem ex una] et DD [Dominos] Ursulam del Pino et Hieronimum friscubaldum [pro omni] cuiuslibet ipsorum Iure et Interesse reos convenctos de et super Venditione cessione traditione et consignatione [domus seu do]munculae positae in Regione Columnae prope bona dicti Illustrissimi Domini actoris et alia latera etc in vim bullae felicis recordationis Gregorii Papae xiij de [aedificiis et Iure] Congrui partibus ex altera Unde viso monitorio pro parte dicti Illustrissimi Domini Actoris obtento executo et in actis legitime reproducto Viso loco differentiae al[ijsque visis videndis] et consideratis considerandis Dicimus Pronuntiamus Sententiamus decernimus et declaramus dictam Dominam Ursulam et eius virum teneri et obl[igatos esse ad] vendendum cedendum tradendum et consignandum dicto Illustrissimo Domino Actori supradictam domum seu domunculam cum omnibus suis Iuribus membris et pertinentij[s prout nos] vigore dictae bullae et alias omni meliori modo etc vendimus et adiudicamus pro pretio per nos ubi tertios in dicta bulla deputatos attenta di[scordia Dominorum] Ioannis Antonij de Pomis et Antonij foliettae peritorum per dd [dictas] partes communiter electorum declarato et aestimato scutorum sexcentorum octu[aginta no]vem baiocchorum 27 monetae computato in dicto pretio augumento ex forma dictae bullae proveniente ac Instrumentum praedictae Venditionis et cessionis cum clausulis et solem[nitatibus necessarijs] et opportunis faciendum pretiumque praedictum una cum dicto eius augumento accipiendum data tamen prius Idonea cautione ad favorem dicti Illustrissimi Domini Actoris de evi[ctione dictae] domus illiusque membrorum Iuriumque etc seu reinvestiendum loco cautionis de evictione eiusdem domus et Iurium praedictorum iuxta formam dictae b[ullae] Coniu-[gibusque praedictis In]strumentum Venditionis facere et precium recipere recusantibus Instrumentum praedictum confici mandamus per nos ex officio [cum clausulis] et cautelis necessarijs in vim facultatum nobis in dicta bulla attributarum preciumque cum dicto augumento dep[oni] penes Sacrum Montem Pietatis ad effectum [illud reives]tiendi in tot bonis stabilibus seu locis Montium non vacabilium iuxta formam dictae bullae et dictum Illustrissimum Dominum Cardinalem in realem actuale[mque possessionem] dictae domus illiusque Iurium fore et esse Immittendum pro ut nos Illum I[mmitti] volumus et man-damus quem etiam condemnamus ad [fabricandum] ad ornatum Urbis et in fabrica predicta erogare ad minus scuta tercentum [sic] et hoc Infra sex menses [Incepisse et Infra annum per]fecisse etc [?] Victosque victori in expensis condemnamus quatenus non acquiescant et quaecunque mandata desuper necessaria et opportuna decer[nimus et relaxamus et ita Dici]mus Declaramus decernimus Pronunciamus et Sententiamus non solum praemisso sed etiam omni alio meliori modo

ita pronunciavi ego Hercules Vaccarius pro Illustrissimo Domino meo Cardinali Aldobrandino habito [voto aestimavi]

ita pronunciavi aestimavi, et [declaravi ego Laurentius Alterius Magister Viarum]

ita pronunciavi aestimavi, et de[claravi ego Petrus Paulonius Judex, et Assessor].

DOCUMENT 6

27 April 1618: note of the notary of the Mastri di strada (AS, Tribunale delle Acque e Strade, vol. 66: *Broliardus anni 1618*, fol. 466v)

Pro DD [Dominis] Ursula del Pino et Hieronimo friscubaldo contra Illustrissimum Dominum Cardinalem Aldobrandinum

In officio etc Idem et dixit nihil fieri nisi facto deposito pensionis domus de qua agitur a die aestimationis usque ad diem depositi omni etc.

DOCUMENT 7

11 May 1618: order for payment of Cardinal Pietro Aldobrandini (ADP, Fondo Aldobrandini, busta 19, interno 59^b: *Registro de Mandati del s.^r Card.^l Aldombrandini* [sic] *dal 1618 al 1620*, fol. 18v)[45]

ss.^ri [signori] Errere e Costa [li piacerà] pagare alli ss.^ri [signori] Provisori del sacro monte della Pieta di roma scudi 689 baiocchi 27 moneta e di pigliarne da loro una cedola del[l']Infrascritto tenore poiche hanno da servire per pagare Il prezzo della Casa In essa espresso, e con le conditioni similmente espressine etc ["]Habbiamo In deposito dall'Illustrissimo et Reverendissimo signor Pietro Cardinale Aldobrandini scudi 689 baiocchi 27 moneta reco contanti disse per l[']Intero prezzo d[']una Casa In piazza colonna contigua all'altri beni di esso signore Cardinale spettante a Donna orsola del Pino e Girolamo Francesco Baldo suo marito [*crossed out*: ogni volta che sara] la quale detto signor Cardinale Intende comprare per Vigor della Bolla della felice ricordanza di Gregorio xiij de Iure congrui, et conforme alla sentenza data a suo favore per li atti del notaro delli ss.^ri [signori] Mastri di strada da pagarsi alli detti Donna Orsola e girolamo francesco suo marito ogni volta che sara fatto l'Istromento della Vendita di detta Casa con sue ragioni a favore del detto Illustrissimo signor Cardinale Aldobrandini con le solite Clausole et Cautele etc et che detta orsola et Girolamo havranno dato Idonea sicurta per li atti di detto notaro per l'evitione di detta Casa overo Il detto prezzo con licenza et consenso del detto signor Cardinale compratore Investiranno In tanti beni stabili, o vero luoghi di monte non Vacabili i quali dovranno stare specialmente surrogati et hipotecati per la detta evitione, o vero restituirli al detto signor Cardinale riportandoci la presente Cedola etc["] che coll'haverne tal cedola saranno ben pagati e li porrete a nostro debito nel conto a parte de denari che ci furno restituiti per li luoghi estratti del monte sisto prima erettione, Della [sic] Villa Belvedere li 11 maggio 1618.

DOCUMENT 8

22 May 1618: contract between the Frescobaldis and Cardinal Pietro Aldobrandini (AS, Notai dell'Ufficio delle Acque e Strade, vol. 51: *1618. Alexius buccamat(ius) not(ari)us*, fols. 493r–498v)[46]

Venditio domus Pro Illustrissimo et Reverendissimo Domino Petro Cardinali Aldobrandino Sanctae Romanae Ecclesiae Camerario

Die Vigesima secunda Maij 1618

Cum sit quod Illustrissimus et Reverendissimus Dominus Petrus tituli Sanctae Mariae in Transtiberim Presbiter Cardinalis Aldobrandinus Sanctae Romanae Ecclesiae Camerarius volens ad Urbis ornatum ac suam suaeque familiae commoditatem emere domum cum cortili et aliis suis Iuribus membris et pertinentijs spectantem et pertinentem ad DD [Dominos] Hieronimum friscubaldum ferrariensem et Ursulam del Pino Coniuges positam Romae in Regione Columnae in via tendente a platea Columnae ad Montem Cetorium iuxta a duobus lateribus bona dicti Illustrissimi Domini Cardinalis ab alio tunc Venerabilis Archiconfraternitatis Charitatis de Urbe in Ecclesia Sancti Hieronimi nunc eidem Illustrissimo per Infradictos DD [Dominos] Iudices per Sententiam adiudicatam pro ut in actis mei etc die [*crossed out:* salvis] 15.ᵃ praesentis mensis Maij seu etc ante dictam viam publicam salvis alijs etc si qui etc dictamque domum praesentis suis bonis unire et Incorporare et in ea et eis murare et fabricare ad ornatum Urbis in vim bullae felicis recordationis Gregorii Papae xiii super Aedificijs et Iure Congrui via monitorij in actis mei etc die prima februarij proxime preteriti seu etc legitime reproducti et contra dd [dictos] DD [Dominos] Hieronimum et Ursulam Coniuges sub diebus 24 Novembris et 8 Decembris 1617 executi coram Illustrissimo et Reverendissimo Domino Cardinali Camerario et Illustribus DD [Dominis] Viarum Magistris contra praedictos DD [Dominos] Hieronimum et Ursulam Coniuges egerit ad sibi vendendum domum praedictam cum suis Iuribus membris et pertinentijs quo monitorio executo Iidem Coniuges in actis mei etc declararunt se velle dictam domum eidem Illustrissimo et Reverendissimo Domino Cardinali vendere cum augumento et alias iuxta formam dictae bullae et propterea ad effectum estimandi [*sic*] dictam domum in peritum suum Iidem Coniuges elegerunt et deputarunt Dominum Antonium foliettam pro parte vero dicti Illustrissimi Domini Cardinalis fuerit electus Dominus Ioannes Antonius de Pomis sub diebus. . . . [*sic*] qui periti sic communiter electi in actis mei etc medio eorum Iuramento tactis etc dederunt suam relationem et cum Inter se fuerint discordes fuerit per dd [dictos] DD [Dominos] Judices uti tertios in dicta bulla deputatos Iustum pretium esse et ascendere computato augumento ex forma dictae bullae proveniente tamquam de domibus locari solitis ad scuta sexcenta octuaginta novem baiocchos 27 monetae et dd [dicti] Coniuges pro dicto precio ut supra declarato vendere condemnatos prout latius ex eorum deffinitiva [*sic*] Sententia lata et promulgata in actis mei etc 3 Aprilis proxime preteriti seu etc ad quam etc.

Modo autem citatis dd [dictis] Coniugibus ad recipiendum precium domus praedictae et de qua agitur et faciendum Instrumentum Venditionis dictae domus et reinvestiendum pretium praedictum iuxta formam dictae bullae alias videndum per DD [Dominos] ex officio et in vim quarumcunque facultatum ac bullae praedictae dicteque declarationis de vendendo per praedictos DD [Dominos] Coniuges ut supra factae confici Instrumentum opportunum dictae domus cum suis Iuribus membris et pertinentijs et de qua actum fuit cum clausulis et cautelis de super necessarijs et opportunis et consuetis pretiumque praedictum mandari deponi penes Sacrum Montem Pietatis Urbis et alia omnia fieri et adimpleri ex forma dictae bullae Instet Excellens Dominus Ioannes Baptista Cioffanus Utriusque Iuris Doctor procurator dicti Illustrissimi Domini Cardinalis et praedictam Venditionem et Instrumentum fieri ex officio omni meliori modo etc praesentibus ibidem dd [dictis] DD [Dominis] Hieronimo friscubaldo marito dictae Dominae Ursulae et Ioanne del Pino patre eiusdem Dominae Ursulae consentientibus ac vendere et predicta omnia velle adimplere declarantibus quibus omnibus per dd [dictos] DD [Dominos] Iudices auditis ac causa cognita et discussa ad maiorem dicti Illustrissimi Domini Cardinalis cautelam ad Infradicti Instrumenti Venditionis celebrationem una cum dictis DD [Dominis] Hieronimo et Ioanne marito et patre respective devenire decreverunt

Hinc igitur est quod coram Perillustre et Reverendissimo Domino Hercule Vaccario Utriusque Signaturae Referendario et Illustrissimi et Reverendissimi Domini Cardinalis Camerarij Auditore et Perillustre Domino Laurentio Alterio Patritio Romano Almae Urbis eiusque districtus a Sanctissimo Domino Nostro Papa Paulo quincto specialiter et expresse deputato Viarum Magistro et votum ut asseruit habente ab eius honorando Collega ac Excellenti Domino Petro Paulonio Utriusque Iuris Doctore eorum Iudice et Assessore Insimul Iudicibus ordinarijs et competentibus vigore bullae praedictae in loco Infradicto sedentibus super sedibus lignei sive coraminis quem locum et sedes quoad hunc actum tantum pro eorum congruo Iuridico et tribunali loco elegerunt et deputarunt ac eligunt et deputant meque notario personaliter Constitutus Suprascriptus Dominus Ioannes Baptista Cioffanus procurator dicti Illustrissimi Domini Cardinalis repetitis in primis et ante omnia monitorio et oblatione de vendendo electione peritorum illorumque relatione alijsque in similibus repetendis petijt et Instetit per eosdem Reverendissimum Dominum Auditorem et DD [Dominos] Viarum Magistros et Assessorem Insimul eadem auctoritate eorum officij vigore suprascriptae Constitutionis Gregorianae ac oblationis praedictae et electionis Instrumentum Venditionis dictae domus cum suis Iuribus membris et pertinentijs cum solitis clausulis cautelis promissionibus et obligationibus una cum dicto Domino Hieronimo friscubaldo marito et dicto Domino Ioanne del Pino patre pro qua de rato ut Infra etc fieri atque confici ad favorem dicti Illustrissimi Domini Cardinalis et predicta fieri non solum predicto sed etiam omni alio meliori modo etc.

Qui Perillustris et Reverendissimus Dominus Auditor et Perillustri DD [Domini] Viarum Magistri et Assessor pro tribunali ut supra sedentes et auctoritate eorum officij qua in hac parte funguntur vigore supradictae bullae et oblationis praemissa in primis et ante omnia per eos expressa protestatione quod per huiusmodi Instrumentum Venditionis dictae domus cum suis Iuribus etc non Intendunt se eorumque haeredes etc et bona aliquo modo obligare sed tantum obligare dd [dictos] DD [Dominos] Hieronimum friscubaldum et Ursulam del Pino Coniuges eiusque heredes etc bona etc Iura etc et non alias aliter nec alio modo etc de quo expresse protestati fuerunt et protestantur quam protestationem pro facta et repetita haberi voluerunt et volunt in principio medio et fine et in qualibet parte et clausula praesentis Instrumenti etc sponte etc ac omni meliori modo etc cum praesentia et consensu dicti Domini Hieronimi mariti dictae Dominae Ursulae et Ioannis del Pino patris eiusdem Dominae Ursulae et pro dicta Domina Ursula de rato et de faciendi ratificare praesens Instrumentum ac omnia in eo contenta etc Vendiderunt etc supradicto Illustrissimo et Reverendissimo Domino Petro Cardinali Aldobrandino Sanctae Romanae Ecclesiae Camerario absenti dicto Domino Ioanne Baptista Cioffano eius procuratore meque etc praesentibus etc dictam domum ut supra positam et confinatam una cum omnibus suis Iuribus membris et pertinentijs adiacentijs usibus Ingressibus egressibus commoditatibus alijsque ad dictam domum spectantibus et pertinentibus tam de Iure quam ex consuetudine et alias omni meliori modo etc tam apparentibus quam non apparentibus et a centro terrae usque ad coelum etc Item ex causa et titulo Venditionis huiusmodi cesserunt etc omnia Iura etc Nullo Iure etc ad habendum etc Ponentes etc Costituentes etc Dantes etc et donec etc Constituerunt etc.

Hanc autem Venditionem Supradicti DD [Domini] Iudices auctoritate eorum officij qua in hac parte funguntur vigore dictae bullae et oblationis ut supra nomine et dd [dicti] DD [Domini] Hieronimus et Ioannes del Pino fecerunt etc dicto Illustrissimo et Reverendissimo Domino Petro Cardinali Aldobrandino absenti dicto Domino Ioanne Baptista Cioffano eius procuratore meque etc praesentibus pro pretio et pretij nomine scutorum sexcentorum octuaginta novem baiocchorum 27 monetae comprehenso et computato in dicta summa augumento ex forma dictae bullae proveniente tamquam de domibus locari solitis iuxta formam dictae bullae sic per dd [dictos] DD [Dominos] Iudices ut supra aestimato et declarato pro quorum solutione Idem Dominus Ioannes Baptista Cioffanus procurator nunc in mei etc ac testium praesentia etc consignavit et cum effectu tradidit dd [dictis] DD [Dominis] Iudicibus pro tribunali ut supra sedentibus cedulam Sacri Montis Pietatis Urbis continentem dictam summam scutorum sexcentorum octuaginta novem baiocchorum 27 monetae tenoris in fine praesentis Instrumenti registrandam quam cedulam ad sese traxerunt etc et deinde mihi notario consignarunt ad effectum Infradicendum quibus stantibus dd [dicti] DD [Domini] Iudices dictusque Dominus Hieronimus maritus et Ioannes pater dictae Dominae Ursulae nominibus praedictis dictum Illustrissimum Dominum Cardinalem emptorem absentem qua supra stipulatione Interveniente de toto et Integro pretio dictae domus ut supra venditae quietarunt etc exceptioni etc speique etc ad cautelam renunciarunt etc per pactum etc quod precium sic ut supra depositatum et in dicta cedula contentum dictus Reverendissimus Dominus Auditor et Viarum Magistri et Assessor consignari mandarunt dd [dictis] DD [Dominis] Hieronimo seu Ursulae Coniugibus data tamen prius Idonea cautione de evictione dictae domus ad favorem dicti Illustrissimi Domini Cardinalis suorumque sive facto legitimo reinvestimento pro evictione dictae domus cum suis Iuribus ut supra venditis in omnibus et per omnia cum scientia et consensu dicti Illustrissimi Domini Cardinalis suorumque in tot bonis stabilibus de quorum evictione Idoneis fideiussoribus sit cautum seu in tot locis Montium non vacabilium iuxta formam dictae bullae ad quam etc quae bona et loca Montium semper et quandocunque et in perpetuum stent et stare debeant et Intelligantur loco dictae domus subrogata et titulo primariae et privilegiatae hippotecae specialiter affecta obligata et hippotecata ad favorem dicti Illustrissimi Domini Cardinalis suorumque etc pro omni et quacunque evictione dictae domus illiusque Iurium etc et pro observatione et adimplemento omnium et singulorum contentorum in praesenti Instrumento ita ut in casum cuiuscunque evictionis et Inobservantiae et non adimplementi contentorum in praesenti Instrumento liceat dicto Illustrissimo Domino Cardinali suisque etc super dictis locis Montium et illorum fructibus et bonis liberum habere recursum et regressum propria auctoritate et sine Iudicis licentia vel decreto et sine vitio spolij et attentatorum secundario vero pro assecuratione et hippoteca dotis dictae Dominae Ursulae illiusque restitutionis etc nullique alteri personae etc super illis aliquod Ius seu aliqua actio etiam minima aquiratur in praeiudicium dicti Illustrissimi Domini Cardinalis suorumque etc sed ipsi semper caeteris alijs praeferri debeant et praeferantur et in dictis Investimentis ut supra fiendis fieri debeat expressa mentio quod pecuniae proveniunt ex dicto pretio ut supra soluto eademque bona stabilia et loca Montium ut supra emenda dd [dicti] Coniuges minime vendere nec alienare quovis modo possint etc nisi data prius Idonea cautione de evictione ad favorem dicti Illustrissimi Domini Cardinalis suorumque pro evictione dictae domus iuxta formam dictae bullae et in eventum [*sic*] extinctionis vel alienationis dicti Investimenti semper et quandocunque dictus casus evenerit et sequatur dictum pretium reinvestiatur in alijs bonis stabilibus aut locis Montium non vacabilium cum scientia et consensu dicti Illustrissimi Domini Cardinalis suorumque et hoc servari debeat toties quoties casus praedictus evenerit et occurrerit quia sic etc et semper cum scientia et consensu ut supra et cum expressa mentione diei et anni praesentis Instrumenti et quod sunt de pecunijs ut supra redactis et cum expressa declaratione et prohibitione praedictis et alias iuxta formam dictae bullae ad quam etc.

Promiseruntque dd [dicti] DD [Domini] Iudices auctoritate qua supra nomine dd [dictorum] Coniugum necnon predicti DD [Domini] Hieronimus et Ioannes maritus et pater respective predictae Dominae Ursulae dictam domum cum suis Iuribus membris et pertinentijs ut supra venditis ad ipsos Coniuges pleno Iure utilis et directi dominij vel quasi spectare et pertinere et esse liberam Immunem et exemptam ab omni et quocunque censu canone responsione servitute aut alio quovis onere etc nullique fideicommisso devolutioni caducitati et prohibitioni alienandi purificatam seu purificandam esse obnoxiam et quatenus dicta bona reperiantur subiecta alicui fideicommisso et prohibitioni alienationis ex nunc dictum fideicommissum et prohibitionem alienationis dictae bullae auctoritate pro concurrenti quantitate Integri pretij dictae domus et illius augumenti transtulerunt in reinvestimento de dicto pretio fiendo Ita quod dicta domus cum suis Iuribus etc de cetero ab omni onere etiam respectu cuiusvis fideicommissi libera et exempta remaneat et dd [dicti] Coniuges dictam domum nulli personae etc in totum nec in partem Vendidisse cessisse concessisse donasse pignorasse permutasse nec alias quomodolibet alienasse alienationis vocabulo latissime sumpto et de ea in totum nec in partem fecisse aliquem alium contractum seu distractum in praejudicium praesentis Instrumenti et contentorum in eo et huiusmodi Instrumento et omnibus in eo contentis facere consentire omnem personam Ius seu actionem aliquam super dicta domo aut qualibet illius parte habentem [?] seu habere quomodolibet praetendentem [?] tam in proprietate quam in possessione ad omnem simplicem et extraiudicialem requisitionem et Interpellationem dicti Illustrissimi Domini Cardinalis suorumque etc quem Illustrissimum Dominum Emptorem suosque promiserunt semper manutenere in pacifica et quieta possessione dd [dictorum] bonorum et ab omni lite molestia et molestante persona etc defendere eximere et liberare etc litemque non Inferre etc qui nimmo ab alijs moventibus tam in petitorio quam in possessorio aut alio quocunque Iudicio avocata et non avocata possessione in quocunque foro et Instantia et qualibet parte Iudicij seu litis in seipsos nominibus quibus supra in quavis Instantia et parte litis suscipere ad omnem simplicem denunciationem requisitionem et voluntatem dicti Illustrissimi Domini Emptoris suorumque etiam non solemniter facta sine Insertione libelli et domi dimissa copia et in eventum absentiae ab Urbe per affixionem ad valvas Curiae vel audentiarum sive per edictum publicum quae ita facta arctet et valeat ac si solemniter et personaliter facta foret illasque prosequi omnibus et singulis dd [dictorum]

Coniugum sumptibus et expensis etc et demum de quacunque dictae domus eiusque Iurium generali et particulari evictione tam in petitorio quam in possessorio Iurisque et facti defensione universali et particulari in forma ita ut si evictio sequatur per Iniustitiam Imprudentiam vel malitiam Iudicanda aut quacunque alia de causa dicti Coniuges se nullatenus excusare possint et ultra praemissa ad omnia damna etc Et cum expresso etiam pacto et condicione quod omnia et singula in praesenti Instrumento contenta reduci debeant et reducta esse Intelligantur ad formam et dispositionem dictae bullae ita ut si plus vel minus hic scriptum vel convenctum sit quod scribi vel conveniri non deberet Id totum pro non scripto vel respective non convencto habeatur quia eorum Intentio fuit et est dictae bullae adhaerere et cum illa confrontare quae omnia dd [dicti] DD [Domini] Iudices auctoritate eorum officij qua in hac parte funguntur vice et nomine dd [dictorum] Hieronimi et Ursulae nec non dictus Dominus Hieronimus maritus dictae Dominae Ursulae et dictus Dominus Ioannes del Pino pater promiserunt habere rata grata valida atque perpetuo firma et ullo umquam tempore dicere venire vel opponere sub quovis praetextu et quavis de causa et occasione etc alias etc de quibus etc Pro quibus etc [dicti Domini Iudices] dd [dictos] DD [Dominos] Hieronimum et Ursulam Coniuges et dictus Hieronimus et Ioannes del Pino usque ad ratificationem se ipsos heredesque et bona etc in ampliori forma Camerae Apostolicae cum clausulis solitis obligarunt etc citra etc renuntiarunt etc Consentientes [?] etc. Unica etc. sic tactis respective Iurarunt etc. super quibus omnibus et singulis tamquam legitime gestis dd [dicti] DD [Domini] Iudices ut supra pro tribunali sedentes suam et dicti eorum officij auctoritatem et decretum Interposuerunt supplendo omnes et singulos defectus si qui forsan in praemissis Intervenerunt omni meliori modo etc super quibus etc.

Actum Romae in Regione Trivij et in aula solitae audientiae dicti Reverendissimi Domini Vaccarij praesentibus ibidem DD [Dominis] Dominico Betto quondam Ioannis Baptistae de Mattellica Camerinensis diocesis et Bernardino Gerardo de Nemo diocesis Albanensis testibus etc.

Ioannes Baptista forcinus rogavit

Tenor cedulae

736 Noi Don Francesco Boncompagni deluna [sic] et l'altra Signatura Referendario Giovanni Battista Bolognetti Fabritio Naro et Nicolò Benigni Provisori del Sacro Monte della Pietà di Roma havemo in deposito dall'Illustrissimo et Reverendissimo Signor Pietro Cardinale Aldobrandino scudi seicento ottanta nove baiocchi 27 moneta hauti da Signori Herrera et Costa [che] recò Piermarino Barnabò lor Cassiere contanti disse depositarli di ordine di Sua Signoria Illustrissima disse per l'Intiero prezzo di una Casa in piazza colonna contigua ad altri beni di detto Signor Cardinale spettante ad Orsola del Pino et Gironimo friscobaldi [sic] suo marito qual Casa Sua Signoria Illustrissima Intende conprar [sic] per vigor della bolla Iuris Congrui et conforme alla Sententia data a suo favore per li atti del notaro dei Signori Mastri di Strade per pagarli a detta Madama Orsola et Girolamo [sic] suo marito sempre che da loro sarà fatto l'Instrumento della vendita di detta Casa con sue raggioni a favor di detto Signor Cardinale con le solite clausule et cautele et che essi Orsola et Girolamo habbino dato Idonea segurtà per li atti di detto notaro per l'evittione di detta Casa [crossed out: con sue raggioni a favor di detto Signor Cardinale] overo il detto prezzo

con scientia et consenso di Sua Signoria Illustrissima Investiranno in altri beni stabili ò Monti non vacabili quali doveranno stare spetialmente surrogati et hippotecati per la detta evittione overo restituirli a detto Signor Cardinale o à chi Sua Signoria Illustrissima li ordinera in pie della presente cedola et in fede questo di 14 di Maggio 1618 scudi 689.27

Alessandro Roncalli Cassiere loco + sigilli Francesco Boncompagni Provisore Pietro Paolo Bonillo Computista.

Notes

1. In seventeenth-century sources the word often is spelled *retratto*. A discussion of the judicial significance of this term is given in Giovanni Battista De Luca, *Il dottor volgare* (Rome: Corbo, 1673), 4:155–71.

2. The documents are transcribed in the appendix to this essay. I shall use the abbreviations AA (Archivio Aldobrandini, Frascati), ADP (Archivio Doria Pamphilj, Rome), AS (Archivio di Stato, Rome), and AV (Archivio storico del Vicariato, Rome). For Frescobaldi's first name, the customary version, "Girolamo," will be used here, although the documents show both this version and the obsolete variant "Gironimo." The composer himself always signed "Girolimo," the spelling that also appears in his baptismal act.

3. Renato Lefevre dealt with the *ritratto* in "Il palazzo degli Aldobrandini a piazza Colonna," *Capitolium* 37 (1962), no. 1: 11–19; "Gli Aldobrandini in piazza Colonna tra il '500 e il '600," *Studi romani* 11 (1963): 417–33; *Il palazzo degli Aldobrandini e dei Chigi a piazza Colonna* (Rome: Istituto di studi romani, 1964); "La costituzione edilizia romana del 1574: Contenuto, valore e applicazione," *Economia e storia* 19 (1972): 20–39; and *Palazzo Chigi* (Rome: Editalia, 1973). The document summarized in "La costituzione edilizia," 31–32, no. 9, and quoted in *Palazzo Chigi*, 57 n. 10, is no. 8 in my appendix. Frederick Hammond refers to the story of the *ritratto* in *Girolamo Frescobaldi* (Cambridge, Mass: Harvard University Press, 1983), 59, 349 n. 7, and in "Cardinal Pietro Aldobrandini, Patron of Music," *Studi musicali* 11 (1983): 61.

4. The original contract (signed 30 September 1616) is held in AS, Notai A.C., vol. 2824, fols. 722r–745r; and a copy appears in AA, tomo 4: *Fabbricati. Palazzo Chigi in Piazza Colonna, interno 2.*

5. *Bullarium diplomatum et privilegiorum Sanctorum Romanorum Pontificum* (Turin: Franco-Dalmazzo, 1863), 8:88–95. The law is discussed at length in Ludwig von Pastor, *Geschichte der Päpste* (Freiburg and Rome: Herder, 1958), 9:819–24; and in Lefevre, "La costituzione edilizia."

6. The other houses belonged to Antonio Francesco De Grassi, the Arciconfraternita di S. Girolamo della Carità, Francesco and Ludovico Angeletti Cerasoli, and Giovanni and Domenico Mancini. Summaries of the cardinal's expenses for the five *ritratti* of 1617–19 can be found in AS, Notai A.C., vol. 6326, fols. 639r–644r: *Invent(ariu)m p(ro) Ex(cellentissi)ma D(omina) Olimpia Aldobrandina; AA, Card(inale) Pietro Aldobrandini. Lib(ro) M(ast)ro H dall'an(no) 1618 al 1628,* fols. 64–lxiv; ADP, scaffale 86 (numero 4: *Primogenitura Pamphilj . . . Parte 2ª,* fol. 35v, and *Parte 3ª,* fol. 49r) and scaffale 88 (numero 45, interno 7: *Palazzo Aldobrandini*

al Corso . . . Nota di case comprate, delle quali alcune furono incorporate al pred(etto) Palazzo). Except for the first, all these items include some mistakes. A fragment of the second one—in which Frescobaldi is named "Girolamo Francesco Baldo," as in document 7 of the appendix—is transcribed in Hammond, "Cardinal Pietro Aldobrandini," 65–66, no. 6. The last two documents have been published in part in Jörg Garms, ed., *Quellen aus dem Archiv Doria-Pamphilj zur Kunsttätigkeit in Rom unter Innocenz X* (Rome and Vienna: Böhlaus, 1972), 43 (no. 147), 118–19 (nos. 486–92); and in the miscellaneous volume *Via del Corso* (Rome: Cassa di risparmio di Roma, 1961), 181 n. 9 (where the first name of Frescobaldi is misquoted as "Domenico").

7. Appendix, documents 1a, 1b, 5, 8 (first paragraph). The increase in the price of the house suggested by these documents was set by the Constitutio gregoriana for rented houses. This leads us to wonder where the Frescobaldi family dwelt in 1617–18. It is possible that they had already moved to the house of the Via Camilliana, where the *stati d'anime* of S. Stefano del Cacco record their presence between 1623 and 1628. On the other hand, I have recently discovered a parish register that shows that in 1616 the Frescobaldis had let their house in the street running from the Piazza Colonna to Montecitorio, and that they lived nearby—probably in the Isola di Colonna. See AV, *S. Maria in Via. 17. St. d'An. 1581–84; 1616,* fol. 4r (on the reverse of the volume).

8. Appendix, documents 1a and 1b.

9. See the plate on p. 31 of Lefevre's *Palazzo Chigi,* in which the author tries to reconstruct the position of the houses bought by Cardinal Aldobrandini on a map of the present Palazzo Chigi. Similar plates were also published by Lefevre in "Il palazzo degli Aldobrandini a piazza Colonna" (p. 18), "Gli Aldobrandini in piazza Colonna" (plate lxxi), and *Il palazzo degli Aldobrandini e dei Chigi* (plate iii). As a matter of fact, the documents of the five *ritratti* record the boundaries of the relevant buildings in a vague and contradictory way. According to the cardinal's expert, for example, the boundaries of Frescobaldi's house were the public street in front, the cardinal's property on one side, and the Arciconfraternita's property on the other side and on the rear. But according to the contract they were the public street in front, the cardinal's property on two sides, and the Arciconfraternita's property on one side. See the appendix, documents 1a and 8 (first paragraph), respectively.

10. This can be easily proved, since the houses dispossessed by the cardinal were still inhabited by some of the people registered five years earlier as the Del Pinos' neighbors. See, for instance, Antonio Arnediglia, whose family is recorded in the *stati d'anime* of 1613 just before the Del Pino-Frescobaldis (AV, *S. Maria in Via. 18. St. d'An. 1610–13,* fol. 86v) and who is quoted in 1619 as a tenant of the Mancini brothers (AS, Notai del Tribunale Acque e Strade, vol. 52, fol. 548v).

11. De Luca, *Il dottor volgare,* 4:173.

12. *Bullarium,* 8:90, paragraph 4.

13. The other owner was Antonio Francesco De Grassi.

14. Appendix, document 5.

15. The price of the house was, according to the cardinal's expert, scudi 623.62 (see appendix, document 1a), and according to the Frescobaldis' expert, scudi 838.53 (see appendix, document 1b).

16. *Bullarium*, 8:94, paragraph 18.

17. Appendix, document 6.

18. Appendix, document 7. It should be noted that the cardinal's bookkeepers recorded all payments made by their master to the owners dispossessed by him. Thus we know that the Arciconfraternita di S. Girolamo della Carità (whose expert had agreed with the cardinal's expert, but whose attorney appealed the verdict of the Mastri di strada) eventually received the rents owed by the other party. ADP, Fondo Aldobrandini, busta 19,interno 59[b]: *Registro de Mandati del s[r]. Card[l]. Aldombrandini* [sic] *del 1618 al 1620*, fol. 54v; and AA, *Card. Pietro Aldobrandini. Lib(ro) M(ast)ro H*, fol. 103.

19. This detail is confirmed by the text of the contract. See appendix, document 8 (fifth paragraph).

20. This clause was literally observed. On 16 July 1618, the price of the Frescobaldis' house was invested in 6.5 *luoghi* of the *monte* "Fabbrica di S. Pietro" and on 1 January 1620 the cardinal's attorney consigned the relevant document to the notary of the Mastri di strada together with those concerning the other owners dispossessed by his master. As a consequence, in July 1683 the musician's daughter Caterina, wishing to buy similar *luoghi di monte* with the fruits of the investment made by her parents sixty-five years earlier, had to ask permission of the prince Giovanni Battista Pamphilj—that is, the permission of the son of the daughter of the nephew of Cardinal Pietro Aldobrandini. See AA, tomo 4: *Fabbricati. Palazzo Chigi in Piazza Colonna*, interno 1, fols. 9r–10v; and ADP, scaffale 92, numero 9: *Registro de memoriali. A. 1683 e 1684*, fol. 22r. (I wish to thank my colleague Renato Bossa for drawing my attention to this last source.)

21. *Bullarium*, 8:94, paragraph 18. Although this provision may strike us as absurd, it was entirely consistent with a law that served to promote the interests of the "Urbis ornatum," since it assured that buildings intended to embellish Rome for centuries to come were protected against any legal threat to their completion and continued existence.

22. We have, on one side, the well-known dedication of the *Recercari*, which hints at the many benefits received by the musician from the cardinal, and, on the other, the absence of the name of Frescobaldi in any extant record of the cardinal's bookkeepers except for the *mandato* quoted above (Appendix, document 7). Moreover, it should be noted that Frescobaldi definitely served the Aldobrandini family after the cardinal had died (on 10 February 1621) (see n. 28 below) but he did not partake of the *Distribuzion del legato fatto per la famiglia . . . di scudi sei milla di m(one)ta* that took place after the cardinal's death (see AA, tomo 10: *Atti di famiglia. Cardinal Pietro Aldobrandini*, fascicolo 34). I am not sure, however, that Frescobaldi is the "Don Gironimo organista" quoted in a *Rollo della Famiglia dell' Ill(ustrissi)mo et R(everendissi)mo Card(ina)l Aldobrandino restata à Roma p(er) la sua partita p(er) Ravenna questo di Dicembre 1620* in ADP, Fondo Aldobrandini, busta 28, interno 87, fol. 370r (as suggested by Hammond in *Frescobaldi*, 45, and "Cardinal Pietro Aldobrandini," 63). As a matter of fact, this would be the only source in which the title preceding the musician's name is *Don* instead of *Signore*—a title ordinarily reserved for noblemen or clergy (the document lists other names preceded by *Signore*). This "Don Gironimo" follows closely after Don Agostino Beruti, Don Antonio *cappellano*, and Don Ottavio Crispi, all of whom appear in similar sources among the clergymen serving Cardinal Aldobrandini and his

nephew Cardinal S. Cesareo as confessors, chaplains, or *caudatari*.

23. Teodoro Amayden, a contemporary biographer, pointed out repeatedly the political background of Cardinal Pietro Aldobrandini's splendors. About the villa at Frascati, which the cardinal wanted to be unmatched in Italy, we are told that, in spite of his stinginess, he had a leaning toward luxury and grandeur ("quamvis enim liberalitate non litasset, attamen erat splendidus et magnificus"). Similarly, speaking of the wedding of a niece of his (which ran the risk of being invalidated unless it were solemnly celebrated), Amayden adds that the cardinal, although he was a miser, on this occasion pretended to be prodigal ("licet avarum, in hac occasione liberalem se ostendere voluisse"): see *I-Rvat* Vat. lat. 13463: *Amideni Vitae Romanor(um) Pontific(um) & Cardinal(ium)*, fol. 140r (modern foliation).

24. The houses in which the Frescobaldis dwelt in Rome in 1623–28 and 1635–45 were called respectively "Casa della signora Laura" and "Casa del Tovaglia" (see AV, *S. Stefano del Cacco. St. d'An. 1 (1623–25)*, fol. 33r, and *S. Lorenzo ai Monti. 26. St. d'An. (1634–49)*, interno 9, fols. 4v and 18v). The same applies to the house in Borgo Vecchio where Orsola died in 1651, which belonged to the Cappella Giulia (I wish to thank Giancarlo Rostirolla for this information). For the rent of the second house mentioned above, Cardinal Francesco Barberini, the last patron of Frescobaldi, used to pay him 30 scudi semiannually; see Hammond, *Frescobaldi*, 81, and idem, "Girolamo Frescobaldi and a Decade of Music in Casa Barberini: 1634–1643," *Analecta musicologica* 19 (1979): 99.

25. Appendix, document 5.

26. On the functions of a Chamberlain of the Holy Roman Church in the seventeenth century see Giovanni Battista De Luca, *Theatrum veritatis, et iustitiae* (Rome: Corbelletti, 1673), 15:68–69. This appointment of Cardinal Aldobrandini, which went back to his uncle's pontificate, is repeatedly mentioned in appendix, document 8.

27. It goes without saying that Cardinal Aldobrandini himself had a patron—the king of Spain, whom he called "benignissimo Padrone della casa mia" in a letter of 29 July 1602 (ADP, Fondo Aldobrandini, busta 7, interno 20, fol. 40r). A systematic approach to the problem of paternalism, whose theoretical relevance was first noted by Max Weber, is provided by John W. Bennett, "Paternalism," *International Encyclopedia of the Social Sciences* (New York: Macmillan, 1968), 9:472–77.

28. See for example two *mandati* paid to Frescobaldi in 1621, which concern sums to be distributed by him to musicians engaged for official banquets (both of them have been published, with some errors in dates and transcription, in Hammond, *Frescobaldi*, 345 nn. 51 and 52, and "Cardinal Pietro Aldobrandini," 66, nos. 8 and 10). The first (24 scudi for seven *musici* and one harpsichord tuner) is dated 18 June and, although recorded in a ledger of the late Cardinal Pietro, was debited to his sister Olimpia (AA, *Card(inale) Pietro Aldobrandini. lib(ro) M(ast)ro H.*, fols. ccxxxxiv and cclxxiv). The second *mandato* (6 scudi for five *musici*) is dated 12 November and was recorded by the bookkeepers of Ippolito Aldobrandini (AA, *Li(b)ro M(ast)ro di D. Ipolito Aldob(randi)ni dal 1614 al 1628*, fol. 75 [left]; and ADP, Fondo Aldobrandini, busta interno 59ᵃ, fol. 7r). It should be noted that the ledgers of subsequent years in AA do not contain any further reference to Frescobaldi, though among them are all those of Ippolito, the nephew of Pietro, who was named cardinal two months after his uncle's death and inherited his leadership of the Aldobrandini family.

29. See the third section of Anthony Newcomb, "Girolamo Frescobaldi, 1608–1615: A Documentary Study," *Annales musicologiques* 7 (1964–77): 134–44.

30. Newcomb, "Frescobaldi, 1608–1615" 141–42; and Hammond, *Frescobaldi*, 15–45. Newcomb speculates that Cardinal Aldobrandini had had in his service only Filippo Piccinini (a hypothesis accepted in Hammond's *Frescobaldi*, 10). This is probably true during the cardinal's absence from Rome in 1606–09. But after the *devoluzione* of Ferrara, all three Piccinini brothers had gone into his service, and they probably followed him to Rome at the end of 1598 (Luzzaschi's stay in Rome in 1601, on the contrary, followed the cardinal's return from a diplomatic mission in France). In the penultimate chapter of the preface to his first book of *Intavolatura di liuto, et di chitarrone* (Bologna: Moscatelli, 1623; reprint, Florence: Studio per Edizioni Scelte, 1983) Alessandro Piccinini speaks of his concertante pieces as compositions performed by him and his brothers during their tenure at the Ferrara court and in the Aldobrandini household (see Lucio De Grandis, "Famiglie di musicisti nel '500. I Piccinini: vita col liuto," *Nuova rivista musicale italiana* 16 [1982]: 226). Concerning the Piccininis' stay in Rome, an anonymous chronicle of the Arciconfraternita della Ss. Trinità de' Convalescenti e Pellegrini reports on the ensemble performances they contributed, on behalf of Cardinal Pietro Aldobrandini, to the Lent sermons of 10 and 19 March 1600 (*I-Rvat* Vat. lat. 6822, pp. 109–10: "Et di poi si è fatta la Musica dove v'intervengono tre Fratelli Ferraresi [*sic*], che stanno con il Signor Cardinale Aldobrandino che sonano eccellentissimamente di leuto, et detto Signor Cardinale ha promesso mandarli tre volte la settimana"; "et poi si è fatta la Musica, con il conserto delli leuti delli retro scritti Fratelli servitori del signor Cardinal Aldobrandino eccellentissimamente"). There is little doubt, therefore, about the identity of the three Bolognese brothers whose salary of 700 scudi per annum is listed among the cardinal's expenses in Pastor, *Geschichte der Päpste* 11:776–79 (the original of this document, which Pastor quotes as an undated one, is held in AA, tomo 7: *Atti di famiglia. Card. Pietro Aldobrandini*, fascicolo 11; and it is clearly dated "l'anno 1598").

31. See, for example, the letter of condolences for Cardinal Pietro Aldobrandini's death, written on 11 February 1621 by Cardinal Domenico Ginnasi (a *creatura* of Clement VIII, who had to do also with Frescobaldi since he held his third son at the baptismal font). Ginnasi addresses himself to Olimpia, Ippolito, and Aldobrandino Aldobrandini, confirming his true *servitù* to their family in terms of a perpetual obligation of his own person and properties ("come loro vero e real servidor' di bon' cuore l'offero me et mei beni in perpetuo servitio della Casa loro Eccellentissima"). ADP, Archiviolo, busta 342, fol. 127r.

32. My reconstruction of the Meldola affair is chiefly based on the following sources: AA, tomo 1: *Atti di famiglia*, interno 5 (*Primogenitura Aldobrandini. Lettere sopra il negotio successo in Meldola*); ADP: scaffali 16 (busta 51) and 91 (busta 50, interno 4); Archiviolo, buste 146 (fols. 449r–567v) and 342 (fols. 429r–430v and 593r); Fondo Aldobrandini, buste 11 (interno 35), 20 (interno 63), 22 (fascicolo "1615"), and 30 (interno 95b); and the erratic volume *Processo fatto dal Fisco contro Gio: Giorgio Aldobrandini per la protettione de Banditi in Meldola à di 14 8bre 1614*. This last source includes the copy of a letter (1 November 1614) in which Cardinal Borghese expresses the pope's satisfaction with the official inquiry held by the Cardinale legato of Romagna into the "successo di Meldola."

33. To be sure, the Meldola affair led the cardinal to consider the possibility of giving up this family leadership. In October 1615, after the end of the affair, he wrote to his sister Olimpia Aldobrandini, hinting at this possibility and complaining about her sons' behavior: "Per l'avenire non credo di fare errore mentre per spatio di venti quattro anni l'attioni mie sono state sempre indirizzate dopo il servitio di Dio al bene et grandezza della casa che vol dire de sua figlioli che meritavano che ci fosse stata un poco più di consideratione hora ch'essi sono in età di poter disporre di se stessi." But his proposal met the pathetic opposition of Olimpia: "et pero signor Cardinale vengo di nuovo con quella magior sommissione possibile a chiederli perdono pregandola per le viscere di Nostro Signore a volermi dar questa consolatione ch'io senta che ella ritorni i mia figli et me stessa nella sua buona gratia et a voler continuare la sua protetione verso l'interessi di casa nostra benche io non lo meriti." See ADP, Archiviolo, busta 146, fols. 559r and 544r, respectively.

34. On the *Primogenitura Aldobrandina* see Renato Lefevre, "Il patrimonio romano degli Aldobrandini nel Seicento," *Archivio della Società romana di storia patria*, 83 (1959), serie 3, vol. 13, 1–24. Between April and May 1615 the concern for the loss of the family's patrimony led Olimpia and Cardinal Pietro to the paradoxical attempt to transfer the *primogenitura* from the firstborn to the youngest of her sons. See AA, tomo 1: *Atti di famiglia*, interno 5.

35. The Cardinal and Frescobaldi left Rome on 14 and 16 February respectively. See *I-Rvat* Urb. lat. 1083 (*avvisi di Roma* of 1615), fols. 90r, 96r, 116v; and the letter of 14 February 1615 by Vincenzo Agnelli Soardi, quoted in Parisi, this volume, n. 46. On the cardinal's arrival in Naples and on his return to Rome see *I-Rvat* Urb. lat. 1083, fols. 111r, 120r, 124r, 127r and 222r, 236r, 251r, 254r, 263r, and 268r.

36. In a letter from Meldola to Naples dated 11 April 1615, Olimpia states that the fear about the ruin of the family (and particularly of her son Aldobrandino Aldobrandini) will drive her mad: "dubito che questa gran tribulatione mi faccia perdere il Cervello et di non potervi durare al certo vedendo la Casa in ruvina et quando penso che quel povero figlio del Priore habbia da perdere il priorato oltre l'altre cose di tanta importanza mi crepa il Core affatto." On the same day, the secretary that the cardinal had sent to Meldola to assist his sister gives him an impassioned picture of Olimpia's attempts to disguise her distress and of his own inability to bring her some relief: "Io vedo questa Signora in gran travaglio, o smania, e se ben fò tutto quelche posso per supperar me stesso in apparenza, tuttavia mi sento cader l'anima, vedendo, che poco giovano, le persuasioni mie per consolar Sua Eccellenza. . . . Si prova Sua Eccellenza di far forza à se medesima quando si lascia vedere, ma nelle camere s'abbandona, e si sbatte . . . sempre s'aggira, e pensa à nuove cose; s'imagina l'estraminio di questa casa, e ne fà caso, come se fosse già presente; non mancarò io di far quanto posso, e supplico Vostra Signoria Illustrissima à scrivere quanto prima lettere che possino consolarla, perche sò che crederà assai à lei" (ADP, Archiviolo, busta 146, fol. 474r, and Fondo Aldobrandini, busta 11, interno 35, fols. 438r–438v).

The *famigli* of the cardinal and the *creature* of his uncle also felt embarrassed and confused. A project of a collective intervention of the *creature*, suggested by Ginnasi but criticized by others, was dismissed as involving the risk of irritating the pope; and isolated attempts to influence the latter were admittedly made (among others, by Ercole Vaccari himself) with fear and anxiety. See ADP, Fondo Aldobrandini, busta 20, interno 63, fol. 28r and 31r–31v. However, an important role in the eventual settlement of the Meldola affair was in fact played by a *creatura:* the Cardinal Giovanni Delfino (see the *avvisi di Roma* of 6 and 17 June and of 4 July 1615 in *I-Rvat* Urb. lat. 1083, fols. 294v, 311v, 337r).

37. The cardinal was expected at Frascati on 14 May 1615 (see the *avvisi di Roma* of 16 May 1615 in *I-Rvat* Urb. lat. 1083, fol. 263r). Frescobaldi's letter was published by Cametti ("Girolamo Frescobaldi in Roma: 1604–1643," *Rivista musicale italiana* 15 [1908]: 721) and by Newcomb ("Frescobaldi, 1608–1615," 155–56).

38. Susan Parisi's chapter in this volume quotes Frescobaldi's last letter to the Duke of Mantua, which also appears in Paola Besutti, "Una lettera inedita di Girolamo Frescobaldi," *Rivista italiana di musicologia* 17 (1982): 207–11, and in Hammond, *Frescobaldi*, 347–48 n. 24. I believe that even this letter of 5 September 1615 is to be correlated with the conclusion of the Meldola affair. At the end of July 1615, after they had submitted themselves to justice and undergone some days of imprisonment in Castel S. Angelo, Paul V gave his pardon to Cardinal Aldobrandini's nephews. But such a happy ending had to be formalized, and this did not happen at once. At the beginning of August 1615 the relevant *breve* was still in preparation; Olimpia Aldobrandini shows that she is informed of the formal acquittal of her sons in a letter of 12 September 1615 (ADP, Archiviolo, busta 146, fol. 531r). At the time she was still in Meldola, and received the news through a letter from her brother. Since it usually took her a week to respond, the last letter from Frescobaldi to the Duke of Gonzaga was probably mailed around the same time as the last one the cardinal wrote to his sister on the Meldola affair. For the conclusion of this affair, see the *avvisi di Roma* of 11, 22, 25, 29 July and 1 August 1615 (*I-Rvat* Urb. lat. 1083, fols. 369v, 372r, 374v, 379r, 393v, 397r, 419v).

39. One should keep in mind that the notion of paternalism involves the idea that a client is like a child, and therefore that he "can be deceived, or treated in such a way as to serve the interest of the 'adult' without becoming aware of this" (Bennett, "Paternalism," 472).

40. The key to the commercial effectiveness of a coat of arms as a sign of support and recognition on the part of some important personage is to be found in the ideal of art expressed by Frescobaldi himself when he dedicated the 1615 edition of the *Recercari* to the cardinal. The author's hope of being forgiven for daring to compensate for the weakness of his music by putting it under the protection of the dedicatee clearly suggests that the cardinal's protection enhanced the intrinsic quality of Frescobaldi's music since appreciation of art was regarded as a privilege of the upper classes: "Cosi confido nella medema humanità, non sia hora per isdegnare, che questo primo, & picciolo parto dell'ingegno mio debole, scorgendosi manchevole di ogni splendore, habbia procurato d'illustrarsi co'l chiaro nome di Vostra Signoria Illustrissima, uscendo sotto la sua protettione." Along these lines we read in another volume of music printed in those years by the publisher of Frescobaldi's *Recercari* that the leading men of the world are fond of music and regard it as an attribute of their social rank ("Quominus mirari solemus Principes viros, quorum est summa in reliquos auctoritas, & quaedam quasi terrestria Numina, Musica delectari, & hanc habere quandam quasi Humanitatis & Nobilitatis accessionem"); see the dedication of Vincenzo Pace's *Sacrorum Concentum . . . liber tertius* (Rome: Bartolomeo Zannetti, 1617).

41. As was the case with the quotations from unpublished sources in previous notes,

these transcriptions retain the spelling of the originals except for the replacement of *u* by *v* when appropriate. The figures for measurements, prices, and fees occasionally have been modernized and the customary sign for the Roman scudi has been replaced with *scudi*. Interpolations in brackets are conjectural readings of elliptical, illegible, or damaged passages. Abbreviations have been resolved; some special abbreviations have been retained and resolved in square brackets.

42. Copies of the valuations concerning the other four houses dispossessed by the cardinal are contained in the same volume. The original valuation of Angeletti's and Mancini's houses are in AS, Notai dell'Ufficio delle Acque e Strade, vols. 51 and 52.

43. This volume and the adjacent ones also include the notary's notes concerning the other four *ritratti*. See, for De Grassi, vols. 65 and 66; for the Arciconfraternita, vol. 66; for the Angelettis, vols. 66 and 67; for the Mancinis, vol. 67.

44. A copy is included in AA, tomo 4: *Fabbricati. Palazzo Chigi in Piazza Colonna*, interno 1, fols. 7v–9r. The originals and copies of the verdicts concerning the other four owners can be found in these same volumes.

45. The *mandati* concerning the other owners are found in the same volume.

46. A copy of the contract is included in AA, tomo 4: *Fabbricati. Palazzo Chigi in Piazza Colonna*, interno 1, fols. 1r–5v. An abstract was published in Lefevre, "La costituzione gregoriana," 31–32, no. 9. Copies and originals of the other contracts are found in the same volumes. Other documents concerning these four owners are in AA, *Card(inale) Pietro Aldobrandini. Lib(ro) M(ast)ro H* and tomo 4 cited above; ADP, Fondo Aldobrandini, busta 19, interno 59[b]: *Registro de Mandati del s.̄ Card.̄ Aldombrandini* [sic] *dal 1618 al 1620*; and AS, Notai dell'Ufficio delle Acque e Strade, vols. 51 and 52.

"Licenza alla Mantovana": Frescobaldi and the Recruitment of Musicians for Mantua, 1612–15

SUSAN PARISI

A
FTER NEGOTIATIONS LASTING from November 1614 to February 1615, Girolamo Frescobaldi was successfully enticed by a lucrative offer and the efforts of the Mantuan recruiting agent, Paolo Faccone, to leave Rome and enter the service of Cardinal Ferdinando Gonzaga, then twenty-seven years old and uncrowned duke of Mantua.[1] But already by early March, only two weeks after his arrival in Mantua, Frescobaldi was disheartened by the atmosphere at court and had begun to complain about his treatment. A short while later he returned to Rome.

This bare outline of the incident, first sketched in 1891 by Antonio Bertolotti,[2] and amended in 1908 by Alberto Cametti, who published the first excerpts from Faccone's and Frescobaldi's letters,[3] represented until recently all that was known of these events. In the last few years, however, a more precise narrative and better understanding of Frescobaldi's character, as well as more documents, have emerged from contributions by Anthony Newcomb,[4] Frederick Hammond,[5] and Claudio Annibaldi.[6] But this excellent work notwithstanding, we are still not well informed about Ferdinando Gonzaga's attitude toward music and musicians, and the prevailing atmosphere in this respect at his court, during the period of Frescobaldi's recruitment and his subsequent brief sojourn in Mantua.

The present essay will examine this aspect of the episode more closely,[7] drawing on new documents from the Mantuan archives[8] and on a Venetian ambassadorial report for interesting details concerning events and recruiting in Mantua, and for insights into Ferdinando Gonzaga's activities and taste. New documents from 1612 that enlarge our perspective on the dismissal of Claudio and Giulio Cesare Monteverdi and reveal a plot to steal Adriana Basile, the court's most prestigious soprano, will also enter into the discussion.

The first documents that must be considered are three new dispatches pertaining to Frescobaldi's recruitment, and one published letter that can now be interpreted more accurately.

Paolo Faccone, a papal singer and the Mantuan court's recruiting agent in Rome for at least twenty-nine years,[9] had written to Ferdinando on 1 November 1614 that he thought Frescobaldi could be induced to serve in Mantua: Frescobaldi claimed that he did not want to leave Rome, but had said he might decide to come if offered an extraordinary salary in the form of property.[10] Ferdinando's reply to Faccone survives in a draft copy. The dispatch, dated 8 November, reads,

> We have seen what you have written us about the demands of the organist, and finding his motives sound we make him an offer of an income of 600 scudi which we will award him in that much realty or property, and which his children will inherit. Thus he can come here happily and see well how much we esteem his virtuosity. And we have in mind for him not to assume any engagement except with us.[11]

Judging from the reply, Ferdinando seems to have been genuinely intent, at least at this moment, not to lose Frescobaldi to another patron.[12] But in his haste he forgot to clarify one matter, and had his counselor, Giovanni Magni, send Faccone a postscript the same day. It states:

> His Highness has ordered me to add that if ever that organist were to ask to leave service the award of 600 scudi of income would be revoked. This your lordship will make clear to him as a condition that specifically has to be included in the contract which is being made with him.[13]

But Frescobaldi was not yet ready to sign a contract, for there were other conditions he hoped would be met. These are enumerated in Faccone's well-known letter of 22 November, of which the main points were that the income would belong to Frescobaldi from the day he left Rome and would pass to his heirs upon his death, even should he die on the way to Mantua; that he would leave Rome only after the printing of his *Primo Libro di Toccate e Partite* was completed, for which he wanted a loan of 300 scudi; and that he be given a house, and, for two years, the use of all utensils and furnishings.[14]

Ferdinando's reply to that letter survives in a draft dated 5 December. The opening gives the impression that Ferdinando had not expected further demands, nor to hear that Frescobaldi's arrival might be delayed; but then every point is conceded:

> Although the demands of the organist Frescobaldi very much alter the offer that we have made to him through you, nevertheless we wish for him to know, so much the more by this expression, how pleased we will be to have him. So that he will go on being certain we hereby affirm that the award in realty, amounting to an income of 600 of these scudi a year, will become his as soon as he sends someone who accepts it in his name. But it would be better, so that the time until his arrival is less, for him to come himself to claim the award. It will be left to go to his heirs whatever accident should happen to him, whether the time he has served has been short or long, unless, however, as we had written to you by Magni, he should leave our service, in which case it is agreed of course that the award will be revoked. The 300 scudi will be delivered to him and he will pay them back as he likes over two years. An adequate house and the loan of general furnishings will be equally provided for his needs. We will arrange for the requisition of three portions of bread and wine for four months.

Ferdinando ends by explaining his agreement to all of Frescobaldi's demands:

> We want to comfort him in everything. In this way we are confident that he will be inspired to serve us well and with all his heart. As we have already done by granting his every request, so we will also try to relieve him of every other worry.[15]

This passage is important, for it provides the missing link to Faccone's next communication, that of 13 December. Faccone must have been suspicious of easy promises—undoubtedly for good reasons—and thus, reacting to Ferdinando's assumption that promising Frescobaldi whatever he wanted would guarantee his dedicated service, issued that pointed warning to Giovanni Magni:

> Let me advise your lordship that it is not enough that our patron has good intentions for his foreign servants to be well treated and lodged. Someone kind and zealous must take charge and carry out this good will. . . . I know that your lordship is wise and understands me.[16]

The very day of this writing, Frescobaldi had accepted Ferdinando's offer and had promised to come to Mantua in the course of the Christmas and New Year holiday.[17]

Sometime between 19 December and 11 January Magni replied to Faccone:

> As for the organist, His Highness will give him the esteem that his skill is worth, and from the others he will also receive courtesy, whereby your lordship can encourage him and tell him confidentially that he will be well received and well treated.[18]

Faccone responded on 17 January:

> These words that your lordship writes in your last letter, I do not know what they are meant to imply. . . . Please favor me with a short explanation because I do not know what you mean by these [words], unless your lordship indeed wants to hint that the bread of remorse has now been eaten; or perhaps this is courtier-like license, or to say it better, Mantuan-style license, which if it should be, I beg your lordship to kindly do me the favor of informing me of it and at the same time, the means of the justification so that one party and the other remain satisfied, for the poor man is already well along [in all this], and as soon as this work of his is printed, which he has dedicated to His Highness, he wants to come to present it personally in Mantua.[19]

Apparently Faccone was not sure of Magni's sincerity and felt compelled to ask whether the court had really resolved to treat Frescobaldi properly ("the bread of remorse has now been eaten") or, on the other hand, was continuing to treat the matter with cavalier nonchalance ("courtier-like license"). His fears in this regard may have been magnified by his knowledge that Frescobaldi still had not left Rome at this time: he might have assumed that Ferdinando and his advisers were disappointed at the delay or even angry at the lack of explanation and apology. However, such a reaction on their part would have betrayed ignorance of the practical problems facing a busy musician of Frescobaldi's reputation seeking to put his professional and personal affairs in order in the middle of the Christmas season for a move to a distant city; it would have been extremely difficult for Frescobaldi to accomplish these tasks and travel to Mantua in a mere three weeks, even though he had agreed to do so. Justified or not, however, Faccone clearly considered the first possibility—that the court was ready to do everything he had requested—the less likely one, and the other—that it had dismissed his message and was continuing to take liberties with Frescobaldi—far more probable.

In fact Faccone's reference to "licenza" may indicate (if its meaning here is dismissal [from a post] rather than license [in behavior])[20] that he feared Ferdinando was no longer interested in Frescobaldi and wished to break off the negotiations. Faced with these possibilities, he seems to have inserted in the midst of his pleas an even more pointed, indeed ominous, warning, embodied in the epithet "licenza alla Mantovana." For, regardless of whether these words referred to the dismissal of persons or to cavalier treatment of them, Faccone's allusion to the Mantuan style of doing this was surely intended to remind Ferdinando and his ministers of a scandalous situation that two-and-a-half years earlier had gained the Mantuan court a reputation for precisely such high-handed treatment of musicians. The details of this episode, an important one in the history of the musical establishment at Mantua, will help to illuminate the background to Frescobaldi's recruitment and thus warrant the digression of a closer examination.

By the late reign of Ferdinando's father, Vincenzo I, the Mantuan duchy was in financial difficulty, but Vincenzo continued to live above his means and to enlarge his staff, placing on the payroll alchemists, dwarfs, and marginal figures who had taken his fancy, and hiring still more actors and musicians, even when his treasury could no longer afford to maintain them. When, following Vincenzo's death in February 1612, Ferdinando's elder brother Francesco came into power, the outstanding debts amounted to 800,000 ducats.[21] To reduce this exorbitant sum, Francesco (who was to rule for only ten months) resolved to apply half his personal income toward the deficit each year, pay more ordinary expenses from his income than Vincenzo during his time had done, and sell jewels and property. He further undertook to avoid traveling and other unnecessary occasions for expenditures, curtail the outlay for the coronation, and dismiss some of the court personnel, then numbering 800 *bocche*.[22]

It was Francesco's intentions concerning the personnel that caused the most concern. His desire to rid the staff of the parasites accumulated by his father—persons he considered to be of little use and a burden on the court's finances—was rumored to be intense; concurrently, there was speculation about arbitrary dismissals. In March the Modenese ambassador reported that not only Vincenzo's favorites, but most of his staff expected to be discharged of their duties; and the Mantuan ambassador in Rome wrote that "they are guessing [in Rome] that in a little while you [= Francesco] will rid yourself of all your father's servants. . . . They conceive of you as enemy to the alchemists, prostitutes, fools, sycophants, and scoundrels."[23] The reports were exaggerated, but not altogether false. After the coronation in June 1612 several high-ranking officials were abruptly sacked,[24] as were a number of musicians, and by the end of the summer the musical personnel had been reduced by one-quarter, from thirty-two to about twenty-four.[25]

A serious rumor about Claudio Monteverdi also surfaced in early June —that he wanted to leave and might be replaced by his brother Giulio Cesare.[26] This news probably came to Francesco's attention; in any case, by 6 July 1612 Francesco had made up his mind to dismiss both of them, and to do it "immediately . . . when they least expect it." Francesco reveals this in a lengthy dispatch of that date to Ferdinando in Rome—a communication written primarily to assure himself of another maestro di cappella before proceeding:

> Your Illustrious Lordship knows how much obligation Monteverdi and his brother have to serve me on account of the honorable stay that they have had in this house for so many years, and because of the great esteem that I have always shown toward both of them; now it appears to me that either to ruin me or for some other reason they have rebelled, and they treat me with every term of disrespect, claiming that other shelter is not lacking to them; and because I would like to take revenge for my reputation I had the idea to dis-

miss both of them immediately from my service when they least expect it; and because I cannot come to this resolution without someone ready who will take over the position in my chapel for any occasion which might come up concerning concerts or musical compositions, I decided to turn to Your Illustrious Lordship and beg you on this occasion. I cannot express to you how much I dearly desire to have the services of the person of Messer Santi Orlandi and if you are not willing to give him to me, at least lend him to me until such time as I can provide myself with a chapelmaster, to which your help in Rome, where there are so many virtuosi and where far more than elsewhere some candidate to fit my plan will be found, will be of great service to me. My thought is to give the said position of chapelmaster to Messer Santi and to treat him well in all ways, since I am very well informed of how greatly he is esteemed in this profession; and if I am indeed aware that Your Lordship will part with him unwillingly, I would in any case hope it will not seem to you that you are depriving yourself of him by giving him to me, and that you would not want to deny me this favor, since there will be no dearth of others there who will serve you to your satisfaction. It is absolutely certain that the greater your inconvenience so much the greater will be my obligation to you, for which I will always show you the effects in other needs. Your Illustrious Lordship should not be surprised that, since Monteverdi is the subject he is, I should condescend to part with him; for if you knew with what hope of advantage and from what ulterior motives he and his brother are dealing with me you would side with me completely. I have charged Marliani to take care of anything else that will be necessary in order to send Messer Santi on the way here, and entrusting the rest to him, I kiss your hand and I wish you God's every kindness. Francesco.[27]

In light of the earlier rumor, Francesco's insinuations ("they treat me with every term of disrespect, claiming that other shelter is not lacking to them"; "if you knew with what hope of advantage and from what ulterior motives he and his brother deal with me") suggest that both Claudio and Giulio Cesare had probably been pressing him for better wages and privileges, letting him know that they could obtain posts elsewhere, [28] presumably in the hope that this would serve as leverage. As he admits, Francesco found their behavior potentially damaging to his reputation; his way of dealing with the situation was to take immediate revenge by firing both of them without warning.

This may appear to be an excessive reaction. But Francesco was under considerable pressure at that moment, not only in his foreign affairs, as he moved closer to a confrontation with the Farnese over his father's honor and the deaths of several loyal Gonzaga supporters accused of conspiracy (in late August he stationed Mantuan troops near the border with Parma in preparation for war), [29] but also in regard to his musicians. Shortly before the problem of the Monteverdi brothers arose, the court's best castrato, Giovan Battista Sacchi, had run away to Florence and sent word that he did not wish to return. On the same day that Francesco wrote to Ferdinando about Monteverdi he also wrote to the Medici requesting their cooperation in finding and returning Sacchi. It can hardly be a coincidence that the two letters express certain similar sentiments. The dispatch to the Medici reads, "His Highness is insisting on this . . . inasmuch as it appears to him that he has been made fun of by a boy who, once away from here, decided to treat him disrespectfully."[30]

The conduct of two other musicians had also been cause for embarrassment. In the previous month the principal wind player, the cornettist Giulio Cesare Bianchi, had approached Cardinal Borghese about entering his service in Rome. Word that he wanted to leave Mantua circulated, and by July even the Mantuan ambassador in Rome had heard the news,[31] though by then Bianchi had already been dismissed by Francesco.[32] Also Adriana Basile had begun to complain in this period. There had been no special performances in which she could sing since Francesco had come to the throne, and she felt shut in: "In six months only once have I seen her Highness Signora Infanta the Duchess," she wrote in July to Ferdinando in Rome, "in this small house, without any of the recreation of the villa as in past years, and with little hope of going out, you can see that I want freedom." And she adds, "even though it is only some months it seems to me a thousand years."[33]

Undoubtedly more disturbing to Francesco than Adriana's restlessness, however, was the rumor of a possible plot to steal her. As early as March, only a few weeks after he had begun to rule, Francesco had been warned by the Mantuan ambassador in Rome, Aurelio Recordati, that Cardinal

Borghese might be trying to obtain her for his service.[34] Then, at the beginning of July, Francesco's principal adviser, Annibale Chieppio, received not only confirmation of a plot but also word that Ferdinando Gonzaga was involved in it. It is not certain that Francesco was given this news right away, since the writer, in adding that the duke "would probably be disgusted" should he find out, implies that this might not happen.[35] Nevertheless, it seems extremely unlikely that a report of his own brother's participation in an intrigue to steal the court's most brilliant singer would not have been relayed to Francesco immediately. And if it was, this would have occurred within a day or two of his writing to Ferdinando about his decision to dismiss Monteverdi and of his need for the services of Ferdinando's maestro di cappella, Santi Orlandi. Francesco's request for Orlandi may thus perhaps have been motivated, at least in part, by his desire to get even with his brother, whose pleasure in music was limitless and whose fondness for Orlandi was such that he professed not to be able "to console myself without him."[36] Within two weeks, in any case, Francesco had definitely heard about the whole matter, for Recordati, writing to him personally on 14 July, reported at length that it was not Cardinal Borghese but Ferdinando who wanted Adriana, having taken it into his head to try to create the best musical establishment in Rome, and having even managed to persuade Adriana to send him a deposit of 1000 scudi as a guarantee that she would come.[37] The plot collapsed, but not before word had spread; and Recordati lamented to Francesco, "It is unfortunate that our Lord Cardinal has been conducting himself in such a manner that he lets the whole world know that between you and him there is not that mutual understanding that there should be."[38]

That Francesco and Ferdinando were not especially close in these months was also reported by the Venetian special ambassador, Pietro Gritti, who was in Mantua from 19 to 25 July for the festivities celebrating the election of Emperor Matthias. In the course of his detailed report assessing Francesco's administration, Gritti noted,

> The Lord Cardinal . . . was in Mantua once after his father's death, and only stayed a few days [Ferdinando departed before the coronation], and they say that there is not a good understanding between the duke and him. Some have it that this is because of their different temperaments, for the cardinal is lavish in his expendi-

tures and more clever [*di maggior vivacità d'ingegno*] than the duke;
and others say that it is the usual habit of all princes not to trust and
to always be suspicious of the one who is closest in succession.[39]

On 19 July Ferdinando nevertheless complied with Francesco's wish,
and though finding it difficult to part with Orlandi, sent him to Mantua.[40]
Meanwhile in Mantua the foreign guests, numbering about four hundred,
had begun to arrive for the imperial celebration. The first evening a
banquet and play were offered; the next night elaborate fireworks displays (*fali*) that had been erected in the main piazzas of the city were lit
by the ducal party on horseback, after which a mock battle was fought to
capture a castle; on Sunday Mass was sung, and in the afternoon there
was a tournament on horseback with musical interludes, representing
the Rape of the Sabines, followed by a banquet; on the last evening the
fireworks constructions were lit again and a concert, featuring Adriana
Basile, was given on Lake Garda.[41] Orlandi did not witness any of these
events, for he only reached Mantua on the evening of 27 July. Two days
later Monteverdi was dismissed; the same day Orlandi was installed as
maestro di cappella, and the following day he was introduced in that
capacity before the Invaghiti Academy.[42] It was thus, in the very abrupt
manner Francesco had proposed to Ferdinando only three weeks earlier,
that Monteverdi was deposed; and, as he himself later described his
departure, "[I] left that Most Serene Court so disgracefully—by God
—after being there for twenty-one years I took away no more than
twenty-five scudi."[43]

The subtle allusion in Faccone's letter of 17 January 1615 to those recent
scandals and the behavior that had brought about the irrevocable loss of
Monteverdi and the near disintegration of the Gonzaga musical establishment—about which there had been so much talk in various cities
—and the implication that Ferdinando and his ministers might dare deal
similarly with Frescobaldi, must have been effective, especially coupled
with the assurances that Frescobaldi was truly coming and had only
been held up by the printing of the *Toccate*. In any case, the communication stirred the Mantuan officials to inform the ambassador in Rome how
he was to handle the transfer of funds.[44] But then, in precisely the
cavalier manner that Faccone knew so well, the amount sent was less

than half of what was needed for the *Toccate*, and included no travel allowance at all. Nevertheless, by 16 February Frescobaldi was on his way, spending his own money on the journey.[45] Faccone remained worried about the impending reception; in his last-minute instructions he again urged the necessity of treating Frescobaldi with kindness—housing him with someone familiar, buying him a proper suit, finding a court position for his relative—and he warned about possible jealousy on the part of the other musicians.[46] However, there is now confirmation that when Frescobaldi reached Mantua, Ferdinando and his officials were favorably impressed, for the Mantuan ambassador in Rome wrote to Magni on 7 March, "I am particularly glad to hear that Frescobaldi, having arrived, has succeeded in pleasing His Highness, especially since he has also won your vote."[47] But it is clear that Ferdinando and those around him immediately reverted to the behavior that Faccone had feared, for within a week Frescobaldi had complained to friends in Rome about his treatment and Faccone had relayed that urgent message to Mantua: "Here there is talk that Signor Frescobaldi is very displeased with the court. . . . After the four or so words that His Highness said to him the first day he arrived it seems no one has looked on him again."[48]

With this evidence of Frescobaldi's displeasure we have arrived at the critical moment in his stay at the Mantuan court, a moment that requires further elucidation, especially with regard to the attitudes of Ferdinando and the ambiance of his court. For this we are fortunate to have the testimony of an eyewitness, the Venetian ambassador Giovanni da Mulla, whose detailed appraisal of Mantuan affairs is set forth in a lengthy report to the Venetian Senate, written shortly after his own return from Mantua in September 1615.[49] Da Mulla analyzes Mantua's difficulties with Savoy, her relationship with Spain, the proposal to exchange Monferrato for Cremona, the state of negotiations to contract a marriage, the line of succession, and the inner workings of the government; he also describes Ferdinando's handling of finances, and some of his personal characteristics. It is Da Mulla's observations regarding the latter points that are of principal interest here.

According to Da Mulla, Ferdinando's annual expenditures amounted to 430,000 ducats, equalling his revenue from both Mantua and Monferrato.[50] Many of the expenses were unavoidable; but others, Da

Mulla points out, were incurred by choice. Expenditures included the maintenance of a large household (numbering 800 *bocche*), personal guards, ambassadors, and the fortress of Casale. There were also expenditures on trips, music, theatrical performances and other entertainment, and the lodging of visiting emissaries. The outlay for the last had been unusually high in the two-and-a-half years of Ferdinando's reign because of the hostilities with Savoy: most of the delegates had been *ambassadori estraordinari* rather than resident ambassadors, and their expenses had been assumed by Ferdinando, not by the courts sending them.[51] In Da Mulla's own case, for example, Ferdinando had arranged for him to be ceremoniously escorted into the city. He and his staff had been lodged in a ducal apartment, were waited on by several servants, and had the use of horsemen, guards, and ten carriages. Ferdinando had entertained him every day, offering a dinner, a hunting expedition, an outing to shoot birds on the lake, music, a play, and, on the last day, a party and ballet in his honor. A necklace had also been given to him. For the return trip five boats with men had been provided, while additional servants accompanied the party ten miles outside Mantua in order to prepare their first meal.[52]

Da Mulla offers the opinion that if Duke Francesco had lived longer, Mantua's debts would probably have been paid off in a short time, since Francesco was concerned about the problem and had managed to curtail some excesses during his brief reign.[53] How Ferdinando will fare is less predictable, though Da Mulla implies he is a spendthrift with regard to certain activities, of which music is one:

> It cannot be said what the present duke will be able to do about this [the financial crisis], for his entrance into office was expensive and very inauspicious [in this regard], whence he has surely not been able in any way to pay off the old debts, and, too, has had to incur new ones, not to mention having pawned most of his jewels and silver, as His Highness himself said it convened him to do. However, he has good intentions: he wants to cut back on expenses, favors decreasing his staff by 100 *bocche*, and he also told me that he has little interest in traveling, or indulging his senses, that he loathes gambling, and that his greatest pleasure is music, on which, however, he spends a lot—some 30,000 ducats a year.[54]

Following this comment Da Mulla turns to Ferdinando's physique, professional training, and intellectual pursuits. Ferdinando's health is adequate but would probably be better if he did not take medications as often as he does ("From what I have heard, whenever he is in the least angry, upset, or a little depressed he immediately resorts to some kind of pill"), a habit which is generally felt to be doing him more harm than good.[55] He has a sharp wit, good mind, and excellent memory, and claims never to forget anything he has read or seen once; indeed, he has considerable aptitude for everything. Da Mulla stresses Ferdinando's training in the legal profession and studies in the liberal and fine arts, and refers specifically to his fluency in languages, his writing in philosophy and theology, [56] and his talent for poetry and music. It is the last which receives Da Mulla's most effusive comments:

> Poetry delights him in an extraordinary way. He always has all the good ancient and modern poets "in hand," as we say. . . . And he writes poetry nicely and loves to talk about what he has written and how his verses are praised. He has great relish for music and is very proficient in it, and himself has skillfully set to music several of his verses, which he has then had sung, and these have been stupendous successes.[57]

Da Mulla confirms Ferdinando's particular fondness for vocal performance:

> Besides a very large choir of singers in his Santa Barbara cappella he also maintains three really exceptional women singers who play and sing excellently.[58] And if this musical recreation costs the duke what I have already said, he nevertheless savors and enjoys it so much that I do not believe he feels the expense. And he told me several times that during the last serious disturbances [i.e., with Savoy] he had no other refuge or solace than music, and that he would already be dead if he had not had that refuge.[59]

Even at nighttime, and upon waking, Ferdinando's mind is occupied with music and literature:

> And truly it is his natural inclination to relish music and poetry so incredibly much. And because he sleeps very little it is thought that compositions form in his head at night; and in the morning when he

leaves his rooms he always has something gracious to say and to talk
about with a literary person, which does not please the rest of his
gentlemen of the chamber and of the court, who were used to being
treated more intimately by Duke Francesco and Duke Vincenzo, and
to whom it appears that the present duke values only those whose
profession is letters.[60]

Da Mulla's report gives us valuable details of Ferdinando's preoccu-
pations. That he genuinely loved music and actively cultivated it was, of
course, already known. Both as a student in Florence and as a cardinal in
Rome he had enthusiastically pursued one musical project after another,
as his association with the Academy of the Elevati and his many letters
about compositions and productions attest.[61] Despite the added respon-
sibilities, the delicate political situation, and the serious financial bur-
dens occupying much of his attention when he assumed control of the
court, it is clear that he continued as intensely as before to bring together
a superior corps of musicians: the personnel had dropped significantly
under Francesco, but Ferdinando soon brought their number again to
thirty-two[62] (not counting the additional musicians at Santa Barbara),
and he avidly sought still more singers from Rome.[63] But what is particularly significant in Da Mulla's portrayal of the man are the insights into
certain of Ferdinando's less admirable qualities: his tendency to live
above his means, his egoism, his nervous, intense, impatient personality.
If these qualities had not already become apparent to Frescobaldi in the
course of the negotiations they must surely have struck him within a
short time of his arrival.

Frescobaldi's arrival in Mantua could not have come at a worse moment,
for Ferdinando was experiencing frustrations on two important fronts.
First there was his marriage. In the early months of 1615 Ferdinando's
marriage plans revolved around three women representing three alliances
then being negotiated.[64] The potential candidates were Margherita of
Savoy (widow of Duke Francesco), one of the Estense princesses of
Modena, and Caterina de Medici of Florence. Not only did Ferdinando
have to juggle the simultaneous negotiations with Savoy, Modena, and
Florence, but he had to deal with the repeated Spanish veto of his
wishes—a situation that was to continue without interruption until Feb-

ruary 1617, when the marriage with Caterina de Medici was finally concluded.[65]

The second problem consuming Ferdinando's attention and energy at the end of February—exactly at the moment of Frescobaldi's arrival —was the turbulent situation in Monferrato. This possession of Mantua, geographically adjoining the duchy of Savoy and coveted by Carlo Emanuele I, duke of Savoy, had already been the subject of dispute, and had been occupied by Carlo Emanuele's troops twice in the past two years.[66] Now Carlo Emanuele was preparing to attack again and Ferdinando invited the participation of Spain, which had its own designs in the area. Although hostilities resumed only on 17 April, already by the end of February intelligence reports had confirmed troop movement on both sides, as well as the emergence of plans of attack.[67] Then, after Carlo Emanuele publicly announced that he had been compelled to increase his forces to deter future Spanish aggression in the area, there was no longer any doubt that another confrontation would ensue. It was not clear when it would take place, but intelligence reports predicted it would be in the middle of April.[68]

Future research may help to determine the precise effect of this crisis on domestic events at court. Letters of 14 and 19 (?) February from two of Ferdinando's three principal advisers, Annibale Chieppio and Alessandro Striggio, give the impression that the marriage negotiations were continuing, though another difficulty had been encountered with Modena.[69] Artistic life appears to have proceeded normally, for Ferdinando had received a visiting emissary, who had been invited to return for a performance of Orlandi's opera *Galatea* and a ballet on a subject proposed by Ferdinando's brother, Vincenzo, both probably staged around 21/23 February.[70] But as is suggested in a letter by Chieppio of 26 February, by which time carnival was at its height—and Frescobaldi had undoubtedly reached Mantua—Ferdinando was nevertheless preoccupied with Monferrato and preparations for war.[71]

Yet Ferdinando arranged for the recruitment of Margherita Basile, the younger sister of Adriana, in Naples in this same period, and despite the fact that fighting had already begun when she arrived in Mantua, her recruitment was apparently executed with care, as were the plans for her reception. Ferdinando personally wrote to Margherita's mother at the beginning of February.[72] To persuade Margherita, he engaged the same agent who had negotiated her sister's contract five years earlier, and had patiently put up with Adriana's whims and frequent changes of mind for over a year until she finally set off.[73] As a further precaution, and to assist in the operation, Ferdinando sent their brother Lelio Basile, a composer already in his service, to Naples, and later he enlisted the help of another relative living there.[74] It had been hoped that Margherita would be on her way to Mantua almost immediately. But it was soon learned that she was planning to marry, and the immediate problem was to persuade her to break off her engagement and enter Ferdinando's service instead.[75] In the meantime, though she had not yet agreed to come, the Mantuan staff nevertheless began arranging her trip, particularly her accommodations along the route with various noble families.[76] Thus, when she did set off at the end of March, traveling first to Rome[77] and then to Florence, there were no last-minute difficulties, as had arisen with Frescobaldi. Margherita gave performances in both Florence and Bologna before various dignitaries and musicians, winning praise and gifts for herself.[78] While there are no details about her reception in Mantua, Ferdinando must have heard her sing almost immediately, for on 1 May when he thanked her various relatives for encouraging her to come, he wrote that she was more talented than he had even imagined and that he would soon demonstrate his esteem of her talents.[79] One month later he arranged a marriage for her, paid the dowry of 5,000 scudi, and stipulated that her husband invest it in property for her.[80]

In the weeks following Frescobaldi's departure, Ferdinando continued to seek more singers for the court. The possibility that Frescobaldi might return to Mantua with his family had arisen in early May,[81] but considering how his interests had been neglected, there is no reason to assume that immediate action was taken regarding the property transferral upon which his return was surely contingent, or that Ferdinando took any pains to persuade him to come back. On the other hand, in this very period Ferdinando ordered Faccone to recruit the tenor-bass virtuoso Giovanni Domenico Puliaschi[82] as well as a young castrato, both of whom were then employed in Roman households.

These initiatives are a further indication of the Mantuan court's, and particularly of Ferdinando's, enthusiasm, indeed overwhelming preference, for singers and for vocal music in the years after Monteverdi's departure.[83] That enthusiasm can be attributed not only to the general popularity that monodies enjoyed in Italy in this period, inspiring Ferdinando to similar compositional efforts of his own, but also to his inherent desire to compete with the musical establishments of Rome and Florence. From 1613 on, apart from Salamone Rossi and the group of string players, Mantuan court music was dominated by singers, among them the monodists Francesco Rasi and Settimia Caccini; Adriana, Vittoria, and Margherita Basile; Francesco Campagnolo; Francesco Dognazzi; Giovan Battista Sacchi; Giulio Cardi; and Lorenzo Sances, some of whom, in the absence of composers and instrumentalists of stature, appear also to have written a significant portion of the repertory performed at court.[84]

In retrospect it is clear that Frescobaldi was brought to Mantua only half-heartedly, and when he arrived found that he had come to serve a patron whose taste strongly favored a medium other than that in which he excelled,[85] one who was preoccupied with frustrating diplomatic negotiations on the one hand and with preparations to meet the threat of hostilities on the other, a man who was vain, fickle, carried along by events. Little wonder, then, that when Frescobaldi also found himself neglected by the rest of the court, he preferred—despite the possible financial advantages of Mantua—to return to the larger world of Rome, a more fertile ground for his talents.

Notes

1. Ferdinando (1587–1626) assumed control of the court while still a cardinal, following the unexpected death on 22 December 1612 of his brother Francesco, but he was not crowned duke until 6 January 1616, after the cardinalate had been transferred to their younger brother, Vincenzo II.

2. Antonio Bertolotti, *Musici alla corte dei Gonzaga dal secolo XV al XVIII: Notizie e documenti raccolti negli archivi mantovani* (Milan: Ricordi, 1891), 91.

3. Alberto Cametti, "Girolamo Frescobaldi in Roma, 1604–1643," *Rivista musicale italiana* 15 (1908): 717–22.

4. Anthony Newcomb, "Girolamo Frescobaldi, 1608–1615: A Documentary Study," *Annales musicologiques* 7 (1964–77): 145–57, which also contains letters not in Cametti, "Frescobaldi in Roma," as well as full transcriptions and English translations of the previously published excerpts. I am indebted to Professor Newcomb for valuable comments and suggestions on an earlier version of this study.

5. Frederick Hammond, *Girolamo Frescobaldi* (Cambridge, Mass.: Harvard University Press, 1983), 47–53. I am most grateful to Professor Hammond for allowing me to read this chapter in his book before it appeared in print, for helpful comments on my work, and for other kindnesses.

6. See Annibaldi, this volume, which discusses the decline of Cardinal Pietro Aldobrandini's power at the time Frescobaldi agreed to enter Ferdinando Gonzaga's service in Mantua, and Aldobrandini's subsequent absence from Rome between February and May 1615. I am indebted to Professor Annibaldi for sending me a typescript of his paper.

7. The question of Frescobaldi's personality and the role this may have played in his early departure from Mantua will not be dealt with here. For discussions of Frescobaldi's character, see Hammond, *Frescobaldi*, and Newcomb, "Frescobaldi, 1608–1615."

8. I owe special thanks to Signora Anna Maria Lorenzoni, Signora Wilma Faberi, and Dottore Carlo Belfanti of the Archivio di Stato of Mantua for their assistance in locating certain documents; and to Signora Lorenzoni, Signora Faberi, Dottoressa Adele Bellù, the archive's director, Dottore Roberto Navarrini, and Signora Anna Maria Mortari-Vanzini, I wish to express my gratitude for their unfailing kindness during my visits to Mantua.

9. Recruiting and hiring practices at the Mantuan court, and Faccone's role in these, are discussed in Susan Parisi, "Virtuoso Performers at the Court of Mantua, 1587–1627: An Archival Study," chapter 3 (Ph.D. diss., Univ. of Illinois, forthcoming).

10. Paolo Faccone in Rome to Ferdinando Gonzaga in Mantua, 1 November 1614 (Mantua, Archivio di Stato, Archivio Gonzaga [hereafter ManAS, A.G.], 1006). The relevant paragraph, the first in the letter, is published in Cametti, "Frescobaldi in Roma," 718; Newcomb, "Frescobaldi, 1608–1615," 145; and Hammond, *Frescobaldi*, 48–49. The continuation concerns the possible hiring of a bass singer with an extraordinary range who was to come secretly to Mantua for an audition. The course of the negotiations for this singer can be followed in the documents transcribed in n. 11 and 14–16 below. My transcription of the entire letter follows; in this and all subsequent transcriptions in this study I have silently resolved abbreviations and adapted *u* and *v* to modern usage.

Serenissimo Signor et Padron mio singularissimo

Ho ritrovato il Signor Hieronimo assai disposto qual oltra l'organo di san pietro e la provisione di Aldobrandino si guadagna scudi 25 al mese; Mi ha risposto che havendo da partirsi di qua più volentieri venir a servire Vostra Altezza che qualsi voglia principe ma che in conclusione non vuole lasciar Roma per provisioni anchorche siano straordinarie, ma si bene si rissolverà quando le sarrà datto da vivere equivalente e che sia stabile, e suo poiche dissegna e vuole stabbilirsi e la casa sua e suoi erredi in perpetuo; e non havere occasione di andare a cercare altra ventura creddo che quando Vostra Altezza si rissolverà dargli questo che senzo dubbio alcuno sarrà il suo.

Ho ritrovato un Basso per camera, si come anche Vostra Altezza mi comando et creddo non le spiacerà: le qualità sue sono queste: la voce e maggiore e più bella di quella di Don Federico; va basso sino al ottava di Dessore intonante in camera; ha buona dispositione e con bravura sicuro, e fa contrapunto, nelle comedie riuscirà bene, in chiesa farrà il debito suo quanto altro basso. Lui e Mastro di Cappella nella

Marca dove ne cava l'anno scudi 200, la casa di bando, e grano, e vino per la sua famiglia. Ha moglie e figlioli; siamo restati d'accordo insieme che quando Vostra Altezza comandi però lui fingerà di andare a spasso e cappitarà a Mantova, accio se a Vostra Altezza non gustasse il povero Virtuoso non perdesse il suo luogo e reputazione insieme; ma bisogna mandargli Denari si per il venire come per il suo ritorno. Circa al soprano io non ho voluto parlare ad Orfeo eunuco in San Pietro perche ho qualche speranza in quello castrato spagnolo meglio di quest'altro. Humiliamente le fo riverenza. Di Roma il primo novembre 1614.

Di Vostra Altezza Serenissima

> Obligatissimo e Devotissimo Servitore
> Paolo Fachoni

11. Ferdinando Gonzaga in Mantua to Paolo Faccone in Rome, 8 November 1614 (ManAS, A.G. 2285):

> Ferdinando
>
> Mantova 8 Novembre 1614

Paolo Facconi/

Habbiamo veduto cio che ci scrivete della pretensione dell'organista et faccendole buone le considerationi sue gli offeriamo partito di sei cento scudi d'entrata che le faremo assegnare in tanti stabili o livelli et che passeranno nei suoi figli, onde puo venir allegramente che ben vede quanto stimiamo la sua Virtù, et habbiamo in consideratione che non riceva danno dal pigliar se ne con Noi. Quanto al Basso approviamo che egli si trasferisca qui onde potiamo sentir come ci riesca se ben attese le qualità che ci riferite di lui crediamo ci sarà di sodisfattione. Ma sarà però bene che non si levi dal servizio in cui si trova prima di trovarsi accordato al nostro per non perder la sua fortuna in caso che non potessimo o volessimo convenir seco, et del danaro per la sua venuta daremo l'ordine opportuno.

12. Ferdinando's offer was generous by Mantuan standards, though not unrealistic in light of what Frescobaldi may have been earning in this period: 72 scudi a year as organist at St. Peter's (document in Cametti, "Frescobaldi in Roma," 710; see also Hammond, *Frescobaldi*, 49); 100–150 scudi from Cardinal Pietro Aldobrandini (as estimated by Newcomb, "Frescobaldi," *The New Grove Dictionary of Music and Musicians* [London: Macmillan, 1980], 6: 827), and perhaps as much as 300 scudi—unless Faccone exaggerates—from teaching, performances, and miscellaneous gifts (document in n. 10 above). On the salaries of Mantuan musicians in this period, see Susan Parisi, "Virtuoso Performers," chapter 2.

13. Copy of a letter of Giovanni Magni in Mantua to Paolo Faccone in Rome, 8 November 1614 (ManAS, A.G. 2285): "Alla lettera che Vostra Signoria vedra dell' Altezza Sua in proposito dell' organista mi ha ordinato ch'io soggunga che quando mai esso organista domandasse licentio dal servizio di Sua Altezza che in tal caso s'intenda revocato l'assegnamento che si gli farà per sei cento scudo d'entrata, volendo in tal caso trovarsi l'Altezza Sua libera dalla promessa et che i beni assegnati ritornino alla camera ducale. Il che Vostra Signoria dovra significarli come fatto che esspressamente ha da esser compreso nell'accordo che si fa della persona sua."

14. Paolo Faccone in Rome to Ferdinando Gonzaga in Mantua, 22 November 1614 (ManAS, A.G. 1006), partially quoted in Cametti, "Frescobaldi in Roma," 718–19, and Hammond, *Frescobaldi*, 49; and completely in Newcomb, "Frescobaldi, 1608–1615," 146–47. The letter is given here in its entirety so that it may be compared with the reply (see next note).

Illustrissimo Signor et Patron mio Singularissimo

Il Signor Geronimo Frescobaldi organista prontissimamente acetta il partito che Vostra Altezza gli offerisse di scudi 600 l'anno in Beni Stabili, quando però lui sia sicuro siano li beni suoi e passino alli suoi erredi; dirchiarando però che fatto il contratto et che lui sia venuto alla servitù che per disgratia in puocho tempo venisse a morte questi tereni habbiano da rimanere alli suoi erredi; e che la provissione sopra detta habbia da incominciare acorergli dal di che lui partirà da Roma per venire a questo servitio.

E perche detto ha gia incominciato a stampare una opera in ramme quale li costarà scudi 500 non vuole partirsi da Roma sin tanto che detta opera non sia finita di stampare quale creddo habbia animo dedicarla a Vostra Altezza.

Supplica anchora che nanzi si parti di qui gli sia fatta questa assignatione a lui o a chi presenterà in nome suo acciò quando arrivarà a Mantova possi andare liberamente al possesso.

Di più supplica Vostra Altezza fargli gratia subbito che sarrà fatto il contratto di scudi 300 anticipatamente a conto della predetta provisione per pottersi più presto sbrigare di queli denari si habbino da scontare in doi anni prossimi a venire.

Supplica anchora che gli sia datto in vitta sua una casa qual sia capace per se e per la sua famiglia e suo padre; e che in prestito per doi anni gli siano datto tutti li utensilli e fornimenti necessari per detta casa.

Supplica anchora che per quattro mesi al di che arrivarà a Mantova Vostra Altezza gli voglia far gratia di tre spese di pane e vino ogni giorno. Queste sono le conditioni e bisogni quali ricerca il Signor Gieronimo quali quando Vostra Altezza si compiacerà di gratiarlo si obligarà di vivere e morire a detto servitio, e quando mancasse per suo licentio tutto questi beni e terreni habbino da tornare alla camera ducale.

Quando Vostra Altezza comandarà che siano datti li denari inviarò a quella volta il Basso.

Humilissamente le fo riverenza. Di Roma alli 22 novembre 1614. Di Vostra Altezza Serenissima

> Devotissimo e fedelissimo Servitore
> Paolo Fachoni

Serenissimo di Mantova

15. Ferdinando Gonzaga in Mantua to Paolo Faccone in Rome, 5 December 1615 (ManAS, A.G. 2285):

> Ferdinando
> Mantova 5 Dicembre 1615

Paolo Facconi

Si ben le pretensioni del Frescobaldi organista alterano assai l'offerta che gli habbiamo fatto per mezo vostro, tuttavia vogliamo che egli conosca tanto più a questa dimostratione quanto siamo per haver grata la sua persona. Onde egli restarà sicuro mediante questa nostra dichiaratione d'haver assegnamento in tanti stabili per sei cento di questi scudi d'entrata l'anno da farseli quando egli mandi persona che l'accetti in suo nome, ma saria meglio che per metter manco tempo alla sua Venuta lui medesimo venissi a pigliar l'assegnamento qual ne lasciarà di passarne suoi heredi per qualsi voglia accidente che avvenisse nella sua persona sia poco o molto il tempo che havesse servito. Mentre però come vi facessimo scrivere per il Magno non lasciasse egli il servigio, che in tal caso s'intenderà senza altro revocato esso assegno li trecento scudi se li faranno rimetter i quali egli incontrarà come desidera in duoi anni. Sarà parimente provisto di casa suffiente col prestito d'utensili grossi per il suo bisogno ne ripararemo nella spesa delle tre bocche di pane et vino per quattro mesi, onde come in tutto lo vogliamo consolare, cosi confidiamo che verrà animato di servirci bene et con tutto l'animo già che col acconsentir ad ogni richiesta di lui cerchiamo di sollevarlo da ogni altra cura.

Without waiting to hear again from Faccone, Ferdinando instructed various Mantuan officials to obtain the travel money and have Faccone expedite Frescobaldi's departure. On 7 December 1614, Giulio Cesare Pavese, probably associated with the treasury, sent this note to another official, perhaps Magni (ManAS, A.G. 2730):

Molto Illustre Signor mio osservissimo
Rimetto a Vostra Signoria le lettere havendo Sua Altezza ordinato che si scriva al Facconi che sollecite la venuta dell'organista e del Basso poiche la prossima settimana farà rimettere trecento Ducatoni per il Viaggio.

16. Paolo Faccone in Rome to Giovanni Magni in Mantua, 13 December 1614 (ManAS, A.G. 1006), published in part in Newcomb, "Frescobaldi, 1608–1615," 148–49, and Hammond, *Frescobaldi*, 49.

Molto Illustre Signor mio osservissimo
Queste due incluse serviranno per risposta del Basso, quale e Mastro di Capella in Osimo. il povero huomo si raccomanda con tanto lecita scrisa che mi pare degno di scusa. Prego Vostra Signoria supplicare Sua Altezza che le perdoni ch'io dal altro canto procurarò di qualche altro soggetto. Sia per aviso a Vostra Signoria che non basta che il padrone nostro habbia buona intentione che gli suoi servitori forestieri siano ben trattati et alloggiati, ma bisogno che qualche amorevole e zelante sia quello che piglia l'impresa; e mette in esecutione questa buona volonta. Voglio dire in mio linguaggio che venendo come verrà questo organista sia raccomandato a qualcheduno che lo tratti bene acciò che non habbia occasione di mala sottisfatione e di ombra di ricevere peggio. So che Vostra Signoria e prudente e mi intende. Pero altro non dirro se non che sto con desiderio di servire all' Signor Magni al quale bacio le mani. Di Roma alli 3 Dicembre 1614. Di Vostra Signoria Molto Illustre

Affetionatissimo Servitore
Paolo Fachoni

Molto Illustre Signor Magni

17. Frescobaldi's letter, ManAS, A.G., *Autografi* 10, is printed in Cametti, "Frescobaldi in Roma," 719–20, and in Newcomb, "Frescobaldi, 1608–1615," 149.

18. Magni's letter is lost but must have been written at the earliest some six days after Faccone's letter of 13 December and at the latest some six days before Faccone's reply of 17 January. In the latter (transcribed in the next note) Faccone quotes verbatim the portion of Magni's letter translated above. Magni's actual words, "Del organista/ ne fara Sua Altezza il conto che merita la sua Virtù; et da gli altri receverà cortesia; onde Vostra Signoria lo può animare, e lui confidare di esser' ben veduto; et trattato," clearly represent the essence, if not the entirety, of his reply; certainly the beginning, "As for the organist," confirms that there was no earlier reference to Frescobaldi in the letter.

19. Portion of letter of Paolo Faccone in Rome to Giovanni Magni in Mantua, 17 January 1615 (ManAS, A.G. 1010); this portion also published in Newcomb, "Frescobaldi, 1608–1615," 149–50, and Hammond, *Frescobaldi*, 50.

> Molto Illustre Signor mio Osservissimo
> Queste parole che Vostra Signoria scrive nella sua ultima; non so che vogliano significare, dico circa al particolare del organista e sono queste: Del organista/ ne fara Sua Altezza il conto che merita la sua Virtù; et dal gli altri ancora riceverà cortesia; onde Vostra Signoria lo può animare; e lui confidare di esser' ben veduto; et trattato; di gratia [Vostra] Signoria mi favorisca un puocho di Glosa perche io non le intendo ne, se però Vostra Signoria non volesse accenare; che si habbia magnato del pane pentito; o forse questa fosse una licenza Corteggianesca—o—per dir meglio—alla Mantovana: il che se fosse prego Vostra Signoria mi faccia gratia avisarmene; et insieme il modo della scusa; acciò l'una parte el altro rimanga sottisfatta: poiche il povero Huomo già è inbarcato bene; e subbito stampato questa oppera sua—qual ha intittolata a Sua Altezza vuole venirsene a dedicarla personalmente a Mantova. . . . Di Roma alli 17 genaio 1615. Di Vostra Signoria Molto Illustre
>
> Servitore Affetionatissimo
Paolo Fachoni   Maestro di Capella del Papa
>
> Signor Magni

20. In his Italian-English dictionary of 1611 (*Queen Anne's New World of Words*, 283; reprint, Menston, England: The Scolar Press Ltd., 1968), John Florio translates *licenza* (spelled *licentia*) "licence, leave, sufferance, permission. Also boldnesse, licenciousnesse, unrulinesse." That the word had also come to mean dismissal, a substitution of the idea of forbidding continuation of service for the idea of permitting service to cease (temporarily or permanently), is, of course, obvious from the context of its very frequent occurrences in documents of this period. But that it was also widely used in this period in extensions of the sense of Florio's first four translations, particularly in connection with the behavior of those having power over subordinates—taking liberties, acting high-handedly (Tasso speaks of "la licenza tirranica")—is confirmed by all historical dictionaries of the language (see, for instance, Nicolò Tommaseo and Bernardo Bellini, *Dizionario della lingua italiana* [Rome: Unione, {1879}], 2:1846–47, no. 10; also Salvatore Battaglia, *Grande dizionario della lingua italiana* [Torino: Unione, {1975}], 9:43–47, nos. 11, 13, 20). I believe Faccone is using

licenza in this sense, though the word's ambiguity surely fitted his purpose.

21. For a summary of the main events of the late reign of Vincenzo I (1562–1612) and that of Francesco (1586–1612), see Romolo Quazza, *Mantova attraverso i secoli* (Mantua, 1933; 2d ed. Torino: G.A.M., 1966), 188–93, and *Mantova: La storia*, ed. Leonardo Mazzoldi (Mantua: Istituto Carlo d'Arco, 1963), 3:83–85. Recent discussions of musical life at the court during Vincenzo's early reign include Iain Fenlon, *Music and Patronage in Sixteenth-Century Mantua* (Cambridge: Cambridge University Press, 1980), 1:121–62; Iain Fenlon, "Monteverdi's Mantuan *Orfeo*: Some New Documentation," *Early Music* 12 (1984): 163–72; Stuart Reiner, "La Vag'Angioletta (and Others)," *Analecta musicologica* 14 (1974): 26–88; see also *The Letters of Claudio Monteverdi*, trans. Denis Stevens (Cambridge: Cambridge University Press, 1980) and Gary Tomlinson, "Madrigal, Monody, and Monteverdi's 'via naturale alla immitatione,'" *Journal of the American Musicological Society* 34 (1981): 60–108. The musical personnel at Santa Barbara in this period is documented in Pierre Tagmann, "La Cappella dei maestri cantori della basilica palatina di Santa Barbara a Mantova (1565–1630): Nuovo materiale scoperto negli archivi mantovani," *Civiltà mantovana* 4 (1969–70): 376–99.

22. In a report entitled "Relazione del Clarissimo Signor Pietro Gritti, ritornato di ambasciator al duca Francesco di Mantoa l'anno 1612," the Venetian ambassador writes as follows: " . . . il signor duca Vicenzo poco tempo innanzi la sua morte, trovandosi debito di 800,000 ducati. . . . A questi debiti si dice che il signor duca pensi di sodisfare, non solo con le contribuzioni che caverà dalli suoi Stati e con l'avanzo che farà delle sue entrate mediante la spesa ordinata e regolata che fa, ma con dar anco esito a una parte delle gioie che le ha lasciato il signor duca suo padre ed anco, vien detto, a qualche parte de' beni stabili." Earlier in the report Gritti writes, "Le spese solevano essere grandi in tempo del passato duca, spendendo lui molto in tenere una gran corte, che ascendeva al numero di 800 boche, assai in suoi gusti e privati piaceri e molto ne' viaggi, che benspesso faceva più per diletto che per necessità. Ora sono grandemente diminuite, perchè sono stati licenziati tutti li alchimisti, si hanno levate molte provisioni superflue a principali donne della città ed a uomini, che non avevano altro carico che di servire ai gusti del prencipe. Si mostra il signor duca alieno dal far viaggi e dall'abbracciare occasioni di spese, e si spende solamente nelle cose necessarie, ed anco in queste con gran regola ed assignazione." Gritti's report is published in Arnaldo Segarizzi, ed., *Relazioni degli ambasciatori veneti al senato*, 4 vols (Bari: Laterza, 1912–16; reprint ed. Angelo Venturi; Bari: Laterza, 1976), 1:111–29. The above excerpts appear on pp. 119 and 118 respectively.

23. From a letter of Dionisio Brutturi in Mantua to the Duke of Modena, 10 March 1612 (Modena, Archivio di Stato, busta 9): " . . . dimani s'aspeta di sentire varie mutationi della Corte del defunto Signore et la maggior parte aspeta licenza, se bene alcuni ma pochi son statto affermati. Il Signor Alessandro Guarini si è licentiato per causa di pretensioni, in che premeva et si dice giustamente desiderato." On the same day, writing from Rome about what was being said there, Aurelio Recordati told Francesco (ManAS, A.G. 1000), " . . . Stimano che fra puoco tempo privarà di tutti i servitori di suo Padre, il che non fa hora per virtù d'una gran destrezza e prudenza. L'hanno in concetto di nemico agli alchimisti, male donne, buffoni, adulatori, e persone vitiose."

24. From a letter of Eugenio Cagnani in Mantua to Alessandro Striggio, 1 June 1612

(ManAS, A.G. 2725): ". . . il prossimo lunedi, che sarà il 4 del corrente, l'Illustrissimo Signor Cardinale nostro partirà per Roma conducendo per aggiunta della sua corte una quantita di cortigiani derelitti, come il Signor medico Bruschi per medico della sua persona, il Signor Vincenzo Bonino per guardarobiero, il Signor Giovanni Bonnasoni Bolognese già scalco di Madama Serenissima di felice memoria per gentilhuomo; andando parimente con esso Signor Cardinale il Conte Carlo Maffei, et il Conte Giulio Agnelli per loro gusto et dello stesso Illustrissimo Signor Cardinale; ma quella nuova nuovissima che più importa è che il Signor Ercole Marliani co' improvisa resolutione (di chi non lo so) anchor lui va a servire detto Monsignore Illustrissimo, e si parte con lo stesso lasciando la corte di Mantova nella quale per tanti negotii più importanti che passano per la lui mani era tenuto per il più caro che havesse Sua Altezza Serenissima." Within a day of having hired several of the ousted employees for his household in Rome, Ferdinando was ordered to rescind some of the appointments, probably in order not to put Francesco in a bad light. From a letter of Eugenio Cagnani in Mantua to Alessandro Striggio, 8 June 1612 (ManAS, A.G. 2725): "Parti l'illustrissimo Signor Cardinale per Roma, ma lascio a dietro il Signor Bonnasoni bolognese stato solo un giorno alla servitù sua, et parimente fu lasciato a dietro da quello il Signor Spinelli, ambi dua suddetti licentiati dicessi per sodisfar al Signor Duca. . . . Il Signor Marliani . . . si dice haverlo licentiato Sua Altezza Serenissima dalla lui servitù per un disgusto ricevuto . . . il medesimo Signor Marliani, dicendomi però che spera debba restar disingannato e dover fra pochi giorni ritornar alla servitù, che però non vien da molti creduto." And on the same day Augusto de Mori da Cena reported from Mantua (ManAS, A.G. 2724), ". . . Il Signor Marliani è andato a Roma col Signor Cardinale, licentiato dal Signor Duca per haver richiesto all' Usciere del Morato una sua figliola, spendendo il nome di Sua Altezza; il Signor Cardinale licentio anch'egli prima della sua partita il Segretario Spinelli, che qui si va trattenendo cred'io per far sgannar il Signor Duca, a richiesta di cui si dice l'habbia il Signore Cardinale licentiato."

25. Apart from the six musicians named by Augusto de Mori in the letter of 8 June 1612 (see n. 26 below) as having been (or in the case of Claudio and Giulio Cesare Monteverdi, as about to be) dismissed by Francesco, the Spanish guitarist known only as Vittorio and the singer Giovanni Battista Marinone left Mantua at this time. For a discussion of the size of the musical establishment during the reigns of Francesco and Ferdinando, see Parisi, "Virtuoso Performers," chapter 2.

26. From the same letter by Augusto de Mori, 8 June 1612 (ManAS, A.G. 2724): ". . . Sua Altezza ha licentiato alcuni Musici, fra i quali è Don Bassano [=Casola], accettato però per capellano, Don Francesco tenore [presumably Dognazzi], Don Anselmo [=Rossi], ch'è andato con il Signore Cardinale, Messer Giulio Cesare dal Cornetto [=Bianchi], e forse anco il Signor Claudio Monteverde, che con molta istanza chiede licenza, in luoga di cui servirà suo fratello."

27. Francesco Gonzaga in Mantua to Ferdinando Gonzaga in Rome, 6 July 1612 (ManAS, A.G. 2279):

6 luglio 1612

Signor Cardinale

Sa Vostra Illustrissima quanta obligatione il Monteverdi et suo fratello tengano di servirmi per l'honorato trattenimento che per tant'anni hanno havuto in questa casa et per la molta stima che ho mostrato sempre fare de l'uno et l'altro di loro, hora parere me che se per farmi saltare o per altro si siano ammutinati et che trattino meco con ogni termine di poca cortesia facendo professione che non manchi loro altro ricovero et perchè vorrei risentirmene con mia riputatione mi è venuto in pensiero di licentiarli tutti due d'improviso dal mio servigio quando meno se lo pensaranno, ma perchè non posso venir a questa risolutione senza haver persona pronta che subentri al carico della mia capella per ogni occasione che mi venga di concerti o compositioni musicali ho preso partito di ricorrere a Vostra Illustrissima et di pregarla per questa occasione che non posso dirle quanto mi sia a cuore a volermi accommodare della persona di Messer Santo Orlandi et quando non voglia darmelo liberamente o prestarmelo almeno sin tanto che Io mi provegga di un Maestro di Capella nel che potrà anche valermi molto l'opera di lei costì in Roma dove sono tanti virtuosi et dove facilmente più che altrove si trovara qualche soggetto al proposito mio; il mio pensiero è di dare detto carico di Maestro di Capella a Messer Santi et di trattarlo bene per ogni conto essendo molto ben informato di quanto egli vaglia in questa professione, et se ben so che Vostra Signoria Illustrissima se ne privara mal volentieri ad ogni modo voglio credere che non le parerà de privarsene dandolo a me et che non vorrà negarmi questo gusto mentre che a lei non mancheranno altri costì che la serviranno a sua sodisfattione, sicura massime che quanto più sara l'incommodo tanto sara maggiore verso lei la mis obligatione di cui in altre occorrenze le farò sempre vedere gl'effetti. Non si meravigli Vostra Signoria Illustrissima che essendo il Monteverdi il soggetto che è Io condescenda a privarmene perchè se sapessi con che vantaggi et come Interessatamente egli et il fratello trattino meco mi darebbe ogni ragione; Al Marliani ho incaricato che habbia pensiero de quel più che occorrerà per incaminar subito esso Messer Santi a questa volta et con riportarmi nel resto a lui bacio a Vostra Signoria Illustrissima la mano et le auguro da Dio vera felicità. Di F[rancesco]

28. On the question of what caused Francesco to dismiss Monteverdi, Denis Stevens (*Letters of Claudio Monteverdi*, 88) has offered a provocative, though speculative explanation: that because of the delicate political situation between Mantua and Parma in 1612, Francesco's wrath could have been aroused by even a hint of a commission or of employ-ment for Monteverdi by the Farnese. However, since other musicians either left or tried to leave Francesco's service in these very weeks for employment in various cities (see notes 26, 30–31, 33–38), an offer to Monteverdi from an establishment other than that of Parma is equally plausible, and such an offer, or for that matter, merely interest on Monteverdi's part to go elsewhere, could also have aroused Francesco's wrath. For more on the political situation, see n. 29 below.

29. Diplomatic relations between Mantua and Parma had been strained since the assassi-nation of Pier Luigi Farnese in the mid-sixteenth century, an incident in which it was rumored Ferrante Gonzaga had a part. Vincenzo Gonzaga's marriage to Margherita Farnese in 1581 re-established family ties and peace, but both were short-lived. The Gonzagas had the marriage annulled three years later, following a lengthy trial involving the testimony of

doctors, lawyers, and theologians, after it was established that Margherita could not bear children; she was subsequently banished to a convent, and in 1584 Vincenzo married Leonora de Medici, further embittering the Farnese. A few years later a fire that destroyed the Mantuan armory and ducal theater was rumored to have been a retaliatory act instigated by Prince Ranuccio Farnese, Margherita's brother. Tensions reached the breaking point in the spring of 1612, not long after Vincenzo Gonzaga's death. In the course of the preceding year Ranuccio, then duke of Parma, had seized prosperous estates in the Piacenza region, which he declared his fiefs. After accusing the landowners of having plotted with Vincenzo Gonzaga and two neighboring princes to have him murdered, Ranuccio imprisoned several of them, including Barbara Sanseverino (Countess of Sala), a patroness of the arts who in her earlier years had been Vincenzo's mistress, and Gianfrancesco Sanvitale, the young lover of Agnes de Argotta (Marchioness of Grana), another of Vincenzo's mistresses and mother of Don Silvio Gonzaga, Francesco's and Ferdinando's half-brother, then aged twenty, and a prominent figure at the Mantuan court. After a lengthy and secret trial, in which torture was used to extract false confessions, Ranuccio's jurors named Vincenzo the principal conspirator and declared all the landowners guilty; the latter were executed in a public square in Parma on 19 May 1612. There was general outrage in Mantua when word of the trials and executions became known; for his part, Francesco vowed to uphold his father's honor. When mediation efforts proved ineffectual, Francesco adopted more aggressive measures, and finally, at the end of August, moved Gonzaga troops to Viadana in preparation for war. The Spanish intervened in September, upholding the Mantuan position, and the dispute was ended; nevertheless, the remaining threads of cordiality between Mantua and Parma had been severed. See Romolo Quazza, "Una Vertenza fra principi italiani nel seicento," *Rivista storica italiana* 47 (1930): 233–54, 369–87.

30. Communication of Francesco Gonzaga in Mantua to Belisario Vinta in Florence, 6 July 1612 (ManAS, A.G. 2279):

6 July 1612

Signor Commendatore Vinta/

Ha servito qui per alcuni anni nella musica di queste Altezze un certo giovanetto castrato fiorentino che si nomina Giovan Battista Sacchi, il quale da un pezzo in qua veste l'habito di chierico; Hora egli dopo ricevute diverse recognitioni et gratia da Padroni et dal Signor Duca presente in particolare ha ricercato di venir costa per certe sue facende dove poi è fermata scrivendo di non voler ritornarsene, cosa che è spiacciuta tanto per altre cose precedute seco in questo soggetto che non può Sua Altezza accommodarsi l'animo a digerirla; mi ha percio commandato che Io scrivo a Vostra Signoria accio si contenti far uffitio gagliardo in nome di lui col Gran Duca perchè gli commandi strettamente che senza dillatione sene ritorni qua solo per segno di ubbidienza che se non vorra poi restare non gli sara impedito il ritorno premendo all'Altezza Sua questa dimostratione quanto le pare di essere stata burlata da un ragazzo s'è pensato fuori di qua usar con lui ogni termine di poco rispetto; confida molto Sua Altezza nella distezza et autorità di Vostra Signoria a cui raccommanda caldamente il negotio et io al fine le bacio la mano et auguro da Dio vera felicità. Di Francesco

31. From a letter of Aurelio Recordati in Rome to Francesco Gonzaga in Mantua, 14 July 1612 (ManAS, A.G. 1000):

Serenissimo Principe
Puo essere circa un mese che un Messer Giulio Cesare di patria Cremonese che suona il cornetto in corte di Vostra Altezza et ha anche un uffitio, cred'io in Magistrato, mi prego far intendere al Signor Cardinale Borghese che essendo a Sua Signoria Illustrissima [= Borghese] morto un servitore chiamato Lodovico che suonava il cornetto eccellentemente, che lui le sarebbe venuto a servire, conoscendo non poter durar in cotest'aria di Mantova, che per altro non trattarebbe mai di partirsi dal servigio di Vostra Altezza, da cui viene con emolumento conveniente assai honorato; Mi rispose Sua Signoria Illustrissima che quando li fosse constato dell'assenso di Vostra Altezza che l'haverebbe preso, ma senza quello in eterno mai, anzi, che ha lui qualche buon musico che tutti li havrebbe dati a Vostra Altezza; del qual Messer Giulio Cesare non ho mai più havuto lettere doppo che li risposi di questo tenere, e m'imagino che l'aria se li sara mostrata più piacevole.

32. Bianchi's dismissal is mentioned by Augusto de Mori in his letter of 8 June 1612 (quoted in n. 26 above). For further on Bianchi, see Parisi, "Virtuoso Performers," appendix 1.

33. From a letter of Adriana Basile in Mantua to Ferdinando Gonzaga in Rome, 20 July 1612, published in Alessandro Ademollo, *La bell'Adriana ed altre virtuose del suo tempo alla corte di Mantova* (Citta di Castello: S. Lapi, 1888), 193–94: ". . . in sei mesi una sol volta ho visto la Signora Infante [= the Duchess], può imaginarsi come la passo, massime essendo io avezza in quei buoni tempi da me giornalmente sospirati, et adesso in questa picciola casa senza nulla recreatione di villa conforme li anni passati, et con poca speranza d'uscir fuore, veda dunque s'io desidero liberta. Il Serenissimo mi corrisponde con i soliti favori, et più ne farebbe se potesse. con tutto ciò il tempo da me prescritto in mente di volere qui dimorare, anchorche siano di pochi mesi, mi parerà mill'anni." The Mantuan documents corroborate Adriana's claim that there was virtually no musical activity during the first six months of Francesco's reign. See Parisi, "Virtuoso Performers," chapter 5.

34. From a letter of Aurelio Recordati in Rome to Francesco Gonzaga in Mantua, 14 March 1612 (ManAS, A.G. 1000): "Subbito che fui giunto Paolo Faccone Basso della Cappella del Papa sotto specie di venirmi a vedere mi addimando con molta instanza se era vero che la Signora Adriana si fosse licenziata da Vostra Altezza e che se ne veniva a questa volta, Io li disse non ne sapere cosa alcuna, il medesimo mi ricerco il Signor Cardinale Borghese, a cui pure l'istesso risposi, il che discorrendo con Montalto, habbiamo concluso che Paolo trattasse di metterla con Borghese in evento che si fosse licenziata da Vostra Altezza, a cui servira questo per aviso."

35. From a letter of Hercole Marliani in Rome to Annibale Chieppio in Mantua, 30 June 1612 (ManAS, A.G. 1001): "Deve anche sapere che si tratta di levare dal servitio del Signor Duca la signora Adriana per metterla in casa del Signor Borghese, et già ne sono passate lettere et il Signor Cardinale nostro, capo di questa opera, ha data la parola a Sua Signoria Illustrissima che venira in breve, et per quanto ho veduto dalla lettera soddetta del Signor

Pavese, egli ci tiene mano costi. Et se Sua Altezza potesse penetrare questo negotio forse resterebbe disgustata; ne fo però motto a Vostra Signoria perchè come suo amico passi quel uffitio (cosi stimando bene) che possa distorlo da questa negotiatione. Ma ben la supplico a non nominar me affinche poi se si risapessi dal Signor Cardinale io non m'havessi da ritrovare tra l'incudine e'l morsello."

36. Ferdinando Gonzaga in Rome to Francesco Gonzaga in Mantua, 19 July 1612 (ManAS, A.G. 1000); see note 40.

37. From a letter of Aurelio Recordati in Rome to Francesco Gonzaga in Mantua, 14 July 1612 (ManAS, A.G. 1000); further excerpts are given in notes 31 and 38. ". . . Hora ho ripigliato questo ragionamento per attacco a discorrere con Sua Signoria Illustrissima [= Borghese] del particolare della Signora Adriana, mostrando essermi stato detto a Roma che lui cercava d'haverla al suo servitio . . . mi diede una risposta che per me non l'havrei voluto sentire. . . . Mi significo che alli giorni passati il Signor Cardinale Gonzaga discorrendo seco di concerti le disse che lui voleva havere il più perfetto corpo di musica che si fosse mai trovato in Roma, perchè oltre le voci eccellenti che haveva et aspettava, teneva poi anche promessa ferma dalla Signora Adriana che ci verrebbe anch'ella. e lui per obligarla a non mancare de la parola data, si fece dare da lei certi denari, che come in deposito li vuol trattenere appreso di se sino al suo arrivo, non credendo però Borghese niente di questi denari, ma che ciò sia stato proferito per maggiormente insinuarli, che possi esser la verità."

That Adriana did actually send 1000 scudi to Ferdinando is confirmed in the following excerpt from her letter to Ferdinando of 20 July 1612 (published in Ademollo, *La bell'Adriana*, 194): " . . . Il Pavese m'ha detto che Vostra Signoria Illustrissima ha ricevuto li mille scudi, essendo cosi, mi fara gratia dirmi con sua lettera se l'ha ricevuti, et del resto faccia tutto quello che li parerà spediente per utile mio."

The Mantuan official who arranged to have the money forwarded to Ferdinando was Antonio Pavese. On 15 June 1612 (ManAS, A.G. 2725) he informed Ferdinando, "Il Signor Mutio Baroni e la Signora Andriana sua moglie m'hano ordinato che giri in faccia di Vostra Signoria Illustrissima tutta la summa del danaro che la casa mia tiene in mano di lor conto. E però domani se ne fara la scrittura [;] e con altra Vostra Signoria Illustrissima sara l'apunto . . ."

From a letter of the same to Ferdinando Gonzaga in Rome, 29 June 1612 (ManAS, A.G. 2725): "Il Signor Mutio la Signora Andriana ambi concordemente m'hano sotto scritto in ordine perchè passi in credito a Vostra Signoria Illustrissima mille scudi monetta di Mantova lire sei l'uno, ho però cosi efetuatto a conto de quali Vostra Signoria Illustrissima faci riscotere li dua crediti de scudi cinque cento l'uno."

38. From the letter of Aurelio Recordati in Rome to Francesco Gonzaga in Mantua, 14 July 1612 (ManAS, A.G. 1000): "Mi duol bene all'anima che il Signor Cardinale nostro con queste cose simiglianti vadi procacciandosi puoca riputatione, e da ad intendere al mondo che tra Vostra Altezza e lui non passo quella reciproca intelligenze che dovrebbe essere."

39. "Relazione," ed. Segarizzi, 1:121 (report of 1612): " . . . signor cardinale, che è il maggiore delli fratelli del signor duca . . . È stato a Mantoa una volta dopo la morte del

padre e vi ha dimorato pochi di, e si dice che tra il signor duca e lui non passi buona intelligenza. Alcuni vogliono che questo sia per le nature differenti, essendo il cardinale profuso nelle sue spese e di maggior vivacità d'ingegno che non è il duca; e altri dicono che è ordinario costume di tutti i prencipi non si fidare ed aver sempre sospetto quello che, come più prossimo, deve succedere nelli Stati."

40. Ferdinando Gonzaga in Rome to Francesco Gonzaga in Mantua, 19 July 1612 (ManAS, A.G. 1000): "Il Marliani conduce seco Santi come mi ricerca Vostra Altezza. Ben la voglio pregare con qual maggiore affetto ch'io possa a rimandarmelo quanto più tosto sia possibile, poiche fra le mie occupationi non ho con che sollevarmi senza lui." On the previous day Hercole Marliani wrote from Rome to Annibale Chieppio in Mantua (ManAS, A.G. 1001): "Verra meco Messer Santi che dal Signore Cardinale è conceduto volontieri a Sua Altezza perchè professa di volerle dare ogni possibil gusto, ma è ben vero che intende che ciò sia per prestito, poiche Sua Signoria Illustrissima [= Ferdinando] non ha altro trattenimento et lasciandolo venire può credere Sua Altezza che cio sia un vero affetto di cortesia."

41. The musical entertainments for the July 1612 festivities are described in more detail in Parisi, "Virtuoso Performers," chapter 5. Monteverdi's role in the celebrations is not known. Denis Stevens (in *Letters of Claudio Monteverdi*, 87) has suggested that Monteverdi could have reworked music he had been composing for a tournament that the Academia degli Intrepidi of Ferrara intended to produce for Carnival in 1612—a project in which Vincenzo Gonzaga had been very much involved—because the tournament "was almost certainly postponed" on account of Vincenzo's death on 18 February. However, the period of postponement, if there was one, was actually very brief, for Vittorio Badini, writing from Ferrara to Francesco Gonzaga on 25 March 1612 (ManAS, A.G. 1268) makes it clear that the first performance of the tournament had taken place. Thus the nature of Monteverdi's contribution to the July festivities must remain an open question.

42. From a letter of Santi Orlandi in Mantua to Ferdinando Gonzaga in Rome, 3 August 1612 (ManAS, A.G. 2725); this same portion published in Stefano Davari, "Notizie biografiche del distinto maestro di musica Claudio Monteverdi desunte dai documenti dell'Archivio storico Gonzaga," *Atti e memorie della R. Accademia Virgiliana di Mantova* (1885), 104–5: "Il lunedi doppo desenare fece ragunare tutta l'Accademia della musica, dove erano oltre a Sua Altezza, i principi, e moltissimi cavalieri, e doppo l'haver cantato e sonato un gran pezzo, il Signor Duca scomparti molti uffizi, sopra de quali tutti me fece capo, dichiarandomi appresso suo Maestro di Cappella, havendo fatto il giorno innanzi licenziare il Signor Claudio e suo fratello. Monsignore Suardo, che era presente, disse a Sua Altezza, sara per questa cosa ad tempus, e Sua Altezza rispose di si, che come havesse trovato un altro buon soggetto, o che gli fosse mandato da Vostra Signoria Illustrissima, che mi rimanderebbe subito." Ferdinando's efforts to find a maestro di cappella for Francesco in Rome are discussed in Parisi, "Virtuoso Performers," chapter 5. Regarding Pietro Maria Marsolo's application for the position, see Lorenzo Bianconi, *Pietro Maria Marsolo, Madrigali a quattro voci sulle monodie di Giulio Caccini e d'altri autori, e altre opere*, in *Musiche Rinascimentali Siciliane*, vol. 4 (Rome: De Santis, 1973), xxxi–xxxv.

43. Letter of 6 November 1615; published in Domenico De Paoli, *Claudio Monteverdi:*

Lettere, dediche e prefazione (Rome: De Santis, 1973), 76; translated in Stevens, *Letters, Monteverdi*, 104, in which Annibale Iberti, and not Alessandro Striggio, is shown to be the recipient. ". . . non staro a dirle le mie fatiche passate . . . ne che mi sia partito da quella Serenissima Corte cosi disgraziatamente che per Dio altro non portai via che venticinque scudi dopo il corso di 21 anni."

44. From a letter of Vincenzo Agnelli Soardi in Rome to Giovanni Magni in Mantua, 31 January 1615 (ManAS, A.G. 1008): "Avertimenti di Vostra Signoria al Signor Paolo Facconi consegnaro il denaro della lettera di cambio per l'organista che Vostra Signoria scrisse et formaro la partita nel modo che lei mi scrive."

45. See Faccone's letters to Giovanni Magni, 7 and 14 February 1615, published in part in Cametti, "Frescobaldi in Roma," 720, and complete in Newcomb, "Frescobaldi, 1608–1615," 150–52, and Hammond, *Frescobaldi*, 50–51; see also the letter to Ferdinando Gonzaga, 16 February 1615, published in Newcomb, op. cit., 152–53.

46. See the latter two letters mentioned in n. 45 and Newcomb, "Frescobaldi, 1608–1615," 153. The ambassador in Rome, Vincenzo Agnelli Soardi, had apparently also been told to hurry along Frescobaldi's departure, for on 14 February he informed Magni (ManAS, A.G. 1008), "Non hieri l'altro hebbi la lettera di Vostra Signoria perch'io disponessi l'organista Frescobaldi a venirsene quanto prima, et però il Signor Facconi mi accerto che sarebbe partito infallabilmente alli 16 di questo che sara postdimani, ma che voleva condurne la sua famiglia, ben aspettava per questo effetto gli contanti."

47. Letter of Vincenzo Agnelli Soardi in Rome to Giovanni Magni in Mantua, 7 March 1615 (ManAS, A.G. 1008): " . . . che il Frescobaldi sia giunto et che della riuscire a gusto di Sua Altezza ne sento particolare contento, et tanto più concorrendovi il voto di lei."

48. Portion of a letter of Paolo Faccone in Rome to Giovanni Magni in Mantua, 14 March 1615, partially quoted in Cametti, "Frescobaldi in Roma," 720; same portion in Newcomb, "Frescobaldi, 1608–1615," 154–55, and Hammond, *Frescobaldi*, 52 (ManAS, A.G. 1010):

> Sarrà poi per aviso che qui si intende che il signor frescobaldi resta molto disgustato da cottesta Corte: È sarrà bene farne avisato il padrone; e se vi è qualche ombra di disgusto farla levare accio il serenissimo al improviso non restasse servito di quel tanto desiderato affetto che cossi ardentamente aspettava: se Vostra Signoria bene si recorderà, nanzi che detto frescobaldi venisse io previddi tutto questo successo; e gliene avisai; perche conosco cossi la corte di Mantova come ancho le qualità sue di puocho esperto fuor di casa sua: però sarrà bene che sua Altezza la dichiari suo servitore assignandogli quello le vuol'dare: che cossi liberara quel huomo dalla grande Agonia in che si ritrova; nanzi che lui di qua partissi gli dissi che allegramente venisse che tutto quello gli era stato promesso immediatamente arrivato gli sarrebbe stato osservato: adesso doppo che lui è arrivato da quattro parole in poi che gli disse il serenissima in quel primo giorno; parmi di intendere che nissuno mai più le habbia guardato addosso. consideri Vostra Signoria in che stato, et affanno si deve ritrovare un pellegrino che è venuto a rompicollo nel fondo dell'inverno fra tante neve et fango; vorrei che la desenzza et prudenza di Vostra Signoria giovasse in simile occasione accio quando sua Altezza comandara in altri soggetti la nostra rettorica in genere deliberattivo

habbia a giovare. le bacio le mani facendo humilmente riverenza al nostro padrone. Di Roma alli 14 marzo 1615 Di Vostro Molto Illustre

> Affetionatissimo servitore
>
> Paolo Fachoni

Signor Magni

49. "Relazione dell'illustrissimo Signor Giovanni da Mulla ritornato di ambassator dal cardinal duca di Mantova Ferdinando, 1615." Da Mulla's report is published in Segarizzi, ed., *Relazioni degli ambasciatori* 1:130–71. All references to Da Mulla's text will be to pages in the Segarizzi edition.

50. Ibid., 137; see also p. 134f.

51. Ibid., 138.

52. Ibid., 163–66, 170–71.

53. Ibid., 138–39. Da Mulla's exact words are "Non è dubio che, se il duca Francesco fosse vissuto, li [= the debts] avrebbe in breve tempo estinti, perche mostrava di esser principe molto pesato ed applicava a questo grandemente il pensiero, e, se bene stava alla grande e nell'apparenza forse anco più onorevolmente del padre, aveva però riseccate tutte le superfluita e voleva che le cose procedessero molto assignamente."

54. Ibid., 139: "Quello mò che possi far il duca presente intorno a questo, non si puo affermare, perche il suo ingresso al ducato è stato molto infausto e dispendioso; onde, come sicuramente non ha potuto in alcuna parte estinguer li debiti vecchi, cosi anzi gli è stato necessario farne di novi, oltre aver impegnata la maggior parte delle sue gioie ed argenti, come disse Sua Altezza di aver convenuto fare di propria bocca. Ha però buoni pensieri, vuol riseccar le spese, essendo per diminuire al presente 100 bocche del suo servigio; e mi disse anco di non aver molta inclinazione a viaggiare ne ad altri piaceri di senso, che il giuco è aborritissimo a lui e che la sua maggior dilettazione è la musica, che li costa però assai, spendendo in essa 30.000 ducati all'anno."

55. Ibid., 139–40: "È sano convenientemente, e sarebbe anco forse più, se, abandonando l'opinione di un suo medico familiare, non frequentasse cossi spesso i medicamenti come frequenta. . . . Ma, per quello che ho inteso, come si sente non dirò indisposto, ma in alcune parti o perturbato o alterato o raffredato un poco, riccorre subito a qualche medicamento . . . per opinione commune, apporta anzi pregiudizio che giovamento."

56. Ibid., 140.

57. Ibid.: "Della poesia si diletta estraordinariamente: ha sempre, come si suol dire, per le mani tutti li buoni poeti antichi e moderni, cosi volgari come greci e latini, e compone leggiadramente e gode di racontar quello che ha composto e che siano commendate le sue composizioni. Ha gusto grandissimo della musica ed e in essa molto versato, mettendo egli stesso con molta facilità diverse delle sue composizioni in musica, che le fa poi cantare; e riescono stupendamente."

58. Although he refers to the Santa Barbara cappella, presumably Da Mulla means the musical establishment in general. There were actually four female singers at court in this period: Adriana Basile, her sisters Margherita and Vittoria, and Settimia Caccini, whom Ferdinando had recruited, together with her husband, Alessandro Ghivizzani, in the spring

of 1613. Regarding the musical activities of these performers, see Parisi, "Virtuoso Performers," appendix 1.

59. Da Mulla, "Relazione," 140–41: ". . . trattenendo, oltre un pienissimo coro di cantori per la sua capella di Santa Barbara, tre donne cantatrici ancora, veramente singolari, che sonano e cantano per eccellenza. E se bene questa ricreazione della musica costa al signor duca tanto quanto ho già detto, ne gusta però e gode anco tanto che non credo senti la spesa; e m'affermo più volte di non aver avuto altro reffrigerio o sollievo in quest'ultimi importantissimi travagli che quello della musica, e sarebbe talora morto se non avesse avuto questo reffrigerio."

60. Ibid., 141: "E veramente l'inclinazione della natura lo porta incredibilmente al gusto della musica e della poesia. E, perche e di brevissimo sonno, si crede che insino la notte formi nella sua mente qualche composizione; e la mattina nell'uscir delle stanze ha sempre qualche cosa di grazioso da dire e da comunicare con alcuna persona letterata. Il che non da satisfazione al resto delli suoi gentiluomini di camera e di corte, che erano soliti di essere più dimesticamente trattati dal duca Francesco e dal duca Vicenzo, parendo loro che il presente duca non faccia stima d'altri che di chi fa professione di lettere."

61. On Ferdinando's musical activities in Florence, see Edmond Strainchamps, "New Light on the Accademia degli Elevati of Florence," *Musical Quarterly* 42 (1976): 507–35.

62. In an account from 1616 ("Nota della spesa che fa ogn'anno Sua Altezza Serenissima nella Casa et Corte," ManAS, A.G. 414) the musicians numbered thirty-two and their combined salaries came to 28,649–10–3 lire, or 4,774–110–3 scudi. No pay list from this period survives, but I have reconstructed the following roster of musicians at court between 1615 and 1618. It is clear that singers made up the largest segment of the personnel. Few, if any, wind players appear to have been employed during Ferdinando's reign; on the other hand, the string players listed here were already in service a decade earlier.

Maestro di cappella	Santi Orlandi
Composers	Don Francesco Dognazzi (also a tenor)
	Alessandro Ghivizzani
	Lelio Basile
Singers	
Sopranos	Adriana Basile
	Vittoria Basile
	Margherita Basile
	Settimia Caccini
	Giovan Battista Sacchi
	Don Giulio Cardi
Altos	Don Giovanni Abbate
	Lorenzo Sanci (left in 1615)
Tenors	Francesco Rasi
	Francesco Campagnolo
	Pandolfo Grande
Bass	Don Matteo Rossi

Voice ranges not known	Don Bassano Casuola
	Annibale Pelizzari
	Don Anselmo Rossi
	Federico Malgarini
Strings	Luigi Farina
	Giovan Battista Rubini
	Oratio Rubini
	Francesco Barbirolo
	Giacomo Cattaneo
	Fabritio Trolandi
	Giovan Battista Barbirolo
	Salamone Rossi
Keyboard and Continuo	
Organists	Pasquino Grassi (left in 1616)
	Girolamo Frescobaldi
	(in service March-May 1615)
	Mutio Effrem (in service 1616–18)
	Ottavio Bargani (began service in 1618)
Clavicembalo	Domenico Richi
Guitars	Pedro Guttierez
	Giovanni Guttierez

63. Faccone's letters of 1612–15 reveal that he pursued singers for Ferdinando in the Vatican, the Lateran, Santa Maria Maggiore, the households of Cardinals Montalto, Borghese, Aldobrandini, Arrigoni, and those of two other persons, referred to as Madame d'Austria and the King of Coffani. The documentation and further details are in Parisi, "Virtuoso Performers," chapter 3.

64. It had previously been suggested that when Monteverdi was invited back to court in January 1615, and Frescobaldi and Margherita Basile recruited in the following month, Ferdinando was already contemplating marriage with Camilla Faa, one of the Monferratan ladies-in-waiting and daughter of one of his statesmen, and wanted these musicians in Mantua for the musical entertainment that would mark the occasion (see Monteverdi's letters of 28 January and 11 February 1615, and the commentary on these by Denis Stevens, in *Letters of Claudio Monteverdi*, 95–97, 103). However, Ferdinando's infatuation with Camilla appears to have taken hold in the course of the summer, for it was in August that she was receiving favors at court, and in early September that she was hastily engaged to a wealthy gentleman, probably to quell rumors of Ferdinando's interest in her. Indeed, her engagement ceremony, in which Ferdinando and his aunt participated, was so hastily arranged that Camilla's father, at the time in Monferrato, was only informed after the event. It was also in this period that Da Mulla lamented Ferdinando's misfortune in not being able to marry whom he wished. See the documentation in Fernanda Sorbelli-Bonfa, *Camilla Gonzaga-Faa* (Bologna: Zanichelli, 1918), 11–29, especially p.20; and Segarizzi, ed., "Relazione," 1:145–46 (report of 1615). That rumors of Ferdinando's interest in Camilla persisted during

the fall of 1615 is confirmed in a letter of Lelio Arrivabeni in Mantua to the Duke of Urbino, 28 October 1615 (published in Ademollo, *La bell'Adriana*, 214); on Ferdinando's secret marriage to Camilla in February 1616, see Sorbelli-Bonfa, *Gonzaga-Faa.*

65. The alliances are discussed in Sorbelli-Bonfa, *Gonzaga-Faa*, 6–9. Regarding Da Mulla's appraisal of the marriage negotiations, see Segarizzi, ed., "Relazione," 1:145–46.

66. For a summary of the dispute over Monferrato, see Quazza, *Mantova*, 193–97, and Mazzoldi, *Mantova* 3:86–91.

67. L. C. Bollea, *Una fase militare controversa della guerra per la successione di Monferrato (April-Giugno 1615)* (Alessandria: G. M. Piccone, 1906), 16, 19–20.

68. Ibid.

69. Excerpt from a letter of Annibale Chieppio in Mantua to Annibale Iberti in Monferrato, 14 February 1615: "Circa il particolare del matrimonio di Modena Sua Eccelente è stata male avisata, et Sua Altezza s'è riputata per cosi dire offesa in essersi creduto di lei che senza l'assenso del Re passasse a cosi fatta deliberatione."

70. Excerpt from the same letter: "Il Comendatore di Villamediana s'attende qui, et si sarà ingannata in credere che la comedia in musica si repliche per conto suo . . . et fu invitato a ritornare et a veder la comedia che in ogni modo s'havera da recitare."

Excerpt of a letter of Alessandro Striggio in Mantua to Annibale Iberti in Casale, 19(?) February 1615 (ManAS, Davari busta 16): "S'aspetta il Signor Commendatore di Villamediana di ritorno da Venezia dimani o l'altro per la cui venuta si prepara la Galatea per recitare nella scena, et un balletto dal Signor Principe don Vincenzo di bellissima inventione."

A month earlier, as was the custom during carnival, members of the Jewish community had prepared a play with musical and humorous interludes in Ferdinando's honor; but at the last moment the play had to be postponed because Ferdinando had decided to see a ballet instead (see Shlomo Simonsohn, *Toledòt ha-Yehudìm bedukhasùt Mantova* (History of the Jews in the Duchy of Mantua), (Jerusalem: Kiryath Sepher, 1962–64; English ed., 1977), 666–67.

71. Excerpt from a letter of Annibale Chieppio in Mantua to Annibale Iberti in Casale, 26 February 1615 (ManAS, A.G. 2733): "Siamo nel colmo del carnevale, che si fa Dio lodato allegramente. . . . i negoci di cotesti Ribelli et loro beni vanno moltiplicando et non so quando saranno a meta tale che si possa trattare del ritorno di Vostra Signoria. . . . Comincia Sua Altezza a pigliar amore alle confische di cotesti Ribelli et non si come più a furia ne dinare, ne per adesso penso che se ne debba far altro. . . . Ho persuasa Sua Altezza a far stare ardisco dire per forza alcuni de suoi Mantovani in cotoro banda et dice che lo fara."

72. Ferdinando's communication of 6 February 1615 to Cornelia Basile in Naples is published in Ademollo, *La bell'Adriana*, 209.

73. On Adriana's recruitment see the documentation in ibid., 89–118.

74. See the letters of Ottavio Gentile and Lelio Basile in Naples to Ferdinando Gonzaga in Mantua, both dated 28 February 1615 (ManAS, A.G. 827). These and the letters cited in nn. 76–79, as well as other details of Margherita's recruitment, are discussed further in Parisi, "Virtuoso Performers," chap. 6.

75. See the same letter of Ottavio Gentile in Naples.

76. From a letter of Ottavio Gentile in Naples to Giulio Cesare Pavese in Mantua, 28

February 1615 (A.G. 827): "Scrivo a Sua Altezza quanto si sia fatto nel negotio della venuta della Signora Margherita sorella della Signora Adriana a cotesto servitù, ma prima è necessario ancora prevedere, et dare qualche ordine anticipata, caso che si risolvesse di venire, perche risoluta subbito la voglio condure, in molti rispetti, et perche non vi saria poi tempo voglio dire adesso quanto mi occorerà. Sarà dunque senon bene et so che questi signori vi havrano gusto particolare, che Sua Altezza scrivesse in Roma alla Signora Donna Costanza Mattei, che l'alogiasse per quella sera o due che si fermasesimo cola, et anco fare l'estesso a Bologna con il Signor Cavaglier Barbazza, et perche a quel tempo le strade non possono esser buone per andare con carozze, lauderei che venesimo in barca sino a ferrara, et che al porte del lagho scuro fosse un bucintoretto. . . . et dovendo passar per ferrara, saria ancor bene che Sua Altezza facesse o Illustrissima Signor Conte Alfonso scrivesse una lettera alla Signora Marchesa Barbara sua sorella, che si alloggiasia cola."

See also Gentile's letter to the same, 7 March 1615 (A.G. 827). Before agreeing to serve Ferdinando, Margherita demanded several small favors. These are outlined in Gentile's letter of 14 March to Ferdinando (ManAS, A.G. 827): "Finalmente si sono supperate tutte le dificultà che non sono state poche per fare che la Signora Margherita venghi a servire a Vostra Altezza Serenissima, havendole fatto conoscere che il matrimonio propostoli haveva fine molto diversi da quelli che li venivano proposti, come poi a boca diro io a Vostra Altezza; in soma lei verà volontieri, havendo condese io ad alcune sue dimande che mi hano passe molto honeste. . . . le dimande sono state un vestito da viaggio, un manto et altre cosette da giovane, come maneghini, cordelle, velli, o cosse simili, un vestito per un suo fratello che viene con lei, et cinquanta scudi a suo Parenti per la piggione della Casa et dattole intentione che con buona occasione Vostra Altezza non lasciarà otioso questo suo fratello per quello sara buono, et che ancora aiutarà il Signor lelio in un suo pensiero, molto raggionevole che ha costì, come lo diro poi a Vostra Altezza di persona, et che havra ancora consideratione al danno che riceveranno li suoi vecchi essendo lei absente; Creddo che tutto sarà approvato da Vostra Altezza per esser tutte cose necessarie, senza le qualli non si poteva spuntar questo negotio et superare tante dificultà; Se potrà havere pronto il danaro come credo partiremo venerdi prossimo. . . . Ho già scritto al Signor Segretario Pavese quello che credo sarà necessario che Vostra Altezza favorischi la Signora Margherita per il viaggio et glielo raccordaro di novo."

77. The following letters concern Margherita's brief stay in Rome: Vincenzo Agnelli Soardi in Rome to Ferdinando Gonzaga in Mantua, 28 March 1615 (ManAS, A.G. 1008), Donna Costanza Gonzaga in Rome to Giovanni Magni in Mantua, 4 and 10 April 1615, and to Ferdinando Gonzaga, 9 April 1615 (ManAS, A.G. 1010).

78. In Florence Margherita sang twice for the grand duke and archduchess, who awarded her a necklace and praised her singing to the effect that she would likely surpass Adriana and any other singer. (See the letter of Carlo Rossi in Florence to an unnamed official in Mantua, 20 April 1615, ManAS, A.G. 1129, and the letter of Ottavio Gentile in Bologna to Ferdinando Gonzaga in Mantua, 22 April 1615, ManAS, A.G. 1171). In Bologna she was escorted into the city by a sizable crowd and was later entertained by Cardinal Capponi. (See the same letter of Ottavio Gentile, the letters of Andrea Barbazza of 22 and 25 April 1615, ManAS, A.G. 1171, and of Cardinal Capponi of 24 April 1615, ManAS, A.G. 1170).

79. Ferdinando's letters to Cornelia, Giovan Battista, and Francesco Basile of 1 May 1615 are published in Ademollo, *La bell'Adriana*, 209–10.

80. The contract, dated 27 (or 7?) June 1615 is printed in ibid., 211.

81. Frescobaldi's letter of 16 May 1615 is published in Cametti, "Frescobaldi in Roma," 721, and Newcomb, "Frescobaldi, 1608–1615," 155–56; an excerpt also appears in Hammond, *Frescobaldi*, 52. His letter to Ferdinando of 5 September 1615 (by which time he had decided to stay in Rome) is published in Hammond, *Frescobaldi*, 347–48, and Paola Besutti, "Una Lettera inedita di Girolamo Frescobaldi," *Rivista italiana di musicologia* 18 (1982): 207–11.

82. In Puliaschi's case, Faccone proposed borrowing him from Cardinal Borghese for Ferdinando's future wedding—then not to have him return. (That Ferdinando accepted such recruiting practices is a further indication of the less than honest manner in which he operated at this time in musical affairs.) Letter of Paolo Faccone in Rome to Ferdinando Gonzaga in Mantua, 13 June 1615 (ManAS, A.G. 1010):

> Serenissimo signor et patrone mio Collendissimo
> Il signor santi orlandi per comissione di Vostra Altezza mi scrisse ch'io dovessi proporre al signor Giovanni Domenico [= Puliaschi] il desiderio che l'Altezza Vostra haverebbe della persona sua alli suoi servitii, et in particolare in questa congiuntura della signora Margaritta. Io non ho voluto cossi alla libera nottificargli la mente di Vostra Altezza, per non dargli occasione d'avantarsi di cossi honorato, et utile partito; et anchora; per non entrare in diffidenza con il Cardinale Borghese; l'ho però scalzato fuori; che la volonta sua non e di attendere alla pretteria; ma più tosto quando le venisse occassione buona di attacarsi; et pigliar moglie; e creddo che l'oppurtuna sarebbe quando che si facessero le Nozze di Vostra Altezza; del che me l'ha accenato haverne grandissima voglia; e mi rendo sicuro che Borghese in quella occasione non lo negarebbe. l'andro mantenendo cossi; e dispondendolo; accio l'Altezza Vostra al suo tempo sia servita: circa al castrattino quando sapro la risposta; et mente di Vostra Altezza avisaro di quanto passa. . . .
> Di Roma alli 13 Giugno 1615
>
> > Devotissimo e fidellissimo servitore
> > Paolo Fachoni
>
> Di Vostra Altezza Serenissima

Regarding Faccone's earlier efforts to recruit Puliaschi for Ferdinando, see Parisi, "Virtuoso Performers," chapter 3. On Puliaschi's extraordinary vocal range, see Vincenzo Giustiniani, *Discorso sopra la musica* [1628], trans. Carol MacClintock, Musicological Studies and Documents 9 (n.p.: American Institute of Musicology, 1962), 71.

83. Adriana's reception five years earlier was, from all accounts, lavish and festive. On her arrival several events took place, including a theatrical production involving sixty performers and elaborate stage machinery, and her own solo recital. Nor was she forgotten after the first few days, for another production was offered in her honor a month later (see the documentation in Ademollo, *La bell'Adriana*, 123–25, 134–37, 157).

84. Parisi, "Virtuoso Performers," chapter 6.

85. On Ferdinando's discriminating but extravagant taste in art, see Paula Askew, "Ferdinando Gonzaga's Patronage of the Pictorial Arts: The Villa Favorita," *The Art Bulletin*, 60 (1978): 274–96. Ferdinando's penchant for beautiful residences was already evident when he was living in Rome, where in the course of three years he purchased and rented several different properties; its culmination (and most visible expression), however, was the construction and embellishment of a magnificent country villa on the outskirts of Mantua, a building project that between 1616 and 1624 came to surpass the vast remodeling of the ducal palace carried out during Vincenzo's reign.

The documents cited by Askew corroborate two critical points in the present study: that Ferdinando favored artists working in Rome, and that in 1615–16, the years under discussion for Frescobaldi, he was dealing capriciously with the very persons whose services he sought. By late 1614 the Roman painter Carlo Saraceni had been asked to decorate a *galleria* in Mantua; but despite his having begun to draw up plans and find workmen in Rome, the project appears soon to have been abandoned by Ferdinando—at least for the moment —and Saraceni's participation ended. In February 1615 Saraceni was still pleading for payment for two paintings he had made for Ferdinando. In the following year Simone Basio, another artist working in Rome, was asked by Ferdinando to find fresco painters. Some months later their official papers and travel money had still not been sent and Basio had incurred debts for works already produced. In this case the travel money was eventually forwarded; he spent the first nine months of 1617 in Mantua, then returned to Rome.

Predecessors, Contemporaries, and Followers

THE DETERMINATION OF the stylistic roots of the keyboard music has remained a major unfinished task of Frescobaldi scholarship. Since little was known regarding keyboard composition in the composer's native Ferrara, earlier scholars searched elsewhere for these roots, particularly in the works of Neapolitan composers. Anthony Newcomb has reconstructed the distinct features of a North Italian—and to some extent indigenous Ferrarese—keyboard school with the aid of a number of neglected or recently recovered sources, and shows that this school indeed exerted a significant influence on Frescobaldi's early keyboard style.

One of Frescobaldi's Ferrarese predecessors, who in fact preceded him both in his move to Rome and in his tenure at St. Peter's, was Ercole Pasquini. Richard Shindle summarizes the little available information on this somewhat shadowy figure, and provides the first detailed discussion of this composer's vocal oeuvre. The special importance of Pasquini's keyboard music for Frescobaldi is taken up by James Ladewig elsewhere in this volume.

The authors of the next three essays turn their attention to Frescobaldi's contemporaries and colleagues; each explores a little-known circle of musicians and each finds there some surprising and important links with the composer.

Victor Coelho looks at the contemporary music for lute and chitarrone, especially the work of J. H. Kapsberger, whose career paralleled

Frescobaldi's in several aspects and who served some of the same patrons. Coelho demonstrates many similarities in the new techniques introduced by Frescobaldi into his keyboard toccatas and by Kapsberger into his chitarrone pieces.

Frescobaldi spent the years 1628 to 1634 in Florence in the service of the Medici, and his publication in that city of his first (and only) collection of accompanied vocal chamber music has hitherto been associated with the well-known interest in that type of music at the Medici court. John Hill, in an examination of the vocal styles of early seventeenth-century composers, concludes that the models of Frescobaldi's compositions are not to be found in the music of the Florentine composers (or in the works of Monteverdi, as has sometimes been proposed) but rather in the music of a group of composers working in Rome some ten years earlier and associated with the noted patron of the arts Cardinal Montalto. Thus, it seems likely that most of the music in Frescobaldi's collection was composed long before he moved to Florence. The clarification of the antecedents of these works enables Hill to place Frescobaldi's own contribution to the genre in a better perspective, and incidentally, to note the importance of some compositions to the later history of the chamber cantata.

With his toccatas, variations, and dances Frescobaldi laid the foundations of the new idiomatic baroque keyboard style, but he also wrote a large number of pieces in a seemingly more conservative manner, adhering to a strict contrapuntal texture. The contrapuntal compositions have been judged as backward-looking and more concerned with display of craftsmanship than with expression; hence they have generated little interest among present-day scholars. The traditional assignments of the two types of works respectively to the new and old styles, or to the "seconda prattica" and "prima prattica," have reinforced this somewhat negative judgment. Sergio Durante argues that the nature and purpose of such works have been misunderstood, and that they belong to an important contemporary genre known as the "artificioso" composition.

He relates this genre to certain fashionable currents of intellectual thought connected with the Hermetic tradition and the Rosicrucians.

Frescobaldi's strong and enduring influence on later composers is generally acknowledged but has not yet been thoroughly investigated. In a comprehensive study of the Frescobaldi *Rezeptionsgeschichte* in the German-speaking countries, Friedrich Riedel shows that the composer's works were widely studied there until well into the nineteenth century, and that, for example, they received particular attention from J. S. Bach and his pupils. Moreover, Riedel makes a case that it was the instrumental counterpoint of Frescobaldi, rather than the vocal counterpoint of Palestrina, that formed the basis of the contrapuntal style of Johann Joseph Fux (and hence, one presumes, of his influential counterpoint treatise, the *Gradus ad Parnassum*).

The Anonymous Ricercars of the Bourdeney Codex

ANTHONY NEWCOMB

O UR EFFORTS TO RECONSTRUCT the tradition against which we should understand and assess Frescobaldi's earliest publications of instrumental music have always been daunted by the lack of surviving instrumental pieces from the Ferrarese-Mantuan tradition in which Frescobaldi was educated. Apel found strong stylistic connections between Frescobaldi and the keyboard music of the Neapolitan school,[1] especially that from the 1590s and the first years of the new century, but he was never able to confront the question of whether the keyboard styles of both Frescobaldi and the Neapolitans Macque, Mayone, and Trabaci had common roots in a Ferrarese style (as did, for example, the madrigal style of the Neapolitan Gesualdo) because there was virtually no music known through which we could gain an idea of this style.

This situation has changed dramatically (and rather improbably) in the past couple of years. First, a manuscript score of Luzzaschi's second book of four-voice ricercars, copied in 1578, has recently surfaced in Umbria.[2] Second, the Bourdeney codex, now in the Bibliothèque nationale in Paris,[3] contains fourteen anonymous imitative instrumental pieces, which, as I shall propose here, are all from the *ingegno* of a certain Giaches—most likely Brumel.

In brief, the situation as regards the Bourdeney codex is this: The codex itself was first summarily described by Nanie Bridgman and François Lesure soon after its acquisition by the Bibliothèque nationale from the heirs of Clarisse Bourdeney in 1954.[4] Oscar Mischiati published a more exhaustive analysis and an inventory of its contents in 1975.[5] (It is this inventory to which the M-numbers throughout this essay refer.) The codex, written in score, is a compilation of often fully texted madrigals, motets, and Masses by composers from Josquin and Mouton through Pallavicino and Marenzio. Mischiati concludes convincingly from an analysis of the repertoire in the codex that it comes from the Po valley, probably the lower Po valley. Connections with Ravenna seem particularly strong.[6] Some jottings at the end of the codex (which have nothing directly to do with its preparation and hence cannot date it precisely) bear the date 1600, which can thus be taken as a *terminus ante quem*. Bridgman and Lesure find the watermark of the paper to be identical with that of paper used in documents of 1575–76 in Fabriano.[7] The codex contains among its later pieces madrigals from Marenzio's second book à 6 (1584) and Pallavicino's third book à 5 (1585). Since neither of these composers seems to have let pieces drift around unpublished for long, we should probably place the copying of at least the latter part of the codex after 1585, the date of Pallavicino's third book.

The codex contains among its 469 compositions a small amount of instrumental music. There are two unattributed pieces labeled *Canzoni da sonare*, which are also to be found in Maschera's collection of (probably) 1582 (M187–88);[8] there are ten pieces (nine complete, one incomplete) without text, title, or attribution concordant with ten of the ricercars in Merulo's first book à 4 of 1574 (M281–90). These are followed, after four pages of five-voice motets (three attributed to Rore and one to Morales), by the series of untexted four-voice pieces beginning with M295 listed in the appendix. This series is interrupted by a five-voice motet by Animuccia —not the only anomaly in pieces M301–4, as we shall see in a moment. But first, to conclude the list of instrumental music in the codex: two more canzonas to be found in Maschera's collection appear, again without attribution, as M386–87; the last piece in the codex, here headed "per sonar Andrea Gabrielli Organista à 8," is the eight-voice ricercar by Andrea Gabrieli published in the *Concerti* of 1587.[9]

To return now to M295–312. My attention was drawn to this group by Mischiati's observation that, nested in the initial six pieces, four pieces are preserved in fascicles 41 and 42 of the miscellany *I-Rvat* Ms. Chigi Q.VIII.206, where they are labeled "Fantasie di Giaches."[10] Edward Lowinsky first called attention to the Chigi pieces in 1960, attributing them to Jacques Brumel and proposing for the fascicles a date around 1560.[11] In 1966 Carol MacClintock pointed out that the pieces were not concordant with others by Brumel as Lowinsky had claimed, and argued that the Giaches in question was not Brumel, but Wert.[12] Lowinsky did not contest the correction, and MacClintock's attribution has stood ever since. We seem to have in the Chigi fantasias, whether by Wert or Brumel, a few pieces of instrumental music from the elusive Ferrarese-Mantuan school in which Frescobaldi was raised. In fact these were, together with the single ricercar by Luzzaschi in *I-Tn* Ms. Foà 2 about which James Ladewig has written recently,[13] the only full-length imitative instrumental pieces surviving from this school, until the discovery of Luzzaschi's second book à 4, whose first piece is the one in Foà 2. Naturally I wondered when I read Mischiati's inventory a few years ago what the anonymous pieces around the Chigi fantasias in the Bourdeney codex were like.

I shall propose here that they form a stylistically unified group, with the exceptions (obviously) of the motet M304 and (less obviously) of the pieces M301–3. A specific attribution makes me exclude piece M302, although style would have done so too. Style and some peculiarities of notation lead me to exclude M301. Style alone (and perhaps the place-ment of the Animuccia motet) suggests the exclusion of M303. A stylistic argument will thus be central to my definition of the repertory here as well as to the connection that I shall propose between it and Frescobaldi's *Fantasie* of 1608. Before I undertake this argument let me demonstrate that the practices according to which the Bourdeney was compiled do not contradict my interpretation of the situation in M295–312.

In summary, this interpretation is as follows: In M295–300 we have six imitative pieces by a certain Giaches, of which the second, third, fifth, and sixth also appear, with attributions, in the Chigi fascicles. The first piece in the Bourdeney series bears the title *Recercare del nono tuono* (the practice of heading—and attributing—only the first piece of a series is common in the codex). In M301–3 we have three untexted imitative pieces by another composer (or other composers), only the second of which has an attribution (in fact this is the only instrumental piece of the entire series M295–312 that has an attribution). This series of extraneous pieces is concluded by the fully texted five-voice motet attributed to Animuccia. The series begun with M295 then resumes with M305–11, a group of untexted imitative pieces each of which is headed, like M295, *R[icerca]re del [—]° Tuono*. This series is concluded with M312, a *R[icerca]re sopra Cantai mentre ch'i arsi di Cipriano* based on the first piece in the first book of madrigals à 5 by Rore, the composer who occupies the highest place in the pantheon of the compiler of the Bourdeney codex.[14] This last ricercar is followed by a group of quite different pieces: eight texted, attributed madrigals, all to be found in the 1582 anthology *Dolci affetti*. What needs particular defense in this interpretation is the idea of a series interrupted and then resumed, and—even more so—the idea that the interruption at M301 is not somehow indicated. (We may see the resumption of the series as indicated by the resumption and continuation of the original formulaic heading.)

First, there is frequent precedent in the codex for putting a small group of unrelated pieces in the midst of a larger, seemingly unified group: the large group of Rore motets, M15–46, has two Porta motets in its midst (M43–44, the first attributed), and the even longer series of Rore madrigals, M78–183, is interrupted twice by single pieces by Porta (M137) and Giovanni Maria Nanino (M177), both with attributions, and twice by single pieces by Willaert without attributions (M164 and 166). In these last two cases we identify the interruption only by concordances. Between a group of madrigals and a group of motets by Palestrina (M184–86; M189–228) are two canzonas by Maschera, again without attribution. In the midst of Palestrina's third book of Masses (M263–71) comes a Striggio madrigal without attribution. A series of motets and madrigals by Porta (M320–47) has in its midst an unattributed motet by Merulo, another interruption that we identify only by concordance. A long series from RISM 1572[2] (M360–410) has two Maschera canzonas in its midst (M386–87), again without attribution.

It looks likely that the compiler entered the pieces into his compendium, often from circulating manuscript sources (since the order often varies from the order in the prints), pretty much as they came to him. If a particular manuscript fascicle was available to him for only a limited time, he would simply enter its contents in the midst of whatever larger project was underway. If he knew whom the pieces were by, he would attribute them; if not, he would not. When there is an interruption in a series but no attribution, a change in genre often makes the interruption clear (e.g., the Maschera canzonas or the Striggio madrigals in the midst of the Palestrina Masses). But sometimes it does not (e.g., the Merulo motet in the midst of Porta motets and the Willaert madrigals in the midst of the Rore), and only concordance enabled Mischiati to spot the interruption. The compiler seems to put an attribution at least at the beginning of a series when he knows the composer. But when he returns to an interrupted series (e.g., the Rore madrigals after the insertion of a madrigal by Porta in M137, or one by Nanino in M177) he makes no new attribution to Rore.

All of this suggests the hypothesis that he might have interrupted the series of ricercar-fantasias by Giaches at M301 with some few pieces of different provenance. He did not know the composer of M301, so he gave no attribution. M302 was attributed to Fabritio Dentice in its source; for M303 there was again no attribution. M304, the Animuccia motet, may have been entered with this group of extraneous pieces, or it may have been entered later, since it fills the bottom systems of the page. M305, headed (for the first time since M295) *Ricercare del [—]° tuono* and beginning at the top of the next page, then resumes the series interrupted at M301. All this is possible according to the habits of the compiler of the codex. Of course, nothing in the makeup of the codex argues compellingly for it. This is better done by stylistic evidence.

In the case of the initial interruption at M301, my hypothesis is supported by notational peculiarity as well. Unlike all the other ricercars in the group, M301 contains mild notated cadential ornaments and uses a face-value approach to notated accidentals—that is, all required accidentals, including even the most obvious cadential leading tones, never indicated in the other pieces, are written in here. This seems clearly to indicate a different provenance for this individual piece, even if style did not likewise distinguish it. The continuation of the extraneous group is marked by the attribution to Dentice; its end is defined by the (visibly extraneous) Animuccia motet. This interpretation puts M303 in the extraneous group as well. Stylistic distinctions, though less clear than in M301–2, support the exclusion of M303 from the group of Giaches pieces.[15]

The specific new attribution of M313 and the beginning there of a new series of madrigals suggests that M312 should be included with the preceding series, as do both the way of labeling it and its general musical style. I shall now turn to the latter question.

The musical style of the proposed group of ricercars is by no means commonplace. They are long—an average of roughly 183 measures of one breve in ¢ or dotted breve in Φ^{3}_{2}. In this they resemble some pieces of the Venetian school of the 1540s and 1550s, especially some pieces of the *Musica nova* of 1540, some by Annibale Padovano, and many by Buus. Also like some of Buus's and Annibale's pieces is the tremendous density of subject entries. To take an example, M311 has forty entries of the six-note subject in the first sixty measures (after which countersubjects come in to divert some of the attention). Less like the midcentury Venetian school, however, are some of the most characteristic features of the Bourdeney pieces:

1. They manipulate their material constantly by means of various learned devices: augmentation, diminution, inversion (both hexachordal and non-hexachordal),[16] and a great many *inganni* (always, of course, hexachordally based).[17] The insistence upon inversion and, especially, the omnipresence of *inganni* is the distinguishing feature here.

2. The prominence of musical thought based on hexachord syllables here is shown not only by the constant *inganni* and the occasional hexachordal inversion, but also by a kind of subject that is without rhythmic character on initial presentation (for example, a subject in even long notes), and which is subject to incessant rhythmic change. Subjects whose rhythmic character is consistent and defining are the exception; wide variation of rhythm and of metric placement is a hallmark of the style. Again, this is present in the earlier Venetian style, but is here carried to a greater degree (see examples 1 and 2; arrows indicate *inganni*).

3. In fact, some of the pieces gain shape by the play between a more usual—that is, more motet-like—style of imitative point, moderately long and with characteristic rhythmic motives, and a style of point that is quite short (four to six notes) and purely hexachordal, without characteristic rhythmic shape or fixed melodic contour (since this last is often altered by inversion and *inganno*). Often such a piece will move from the first to the second style as it progresses (M298, M305, M309).

4. In economy of material the Bourdeney pieces exceed any collection of the century. Five of the thirteen pieces here have one subject; two have two; three have three; three have four (I include among these last M306, which treats the four phrases of *Ave maris stella* as a succession of subjects). In my tabulation of subjects (see appendix) a subject is counted as new

Example 1   Rhythmic variation on a rhythmically neutral subject (Mischiati 311)

Example 2   *Inganni* on a subject: "R[icerca]re del 2do T[on]o (Mischiati 308)

only if it is thus presented successively. When a subject and a characteristic bit of accompanying material (which I shall call a countersubject) are presented together simultaneously in two voices at the outset of the piece, I call such a unit a double point. When the second part of a subject is later split off and used as a separate bit of material in combination with the subject, I call such a subject a double subject (in agreement with the English edition of Apel's *History of Keyboard Music*).[18] Both occur in Bourdeney pieces, as the appendix shows.

5. The successive subjects of a piece are almost invariably generated by evolving variation, most often using *inganno*, inversion, or augmentation of part or all of the preceding subject or countersubject in order to produce a new shape, which is then taken as the definition of the new subject of musical discourse. I have discussed this procedure in some detail elsewhere, as part of a fairly detailed analysis of M299, based on a transcription from the Chigi fascicles.[19] Example 3 offers a straightforward example of the evolving variation in this piece. The repeated note of subject 1 is suppressed, and an *inganno*, or hexachord change, is made between the first note, the *fa* of the natural hexachord, and the second, changing it from the *la* of the natural hexachord to the *la* of the hard hexachord. The rhythmic values of the subsequent *sol* and *fa* are also changed and a short new tail is added, in order to generate the new subject used for the next fifty-some measures.

6. No matter how many subjects a piece may have, distinctive countersubjects are almost always present, either generated from the subject by motivic variation or picked out from the free voices and elevated to the status of countersubject by repetition. In the case of multisubject pieces such as the *Ave maris stella* ricercar (M306) or M309, the countersubjects often serve as binding material between sections—the countersubject of one section prefiguring the subject of the next, or the subject of one section serving also as the countersubject of the next. In pieces with only one subject (e.g., M311), the succession of countersubjects helps to create variety and to clarify sectional articulations.

The countersubjects may also help to create the extraordinary sense of clear overall design that several of these pieces project. In spite of their insistence on a strictly limited amount of material, most of the pieces do not give the impression of a directionless stroll through the syllables of the hexachord, which might be stopped at almost any point. They use various devices to create a sense both of climax toward the latter part, and of rounding off at the end.[20] A typical device is to recall, in the accompanying material at the close of the piece, the motivic guises of the opening, or to return at the end, by means of continuing evolving variation, to a subject that is close to the original one. M298, M299, M305, M307, and M311 all offer clear examples of this technique of overall shaping; one instance of the return by evolving variation to an earlier subject at the end of the piece is given in example 4.

A sense of building toward a climax in the latter part of the piece is created in almost all of the pieces by some sort of progression of technique.

Example 3   *Inganni* to generate new subject (Chigi no. 58, Mischiati 299)

Example 4   *Inganni* and evolving variation to generate new subjects (Mischiati 307)

The most obvious example is the triple-meter section toward the end of many pieces, or the section in which the subject is presented in each voice in augmentation, as a long-note cantus firmus. Subtler techniques also found here include the erosion of the characteristic rhythmic and melodic contours of the subject through *inganno* and rhythmic variation, leading to the typical cantus-firmus presentation, or the gradual accumulation of rhythmic motion in the accompanying voices as a way of leading toward the typical dance-like triple-meter section, or a gradual increase in either the number of distinct countersubjects or the density of entries as a way of building tension toward the end. All of these devices simply carry further techniques adumbrated in the style of the Venetian ensemble ricercars of the 1540s and 1550s.

It is no surprise that overall shape in these pieces is not described by a single tonal arch. Still, the composer is careful to obtain some tonal variety. The longest of the pieces, M308 with its 251 breves in G-dorian on one double point, cadences (by my count) once on B-flat, twice on A, five times on C, five times on D (once by phrygian cadence), and seven times on G.

A stylistic refinement that one comes to appreciate in pieces of this length is the skill with which the completion of the cadence is avoided —that is, the skill with which the completion of the two-voice sixth-to-octave or third-to-unison formula is avoided in whichever voices it may occur. Such skill, a tribute to Rore's example, is no surprise in pieces attributable either to a colleague of Rore's at the Ferrarese court or to the greatest of Rore's direct successors.

It also makes M312, a recomposition (usually an expansion) of each successive idea from the famous opening madrigal in Rore's first book à 5 of 1542, a particularly fitting close to this group of ricercars. The individual procedures in M312 are quite different from the others in the group: there is in M312 no erosion of melodic contour by *inganni* and inversion, no denial of characteristic rhythmic motives by persistent rhythmic variation, no long-note cantus firmus or triple-meter section, no linking or articulation of sections by distinctive countersubjects, and so on. But the skill with which the material is reworked, the sure sense of the changed demands of overall architecture in a now-textless piece,[21] and the considerable dimensions of the whole all point to the composer of M295–300 and M305–11.

M301–3, on the other hand, are stylistically quite different from the group of thirteen just discussed. They are all markedly shorter than the average of the other pieces. The contrast between M301–3 and the main group is most striking in the two ricercars on *Ave maris stella*: M301 is 73 breves long as opposed to the 220 breves of M306. The imitative elaborations of the four successive phrases of the hymn are 21, 14, 15, and 23 breves in M301; in M306 they are 35, 80 (including a long-note treatment of this phrase in all voices), 53, and 50 breves.

From breve to breve the style of M301–3 is quite different as well. All are pieces with a number of usually unrelated subjects. Thus their density of imitative entries and economy of material is much less. The average length of a section on a single subject is well under 25 breves; a point enters only four to eight times in a section. In the long-note sections at the ends of M302 and M303, imitative structure disappears almost entirely in the surrounding voices, where it is replaced by a free motivic play recalling the accompanying voices of a Ruffo capriccio or a Conforti ricercar. The points are long (ten to twenty notes) and have characteristic rhythmic motives and melodic contours. Melodic evolving variation, where it exists at all (the last sections of M302 and M303) is rather free —that is, it does not proceed by application of the learned devices characteristic of the other pieces. In fact there is very little use of learned device at all in M301–3.

M303 is unlike the previous two in using inversion right away in both its sections. Its sections are also longer (35 and 37 breves as opposed to the 14–28 breves of M301–2) and it makes a slight attempt to interrelate its two sections by means of the countersubjects in the second. It seems the closest in style to the pieces of the main group, yet it has little of their severe intellectuality or density of thought, and it has moments of clumsiness in rhythm and counterpoint which are nowhere part of the other pieces. All these things tend to exclude it from the main group of M295–300 and M305–12. There is no reason, of course, to believe that M301–3 form a unified group. Each of the three may be by a different composer.

On the other hand, the remaining group of ricercars is quite unified in style. And the hypothesis that they should all be attributed to Giaches is buttressed by the observation that the widest stylistic variety in the entire group (that between the two pieces M296 and M300) is encompassed within the four pieces specifically attributed to Giaches in the Chigi fascicles.

Nor can the style of this main group of pieces be dismissed as common coin. As I have asserted and tried to demonstrate, it is an unusual style for instrumental music in the later sixteenth century. Its most distinctive element is a kind of contrapuntal play that places as its challenge the making of the entire texture from one small set of materials. In this the closest ancestors of these pieces are the *Fantasie et Recerchari* of Tiburtino (1549) discussed by James Haar in an article of some ten years ago and the *Ricercari* of Chirstofano Malvezzi (1577).[22] The manuscript ricercars by Macque (now in the Biblioteca nazionale in Florence), to which we shall return below, are their close heirs.[23] In fact, I shall want to assert that the closest heirs to the Bourdeney ricercar-fantasies are Frescobaldi's *Fantasie* of 1608.

In working toward this assertion, I shall summarily review the ricercar style of the later sixteenth century, abandoning in the process Apel's rigorously maintained distinction between ensemble and keyboard music, since Frescobaldi's collection, although its notation in open score and its lack of idiomatic keyboard ornamentation would normally lead Apel to reject it as keyboard music, is explicitly referred to as keyboard music in the dedication, as are many Venetian ensemble ricercars of midcentury (e.g., the *Musica nova* of 1540 and Buus's first and second books). It is in fact to this Venetian tradition of ensemble ricercars (one can hardly speak of Tiburtino as part of a tradition) that the Bourdeney ricercars are closest.

From this tradition they take and exaggerate certain aspects. The length, the economy of material, the frequent presentation of a theme in even long notes (breves, longs, or even *maximae*), the careful drawing of a new subject from the preceding material by what I have called evolving variation are all to be found in the 1540 *Musica nova*, as are the occasional triple-meter section near the end and the frequent use of inversion. On the other hand, the early Venetian repertoire does not show the insistent hexachordal thought that most often keeps the hexachordal position of the theme the same, the omnipresent *inganni*, the tremendous density of entries, the frequent immediate inversion, and the delight in constant rhythmic and metrical variation. These last are to be found, other than in the Bourdeney pieces, only in Tiburtino.

Surprisingly, most are not to be found in the recently uncovered second book of ricercars by Luzzasco Luzzaschi, which I would assume
comes from the decade before 1578 (1578, the date of the manuscript
copy, is the *terminus ante quem*). Luzzaschi's pieces are much shorter than
the Bourdeney pieces (about 100 breves, with little variation around this
average), and his subjects are longer, with a characteristic rhythmic shape
that is usually maintained throughout the series of entries. These are the
principal differences from the Bourdeney pieces. Like the composer of
the Bourdeney pieces, Luzzaschi is intellectually rigorous. He uses a
great deal of stretto, inversion, and evolving variation; he also uses
inganni, though considerably less than the composer of the Bourdeney
pieces. The number of entries of his longer subjects is fewer in a section
of a given length, thus the impression of contrapuntal density is less.
And he does not so frequently play the textural game that I have referred
to above, making the entire fabric out of a limited number of motivic
fragments. This we see more often in the Bourdeney pieces, in Macque's
ricercars, and in Frescobaldi's *Fantasie*.[24]

Thus the proposed Ferrarese-Mantuan style is not monolithic, and the
style of the Bourdeney pieces is not exactly like Luzzaschi's. It is even
less like Andrea Gabrieli's, which is enough written about to need no
review here. And it is not even vaguely similar to the style of the keyboard ricercars of the Neapolitans Rocco Rodio (1575) and Antonio Valente
(1576). Not only are these latter much shorter (50–100 breves), but they
are less hexichordally conceived, and much less learned and rigorous.[25]
The four-voice *Fantasia* of Costanzo Porta in the Bourdeney codex (M325)
and his related four-voice ricercar in *I-Bc* Ms. Q38 are pieces similar to
textless motets in structure, of 61 and 73 breves and with two to three
successive sections, each with its own subject evolved from the previous
by free variation.[26] Though these pieces show considerable contrapuntal
mastery, they lack several crucial features of the Bourdeney pieces: the
length, the hexachordal thought (evidenced by *inganni* and by lack of
consistent rhythmic and melodic contour in the subjects), and the mosaic-
like texture made up by vertical and horizontal rearrangement of strictly
derived contrapuntal fragments. One must come to similar conclusions
after looking at the other ensemble ricercars of the 1570s, 1580s, and
1590s (by Merulo, Malvezzi, Bassano, Raval, and Sponga).[27] None of

them speaks this distinctive dialect of the primarily Venetian ricercar around 1550—none until Frescobaldi's *Fantasie* of 1608.

Frescobaldi's *Fantasie* are much more modern than the Bourdeney pieces in their clearer sectionalization and greater brevity; but their general layout—a regular imitative exposition leading to a long-note section or a triple-meter section—and their basic techniques of thematic manipulation—the constant use of *inganni* and rhythmic variation as a way of finding new guises for the one multiple subject presented at the beginning, which is then combined with itself in dizzyingly tight strettos—are but a further exaggeration of the distinctive elements of the Bourdeney pieces. (Compare example 5 with example 4.) To this style, Frescobaldi adds some early seventeenth-century characteristics—chromaticism and a wider variety of rhythmic values (especially an antic section in semiminims and *fusae* found in most of the *Fantasie*). But the principle and the procedures remain the same.[28]

The ancestry hitherto given for Frescobaldi's imitative style has been the Neapolitan style of Macque, Mayone, and Trabaci.[29] The Bourdeney ricercars suggest rather that the Neapolitan ricercars (that is, those of Mayone and Trabaci, for Apel excluded the manuscript ricercars of Macque now in Florence because he considered them ensemble music) represent a stage between the Bourdeney style and Frescobaldi's fantasias. They use the same range of essential note values as the Bourdeney pieces, while the inversions and *inganni* that they advertise so proudly are already among the most distinctive characteristics of the Bourdeney pieces. Even the multiple subjects exposed at the outset of each of Trabaci's pieces are not far from the Bourdeney style. Trabaci's ricercar *del terzo tuono con tre fughe*, for example (book 1, no. 3), has what I would call a double subject with a tonal answer to the first part of the subject; that *del settimo tuono con due fughe* has a double subject. Trabaci's pieces are much shorter and less contrapuntally dense than the Bourdeney pieces, but this is part of their modernity. In view of the close connection between the musical worlds of Ferrara and Naples in the 1580s and 1590s, it seems reasonable that the Neapolitan style should have taken inspiration from a proposed Ferrarese-Mantuan style, which we see in the Bourdeney pieces.[30] Two bits of evidence help to support this theory.

First, we see continuing, though somewhat pale, reflections of the proposed style in instrumental pieces written in the area during the last

Example 5 *Inganni* and evolving variation to generate new subjects
(Frescobaldi, ''Fantasia seconda'')

years of the sixteenth century. The four-voice fantasia by the Modenese
Orazio Vecchi,[31] published in his *Selva di varia ricreatione* of 1590, skill-
fully imitates many of the extrinsics of the Bourdeney style while utterly
changing its intrinsic meaning. Vecchi mimics the constant rhythmic
variation, the use of motivic development to generate new countersubjects, the long-note and triple-meter sections, and the greater density of
subjects and entries at the end in order to generate a sense of climax; he
even uses a hint of hexachordal variation. But his subject itself is a
passaggio on a triad, not a hexachordal set; and his triple-meter section,
though it is contrapuntally derived, ends up sounding like dance homo-
phony. The letter may be the same but the spirit is quite different.

While Vecchi's piece is a gentle and clever mockery of the style, the
eight four-voice ricercars by the Ferrarese organist Luigi Mazzi (1596) are
a clumsy, dutiful imitation.[32] Alone among the ricercars of the end of the
century, Mazzi's, most of them between 160 and 200 breves long, are
comparable in length to those in the Bourdeney. Like the Bourdeney
pieces, they show economy of material, insistent rhythmic variation, a
tremendous number of entries per section, a penchant for learned device
including even occasional *inganni*, and triple-meter and long-note sections.
But they cannot make the style work. The subjects are longer and more
diffuse than those of the Bourdeney pieces; the lines in general are

shapeless, and use more triads and scalar passage-work. Beyond this the counterpoint is often clumsy, even to the point of occasional parallel perfect intervals, and avoids difficult situations by inserting a rest in a voice for a minim or two, leaving awkward holes in the sonority. Whatever their aesthetic merit, Mazzi's pieces, in their earnest clumsiness, can testify to the continuation of a style like that of the Bourdeney pieces in Ferrara in the 1590s.

Second, the pair of ricercars in the Bourdeney codex based on the four phrases of the hymn *Ave maris stella* (although not explicitly so headed) seem the closest antecedents for a kind of piece that appears again only in the publications of the Neapolitans and of Frescobaldi in the early seventeenth century. Girolamo Cavazzoni in 1543, then a number of Spanish vihuela and keyboard composers around 1550 (Valderrabano, Pisador, Fuenllana, Bermudo, Henestrosa-Cabezon) wrote a series of short pieces based on the *Ave maris stella* in some form.[33] The first two Spaniards include intabulations of sections of Josquin's Mass, and I hoped to find an Italian tradition beginning with Cavazzoni and based on either imitations of sections of Josquin's counterpoint, or perhaps of sections from Willaert's settings based on the hymn tune. But no such tradition turned up. Aside from the explicit intabulations, all the pieces, both Spanish and Italian, appear to be independent of pre-existent models in vocal polyphony. The Bourdeney pieces differ from the (presumably) earlier Spanish pieces based on the hymn in that they are constructed as through-imitative ricercars on subjects that paraphrase one or all of the phrases of the hymn, instead of confining the hymn to one voice as a long-note cantus firmus. Mayone (1606—like Bourdeney, with no comment on the source of the subject) and then Frescobaldi (1627) follow the Bourdeney practice, but no other pieces in the Italian tradition join this trio. The Neapolitan Rocco Rodio published a ricercar on the hymn in his publication of 1575, but it is a relatively simple cantus-firmus piece, aligning Rodio with the Spanish tradition rather than with the one of dense imitative paraphrase leading from the Bourdeney pieces to Mayone and Frescobaldi. In fact, the use of the *Ave maris stella* tune as a basis for a display of sustained contrapuntal artifice, a strong tradition in the early seventeenth century,[34] seems not to have established itself until after Frescobaldi's arrival in Rome in the first years of the century. Thus here again the pieces of the Bourdeney codex may be seen as presenting a style unusual in instrumental music of the late sixteenth century, which then appears later in both the early seventeenth-century Neapolitans and in Frescobaldi.

The other source for the styles of both Frescobaldi and the early seventeenth-century Neapolitans is the group of ricercars by Macque in the manuscript *I-Fn* Magliabecchiana XIX, 106[b].[35] Macque's pieces, like Trabaci's, always begin with from two to four distinct pieces of thematic material stated at the outset—usually a double subject plus an accompanying countersubject. These bits of material are varied by *inganni* and occasional inversion. They almost always have a characteristic head-rhythm, though the tail of the subject may be varied rhythmically. Distinctive about Macque's pieces is the mosaic texture, in which the contrapuntal fabric is made up almost entirely—in some sections entirely—of the vertical and horizontal reordering of those fragments of material presented at the outset of the piece. This particular aspect of the Bourdeney style, among its most distinctive elements, is taken yet further by Macque before being picked up by his Neapolitan disciples and by Frescobaldi's *Fantasie*. On the other hand, there is in Macque only one instance of long-note or triple-meter sections, and Macque's pieces lack the continuity of the Bourdeney pieces and tend to be only about 80 breves long. Thus the Bourdeney pieces are not twins to Macque's style, though they are close relations.

The date of Macque's pieces is uncertain. We know that he had written some ricercars by 1586, before he went from Rome to Naples. But no one as yet has been able to state whether any of the ricercars in the 1586 print, of which only one partbook survives (in private hands), are concordant with those in the Florence manuscript.[36] That Macque's pieces should be closely related to both Frescobaldi's and the Bourdeney style is not strange when one considers that Macque seems to have maintained close relations with Ferrarese court musical circles at least since the early 1580s. His madrigals were included with those of a predominantly Ferrarese group of composers in the two anthologies assembled and printed in 1582–83 in Ferrara for the Ferrarese court soprano Laura Peverara.[37] These relations do not seem to have lapsed when Macque moved from Rome to Naples in 1585. His students Rinaldo dall'Arpa, Fabrizio Filomarino, and Scipione Stella are specifically recorded as having come to Ferrara with Gesualdo's entourage in 1594–96, in at least one case specifically to study with Frescobaldi's teacher Luzzaschi. Macque's third book of madrigals à 5 (1597), dedicated to Duke Alfonso d'Este of Ferrara, was among the few music prints to come from the presses of the Ferrarese court printer Vittorio Baldini.[38]

Even as we recognize the historical and aesthetic importance of the main group of Bourdeney ricercars discussed here, we must also recognize that the question as to their composer and approximate date is far from settled. When the four concordant pieces attributed to Giaches in the Chigi miscellany first drew the attention of Edward Lowinsky around 1960, he proposed that the Giaches in question was Brumel, a Fleming who was organist at the Ferrarese court from 1533 until his death in 1564, and who was widely famous as an organist already in documents of around 1550.[39] Carol MacClintock, in an article of 1966, pointed out that the two concordances claimed by Lowinsky between the Giaches fantasias in the Chigi collection and pieces thought to be by Brumel in manuscripts of Castell'Arquato and Uppsala were not correct.[40] On the basis of the patent lack of similarity of style between the Chigi fantasias and both the early organ pieces in the Castell'Arquato manuscripts (Jeppesen dates these from the 1530s or 1540s) and the lute piece in the Uppsala manuscript, MacClintock took the Chigi pieces away from Giaches Brumel and assigned them to Giaches Wert (for whose activity as an instrumental player or composer we have no evidence).

Her stylistic evidence is not compelling. That parallel sixths as "bridges from one imitative point to another," or a climax made near the end of the piece by "close stretto imitation and increased richness of sound" can be distinctive enough in themselves to constitute "almost a signature in Wert's music," and can be thus used to pin the pieces to him, seems doubtful. MacClintock's thrust is in fact to find in the Chigi pieces "certain features which [are] similar to practices current in the third quarter of the century," as she herself summarizes it.[41]

Alexander Silbiger has already questioned the source-related evidence by which MacClintock transferred the Chigi pieces to Wert.[42] That the two names Giaches and Lucciasco in juxtaposition would inevitably have suggested to a contemporary Wert, not Brumel, as MacClintock claims,[43] is by no means clear—at least not in the early 1560s, when Luzzaschi and Brumel were the first and third organists at the Ferrarese court

(Luzzaschi from May 1561, Brumel till March 1564). Indeed it seems likely that the fledgling Luzzaschi was Brumel's pupil as organist and instrumental composer at this time, for Brumel was a renowned teacher.[44]

While assessing the appearance of the Giaches fantasias from the Chigi miscellany among the anonymous ricercars in the Bourdeney codex, we can bring a bit more circumstantial evidence to the argument concerning their authorship. First, the style of the pieces certainly does not exclude composition in Brumel's lifetime. As we have seen, there is nothing in these pieces that could not have been written around 1560; in fact the length and continuous overlapping imitative texture of the pieces are extremely rare among dated ricercars of the last three decades of the century.[45] Long-note expositions, the number of entries of the principal themes, ricercars on pre-existent vocal models, and a ricercar on *la-sol-fa-re-mi* all point to the 1550s. The extensive, systematic application of inversion and *inganni* may point to a period slightly later than that of the Padovano ricercars of 1556—something more toward Andrea Gabrieli's ricercars, some of which presumably were written in the 1560s. One might thus hypothesize that the circulating fascicles from which the Chigi gatherings and the Bourdeney codex were presumably copied contained Ferrarese music of the early 1560s, pieces some twenty-five years later than Brumel's ricercars in the Castell'Arquato manuscript and, not surprisingly, rather different in style. In support of this, one might note that Claudio Merulo's prospectus of future publications, issued with his *Ricercari d'intavolatura* of 1567, included a volume of ricercars by Giaches da Ferrara. Thus such a collection existed, presumably unpublished, in 1567.[46]

Of course, even if the Bourdeney pieces were written around 1560, they might still be by the young Wert. Since we have no authenticated examples of Wert's instrumental style at any period in his life with which to compare the Bourdeney pieces, stylistic analysis cannot help us. But two small biographical details may suggest a connection between the Bourdeney pieces and Brumel. First, Cristofano Malvezzi—the author of a collection of highly skillful four-voice ricercars printed in 1577, in which the use of *inganni*, ubiquitous rhythmic variation, thematic evolution, density of thematic entries, mosaic-like thematic combinations, and love of inversion and augmentation recall some aspects of the style of the Bourdeney pieces in a briefer, less intellectual form—is said to have been a pupil of Brumel at the end of the 1550s.[47] Second, Mischiati has noted the close connections between the Bourdeney codex, probably compiled in the 1580s, and Ravenna. The organist of the cathedral of Ravenna from August 1572 was a certain Virginio, son of an unspecified Giaches.[48] By November 1580 the post had been assumed by "M. Giaches, hora organista del nostro duomo, figliuolo di quel gran Giaches Brunelli, francese che morì in Ferrara, musico del quel serenissimo duca."[49] The younger Giaches remained in this post through 1594, during the very years in which the Bourdeney codex was likely to have been compiled.[50] Thus the music of Giaches Brumel would certainly not have been forgotten in Ravenna in the 1580s.

In sum, it seems by no means certain that the Giaches fantasias of Chigi need to be taken away from Giaches Brumel, whether father or son. For stylistic reasons, I am inclined at present toward Lowinsky's initial hypothesis that the pieces were written by the elder Brumel around 1560. But the issue remains open. It does not deeply affect the essential point here: that the Bourdeney codex contains a unified group of thirteen imitative instrumental pieces of the highest quality; that these skillful, playful, yet deeply cerebral pieces more than double the number of surviving pieces that we have from the school of instrumental composition around Ferrara in the later sixteenth century, and that, together with the Macque ricercars in the Florence manuscript, they offer the closest model for those outrageously virtuosic productions of the young Frescobaldi, the *Fantasie* of 1608.

Appendix: The Anonymous Ricercari in the Bourdeney Codex
(F-Pn Rés VmA ms 851)

M 295. Recercare del Nono Tuono. 201 breves; 1 subject, 2 countersubjects.

re   fa   sol la   fa   la

M 296. [terzo tono]. 200 breves; 1 subject, 3 countersubjects; Chigi no. 60.

la   sol fa   re   mi

M 297ª. [terzo tono]. 132 breves; 2 subjects (1st double); Chigi no. 59.

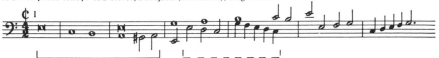

M 298. [nono tono]. 138 breves; 4 subjects by evolving variation.

M 299. [quinto tono]. 131 breves; 3 subjects by evolving variation; Chigi no. 58; cf. *Studi musicali* 7:85–102.

M 300ª. [dodicesimo tono]. 116 breves; 2 subjects (2nd canzona-like); almost no learned device; Chigi no. 57.

M 301. [primo tono]. 73 breves; 4 subjects (*Ave maris stella*).

a. Published in Giaches de Wert, *Fantasias à 4*, ed. Carol MacClintock (Macomb, Ill.: Roger Dean, 1974).

M 302. Di Fabritio Dentice [settimo tono] . 92 breves; 3 unrelated subjects.

M 303. [secondo tono] . 71 breves; 2 subjects (1st double).

[M 304. Paulo Animutia à 5 voci. Laudem dicite Deo nostro. Fully texted; fills last 2½ systems on the page.]

M 305. R.^re del p.^o T.^no. 204 breves; 3 subjects, first and last with detachable countersubjects.

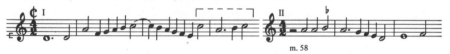

M 306. R.^re del p.^o T. 220 breves; 4 subjects *(Ave maris stella),* 3rd and 4th with countersubjects.

M 307. R.^re del 2.do T.^no. 200 breves; 3 subjects by evolving variation.

M 308. R.^re del 2.do T. 252 breves; 1 double point; many learned devices.

M 309. R.^re del 3.º Tuono. 240 breves; evolving series of 4 subjects, successive ones introduced as countersubjects to preceding, without sectional articulation.

M 310. R.re del 4.to Tuono. 204 breves; 1 double subject with 2 very short parts subjected to both learned device and rather free contour variation.

M 311. R.re del duodecimo Tuono. 179 breves, 3 countersubjects.

M 312. Rre sopra Cantai mentre ch'i arsi di Cipriano. 146 semibreves (in C instead of ₵); reworks each successive point of Rore's *Cantus*, with frequent admixture of the lower parts.

Notes

1. Willi Apel, "Neapolitan Links between Cabezon and Frescobaldi," *Musical Quarterly* 24 (1938): 419–37, and idem, *The History of Keyboard Music to 1700*, trans. Hans Tischler (Bloomington: Indiana University Press, 1972).

2. Luzzasco Luzzaschi, *Il secondo libro de ricercari à quattro voci*, ed. Michelangelo Pascale, Musica Rinascimentale in Italia, vol. 6 (Rome: Pro Musica Studium, 1981). I am grateful to Dr. Pascale for sending me a copy of his edition.

3. Rés VmA ms 851.

4. Nanie Bridgman and François Lesure, "Une anthologie 'historique' de la fin du XVIe siècle: Le manuscrit Bourdeney," in *Miscelánea en homenaje a Mons. Higinio Anglés* (Barcelona: Consejo superior di investigaciones científicas, 1958) 1:161–74.

5. Oscar Mischiati, "Un'antologia manoscritta in partitura del secolo XVI," *Rivista italiana di musicologia* 10 (1975): 265–328.

6. Both the predominance of the works of Porta and a motet and a madrigal for local saints and civic dignitaries point to Ravenna; see Mischiati, "Un'antologia manoscritta," 266–67.

7. Bridgman and Lesure, "Une anthologie 'historique,'" 162.

8. Cf. Howard Mayer Brown, *Instrumental Music Printed before 1600* (Cambridge, Mass.: Harvard University Press, 1967), [1582]4.

9. Neither Mischiati nor I has checked to see whether the Bourdeney versions of the Maschera, Merulo, or Gabrieli pieces are identical in every detail with those in the prints and most likely taken from the prints. The order of the Merulo pieces in the codex, which bears no resemblance to their order in the print, makes this latter seem unlikely. In the one case that Mischiati checked, the hymns of Porta, he found the Bourdeney versions to be significantly different from the readings in the print of 1602. See Mischiati, "Un'antologia manoscritta," 274.

10. Cf. H. Lincoln, "I manoscritti chigiani di musica organo-cembalistica della Biblioteca Apostolica Vaticana," *L'Organo* 5 (1964–67): 78–80.

11. Edward E. Lowinsky, "Early Scores in Manuscript," *Journal of the American Musicological Society* 13 (1960): 135–36.

12. Carol MacClintock, "The 'Giaches Fantasies' in MS Chigi Q VIII: A Problem in Identification," *Journal of the American Musicological Society* 19 (1966): 370–82.

13. James L. Ladewig, "Luzzaschi as Frescobaldi's Teacher: A Little-Known Ricercare," *Studi musicali* 10 (1981): 241–64. The ricercar in the Foà manuscript is in fact the first one in the recently uncovered second book (see n. 2 above), which collection will be discussed in general terms below.

14. The codex is decorated by several gratuitous expressions of enthusiasm for Rore, such as this caption for M115: "W [Viva] Cjpriano Rore Mai morirà ne mai nascerà un altro."

15. M303 occasionally gives the impression of contrapuntal clumsiness (e.g., mm. 14–15, 40, 64) and lack of rigor (e.g., it casually changes the hexachordal position of the subjects and does not stay for long with one version of a subject, varying it through rather free processes instead of the rigorously defined ones typical of the main group).

16. For this term, see Ladewig, "Luzzaschi as Frescobaldi's Teacher," 247ff.

17. The concept of *inganno* (deception), according to which the solmization syllables sung to a series of notes remain the same while the melodic contour and interval content of the series changes, sometimes drastically, is exposed and developed in the context of one of the present ricercars in my article "Form and Fantasy in Wert's Instrumental Polyphony," *Studi musicali* 7 (1978): 85–102.

18. Apel, *History of Keyboard Music*, 179 and passim.

19. See Newcomb, "Form and Fantasy."

20. Ibid.

21. For example, the drastic reduction of a declamatory section in the original, replacing it with a new and extensive imitative section (still using Rore's melodic material) at a point just past the middle of the piece. The tradition for such parody-ricercars, which seems to die out in the 1560s, at least in Italy, is outlined in John M. Ward, "Parody Technique in 16th-century Instrumental Music," *The Commonwealth of Music*, ed. Gustave Reese and Rose Brandel (New York: Free Press, 1965), 208–28.

22. James Haar, "The *Fantasie et Recerchari* of Giuliano Tiburtino," *Musical Quarterly* 59 (1973): 223–38; for the Malvezzi pieces, see the sources given in n. 27 below.

23. See p. 113.

24. Luzzaschi's book of ricercars merits a study of its own, which Ladewig has begun with "Luzzaschi as Frescobaldi's Teacher."

25. For the Andrea Gabrieli, see Apel, *History of Keyboard Music*, 177–82; for Rodio and Valente, see ibid., 185–87, both sections including citations of modern editions.

26. For a modern edition see Costanzo Porta, *Opera omnia*, ed. Siro Cisilino and Giovanni Luisetto (Padua: Biblioteca Antoniana, 1970), 18:17–22. The five ricercars printed in Corpus of Early Keyboard Music, vol. 41, ed. Bernhard Billeter (n.p.: American Institute of Musicology, 1977) are not by Costanzo but Francesco Porta, an early seventeenth-century composer; see Oscar Mischiati, "L'Intavolatura d'organo tedesca della Biblioteca Nazionale di Torino," *L'Organo* 4 (1963): 63 n. 76.

27. For descriptions of these pieces together with transcriptions of many of them, see Milton A. Swenson, "The Four-Part Italian Ensemble Ricercar from 1540–1619" (Ph.D. diss., Indiana University, 1971); and a more recent summary in Cristofano Malvezzi, Jacopo Peri, Annibale Padovano, *Ensemble Ricercars*, ed. Milton Swenson, Recent Researches in the Music of the Renaissance, vol. 27 (Madison: A-R Editions, 1978).

28. There are two possibly chromatic passages in the Bourdeney pieces; they are transcribed in example 6 below.

Example 6 Chromatic half-step?
a. Mischiati 295

b. Mischiati 306

It is possible that these particular accidentals refer both forward and backward, as is occasionally the case especially in cadential alterations. It would be strange if in some two thousand breves of music, chromaticism were neither rejected nor embraced, but turned up only twice, and then somewhat casually.

29. Cf. n. 1 above. Macque's instrumental music survives only in manuscript: see Alexander Silbiger, *Italian Manuscript Sources of Seventeenth-Century Keyboard Music* (Ann Arbor: UMI Research Press, 1980), 165–70. For the publications of Macque and Trabaci, see Claudio Sartori, *Bibliografia della musica strumentale italiana* (Florence: Olschki, 1952), 1603b, 1606c, 1609f (Mayone); 1603c and 1615c (Trabaci).

30. See Anthony Newcomb, "Carlo Gesualdo and a Musical Correspondence of 1594," *Musical Quarterly* 54 (1968): 409–36, and idem, *The Madrigal at Ferrara: 1579–97* (Princeton: Princeton University Press, 1980), 1: 113–53, 191–211.

31. Modern edition in W. J. v. Wasielewski, *Geschichte der Instrumentalmusik im XVI. Jahrhundert* (Berlin: J. Gattentag, 1878), Musikbeilage 26.

32. Transcriptions in Swenson, "The Four-Part Italian Ensemble Ricercar," 2:447–591.

33. The *Ave maris stella* pieces that I have encountered so far occur in the following sources (dates with number subscripts refer to Brown, *Instrumental Music*; those with letter subscripts refer to Sartori, *Bibliografia*). First is an Italian source, 1543_1 (Cavazzoni); then follows the series of Spanish sources 1547_5 (two pieces), 1552_7, 1554_3 (two pieces), 1555_1, and 1557_2 (seven pieces), to which might be added 1578_3, Cabezon's posthumously published *Obras de musica* (ten pieces). Italian sources pick up again with the Bourdeney pieces (1560–85?) and Rocco Rodio (1575_5), but become particularly important only with Mayone's 1606_c (one piece) and 1609_f (one piece). In 1610 appeared Francesco Soriano's *Canoni et oblighi di 110 sorte sopra L'Ave maris stella* (Rome: G. B. Robletti). Frescobaldi's imitative versets appeared, of course, in 1627. Other pieces based on *Ave maris stella* appear in the early seventeenth-century South German source *D-Mbs* Ms. Mus. 1581 (edited by Clare G. Raynor in Corpus of Early Keyboard Music, vol. 40 [n.p.: American Institute of Musicology, 1976]). A seminar paper by Brian G. Newhouse at the University of California, Berkeley, both compiled these sources and established the unusual position of the Bourdeney pieces in the sixteenth-century repertoire. His field of investigation included all accessible first-mode ricercars, not just those headed "sopra Ave maris stella."

34. See the essay by Sergio Durante in the present volume.

35. On this source, see Silbiger, *Italian Manuscript Sources*, 101–3. I am grateful to Prof. James Ladewig for providing me with transcriptions of these pieces. The author uncovered in the summer of 1986 a copy by Karl Proske of an additional collection of ricercars that can be attributed to Macque on stylistic grounds. Both these newly discovered ricercars and the Florentine ones are to be published in the Yale University Collegium Musicum series, edited by James Ladewig.

36. The partbook, which is for sale by a private citizen in Milan, had been opened to the view of none of the scholars at the 1983 conference. Stylistically, there is no reason to say that the manuscript ricercars could not have been written in the middle of the 1580s.

37. On these anthologies, see Anthony Newcomb, "The Three Anthologies for Laura Peverara, 1580–83," *Rivista italiana di musicologia* 10 (1975): 329–45.

38. A recent study of mine has led to similar conclusions about the stylistic ancestry of Frescobaldi's *Toccate I*. Its closest ancestors seem to be Macque on the one hand and an indigenous Ferrarese school, in this case represented by Ercole Pasquini, on the other. See Anthony Newcomb, "Frescobaldi's Toccatas and Their Stylistic Ancestry," *Proceedings of the Royal Musical Association* 111 (1984–85), 28–44.

39. Lowinsky, "Early Scores in Manuscript." Knud Jeppesen, "Eine frühe Orgelmesse aus Castell'Arquato," *Archiv für Musikwissenschaft* 12 (1955): 193, quotes a letter of 23 April 1552 to the Duke of Ferrara, which extravagantly praises a young musician in the household of the Cardinal of Trent by saying that he not only sings beautifully but also "plays the harpsichord as well as the best pupil that Master Giaches ever had."

40. MacClintock, "The 'Giaches Fantasies.'"

41. Ibid., 375, 374, 377.

42. Silbiger, *Italian Manuscript Sources*, 132–33.

43. MacClintock, "The 'Giaches Fantasies,'" 380.

44. He is known to have taught Jacopo Corsini (Corfini) (see Jeppesen, "Eine frühe

Orgelmesse," 193) and Malvezzi (see *Ensemble Ricercars*, ed. Swenson, p. ix). See also the letter of 1552 quoted in n. 39 above. It might in fact explain the rather tentative and clumsy style of the *versetti* grouped with the "Giaches Fantasies" and ascribed to Luzzaschi in the Chigi miscellany to see them as student works, circulating with work from the early 1560s by Brumel, who would at that time have been Luzzaschi's colleague and, as I am proposing, his teacher-sponsor.

45. Padovano's ricercars (1556) average ca. 140 breves, Malvezzi's (1577) and Luzzaschi's (ca. 1575?) ca. 100 breves, Macque's (1585–1605?) ca. 80 breves. Only Luigi Mazzi's (see discussion above) are close to the Bourdeney pieces in length.

46. The "Fantasie di Giaches" in the Chigi miscellany and the concordant "Recercari" in the Bourdeney codex were probably not copied from the same source, for there are small differences of rhythm, producing differing but equally sensible readings, and an occasional difference of pitch, involving the inclusion of the third in the final chord, as well as a number of differences in notated accidentals (presumably not significant for the purpose of filiation). For Merulo's (largely unfulfilled) prospectus, see Gaetano Cesari, "Origini della canzone strumentale detta 'alla francese,'" in *Andrea e Giovanni Gabrieli e la musica strumentale in San Marco*, tomo 2, Istituzioni e monumenti dell'arte musicale italiana (Milan: Ricordi, 1932), 2:xliii–xliv.

47. See n. 44 above. Malvezzi's collection of 1577 also includes a ricercar on *la sol fa re mi*. For transcriptions, see the source cited in n. 27.

48. R. Casadio, "La cappella musicale della cattedrale di Ravenna nel secolo XVI," *Note d'Archivio* 16 (1939): 150.

49. Ibid.

50. Paolo Fabbri, "Vita musicale nel cinquecento ravennate," *Rivista italiana di musicologia* 13 (1978): 48. Casadio, "La cappella musicale," suggests that Virginio and Giaches might have been two sons of Giaches Brumel, though no evidence confirms this.

The Vocal Compositions of Ercole Pasquini

W. RICHARD SHINDLE

T HE first important assessment of Ercole Pasquini as a predecessor to Girolamo Frescobaldi appeared in Willi Apel's *Geschichte der Orgel- und Klaviermusik bis 1700*.[1] Prior to its publication in 1967, historians merely mentioned Pasquini's name as Frescobaldi's immediate predecessor as organist to the Cappella Giulia at St. Peter's in Rome. One of the major obstacles in assessing Pasquini's keyboard music is the lack of satisfactory and authoritative sources.[2] The assessment of his vocal compositions, on the other hand, presents a different set of problems. Of the five extant compositions, four were published during his lifetime and one shortly thereafter (see table 1). Each of the preserved compositions represents a different genre: a madrigal and a spiritual madrigal, a five-voice motet, a polychoral motet, and a four-voice motet with organ.

That Pasquini's vocal output was more extensive is verified by an inventory of the music collection of Archduke Sigmund Franz of Tyrol in Innsbruck taken upon his death in 1665:[3]

No. 1   Messa a 10 voci di Hercole Pasquini
No. 2   Messa a 3 Chori sopra Vestina colli di Hercole Pasquini[4]
No. 93   Opera 16 libro tutto di Hercule Pasquini
No. 131 No. 8. Madr. a 5 alla Sma. Vergine di Hercole Pasquini

This collection, from the estate of Antonio Goretti of Ferrara, had been sold to the Innsbruck court by his heirs.

Three of the extant works under discussion were published while Pasquini was still in Ferrara, a period of his life for which there is only

Table 1   Pasquini's extant vocal compositions

1. Madrigal

Mentre che la bell'Isse a5
a. *Giardino de musici ferraresi madrigali a cinque voci*
(Venice: Giacomo Vincenti, 1591) RISM 1591[9]
b. *Paradiso musicale di madrigali et canzoni a cinque voci . . .
racolti da P. Phalesio* (Antwerp: Pierre Phalèse, 1596)
RISM 1596[10]

1b. Contrafact motet

Sanctus Sebastianus a5
*Hortus musicalis, variis antea diversorum authorem Italiae
. . . authore R. P. Michael Herrerio* (Passau: M. Nenninger,
1606) RISM 1606[6]

2. Motet

Jubilate Deo a5
Raphaela Aleotta ferrariensi. *Sacrae cantiones quinque,
septem, octo, & decem vocibus . . . liber primus* (Venice:
Ricciardo Amadino, 1593)
RISM A 821

3. Motet

Quem vidistis, pastores? a 10
see Jubilate Deo (preceding entry)

4. Spiritual madrigal

M'empio gli occhi di pianto a5
*Musica de diversi eccellentiss. autori. A cinque voci. Sopra
i pietosi affetti, del M.R.P.D. Angelo Grillo; raccolta per
il Padre D. Massimiamo Gabbiani da Brescia, monaco
cassinese* (Venice: Angelo Gardano, 1604) RISM 1604[8]

5. Motet

Jesu decus angelicum a4 with organ
*Scelta di motetti di diversi eccellentissimi a2, a3, a4, et a5,
posti in luce da Fabio Costantini . . . Libro secondo, opera
quarta* (Rome: B. Zannetti, 1618) RISM 1618[5]

sketchy documentation. Agostino Superbi (see document 1) states that Pasquini studied with Alessandro Milleville and played organ for many years in Ferrara before moving to Rome. Other evidence indicates that he was organist at the Accademia della Morte in Ferrara in the 1590s, succeeding Luzzasco Luzzaschi and preceding Girolamo Frescobaldi in that post.[5] His name does not appear in the records of the Ferrarese court, and there is no evidence he ever played there.[6]

In preparation for the wedding festivities of Eleonora d'Este and Don

Carlo Gesualdo, Pasquini wrote a *favola boscareccia* entitled *I fidi amanti*. It is clear from the letter of dedication to his patroness Eleonora d'Este (document 2) that he considered the writing of verse a weaker part of his talent. If he also wrote music for this occasion, it has not been preserved. This play was published by the Veronese printer Girolamo Discepolo in 1593, the year before Gesualdo's arrival in Ferrara for the wedding.[7] Eleonora d'Este's brother, Don Cesare of Modena, had made an unsuccessful attempt two years earlier to secure a position for Pasquini as organist at Santa Casa in Loreto.[8]

Pasquini's other known activities during these years were connected with his role as teacher of composition to the daughters of Giovanni Battista Aleotti, court architect and engineer to the Duke of Ferrara. In 1593 Aleotti published a book of madrigals by his daughter Vittoria. In the same year a book of motets was published by Raphaela Aleotti in which she named Ercole Pasquini as having taught her in that art, and in which two motets by him were included. There have been conflicting interpretations of Aleotti's letter of dedication in the madrigal volume regarding the identity of Vittoria and Raphaela.[9] According to the letter, Ercole Pasquini discovered the talents of the four-year-old Vittoria when she was present at her older sister's lessons in harpsichord and composition. Under Pasquini's instructions, Vittoria made such progress that he recommended her to be sent to the convent of San Vito. There she participated in concerts given by the nuns, which were highly praised by Ercole Bottrigari and Giovanni Maria Artusi.[10] At the age of fourteen, Vittoria decided to take vows herself. Aleotti's reference in the letter to Pasquini as a "buon vecchio" indicates that the musician was born earlier than previously thought.

An anonymous document (Antolini 56) preserved at the Biblioteca Communale Ariostea at Ferrara includes in a list of nuns at San Vito the names of both Raphaela and Valeria Aleotti. Another source, overlooked until recently, Luigi Napoleone Cittadella's 1847 edition of G. B. Aleotti's *Dell'interrimente del Po di Ferrara*, sheds new light on this issue.[11] In his preface, Cittadella presents a documentary account of G. B. Aleotti, including several pages on the family. Cittadella did not know of the existence of either the madrigal or the motet books, and therefore was unacquainted with Aleotti's letter of dedication. He drew upon a number of primary documents, including Aleotti's will of 1631 and the account of

Marcantonio Guarini of 1621.[12] The only son, Giambattista, died at age four, and, in addition, there were five daughters. The order given by Cittadella is Beatrice, Cinthia, Armanda, Raphaela, and Valeria. Only four daughters, however, are mentioned in the will: one a nun at San Vito, R[everen]da Suor Raffaela; the two living married daughters Cinthia and Beatrice (the latter a widow in 1631); and his deceased daughter Armanda, who had left several grandchildren. Valeria, who according to Cittadella had been a nun at San Vito and had died in 1625, is not mentioned in the will.[13]

More important to this study, Cittadella mentioned a receipt dated 5 May 1588, from the shopkeeper Biassini to G. B. Aleotti, for purchases made in connection with the latter's fourteen-year-old daughter becoming a nun. Cittadella connected this receipt with Beatrice's taking vows at San Vito, which, according to Cittadella, she subsequently left to marry the physician Orazio Nigrelli. But the father's pride, exuded in his letter of dedication, in Vittoria's becoming a nun at fourteen, makes it seem more likely that the receipt is concerned with her rather than Beatrice. If so, Pasquini's instructions to the daughters of Aleotti should perhaps be backdated to 1578, when Vittoria would have been four years old.

Pasquini's first published madrigal, "Mentre che la bell'Isse," appeared in the anthology *Giardino de musici ferraresi* in 1591, which was dedicated to Duke Alfonso II of Ferrara. In the same collection appeared also the first published composition of Vittoria Aleotti, the madrigal "Di pallide viole," where her name is given in the masculine form Vittorio Aleotti. Only three partbooks are extant in the single copy at the Biblioteca Estense in Modena in which the name has been changed in ink to Vittoria. Pasquini's madrigal was reprinted in the Antwerp anthology *Paradiso musicale*, published by Pierre Phalèse in 1596: it was made over into a motet, "Sanctus Sebastianus," by Michael Herrer in the anthology *Hortus Musicalis* of 1606.[14] The music is exactly the same for both versions, except for a minor adjustment in the "quinto" voice to accommodate a triple repetition of the name "Dioclitianus."

> Mentre che la bell'Isse
> Tra perl'e bei rubini
> De baci una ghirland'ab inordisce
> Venere sol'assisa

Ne begl'occhi divini
Sciolta la lingua favellom'e disse
Se vuoi far liet'il core
Felicissim'Amante
Mira contempl'e baccia
La poma del nel sen nido d'Amore.

Sanctus Sebastianus
carbuncili ad instar
refulget circundatus praeclara stola
militat et nunc Deo
infelici a quondam
castra secutus Dioclitianus
nec sanguinis formidat
fundere mille libras
cuius ad Catacumbas
corpus recondidit pia Lucina.

Some accidentals left to the singer's discretion in the madrigal version were printed in the motet contrafact.

The placement of textual accents in the first six lines, with the exception of the third, is generally in agreement in the two versions. No attempt was made in the remaining lines to adjust the musical setting of the contrafact to the text accents. For example, the final line in the madrigal is a hendecasyllable with a caesura falling after the sixth syllable. The accents are placed on syllables 2 and 6 in the first part and on 7 and 10 in the second:

Le pō-ma del bel sēn / nī-do d'a-mō-re.

The contrafact text employs a dactyllic hendecasyllable with text accents on 1, 4, 7, and 10:

cōr-pus re-cōn-di-dit pī-a Lu-cī-na.

In her *Sacrae Cantiones* of 1593, Raphaela Aleotti included two motets by her teacher Ercole Pasquini: "Jubilate Deo" for five voices and "Quem vidistis, pastores?" for ten voices. A brief examination of Raphaela's motets from this same volume may help us to assess more fully those by her teacher. Ann Carruthers-Clement noted that Raphaela drew heavily on psalm texts and responsories, especially those associated with the Augustinian order.[15] Her five-voice motets fall into two groups. In the first group are those that are basically continuous and primarily imitative. They are written in the older tradition of successive points of imitation for each textual unit, with occasional interruptions of antiphonal, homophonic, or declamatory passages. In the second are those that are sectional, with greater contrast in texture. They reflect a more progressive attitude toward rhythm, harmony, and texture. Passages in imitation are interrupted by homophonic sections, in which the bass line begins to assume harmonic rather than melodic function. Sections in *proportio tripla* punctuate the more normal binary mensuration. The overall pace is varied by passages in rhythmic diminution. Great attention is given to portraying the text.

Pasquini's five-voice motet "Jubilate Deo" (Ps. 99: 1–2) falls more or less into the second group. The first verse begins in sprightly imitation terminated by a rest, after which the text "servite Domino" is presented in *proportio tripla* and in homophonic texture by the three higher voices, and then in duet imitation, cadencing in the more normal binary mensuration (see example 1).

Pasquini's impressive polychoral setting of the third responsory for Christmas morning, "Quem vidistis, pastores," retains the structure of the responsorial motet (aBcB).

a. Quem vidistis, Pastores?
   dicite, annuntiate nobis, in terris quis apparuit?
B. Natum vidimus, et choros Angelorum collaudantes Dominum:
c. dicite, quidnam vidistis?
   et annuntiate Christi nativitatem.
B. Natum vidimus, et choros Angelorum collaudantes Dominum.

This motet comprises two choirs of five voices each in contrasting tessitura, high voices for the first choir and low voices for the second choir. The texts "in terris quis apparuit?" and "collaudantes Dominum" are set in an impressive ten-voice texture, while the remaining portions are divided between the two choirs.

On 6 October 1597, Pasquini was elected organist to the Cappella Giulia at St. Peter's in Rome.[16] During the summer and fall of 1604, he was also organist at the nearby Santo Spirito in Saxia.[17] Beginning in

Example 1.   Jubilate Deo, beginning

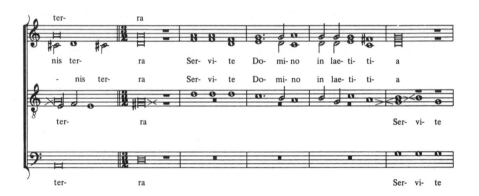

September of 1603, there appears to be some irregularity in Pasquini's signing for his payment from the Cappella Giulia.[18] Nicolo Pasquini, a son or a brother, signed in September of that year, and his signature appeared from time to time over the next two years. During the summer of 1605, the maestro di cappella, Francesco Soriano, signed for Pasquini, and in November and December, an attendant from the hospital where Pasquini was being treated signed for him. On 19 May 1608, Pasquini was dismissed from his post for "just causes."[19] Superbi states that Pasquini died under unfortunate circumstances (document 1). But, according to Faustini, he became insane (document 3).[20] Writing a quarter-century after Pasquini's death, Faustini is not always reliable; for example, he suggests that Pasquini moved to Rome in 1597 because there was no position for him at the court of Ferrara, since older musicians such as Luzzaschi and Milleville were still active at the time. This seems to be contradicted by Superbi's statement that Pasquini played the first organs in Ferrara for many years, and G. B. Aleotti's reference to him as a "buon vecchio" in 1593.

Pasquini's spiritual madrigal on a text by Angelo Grillo appeared in the anthology *Musica de diversi eccellentiss. autori* in 1604, about the time the symptoms of his final illness began to be apparent. The anthology was compiled by the Cassinian monk, Don Massimiano Gabbiani of Ravenna. The entire collection is based upon "i pietosi affetti" of Grillo, and was dedicated to Cardinal Montalto in Rome.[21] Gabbiani called upon three different groups of composers: (1) two fellow monks, Don Serafino Cantone and Don Gregorio Zucchini; (2) composers from northern Italy: Giulio Belli, Lelio Bertani, Giovanni Cavaccio, Giacomo Gastoldi, Luzzasco Luzzaschi, Benedetto Pallavicino, Costanza Porta, and Paolo Virchi; and (3) composers established in Rome: Giovanni Francesco Anerio, Arcangelo Crivelli, Ruggiero Giovannelli, Asprilio Pacelli, and Ercole Pasquini. The "pietosi affetti" of Angelo Grillo in the madrigal set by Ercole Pasquini are those in contemplation of the martyrdom of Christ and the renewal of the spirit:

> M'empio gli occhi di pianto il tuo martiro
> Mentre mio Gesù il miro
> E di sospir la bocca
> Mentre ne pensa il core
> Ma se con man d'amore
> L'alma giamai lo tocca
> Ne resterà ferita
> E m'empierà le man d'opre di vita.

The final work, "Jesu decus angelicum," published in Fabio Costantini's *Scelta di motetti* (1618), gives an added dimension to Pasquini's extant vocal compositions. It is a four-voice motet with organ as a *basso seguente*. The text, in two strophes of octosyllabic quatrains, had been set previously by Felice Anerio as a *canzonetta spirituali* in Simone Verovio's *Diletto spirituali* (1586):

Jesu decus angelicum
in aure dulce canticum
in ore mel mirificum
in corde nectar caelicum.

Tu fons misericordiae
tu vere lumen patriae
pelle nubem tristitiae
da nobis lucem gloriae.

The verse accent falls on the antepenultimate syllable of each line, similar to the *settenario sdrucciolo* of vernacular poetry, and thus ends with the dotted, or *sdrucciolo*, rhythm. Contrary to the practice in the Verovio prints, in which the same music serves both strophes, Pasquini gives each strophe a separate setting. The first quatrain retains the canzonetta format of AAB, often found in the Verovio prints. The second strophe is through-composed, except for a triple repetition of the final verse.

The choice of text in this motet and the simpler, more direct style of setting are our only indications that Ercole Pasquini, like many of his Roman contemporaries, was involved either directly or indirectly with the oratorio movement born of the religious fervor of the Counter-Reformation. It was most probably written during his years in Rome, but before his final illness; therefore, between 1597 and 1605.

Pasquini's career parallels that of Frescobaldi in that both composers were from Ferrara and moved to Rome. Both held positions as organist to the Accademia della Morte in Ferrara, and as organist to the Cappella Giulia at St. Peter's and at Santo Spirito in Saxia in Rome. The style in Pasquini's thirty-some keyboard compositions, however problematic the extant sources are, clearly indicates that he was a highly original composer and must be counted as one of Frescobaldi's more important predecessors.[22] The extant vocal compositions, though small in number, remind us on the other hand that Pasquini was a composer of the late Renaissance. His career ended while Frescobaldi's was ascending. In 1608, the year of Frescobaldi's first publications, the younger composer replaced Pasquini as organist at the Cappella Giulia. Based upon Pasquini's connection with the Aleotti family, and G. B. Aleotti's reference to him as a "buon vecchio" in 1593, Pasquini was probably born earlier than previously believed. He should be regarded as a slightly younger contemporary of Frescobaldi's teacher, Luzzasco Luzzaschi, and probably was some forty years older than Frescobaldi himself.

Had the Goretti collection remained intact at Innsbruck, we would be in a better position to assess Pasquini's vocal compositions. We can only regret the tragic loss, for works by composers other than Pasquini were represented by a large number of works not preserved elsewhere. The extant works only hint at our loss, and give us but a glimpse into the enigma of Ercole Pasquini.

Documents

1. Agostino Superbi. *Apparato de gli huomini illustri della citta di Ferrara* (Ferrara: Francesco Suzzi, 1620), 132.

    Similmente Ercole Pasquini, è stato molto spiritoso, & eccellentissimo nella Musica, & nell'Organo; fù Discepolo d'Alessandro Milleville; molt'anni nella Patria suono i primi Organi; e poi molt'anni in Roma in S. Pietro fù organista; aveva una mano delicatissima, & velocissima; suonava alla volte tanto eggregiamente, che rapiva le persone, e faceva stupire veramente. Morì non dimeno poco fortunato in Roma.

    Similarly Ercole Pasquini was a most clever and most excellent musician and organist; he was a pupil of Alessandro Milleville; for many years he played the first organs in his own country; then for many years he was organist in Rome at St. Peter's; he had a very delicate and nimble hand; and sometimes played so splendidly that he enraptured the people and truly amazed them. Nevertheless, he died in Rome under unfortunate circumstances.

2. (Title page) I FIDI AMANTI/ FAVOLA BOSCARECCIA/ DI HERCOLE PASQUINI/ DA FERRARA/ Dedicata nel preparamento delle felicissime/ nozze de gl'Illust.^{mi} & Eccel.^{mi} Sig./ D. CARLO GESUALDI, ET/ D. ELEONORA ESTENSE./ (NATURA IUBENTE ET ARTE EXEQUENTE)./ IN VERONA,/ Appresso Girolamo Discepolo./ M D XCIII.

    (Dedication) ALL'ILLUSTR.^{MA} ET/ ECCELL.^{MA} S.^{RA} D. ELEO-/NORA DA ESTE, Signora & Patrona mia/ colendiss.

    Mando sotto l'ombra di sua Eccellentia in luce il presente primo, e debole parto del mio ingegno, come quello, che essendo già a principio della generation sua dedicatosi a lei, non dovea sotto altre ali adombrarsi; Et come quello, che co'l scoprirsi quasi troppo frettloso, & arrogante precursore al suono delle fortunatissime sue nozze, dovea dargli aperto segno della mia eccessiva osservanza, & servitù, che a ponto non potea scoprirsi, ne esser dalla debolezza mia in una minima parte resa uguale all'infinità de i meriti suoi, se non con l'eccedere impatientemente il tempo, e l'opportunità di scoprirsi; cercando in tal guisa d'avanzare cosi con le attioni ogn'altro suo più fido servo, come mi persuado di far con l'animo. So che molti estimaranno questo frutto non tanto lontano quanto inaspettato dalla profession mia; ma perche so anco, che all'altissimo giuditio di sua Eccellentia non possono occorrere simili pensieri, poco estimarò cosi fatta opinione, rendendomi certo, che per la perfetta intelligenza ch'ella ha della Musica, conoschi chiaro quanto siano ad un Musico necessario la cognitione, et esercitio del verso. Gradisca sua Eccellentia la fatica conforme alla natural affabilità sua, ch'io fra tanto, publicati che havrò alcuni miei musicali componimenti, con l'andar volgendo l'animo a fatiche maggiori, farò conoscere al mondo, che se non degno, non sono anco otioso servo di sua Eccellentia.

Di sua Eccell. Illustriss.

Affettionatiss. servitore

H[e]rcole Pasquini

3. Agostini Faustini. *Aggiunta* to Gasparo Sardi, *Libro delle Historie Ferraresi* (Ferrara: Giuseppe Gironi, 1646), 97.

. . . Hercole Pasquini, perche essendo questo valente Organista, ma non pero adoperato in Corte perch'era giovine, & vivevano il Milleville, il Luzzaschi, & altri più vecchi di lui, passando a Roma, con la perdita della gratia del suo Principe, finamente impazzitosi, morì miserabile Organista di San Pietro in quella Città.

. . . Ercole Pasquini, while being a valuable organist, but not adopted in court because he was young and Milleville and Luzzaschi and others older than he were living, passed on to Rome with a loss of favor of his Prince. Finally going insane, he died wretchedly as organist of St. Peter's in that city.

Notes

1. Willi Apel, *Geschichte der Orgel- und Klaviermusik bis 1700* (Kassel: Bärenreiter, 1967), 412–15. English translation and revision by Hans Tischler, *The History of Keyboard Music to 1700* (Bloomington: Indiana University Press, 1972), 421–23.

2. Ercole Pasquini, *Collected Keyboard Words*, ed. W. Richard Shindle, in *Corpus of Early Keyboard Music* 12 (n.p.: American Institute of Musicology, 1966); Alexander Silbiger, *Italian Manuscript Sources of Seventeenth-Century Keyboard Music* (Ann Arbor: UMI Research Press, 1980).

3. Franz Waldner, "Zwei Inventarien aus dem XVI. und XVII. Jahrhundert über hinterlassene Musikinstrumente und Musikalien am Innsbrucker Hofe," *Studien zur Musikwissenschaft* 4 (1916): 128–47; Walter Senn, *Musik und Theater am Hof zu Innsbruck* (Innsbruck: Österreichische Verlagsanstalt, 1954), 344–46.

4. An anonymous *Missa vestiva i colli* for twelve voices exists in the former collection of the Archivio di Santo Spirito in Saxia in Rome where Pasquini was organist in 1604; see Antonio Allegra, "La Cappella musicale di S. Spirito in Saxia di Roma, Appunti storici

(1551–1737)," *Note d'archivio per la storia musicale* 17 (1940): 26–38. This collection was dispersed c. 1937, at which time the manuscript in question was bought by Evan Gorga; see Guido Mattei-Gentili, *Membra disjecta dell'archivio musicale di Santo Spirito in Saxia* (Rome: Nova et Ventura, 1937); and Raffaele Casamiri, "Il disperso archivio musicale di Santo Spirito in Saxia," *Note d'archivio per la storia musicale* 25 (1938): 140–44. It was acquired by Laurence Feininger in 1963, and is presently housed at the Museo Provinciale d'Arte in Trent.

5. Silbiger, *Italian Manuscript Sources*, 178.

6. Anthony Newcomb, *The Madrigal at Ferrara: 1579 97* (Princeton. Princeton University Press, 1980), 1:179.

7. Glenn Watkins, *Gesualdo: The Man and His Music* (Chapel Hill: University of North Carolina Press, 1973), 48.

8. Newcomb, *Madrigal* 1:179.

9. Robert Eitner in his *Quellen-Lexikon* assumed Raphaela and Vittoria were the same person. Adriano Cavicchi in his articles in *The New Grove Dictionary of Music and Musicians* (London: Macmillan, 1980) gives separate entries under the two names. The letters of dedication in both the madrigal and motet volumes will be reproduced in following forthcoming publications edited by C. Ann Carruthers-Clement: Raffaella Aleotti, *Sacrae cantiones quinque, septem octo, & decem vocibus, . . . liber primus (Venice: Ricciardo Amadino, 1593)* (The Broude Trust); and Vittoria Aleotti, *Ghirlando de madrigali a quarto voci (Venice: Giacomo Vincenti, 1593)* (The Broude Trust).

10. Ercole Bottrigari, *Il desiderio* (Venice: Bellagamba, 1594), trans. Carol MacClintock, Musicological Studies and Documents 9 (American Institute of Musicology, 1962); Giovanni Maria Artusi, *L'Artusi overo delle imperfettioni della moderna musica* (Venice: Giacomo Vincenti, 1600).

11. Luigi Napoleone Cittadella, preface to Giovanni Battista Aleotti, *Dell'interrimento del Po di Ferrara . . . di Ficarolo; le memorie per servire alla biografia dell'autore* (Ferrara: D. Taddei, 1847), 54–55.

12. Marcantonio Guarini, *Compendio historico delle chiese di Ferrara* (Ferrara: Baldini, 1621).

13. G. B. Aleotti's will is in the Archivio di Stato in Ferrara (Archivio notarile antico di Ferrara, Notaio Mainardo Guarini, Martricola 852, Pacco 23, Anno 1631, folo. 217 22). I wish to express my gratitude to Jane Bowers for providing me with a photographic copy.

14. I am grateful to Friedrich Wilhelm Riedel for clarifying the role of M. Herrer. Prof. Riedel provided me with the information that Saint Sebastian was greatly venerated at Passau, where *Hortus Musicalis* was published.

15. C. Ann Carruthers-Clement, "The Madrigals and Motets of Vittoria/Raphaela Aleotti" (Ph.D. diss., Kent State University, 1982), 87, 95–96.

16. Alberto Cametti, "Girolamo Frescobaldi in Roma," *Rivista musicale italiana* 15 (1908): 709 n. 3.

17. Allegra, "La Cappella musicale."

18. James Leslie Ladewig, "Frescobaldi's *Recercari, et Canzoni Franzese* (1615): A Study of the Contrapuntal Keyboard Idiom in Ferrara, Naples, and Rome, 1580–1620" (Ph.D. diss., University of California at Berkeley, 1978), 303.

19. Cametti, "Frescobaldi in Roma," 710.

20. Agostini Faustini, *Libro delle historie ferraresi* . . . *di G. Sardi con le aggiunte di A. Faustini* (Ferrara: Girono, 1646), 97.

21. Alfred Einstein, "Abbott Angelo Grillo's Letters as Source Material for Music History," *Essays on Music* (New York: W. W. Norton, 1956), 153–73.

22. See Ladewig, this volume; Silbiger, *Italian Manuscript Sources*, 178–86.

Frescobaldi and the Lute and Chitarrone
Toccatas of "Il Tedesco della Tiorba"

VICTOR COELHO

T HE scope of current research into the origins and impact of Frescobaldi's keyboard music can be substantially augmented through a consideration of Italian music for the seventeenth-century lute and chitarrone. This corpus of music—much of it preserved in printed tablatures, but a good deal of it transmitted in hastily scribbled commonplace books as well—has never been examined in this light, despite the fact that lute and keyboard music enjoyed a close partnership in seventeenth-century English and French repertories.[1] Much of this neglect can be attributed to the present lack of bibliographic control over the lute and chitarrone sources.[2] Moreover, it is difficult to assess the impact of a body of music when the extant sources represent only a small fraction of the original repertory. Nevertheless, the conclusions offered by the music contained in the sources I have examined strongly suggest that a fertile field of research lies ahead.[3]

Specifically, between 1600 and 1650 there existed in Italy a cross-pollination of musical styles, repertories, forms, and compositional techniques between the keyboard and the lute (both long- and short-necked).[4] For Frescobaldi's keyboard music, the relationships between these instruments and their repertories assume a special significance. The composer had long personal contacts with the two most influential lute and chitarrone virtuosos in Italy: Alessandro Piccinini (1566–ca. 1638) and Johann Hieronymus (Giovanni Girolamo) Kapsberger (1580–1651).

Piccinini was born into a family of lutenists, all of whom worked for Duke Alfonso II d'Este of Ferrara until the dissolution of the Ferrarese court in 1597.[5] We can assume that there was contact between Piccinini and Frescobaldi during this time; they could scarcely have missed each other in Rome. Documents show that shortly after 1600, Piccinini entered the service of Guido Bentivoglio and possibly that of Cardinal Pietro Aldobrandini, both of whom patronized Frescobaldi during his early years in Rome.[6] While the rather conservative nature of Piccinini's works suggests that there was little or no actual transference of style between Frescobaldi and Piccinini, the lutenist may have introduced Frescobaldi to the music of other fine lute and chitarrone players working in Italy.

Among these musicians was Johann Hieronymus Kapsberger, the most prolific composer of lute and chitarrone music in the seventeenth century.[7] The Venetian-born Kapsberger, who was popularly known as "Il Tedesco della tiorba," settled in Rome shortly after 1604, and in late 1624 entered the service of Frescobaldi's last patron, Cardinal Francesco Barberini, nephew to the reigning Pope Urban VIII.[8] Moreover, Kapsberger is mentioned in two letters by Vincenzo Landinelli in Rome to Enzo Bentivoglio in Ferrara (1610, 1611), which, at any rate, suggests at least a peripheral relationship with Frescobaldi's first Roman patrons.[9] This similarity in backgrounds is coupled with a congruity in the two composers' musical styles. In this paper, then, I would like to open up new lines of investigation into an unexplored area of Frescobaldi research by concentrating on the similar approaches toward chromaticism, formal construction, and textural makeup in the toccatas of Frescobaldi and the lute and chitarrone toccatas of Kapsberger. My aims are to increase our limited knowledge of the sources, transmission, and impact of the seventeenth-century lute and chitarrone repertory in general, and specifically, to contribute new thoughts concerning the performance of Frescobaldi's toccatas.

In 1604, Kapsberger published his first and perhaps most important work, the *Libro primo d'intavolatura di chitarrone*. It is the only work of Kapsberger that was published in Venice. For its novelty as the first printed book of chitarrone music, and because it contained a short but very valuable list of *avertimenti* for the player, the *Libro primo* was probably the most important of the seventeenth-century chitarrone and lute tablatures. It seems to have remained in use for at least twenty years, since some of its contents appear in manuscripts copied as late as 1627.[10]

Of special interest are the six brilliant toccatas that open the *Libro primo*. Similar to Frescobaldi's toccatas in style, but anticipating them by eleven years, these works display an attunement to the expressive and dramatic style of the *seconda prattica* through the daring use of chromaticism and by the introduction of various improvisatory techniques within a declamatory musical texture.

The toccatas from the *Libro primo* are also of great historical significance because they combine elements of Renaissance lute music and the emerging baroque keyboard style. The playing technique of the chitarrone and its tuning are both refinements of the sixteenth-century lute style, but the formal designs, textures, and ornamentation of Kapsberger show a closer affinity to keyboard music. It thus seems likely that Kapsberger's and Frescobaldi's toccatas have common antecedents in the toccatas composed by the Venetians Andrea Gabrieli, Annibale Padovano, and Claudio Merulo. The Venetian toccatas represent a significant departure from previous instrumental music in their introduction of virtuoso passagework and contrasting chordal episodes, and in their well-defined harmonic motion and formal clarity.[11]

That Frescobaldi should have been drawn to the Venetian repertory is to be expected in view of his early sensitivity to current styles of playing and also because of the proximity of Ferrara to Venice, which was then the center of toccata activity. Kapsberger's absorption of the Venetian style, on the other hand, was the culmination of a certain progressive trend in sixteenth-century lute music, which from midcentury showed the influence of keyboard music. Significantly, this influence coincided with a period of heightened activity in the publication of keyboard music. In the lute manuscript *B-Br* II.275 (dated 1590), one of fifteen anonymous ricercars is based on a *fuga* by Merulo.[12] Copied in roughly the same period as Venetian publications of keyboard works by Bertoldo (1591), Merulo (1592), Radino (1592), Diruta (1593), and Giovanni and Andrea Gabrieli (1593), this manuscript is the first to acknowledge the lutenists' growing awareness of keyboard music and may even point to the possibility that some musicians played both instruments. This is certainly the case with Radino, whose 1592 keyboard print was republished by Vincenti in an arrangement "per sonar di liuto" later in the same year.[13] Both versions were published in Venice, which was the center of keyboard and lute music as well as the city where Kapsberger published his *Libro primo*.[14]

It thus appears that Venice was also the focus of this progressive trend of lute music. Radino's arrangements, which clearly show how keyboard style can be transferred to the lute, were a watershed in this trend, which culminated with the publication of Kapsberger's *Libro primo* in 1604. The simultaneous presence of keyboard and lute music in the manuscripts *D-Ngm* Ms. 33.748/M.271 and *I-Bc* AA/360, both of which date from after 1604, show that this trend continued well into the seventeenth century.[15] Finally, the lute manuscript *A-KR* L64, copied after 1609, contains excerpts from part 2 of Diruta's *Il Transilvano* of 1609. Diruta's treatise apparently held great interest for lute players, and Kapsberger's discussion of *accenti* in his *Libro quarto* (1640) has its origins in part 2 of Diruta's book.

Kapsberger's toccatas of 1604 become even more significant when compared with what might be the only contemporaneous source of solo chitarrone music. In the back of a rather ordinary seventeenth-century lute manuscript now owned by the University of California at Berkeley, an addition, probably dating from around 1605–10, contains among other pieces six toccatas, and these toccatas provide an ideal index for comparison with Kapsberger's work.[16] The Berkeley toccatas show none of the predilection for textural contrast and virtuosity characteristic of the Venetian keyboardists' and Kapsberger's work (see example 1).

Example 1   Toccata from *US-BE* Ms. 757, fol. 33v

In short, Kapsberger's 1604 toccatas are unique examples in the plucked-string repertoire of the adoption of the progressive tendencies of the Venetian keyboard school. But beyond this, with his many innovative departures from the keyboard mold, Kapsberger demonstrates his ingenuity, and ultimately his link with the toccatas of Frescobaldi.

When comparing Kapsberger's list of *avertimenti* that appears in the *Libro primo* and in an expanded version in the *Libro quarto* (see plate 1), with Frescobaldi's own instructions to the player from his *Toccate* of 1615, one becomes immediately aware of the composers' common conceptual approach toward performance. Both attempt to set forth a guide which, in essence, warns against a strict interpretation of notated music in favor of a more improvisatory approach. As for specific connections between

Plate 1. Expanded avertimenti from the *Libro quarto* (1640)
(London, British Library)

Kapsberger and Frescobaldi, their discussion of something so seemingly unimportant as the arpeggio underlines the congruities in their styles.

In his preface Kapsberger describes an arpeggiation pattern which is to be used on all chords of four or more notes, and occasionally for chords of three notes. On the one hand, Kapsberger was simply providing a solution to the problem of voicing chords on an instrument with re-entrant tuning. According to Kapsberger (1640) (see plate 1) and Kircher, among others, the chitarrone was tuned as shown in example 2.[17]

Example 2

Since the top two courses are tuned an octave lower than on the lute, the third course has the highest pitch. Thus, a simple arpeggio from lowest strings to highest causes the highest note to sound somewhere in the middle of the arpeggio (see example 3).

Example 3

However, by employing Kapsberger's method—his "propria et sola inventione"—arpeggiated chords sound in a normal fashion, as shown in example 4.

Example 4

But there must have been other reasons as well for Kapsberger's method, since on certain chords it is the pattern itself that causes the tones to sound "out of order" (see example 5).

Example 5

It appears that proper chord voicing in an arpeggio was a secondary consideration to the use of the arpeggio as an effect, or, more precisely, an *Affekt*, which formed part of the general musical aesthetic of the time. In his *Della prattica musica vocale, et strumentale*, Scipione Cerreto alluded to the expressive quality of the arpeggio when, in his chapter on the guitar, he wrote, "And when one plays this instrument *arpeggiando* with the fingers of the right hand, it also has a beautiful effect, but one can learn this style of playing only through long practice."[18] Cerreto's comment on the difficulty of mastering this technique suggests that arpeggios were played not as simple rolled chords, but in a more complex manner, as indicated by Kapsberger. Kapsberger's rules, which offered practical solutions to the problem of arpeggiation, standardized this technique, and his method was quickly adopted by other instrumentalists. Piccinini employed Kapsberger's method in his book of 1623—albeit with some modifications—but he failed to cite its inventor. Such was not the case with the guitarist Francesco Valdambrini, who used the technique in his guitar books of 1646 and 1648 and acknowledged his debt to Kapsberger.[19]

It was Kapsberger, then, who was the founder of this particular arpeggiated style, and his methods gained widespread use first through his own chitarrone publications, and then through the guitar repertory. Moreover, in exploiting the arpeggio as an affective device, Kapsberger could employ it as a means of heightening the dramatic tensions of the toccata. Indeed, one of the most important aspects of the *Libro primo* toccatas is Kapsberger's creation of this drama, not only through the alternation of chordal and figural elements, but also through the contrast between arpeggiated and unarpeggiated sections (see example 6).

Frescobaldi's rules bear strong resemblances to Kapsberger's. In his third rule, which states that the opening of the toccatas "should be played slowly and with arpeggiation," Frescobaldi seems to be striving

Example 6   Toccata III from the *Libro primo di chitarrone* (1604)

* Dotted line indicates that original passage is to be slurred.

t = *trillo*

Example 7   Toccata VII (1615)

Example 8   Kapsberger, Toccata IV (1604)

t = *trillo*

for a lightly strummed lute-like sonority.[20] This rule would have been applied, for example, to the passage in example 7. The actual execution of the arpeggios is left to the player; Frescobaldi gives no examples. Frescobaldi's ideal, however, may have been the sound of Kapsberger's chitarrone arpeggios. Furthermore, almost all of Kapsberger's toccatas begin "slowly and with arpeggiation" (see example 8).

These chordal beginnings have their origins in the sixteenth-century preludial forms used by lutenists to set the mode, warm up, check the tuning of the instrument, or alert the audience that music was about to begin. These pieces, many of which have titles such as "tastar de corde," "praeludium," "tochata," but others of which are simply nonimitative ricercars, functioned as preludes to more "learned" pieces such as imitative ricercars, fantasias, canzonas, or intabulations of vocal works.[21] In his toccatas, Kapsberger retains this improvisatory and ultimately practical element by writing out a prelude and integrating it into the toccata as an opening section that precedes an imitative one. The beginning of Toccata 5 from the *Libro primo*, to give but one example, is essentially a prelude consisting of primary chords sounding over long tonic pedals in the bass. This static opening has no musical function other than to set the mode of the toccata and to check the tuning of the instrument. The opening G chord, for example, is fingered in three different positions —all of them retaining the original spacing—so that the player can check the relative tuning of the strings, and make sure that the frets are properly aligned (see example 9). In performance, these chordal *exordia* create a sonorous, rhythmless texture, which contrasts nicely with the

Example 9   Kapsberger, Toccata V (1604)

introverted and severely disciplined imitative sections that follow. In addition, these preludes exploit the resonance and sympathetic vibrations that naturally occur from the lingering sound of unmuted bass notes. The beginning chordal sections in Frescobaldi's toccatas, when played "arpeggiando," achieve the same quality of sound—a kind of resonant harmonic blur that gradually focuses into rhythmic clarity (see example 10).

The influence of Kapsberger's use of the arpeggio is also evident in the last two points of Frescobaldi's third rule. He continues, "Where suspensions occur, even if this is in the middle of the piece, these too should be arpeggiated so that the instrument is not left empty; these arpeggios may be repeated at the discretion of the player."[22] The arpeggiation of strict chordal passages, or *botte ferme*, that contain dissonances, constitutes the most expressive use of the arpeggio, for it allows the player to restrike the suspensions, prolong the dissonances, and thus heighten the harmonic tension. In Frescobaldi's work, such chordal episodes are sprinkled throughout the toccatas (see example 11).[23]

A likely predecessor of these passages is Kapsberger's Toccata *Arpeggiata* from the *Libro primo*. Written in long note values, one chord to a bar, the work requires the arpeggiation of every chord—a technique that further dramatizes the effect of the ambiguous, suspended harmonies (see example 12). The use of a slow rhythm is also indicative of the tempo at which the toccata should be played. Frescobaldi employed a similar procedure to show tempo relationships, in which the slow introductions to his toccatas suggest a change in tempo between the introductions and the sections that follow.[24] The slow-moving, murky harmonies of the *Arpeggiata* toccata might also have a parallel in Frescobaldi's Toccata VIII, "of dissonances and suspensions," from the 1627 *Toccate*. Here Frescobaldi writes a toccata similar to Kapsberger's in which the resultant chordal texture is chiefly effective by being dramatically conditioned through a sophisticated and adventurous harmonic vocabulary (see example 13).[25]

Finally, in setting the Toccata "Arpeggiata" to a slow rhythm, Kapsberger, like Frescobaldi, promotes the element of improvisation by leaving space within each bar for the player to embellish or restrike the chord. This intention is confirmed in Kapsberger's *avertimenti*, where he states that the arpeggio can be repeated "for as long as the time indicated above."[26]

Example 10 Frescobaldi, Toccata XI (1615)

Example 11 Frescobaldi, Toccata IX (1627)

Example 12 Kapsberger, Toccata II "Arpeggiata" (1604)

Example 13 Frescobaldi, Toccata VIII "di durezze e ligature" (1627)

This appears to be a clear foreshadowing of Frescobaldi's suggestion that chords can be repeated "at the discretion of the player," and the earliest anticipation of Frescobaldi's warning against "leaving the instrument empty."[27]

Chordal textures, however, were often more effectively used in the middle of a toccata in conjunction with other contrasting elements, rather than at the beginning or throughout the piece. In emphasizing the "nuova maniera" and the "novita d'artificio" of his 1627 *Toccate*, Frescobaldi employed new modes of textural contrast, of which the use of dance-like triple-meter sections in tandem with chordal episodes was a major component. This feature was indeed part of the "novelty" of the 1627 book, since triple-time sections did not appear in the 1615 collection nor were they all that common in the toccatas composed by the Neapolitans Macque, Mayone, and Trabaci. They were, however, important features in both Kapsberger's and Piccinini's toccatas. In Toccata V from the *Libro primo*, the triple section—framed on both sides by two measures of arpeggiated chords—assumes the characteristic rhythm of the Italian corrente (see example 14).

Example 14   Kapsberger, Toccata V (1604)

A triple-meter section in galliard rhythm appears in a toccata in the chitarrone manuscript *I-MOs Busta 4* (attributed to Kapsberger)[28] (see example 15).

Example 15   [Toccata] from *I-MOs Busta 4*, chitarrone Ms., fol. 2v

A final point of contact between Frescobaldi and Kapsberger concerns their similar approach toward chromaticism. While this is not the place for an extensive discussion, a brief review may point the way to further study in this area.

The use of chromatic subjects had become fashionable in early seventeenth-century keyboard music. The often-cited Neapolitan influence on Frescobaldi seems most persuasive here, since chromatic subjects appeared early in the keyboard music of Trabaci and Macque.[29] It is far more difficult to explain the appearance of chromatic subjects in Kapsberger's work. There was no tradition of Roman or Venetian lute music that could have stimulated this style. Nor was vocal music a factor, since such an influence should have been noticeable in Kapsberger's *Madrigali* of 1609. Is it possible that the Neapolitan influence extended to the lute and chitarrone repertory as well? This question is difficult to answer, but in view of the seventeenth-century lutenists' awareness of contemporary keyboard styles, this relationship may prove to be a promising area of inquiry.

Roland Jackson has shown that one of the most indisputable claims to a Neapolitan influence in Frescobaldi's music is the sudden chromatic lowering of tones at the end of phrases (see example 16).[30]

Example 16 Frescobaldi, Toccata XI (1627)

In the above example, the lowering of the E on the third beat effectively obscures the V_5^6–I cadence that has been set up, by deflecting the resolution to the tonic minor. In Kapsberger's work we see similar chromatic maneuvers in the toccatas of the 1611 lute book (see example 17).

Example 17 Kapsberger, Toccata V (1611), mm. 10–13

Here Kapsberger sets up a cadence on the dominant of C minor, which should resolve to a major chord. Even though the resolution to the major is anticipated by the B-natural in the previous measure, Kapsberger surprisingly cadences on the dominant minor, which fails to relieve any of the harmonic or rhythmic tension generated prior to that point. This ambiguity provides the structure of the entire first section of the toccata, for Kapsberger repeats the whole sequence only a few measures later. This time, a cadence on the secondary dominant of D is similarly resolved with a lowered third, despite the presence of the F-sharps in the previous three measures (see example 18).

Example 18   Kapsberger, Toccata V (1611), mm. 20–23

A similar approach also dictates the method by which Frescobaldi and Kapsberger employ chromatic motives to promote musical and dramatic development. This is normally achieved by the use of a single chromatic subject, which is gradually lengthened during the course of the work, often moving through different voices. In the absence of contrasting figural material, however, it is precisely this technique that is responsible for the forward motion and dramatic tensions of the chromatic toccatas. A good example is offered by Frescobaldi's Toccata VIII from the 1627 *Toccate*. As the following example shows, chromatic or semichromatic lines spanning a fourth appear early (see example 19a) and are gradually lengthened to a fifth (example 19b), sixth, seventh, and finally a tenth (example 19c) to climax the work.

This underlying element of growth becomes the structural fabric of the work and is felt as a dramatic succession of events. Once again, this method of construction can be found in Kapsberger's work, particularly in the toccatas from the *Libro primo di lauto*. In Toccata III, Kapsberger begins the imitative second section of the work with a chromatic subject descending a minor third from C to A (mm. 21–22). This subject is

Example 19   Frescobaldi, Toccata VIII (1627)

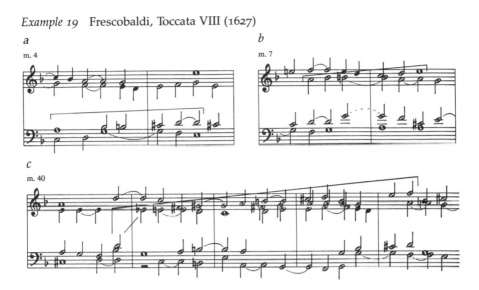

immediately echoed with an answer spanning a fifth from F down to B-flat (mm. 22–25). In the stretto climax of the work, both motives are augmented: the subject, from a third to an octave and a half, while the answer, now real, spirals two octaves down to a low C, played on the tenth and lowest course of the lute (see example 20).[31]

Does the lute and chitarrone repertory, and Kapsberger's contribution in particular, represent no more than a peripheral area of Italian instrumental music of the *seicento*? I have suggested that it does represent more. Many of the modes of dramatic expression implicit in Frescobaldi's toccatas may well be the result of Frescobaldi's adaptation or even imitation of the idiomatic characteristics common to the central lute and chitarrone repertory of the early seventeenth century. With regard to the use of the arpeggio as a means of contrast, and in the appearance of triple-meter sections as contrasting episodes, Kapsberger's influence on Frescobaldi seems strong. The appearance of chromatic subjects in Kapsberger's work is also interesting, for it may indicate that Kapsberger was a point on the line that connects the important Neapolitan keyboardists with Frescobaldi.

In assessing the significance of the relationship between Kapsberger and Frescobaldi, however, we must keep in mind that the sources available for study were all written before the period during which they had

Example 20   Kapsberger, Toccata III (1611)

the most direct contact with each other's music. It is both puzzling and unfortunate that their period of employment under Cardinal Francesco Barberini has yielded no significant information of any contact in their musical activities. Thus, this paper stops short of being an exhaustive study of either Kapsberger's influence or of the intertwining strands of baroque music. It does draw attention, however, to some little-known but important sources, and will perhaps form a basis for further research into some of the larger connections that undoubtedly exist between Italian lute and keyboard music of the seventeenth century.

Notes

1. See, for example, the lute versions made from some of William Byrd's keyboard works, in Nigel North, ed., *William Byrd: Music for the Lute* (London: Oxford University Press, 1976). Some French sources of the seventeenth century contain lute music transcribed into staff notation; Perrine's *Pieces de luth en musique* . . . (Paris, 1680), for example, contains six pieces by Gaultier (le vieux) transcribed expressly for keyboard performance. This trend seems to have continued into the eighteenth century, for in the keyboard manuscript *S-Sk* Kalmar Läroverks, Ms. 4a, there appear nine pieces by the Bohemian lutenist Johann Anton Losy, "reintabulated" into keyboard tablature; see Emil Vogl, "The Lute Music of Johann Anton Losy," *Journal of the Lute Society of America* 14 (1981):5–58.

2. On the gross inadequacies of the RISM volume *Handschriftlich überlieferte Lauten- und Gitarrentabulaturen des 15. bis 18. Jahrhunderts*, Répertoire international des sources musicales, D/VII, ed. Wolfgang Boetticher (Munich: Henle, 1979), see Arthur Ness's review in the *Journal of the American Musicological Society* 34 (1981):339–45. Addenda and corrigenda to Boetticher's volume appear in Victor Coelho, "Communication" in the *Journal of the American Musicological Society* 35 (1982):201–2; and Dinko Fabris, "Prime aggiunte al Volume RISM B/VII—Intavolature mss. per liuto e chitarra," *Fontes artes musicae* 29 (1982):103–21.

3. I am currently preparing a complete study of the manuscript sources of seventeenth-century music for the Italian lute and chitarrone.

4. I use the word "lute" here as a generic term, to cover the many lute-related instruments that were popular in seventeenth-century Italy, such as the chitarrone (or *tiorba*), the *liuto attiorbato*, *tiorbino*, and the *colascione*. For an explanation of the confusing terminology surrounding some of these instruments, see Douglas A. Smith, "On the Origins of the Chitarrone," *Journal of the American Musicological Society* 32 (1979):440–62. Kevin Mason has reached slightly different conclusions regarding the chitarrone's origins; see his "The Chitarrone and its Repertoire in Early Seventeenth-Century Italy" (Ph.D. diss., Washington University, 1983), 13–26.

5. See Lucio De Grandis, "Famiglie di musicisti nel '500. I Piccinini: vita col liuto," *Nuova rivista musicale italiana* 16 (1982):226–32.

6. See Anthony Newcomb, "Girolamo Frescobaldi, 1608–1615: A Documentary Study,"

Annales musicologiques 7 (1976–77):139–41. Although Newcomb suggests that it was probably not Alessandro but his brother Filippo Piccinini who entered the service of Cardinal Pietro Aldobrandini, Claudio Annibaldi, this volume, claims that both Piccininis worked for the cardinal. A good synoptic account of Aldobrandini's activities as a patron is given in Frederick Hammond, "Cardinal Pietro Aldobrandini, Patron of Music," *Studi musicali* 12 (1983): 53–66.

7. The most comprehensive and up-to-date biography of Kapsberger is this author's "G. G. Kapsberger in Rome, 1604–1645: New Biographical Data," *Journal of the Lute Society of America* 16 (1983):103–33.

8. For a study of the cultural and musical milieu in which Frescobaldi and Kapsberger worked, see Frederick Hammond, "Girolamo Frescobaldi and a Decade of Music in Casa Barberini: 1634–1643," *Analecta musicologica* 19 (1979): 94–124.

9. In a letter dated 3 November 1610 (Ferrara, Archivio di Stato, Archivio Bentivoglio, M. 9-55, fol. 524v), Landinelli mentions that Kapsberger performed for some of Enzo Bentivoglio's guests; in another letter, dated 2 January 1611 (Archivio Bentivoglio, M. 9-58, fols. 30-30v), Landinelli writes that Kapsberger will give him the *buco* that Enzo requested be sent to him. The letters are quoted and translated in Victor Coelho, "G. G. Kapsberger in Rome," 114–15. I record here my thanks to Dinko Fabris of Bari, Italy, for drawing my attention to these documents.

10. Concordances are contained in the following manuscripts: *US-BE* Ms. 757, (dated ca. 1600–1605), fol. 40v; *I-MOs* Ms. Ducale Segreto Busta 4 (dated 1619), fols. 21v–22; *FPn* Rés. Vmd. Ms. 30 (dated 1626), fols. 21v, 25; and *I-Rvat* Barb. Lat. 4145 (dated 1627), fols. 4–9. An edition of the Modena and Paris manuscripts, edited by this author, is forthcoming: *Chitarrone Music Preserved in Manuscript Sources* (Madison: A-R Editions).

11. See Murray Bradshaw, "Tonal Design in the Venetian Intonation and Toccata," *Music Review* 35 (1984): 101–9.

12. A description of this manuscript (without an inventory) appears in *RISM B/VII*, 57–58 (cf. n. 2, above); see also Arthur J. Ness, "Sources of Lute Music," *The New Grove Dictionary of Music and Musicians* (London: Macmillan, 1980), 17:736.

13. For a modern edition of the keyboard print see Giovanni Battista Radino, *Il primo libro d'intabolatura*, Corpus of Early Keyboard Music 33, Susan Ellingworth, ed. (n.p.: American Institute of Musicology, 1968). The *Intavolatura di balli per sonar di liuto* has been published in modern transcription, edited by Giuseppe Gullino (Florence: Edizioni Musicali ditta R. Mauri, 1949).

14. I should also mention here the vocal works published in Rome by Simone Verovio, since they contain accompaniments that can be played on either harpsichord or lute (tablature is provided); see Howard Mayer Brown, *Instrumental Music Printed before 1600*, 2d ed. (Cambridge, Mass.: Harvard University Press, 1979), 1586$_8$, 1589$_8$, 1591$_{11}$, 1592$_{11}$, 1595$_{10}$. It is interesting to note that the Verovio family lived in the parish of San Lorenzo in Damaso through at least 1600 (Rome, Archivio del Vicariato, San Lorenzo in Damaso, *Battesimi*, IV (1591–99), fol. 35v, fol. 238; *Battesimi*, VI (1599–1606), fol. 65v). This is the same parish in which two of Kapsberger's three children were born (see Coelho, "G. G. Kapsberger in Rome," 115 n.40). I am indebted to James Chater for this information.

15. These manuscripts are described in Alexander Silbiger, *Italian Manuscript Sources of Seventeenth-Century Keyboard Music* (Ann Arbor: UMI Research Press, 1980), 84–85, 94–95.

16. See Coelho, "Communication."

17. See Athanasius Kircher, *Musurgia universalis* (Rome: Corbelletti, 1650), 476; also Marin Mersenne, *Harmonie universelle* (1636), trans. Roger Chapman (The Hague: M. Nijhoff, 1957), 73.

18. Cerreto, *Della prattica musica vocale, et strumentale* (Naples: Carlino, 1601), 321: "E quando tale Strumento si sonora arpiggiando con tutte le dita della mano destra, fara anco bello effetto, ma questo modo di sonare si puo imprare con lunga prattica."

19. See James Tyler, *The Early Guitar* (London: Oxford University Press, 1980), 99.

20. "Li cominciamenti delle toccate siene fatto adagio, et arpeggiando . . ." On Frescobaldi's rules and their interpretation in general, see Etienne Darbellay, "Liberté, variété, et 'affetti cantabili' chez Girolamo Frescobaldi," *Revue de musicologie* 61 (1975): 197–243.

21. For a provocative interpretation of the general humanistic concept of the ricercar's preludial function, see Warren Kirkendale, "Ciceronians versus Aristotelians on the Ricercar as Exordium, from Bembo to Bach," *Journal of the American Musicological Society* 32 (1979): 1–44.

22. "È così nelle ligature, ò vero durezze, come, anche nel mezzo del opera, si batterano insieme, per non lasciar voto l'Istromento: il qual battimento ripiglierassi à bene placito di chi suona."

23. Piccinini also advocated this style, in which during a dissonant passage, the dissonances can be struck repeatedly, either piano or forte, the number of times depending on how strong the dissonance is, "playing as they do in Naples." See chapter 3 of the preface to his *Intavolatura di liuto et di chitarrone* (Bologna: Moscatelli, 1623; reprint, Florence: Studio per Edizioni Scelte, 1983).

24. Cf. Darbellay, this volume.

25. It may be worth mentioning that works bearing the name "Arpeggiata," of which Kapsberger's was the first, became a small genre during the seventeenth century in both lute and keyboard music. A chitarrone piece entitled "Arpeggiata a mio modo" appears in Castaldi's *Capricci a due stromenti* . . . (1622; reprint, Geneva: Minkoff, 1981), and a keyboard piece entitled "Tastata arpeggiata longa" (possibly by Bernard Pasquini) appears in the manuscript *I-Rvat* Vat. mus. 569, 45–46 (see Silbiger, *Italian Manuscript Sources*, 175–77).

26. "Segno dell' Arpeggiare ÷ (qual'e di diretto contrario al pizzicicare) si fa in diverse maniere toccando le corde di quel' colpo separate . . . reiterando il colpo quanto durera il tempo soprascrittoli."

27. See Luigi Ferdinando Tagliavini, "L'arte di 'non lasciar vuoto lo strumento': Appunti sulla prassi cembalistica italiana nel cinque- e seicento," *Rivista italiana di musicologia* 10 (1975): 360–78; English translation in *Early Music* 11 (1983): 299–308.

28. Almost all the pieces in this section of the Modena manuscript are headed by the initials "HK" (Hieronymus Kapsberger) or "AP" (Alessandro Piccinini?). However, the initials appear in a different, later ink, and have been found to be not entirely accurate.

29. See Roland Jackson, "On Frescobaldi's Chromaticism and Its Background," *Musical*

Quarterly 57 (1971): 255–69.

30. Ibid., 256–57.

31. [Alternatively, one can interpret the lower voice as representing pseudo-polyphony, with the tenor entering with the subject in m. 40, and the bass on the third beat of m. 41. These two entries, together with the soprano entry in m. 39 and an alto entry commencing on the fourth beat of m. 42, form a final stretto on the subject.—*Ed.*]

Frescobaldi's *Arie* and the Musical Circle around Cardinal Montalto

JOHN WALTER HILL

I WOULD like to begin with a problem formulated by Frederick Hammond in his recent book on Frescobaldi. His words are, "The general stylistic orientation of [Frescobaldi's] *Arie musicali* is difficult to explain," although, as he says in another place, their style "suggests some strong external influence."[1] Monteverdi is offered as a possible model for one aria, and Roman monodists of ca. 1615–20 are mentioned in relation to a few others. The purpose of this paper is to examine the relevance of a monody repertoire and of some letters that have come to light in the course of my research on the musicians in the circle around Cardinal Montalto. I hope they will contribute something to our continuing search for Frescobaldi's sources and models as monody composer.

The feature that suggested strong external influence to Hammond was the prominence in Frescobaldi's *Arie* of eleven solo songs written entirely in pure recitative style. By 1630 this was an oddity. Florentine monody collections of the 1620s, by Filippo Vitali and Giovanni Battista da Gagliano, were dominated by strictly metrical, strophic arias.[2] Nor had recitatives been found in Roman or Venetian monody collections of recent years. Stranger still, seven of Frescobaldi's recitatives are settings of sonnets.

I think it likely that these sonnet settings were in view when the Florentine music theorist G. B. Doni wrote in his *Compendio*, published in 1635,

> Sonnets, which correspond so well to the hymns, paeans, nomi, and similar Greek poems, normally should be set for one solo voice, but in madrigalian style (as to the variety of pitches and intervals)

rather than in recitative, which, as the simpler and easier style, is above all suited to *ottava rima* and to heroic poems, to long poems like the *Gerusalemme* by Tasso, or short ones like the "Oronta" by Preti.[3]

The idea of warning composers not to set sonnets in recitative style would likely never have occurred to Doni were it not for Frescobaldi's *Arie*, which were published in Doni's native city at about the time of his writing. Other composers overwhelmingly had been setting sonnets in the form of four strophic variations, one each for the two quatrains and two terzets. In these variations the bass is normally neither static nor metrically rhythmic. The vocal line usually mixes somewhat melodious and expressive declamation with ornamental melismas. This sort of vocal line and that kind of bass combine to form a style aptly designated by Nigel Fortune as "florid madrigalian arioso"—precisely the style suggested for sonnets by Doni.[4] Monteverdi's sonnet "Tempro la cetra" in his seventh book typifies this style and format well enough.

Later, in a letter to Mersenne of 1640, Doni criticized Frescobaldi's lack of literary cultivation.[5] Perhaps he was remembering Frescobaldi's sonnets in recitative style, which he would have viewed as a breach of literary propriety.

For Doni, each of the three styles of recitative had its proper application to specific types of poetry. The narrative style, or recitative proper, he says, is apt for the narrations of messengers in stage works, for descriptions, and for similar calm conversations as well as for the singing of heroic poems or romances. It uses a lot of pitch repetition and rapid speech-like rhythms. His examples are the narration of Euridice's death in Peri's opera and Monteverdi's *lettere amorose*.[6]

Special recitative, according to Doni, is for reciting prologues to dramas or for heroic poems and rhapsodies, but is not to be used within the drama proper. This is because special recitative does not imitate human speech as closely as the narrative style or the third style, discussed below. Doni says special recitative is more *ariosa*, which I take to mean more structured and more premeditated, more flowing and more formulaic. In particular, Doni points out that it uses formulas for verse endings, which can become tedious. His example is the prologue to Peri's *Euridice*.[7]

The third recitative style, the expressive, is best suited for stage works, especially where the expression of *affetti* is called for. According to Doni it imitates the accents of pathetic speech, and thus is the only one of the three that is entirely dramatic. Monteverdi's lament of Arianna is his example.[8]

All three styles are recitative because they use speech-like rhythms, rather rapid delivery of syllables, and only a few short ornaments.[9]

It is interesting that the expressive style is the best for dramatic poetry, in which the words belong to a specific personage. Narrative style goes with narrative or descriptive poetry. And special recitative is for formal recitation rather than for the imitation of dramatic speech or for narration. None of the three styles of recitative is thought suitable for lyric poetry, in which the words of the poet are heard not in narration or description but in the expression of his own passions—not those of a specific dramatic personage, but his own, in words addressed to no particular interlocutor.

A sonnet is usually, though not always, just a sort of lyric poem. And this, I believe, is the reason why Doni advises against setting sonnets with any sort of recitative style.

In reality, composers mixed elements of the three styles, producing recitatives slightly more or less expressive, more or less formulaic. And this is true of Frescobaldi. His setting of the dedication sonnet in his first book of *Arie* (1630), example 1, shows this. As in all recitatives, the bass is predominantly slow-moving and sometimes static for the length of a breve. The monotone recitation and rapid speech rhythms of the narrative style are used. But the naturalness of the speech is moderated by the repeated-pitch formulas at verse endings, as is typical of the special recitative style. And at the same time, some of the more pronounced melodic inflections, chromaticism, and dissonance from the expressive style are mixed in as well. There is even more of the expressive style in some of Frescobaldi's other recitatives, such as the spiritual sonnet *Maddalena alla croce,* the *lettera amorosa* "Vanne, o carta amorosa," and "Ben veggio, donna."

Other salient features of Frescobaldi's recitative style shown in example 1 are the rests, which, for the sake of syntactical clarity, frequently break up the poetic verses, producing a breathless style; the use of syncopation for secondary syllable accents; the rather narrow range and

Example 1 Frescobaldi, "Signor, ch'ora fra gli ostra," Sonetto in stile recitativo, *Arie I* (1630)

avoidance of exaggerated pitch inflections; and the occasional substitution of a dotted rhythm for the two even notes in the formulaic pitch repetition that marks the trochaic endings of phrases, clauses, or verses. To these may be added the important observation that Frescobaldi's eleven songs entirely in recitative style are all through-composed, using no variation technique, and are unrelieved by either melismas or accelerated bass motion.

Seven of these recitatives set sonnets, three of them set strophic poems (but without repetition or variation), and one sets a *lettera amorosa* in *versi sciolti*.[10]

Where and when might Frescobaldi have encountered similar settings that he could have used as models?

Of all monody composers, Sigismondo d'India made the most extensive use of recitative styles, and his works are the logical place to look for Frescobaldi's models for that reason. India's first book of *Musiche* (1609) actually contains two sonnet settings in recitative style, but these consist of two strophic variations each, one for the quatrains, the other for the terzets.[11] Frescobaldi's sonnets, as I have said, are through-composed. India's sonnets represent special recitative style, as their rubric, *aria da cantar sonetti* suggests. Frescobaldi's are more nearly in the narrative style. The same collection by India includes two *madrigali in stile recitativo*.[12] One, however, includes a measured section in triple proportion, while the other uses the expressive more than the narrative style. Similarly expressive is India's through-composed *ottava in stile recitativo*, "La tra'l sangue e le morti," while his "Forsennata gridava" is an *aria da cantar ottave* using special recitative and variation procedure.

India's third book of *Musiche* (1618) includes two through-composed sonnets in recitative style, one described as the *introductione dell'opera*, which is also the function of Frescobaldi's sonnet given as example 1.[13] However, this one and also the setting of Petrarch's sonnet "Tutto il dì piango" close with a melisma and a running bass. Another through-composed sonnet in this collection, "Donna siam rei di morte," a text by Marino that Frescobaldi also set, is really a mixture of recitative and madrigalian arioso.

Finally, in the fifth book of India's *Musiche* (1623) there are three laments in recitative.[14] But they are in the expressive style. Here and in the other recitative settings that are not aria formulas, India employs a highly personal style that features large ranges, wide intervals, and sweeping contours that dramatize his text in a way that finds no echo in Frescobaldi's settings.[15] Nor is there any biographical reason to believe that Frescobaldi had any special contact with India's monodies. We must look elsewhere for his models.

Pietro Benedetti's second book of *Musiche* (1613) includes one through-composed *sonetto spirituale*, but in the expressive style, with a few melismas, and no vestige of the special recitative formulas.[16] Benedetti's octave "Giunt' alla tomba" mixes melismas with recitative. And his setting of "Ch'io non senta" is called an *aria per ottave* in keeping with its formulaic, largely monotone, special recitative style. Therefore, none of them is exactly like Frescobaldi's.

Each of Francesco Rasi's two printed monody collections of 1608 and 1610 contains a through-composed sonnet set mostly syllabically, with some monotone declamation, and verse-ending formulas.[17] In both, however, the bass is much more active than in Frescobaldi's recitative—in fact more active than in anyone else's.

Claudio Saracini's *Seconde musiche* (1620) includes one through-composed sonnet, which, however, uses a type of expressive recitative very close to India's.[18] The same style is used in his *madrigale in stile recitativo*, "Ite amari sospiri." And his *lamento della Madonna*, subtitled *Christo smarito in stile recitativo*, includes melismas and passages in arioso style.

Other through-composed sonnets include Jacopo Peri's "Tutto'l dì piango" and Marco da Gagliano's "Valli profonde," but both employ almost enough melismas to qualify the settings as madrigalian ariosos. Peri's sonnet "In qual parte del ciel" has a vocal line that resembles the style that I am looking for, except for a few very short ornamental melismas. But the four *parti* into which Peri's setting is divided show vestiges of variation relationship, inasmuch as the bass in each one outlines the descending tetrachord g-f-e-d and cadences on G. Frescobaldi's quatrains and terzets always begin on different pitches and show no such vestiges of variation procedure.

Two other through-composed sonnets before Frescobaldi's that I know of are by Antonio Cifra; these, however, are in madrigalian arioso and certainly not in recitative style at all.[19]

Before finally coming to my candidates for Frescobaldi's models, I should like to point out that among all the sonnet settings so far mentioned, those most similar to Frescobaldi's are by India, Benedetti, Rasi, Saracini, Peri, and Gagliano—either Florentines or composers with important Florentine connections at some point in their lives.

The sonnet settings closest of all to Frescobaldi's are also by a Florentine, but one who moved to Rome in 1616. They are found in the third book of *Varie musiche* by Raffaello Rontani, published in Rome in 1619.

In the two through-composed sonnets, "Tu god'il sol" and "Non credete ch'io v'ami," examples 2 and 3, I find the same level of bass activity; the same mix of monotone, stepwise motion, and narrow leaps; the same

Example 2 Raffaello Rontani, "Tu god' il sol," *I-Vc* "Grilanda musicale," fols. 100r–101r

Tu go- d'il sol ch'a- gl'oc- chi miei s'a- scon- de In vi- do

Re de fiu- mi e quel te- so- ro Ric- co m'in- vo- li

on- d'hai l'a- re- ne d'o- ro E di fre- schi sme- ral- di

am- bo le spon- de Hor le sei spe- chio

hor for- te hor fior hor fron- de Tes- si per far- le al crin

va- go la- vo- ro Men- tr'el- la in dol- ce et a- mo-

ro- so co- ro So- lea le tue be- a- te e pal- vi-

uses of verse- and phrase-ending formulas, the same restricted contours, the same breathless use of rests within verses for syntactical clarity, and the same moderate use of chromaticism and expressive dissonance that characterize Frescobaldi's recitatives. Syncopation is used in them, though Frescobaldi uses a bit more. Only Frescobaldi's dotted-rhythm modification of the verse-ending formula finds no precedent in these sonnets by Rontani.

Rontani may have conceived of through-composed sonnets in recitative style in imitation of the settings by the Florentine-related composers mentioned earlier. Indeed, his first book of *Varie musiche* (Florence: Pignoni, 1614) includes one such sonnet.[20] It, however, has much less monotone declamation and fewer rests than his settings published in Rome.

In terms of stylistic congruency, Rontani's two sonnets published in 1619 are easily the best candidates for Frescobaldi's immediate models. In the print, by the way, both are called *sonetto recitativo*, which is the only combination of those two words in any monody collection I have seen, except for Frescobaldi's two books of arias.

Now, the two recitative sonnet settings published by Rontani are also found in a Roman manuscript, the "Grilanda musicale di diversi eccel[entissi]mi hautori scritta da Francesco Maria Fucci Romano."[21] It is the largest and most central of eight monody manuscripts that preserve music by composers associated with Cardinal Montalto.[22] It contains music composed, for the most part, between 1611 and 1619. What little of it was printed came out mostly after Montalto's death in 1623. Exceptions are pieces by composers such as Rontani who were not actually in Montalto's household. Given this pattern and the type of variants between the manuscript and printed versions, I presume that Rontani's sonnet settings were collected by Montalto in manuscript before the 1619 printing, perhaps soon after Rontani's arrival in Rome in 1616.

Frescobaldi was in contact with the composers in Montalto's circle, in contact with several composers represented in the "Grilanda" manuscript, at least as late as the summer of 1615. This is documented in letters that I was lucky enough to find in Ferrara, following leads generously provided by Frederick Hammond and Anthony Newcomb. Newcomb, in his recent article in *Annales musicologiques*, has shown that Frescobaldi must have had extensive contact with Montalto's musicians when he was a musician in the Roman household of Enzo Bentivoglio in 1608 and 1609.[23] Letters tell us that Montalto and Bentivoglio shared musical evenings at each other's palaces. In fact, Enzo Bentivoglio was something of a satellite around Cardinal Montalto, especially in musical matters. The new letters show that Frescobaldi's contacts with Montalto's circle as well as his service to Bentivoglio did not cease after Frescobaldi entered the household of Cardinal Pietro Aldobrandini in 1612 and his subsequent stay in Mantua. The twelve surviving letters in this new series continue from 8 June to 29 August 1615.[24] They were written to Enzo Bentivoglio in Ferrara by his secretary in Rome and report on a crash program for training a boy named Baldassarre, who was supposed to sing in an unnamed *comedia* to be given in Ferrara. The letters tell us that Baldassarre's teachers were Giovanni Bernardino Nanino, the monodists Ippolito Macchiavelli and Cesare Marotta, and Marotta's wife, the celebrated singer Ippolita.[25] These four were musicians in Cardinal Montalto's household. Baldassarre's other two teachers were Ottavio Catalani, who was in the service of Prince Marc' Antonio Borghese, and Girolamo Frescobaldi. At the height of the training program, Baldassarre was taken on a daily round of lessons given by each of these six musicians. The lessons included vocal production, sight-singing, repertoire coaching, written and improvised counterpoint, composing, figured-bass realization, guitar playing, and general keyboard performance. For keyboard lessons, Baldassarre went to Frescobaldi every morning at 10 o'clock.

His teachers constantly lament that Baldassarre has an insurmountable defect with respect to intonation, which I take to mean placing his voice. They say that his voice is changing, inasmuch as he is older than Bentivoglio had been told he was. In the end they are resigned that Baldassarre, unable to sing well enough, will have to become a composer.

We have had little information about Frescobaldi as a teacher, so it is interesting that one of these letters refers to his *scuola di sonare*. But for my purposes it is important to note that Frescobaldi's colleagues in this enterprise, Marotta, Macchiavelli, Nanino, and Catalani, are the dominant composers in the eight monody manuscripts that preserve the music by Montalto's composers and the music for his stage productions. Two other important composers in the manuscripts, Giuseppino Cenci and Domenico Pugliaschi, are mentioned in the 1615 letters on account of their illnesses.

Example 3   Raffaello Rontani, "Non credete ch'io v'ami," *I-Vc* "Grilanda musicale," fols. 99r–99v

ne mi ve- de- te   oh Di- o   Quai se- gni vi da- ro d'es- ser a-

man- te   Se non vi ba- sta il pian- to   o mio te- so-

ro Se non vi ba- st'il pal- li- do sem bian- te   Ec- co di- nan- z'a

voi   be- gl'oc- ch'io mo- ro   Se- gni que- sti sa-

ra for- se ba- stan- te   A di- mo- strar s'io v'a- mo

e   s'io v'a- do- ro.

These connections lead me back to the Montalto monody manuscripts. It is striking that in them are sufficient models for nearly all of Frescobaldi's other monodies, and not just the sonnets in recitative style.

Most similar to these sonnets are Frescobaldi's settings of other poetic forms in recitative style. His *lettera amorosa*, "Vanne, o carta amorosa," example 4, takes the poetic form of a madrigal and finds its counterpart in the anonymous madrigal "Ch'io t'ami et ami piu della mia vita," example 5, set in precisely the same recitative style as the sonnets and found just two folios away from them in the "Grilanda" manuscript. Perhaps it, too, is the work of Rontani. By comparison with Frescobaldi's *lettera* and this anonymous madrigal in recitative style, Monteverdi's *lettera*, "Se i languidi miei sguardi," in his seventh book (1619), uses more monotone recitation, but also uses larger-scale contours and greater variety of pacing; it also uses fewer rests within verses. Monteverdi's *partenza amorosa*, "Se pur destina," which was called a *lettera amorosa* when reprinted in 1623, is even less breathless than "Se i languidi miei sguardi." It often runs two verses together without a pause.

For Frescobaldi's three through-composed, nonsectional recitative settings of two or three stanzas of *canzonette*, I find no precedents or successors. The musical style in them, however, is no different from the sonnets and the *lettera*.

For Frescobaldi's romanesca and ruggiero variations with their florid, madrigalian arioso and moderately slow, varied basses, there is a surplus of potential models. Suffice it to say that the Roman sources, including the Montalto manuscripts, are full of precedents.

The case with Frescobaldi's other strophic variations is much more interesting. These are "Se l'onde, ohime," "Non mi negate, ohime," and "Se l'aura spira" in the first book of *Arie* (1630), and example 6, "O bell'occhi che guerrieri," which appeared in a Roman anthology in 1621. These four are distinguished from the two other strophic variations by a faster-moving bass, which remains unvaried from strophe to strophe, and a more nearly syllabic vocal part with only the occasional brief and modest melisma. Fortune compliments "O bell'occhi che guerrieri" by saying that it represents "strophic variations on the point of turning into strophic-bass cantatas."[26] It would come as a surprise to Fortune that there are many similar sets of strophic variations in the Montalto manuscripts. Of these, the earliest that can be dated is by Cesare Marotta,

Example 4 Frescobaldi, "Vanne, ò carta amorosa," *Arie II* (1630)

Example 5   Anon., "Ch'io t'ami," *I-Vc* "Grilanda musicale," fols. 97r–97v

Example 6   Frescobaldi, "O bell'occhi," *Giardino musicale di varii eccellenti autori*
(Rome, Robletti, 1621)

Montalto's principal composer and one of Frescobaldi's teaching colleagues during that summer of 1615. The piece is mentioned in a letter of 1611, which makes it the earliest datable exemplar of this type after Caccini established it with "Ard'il mio petto" in his 1602 *Nuove musiche*.[27] As a particularly good example to compare with Frescobaldi's "O bell'occhi che guerrieri," I offer example 7, "Ama pur ninfa gradita" by Ippolito Macchiavelli, another Montalto composer and teaching colleague of Frescobaldi. The date of Macchiavelli's composition is unknown, but the composer died in 1619, well before Grandi and Berti began publishing similar so-called *cantade* in Venice during the 1620s.[28]

Even more interesting is example 8, Frescobaldi's "Alla gloria alli honori," published in another Roman anthology in 1621. In this composition, the six stanzas of the *canzonetta* are set in a pattern of interlocking variations: stanzas 1 and 5 are set to the same bass, stanzas 4 and 6 to a different bass; while 2 and 3 are independent, using two different basses, neither of them identical with the other two patterns. The earliest examples of this mixture of variations and independent strophes, as far as I know, again are found in the Montalto manuscripts. One of them is example 9, Cesare Marotta's "O dell'ombrosa notte." In this piece, stanzas 2 and 4 use the same bass as Marotta's strophic variations mentioned in the letter of 1611. Stanzas 1 and 5 form a separate pair of variations. And stanza 3 is musically independent of the others. The same procedure of mixing strophic variations with nonvariation stanzas is found in Puliaschi's "La gloria di colui che tutto muove," from the *veglia, Amor pudico,* produced in 1614 by Cardinal Montalto for his brother's wedding.[29]

Example 7   Don Ip[p]olito [Macchiavelli], "Ama pur ninfa gradita," *I-Vc* "Grilanda musicale," fols. 1r–4v

di- ta, nin- fa gra- di- ta.

P.te seconda
A- ma pur nin- fa vez- zo-

sa, nin- fa vez- zo- sa, Hor ch'il

ciel, hor ch'il ciel sue gra- tie spi-

ra sue gra- tie spi- ra,

Che sel tem- po gl'an- ni gi- ra Ahi ch'in

van sa- rai pie- to- sa A- ma pur, a- ma

Example 8 Frescobaldi, "Alla gloria alli honori," *Ghirlandetta amorosa*, comp. Fabio Costantini (Orvieto: Fei, 1621)

di fio- ri Qui tut- to in- tor- no in- tor-

no, Ri- mi- ro al- mi splen- do- ri, Ma non so do-

ve si-

a, Co- ril- la a- ni- ma mi- a.

[Parte sesta]

Ahi- me chi mi t'a- scon- de, Co- ril- la hai fie- ra sor-

te Ti ce- li tra le fron- de For- se per che la mor- te Con

più gra- vi mar- ti- ri, Mi fac- ci hor hor mo- ri- re.

Example 9 [Cesare Marotta], "O dell'ombrosa notte," *I-Vc* "Grilanda musicale," fols. 103v–105v (rebarred)

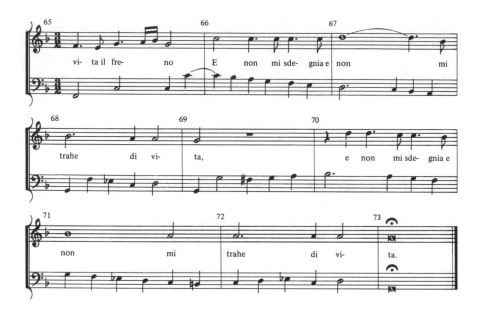

Finally, each type of strophic aria in Frescobaldi's books can be found earlier in the Montalto manuscripts. These include strophic arias split between duple and triple meter and strophic arias split between recitative and measured styles.

With that I have accounted for every category of solo song by Frescobaldi known to survive except for one, "Così mi disprezzate?" called an *aria di passacagli* in his first book of arias. This is a setting of five stanzas of a *canzonetta* of which stanzas 1, 3, and 5 are composed in triple-meter aria style over repetitions, variations, and transpositions of the passacaglia ostinato, while the second and fourth stanzas are set in recitative style. The sectional settings of strophic poems from the Montalto repertoire provide potential models for two formal elements used here: alternation of related with unrelated settings of stanzas, and contrast between recitative and measured aria styles in a through-composed work. On the other hand, precedents for building an aria upon repetitions of a short ostinato were few before 1630. There is the anonymous "Bella mia questo mio core" in Stefani's anthology, *Affetti amorosi* of 1618. It is said to be set *sopra l'aria della ciaccona* in the print, though the ostinato is actually the primitive passacaglia I–IV–V–I, repeated without interruption. The actual ciaccona pattern is used, likewise without relief, in Domenico Crivellati's

"Luci belle," among his *Cantate diverse* (Rome: Robletti, 1628). The only mixture of recitative with ostinato aria sections published before Frescobaldi's, as far as I know, is "T'amai gran tempo" in Stefano Landi's second book of *Arie* (Rome, 1627). Landi's setting, however, is strophic, the same recitative and ciaccona sections being used for each stanza of the text.

Incidentally, two of the manuscripts preserving the music of Cardinal Montalto's composers also include music by Stefano Landi.[30] Although I have found no documents that link Landi directly with Montalto's circle, I note that his connections with the Collegio Germanico, the Collegio Romano, the Borghese family, and Paolo Savelli associate him with several composers who did have firm links to Montalto.

Vocal compositions aside, the most obvious possible model for Frescobaldi's *aria di passacagli* are his own *partite sopra passacagli* for keyboard, which he published three years earlier in his second book of toccatas (1627). The aria, however, uses transpositions and inversions of the ostinato, whereas the *partite* do not. And the aria uses recitative to set every other stanza of the poem, a procedure without parallel in the *partite*.

In the end, I find no single model or precedent for Frescobaldi's *aria di passacagli*, but only the use of the ostinato in some works and the use of recitative and measured styles for alternate stanzas of a strophic poem in other works in the Montalto manuscripts.

Frescobaldi's *aria di passacagli* seems to have spawned imitations. Indeed, I am ready to credit Frescobaldi with the introduction in Florence of the new fashion for ostinato arias. Bologna Q49, a Florentine monody manuscript produced just after Frescobaldi's return to Rome, contains five compositions using one or the other of the new ostinato patterns.[31] Meanwhile in Rome, Giovanni Felice Sances, a former Montalto musician, began in 1633 to bring out a series of cantatas mixing recitative with ostinato aria sections. The same can be found in the works by Luigi Rossi and other early cantata composers.[32]

While I can offer no completely sufficient models for Frescobaldi's *aria di passacagli*, the background to his other solo songs seems more nearly apparent. For Frescobaldi's sonnets that are through-composed in recitative style, there are a number of possible models, but none nearly as similar in style, format, and rubric as Raffaello Rontani's, found in the central manuscript preserving the Montalto monody repertoire and published in Rome in 1619. The same manuscript contains an anonymous madrigal in the same style, a sufficient model for Frescobaldi's *lettera amorosa*. Frescobaldi's strophic variations with rhythmic, unvaried bass, and his aria that mixes strophic variations with musically independent strophes have their earliest precedent in the Montalto repertoire as well. Frescobaldi's ruggiero and romanesca variations are far less unusual; plenty of models for them are found in the Montalto manuscripts and elsewhere. The same is true of the various types of strophic arias by Frescobaldi. All of these potential models are found in a repertoire that was unstudied and nearly unknown until a couple of years ago. The letters of 1615 show that Frescobaldi was collaborating with the composers of this repertoire around the time of its creation. It is a suggestive combination of circumstances.

If I am correct in suggesting that Frescobaldi formed his solo vocal styles on models encountered within the musical circle around Cardinal Montalto, this leads to a nice paradox. Montalto, whose musicians had participated in the earliest Florentine opera performances, was the willing vehicle by which Florentine monody and especially Florentine recitative styles were introduced in Rome.[33] Frescobaldi, having learned these styles in Montalto's circle, perhaps thought to ingratiate himself in Florence by showing his mastery of them in his *Arie* of 1630. But he also brought along some newer types of solo song, which had meanwhile emerged in Rome. With these and his own recombination of their elements in his *aria di passacagli*, he contributed handsomely, though certainly without knowing it, to the emergence of a new and particularly Roman phase of solo song composition epitomized by the multipartite chamber cantata.

Notes

1. Frederick Hammond, *Girolamo Frescobaldi* (Cambridge, Mass.: Harvard University Press, 1983), 265–66.

2. Giovanni Battista da Gagliano, *Varie musiche libro primo* (Venice: Alessandro Vincenti, 1623); and Filippo Vitali, *Arie a 1., 2., 3. voci libro quarto* (Venice: Gardano, 1622) and *Varie musiche a 1, 2, 3, 4 . . . libro quinto* (Venice: Gardano, 1625).

3. Giovanni Battista Doni, "Discorso sopra la perfettione de' concenti," *Compendio del trattato de' generi e de' modi della musica* (Rome: Fei, 1635), 118: "I Sonetti, che corrispondono

assai à gl'Inni, Peani, Nomi, e simil Poesie Greche, comunemente si doverebbono modulare à una voce sola; ma più tosto in Stile Madrigalesco (quanto al ricercare molte corde, & intervalli) che Recitativo: il quale, come quello ch'è più semplice e facile, sopratutto s'accomoda all'Ottava rima, & à' Poemi Heroici; ò siano quei lunghi, come la Gierusalemme del Tasso; ò brevi, come l'Oronta del Preti."

4. Nigel Fortune, "Italian Secular Song from 1600 to 1635: The Origins and Development of Accompanied Monody" (Ph.D. diss., Cambridge University, 1953), 274–78, 329–30.

5. Cornelis de Waard, ed., *Correspondance du P. Marin Mersenne religieux minime*, vol. 9 (Paris, 1965), 488.

6. Giovanni Battista Doni, *Annotazioni sopra il compendio de' generi e de' modi della musica* (Rome: Fei, 1640), 60; and "Trattato della musica scenica," *Lyra Barberina Amphichordos*, ed. Antonio Francesco Gori, vol. 2 of *De' trattati di musica di Gio. Batista Doni tomo secondo* (Florence, 1763), 27, 33–34. These passages and those cited in the next three notes are discussed by Margaret Rosso Grossman, "G. B. Doni and Theatrical Music" (Ph.D. diss., University of Illinois, 1977). I gratefully acknowledge the help I received from reading her dissertation.

7. Doni, *Annotazioni*, 61, 363; "Trattato della musica scenica," 33, 185.

8. Doni, *Annotazioni*, 60–62; "Trattato della musica scenica," 26, 30.

9. Doni, "Trattato della musica scenica," 20–30.

10. Frescobaldi's sonnets in *stile recitativo* are "Signor, c'ora fra gl'ostri," "Dove, dove, Signor, quieto ricetto," "Dopo si lungo error," "A pie della gran croce," "Oscure selve ore giammai non luce," "Ohimè, che fur, che sono," and "Dove, dove sparir si ratto i dì sereni." The three strophic poems in *stile recitativo* are "Degnati, o gran Fernando," "Ardo, e taccio il mio mal," and "Ben veggio donna omai che più non sono." The *lettera amorosa*, "Vanne, o carta amorosa," sets only the first stanza of "L'amante timido," published under the rubric "Idillio terzo" in Girolamo Preti, *Rime* (Venice, 1614), with the explanation that this *idillio* was written to his beloved by a lover no longer able to hide his love.

11. These are "Io viddi in terra angelici costumi" and "Mirate dal gran tronco."

12. "Ferma, Dorinda mia" and "Forse vien fuor l'aurora."

13. The two sonnets in India's third book of *musiche* are "Voi che ascoltate in rime" and "Tutto il dì piango."

14. *Lamento di Didone, Lamento di Giasone,* and *Lamento di Olimpia.*

15. In this I concur with John Joyce, "The Monodies of Sigismondo d'India" (Ph.D. diss., Tulane University, 1975), 136–43.

16. This is "Io vo piangendo."

17. "Che fai alma che pensi?" in his *Vaghezze di musica* (Venice: Gardano, 1608) and "Ferma Tersilla mia" in his *Madrigali di diversi* (Florence: Marescotti, 1610).

18. This is "Intenerite voi donne e donzelle."

19. These are "In qual parte del ciel" and "Cantai hor piango" in *Li diversi scherzi*, book 5 (Rome, 1617).

20. "Mentre che il caro pargoletto estinto."

21. *I-Vc* inventory no. 2952. For a general description of the manuscript see Irving Godt, "A Monteverdi Source Reappears: The 'Grilanda' of F. M. Fucci," *Music and Letters* 60 (1979): 428–39.

22. These manuscripts, some never mentioned in print, the others never truly described or identified as to contents, were the subject of my paper "Early Roman Monody from the Circle of Cardinal Montalto," presented at the meeting of the American Musicological Society, Boston, 1981. I hope that an expanded presentation of this material will appear in print at about the same time as this conference volume.

23. Anthony Newcomb, "Girolamo Frescobaldi, 1608–1615: A Documentary Study in which Information Also Appears Concerning Giulio and Settimia Caccini, the Brothers Piccinini, Stefano Landi, and Ippolita Recupita," *Annales musicologiques* 7 (1964–77): 111–58.

24. *I-FEas* Archivio Bentivoglio, Mazzo 80, nos. 9-12, 25-26, 45-48-46-47, 206, 236-237-238, 268, 280-281-282, 346, 492, 580-581-582, 616, and 620-621.

25. Marotta and his wife are the subject of Alberto Cametti, "Chi era l' 'Hippolita', cantatrice del cardinal di Montalto," *Sammelbände der Internationalen Musikgesellschaft* 15 (1913–14): 111–23.

26. Fortune, "Italian Secular Song," 374.

27. *I-FEas* Archivio Bentivoglio, Mazzo 62, no. 548, 14 Oct. 1611.

28. Macchiavelli's death on 14 May 1619, is documented by Paul Kast, "Biographische Notizen zu römischen Musikern des 17. Jahrhunderts," *Analecta musicologica* 1 (1963): 49.

29. *I-Bc* Q 140, fols. 7r–9r; text and attribution in *Amor pudico* (Viterbo, 1614), 27–28, and the appended *Copia d'una lettera del Sig. Romolo Paradiso* (Rome, 1614), 64–66.

30. *I-Ru* Ms. 279; *I-Baf* Ms. 1424.

31. These are anon., "Amor crudo, fier tirranno"; Parma, "Niegami un bacio"; Luigi Rossi, "Questi caldi sospiri"; Alessandro Ghivizzani, "Lilla tu mi disprezzi"; and Ghivizzani, "Vago mio viso." Concerning the date, provenance, and repertoire of Q49, see Nigel Fortune, "A Florentine Manuscript and Its Place in Italian Song," *Acta musicologica* 23 (1951): 124–36. All five are also found in the sister manuscript to Q49: *CS-Pnm* Ms. II.La.2, the so-called Roudnici manuscript. For a description see Paul Nettl, "Über ein handschrift- liches Sammelwerk von Gesängen italienischer Frühmonodie," *Zeitschrift für Musikwissen- schaft* 2 (1919–20): 83–93.

32. In addition to Rossi's "Questi caldi sospiri," cited in the previous note, see, for example, his "Se non corre," *I-Rcas* 2466, fols. 209–16. For a general view of cantatas combining recitative sections with ostinato aria passages, see Jan Racek, *Stilprobleme der italienischen Monodie* (Prague: Státní pedagogické Nakladatelství, 1965), 170–73. Essentially the same discussion was published earlier in idem, "Die italienische begleitete Monodie und das Problem der Entwicklung der italienischen Solokantate," in *Liber amicorum Charles Van Den Borren*, ed. Albert Vander Linden (Antwerp: Imprimerie Lloyd Anversois, 1964), 180–82.

33. See Cametti, "Chi era l' 'Hippolita', cantatrice del cardinal di Montalto"; Vincenzo Giustiniani, "Discorso sopra la musica de suoi tempi," in Angelo Solerti, *Le origini del melodramma* (Turin: Fratelli Bocca, 1903), 110–11 (English translation by Carol MacClintock, together with Hercole Bottrigari, *Il desiderio*, in Musicological Studies and Documents, vol. 9 [n.p.: American Institute of Musicology, 1962], 71).

On *Artificioso* Compositions
at the Time of Frescobaldi

SERGIO DURANTE

T HIS ESSAY CONCENTRATES on a relatively little-known part of the Italian musical repertory of the first half of the seventeenth century, specifically those compositions that I shall term *artificioso*. The use of this term could lead to misunderstanding, since during the period in question it had several different meanings.[1] It commonly was used in connection with quite different types of compositions, with the rather vague meaning of "well-constructed" or "refined."[2] But the substantive form (*artificio*) was used more specifically to denote a musical procedure that governed the construction of a piece, but at the same time became both its end and its means.[3] I will use the term mainly in this latter sense.

Table 1 gives a list, in chronological order, of the group of works with which I shall be concerned here. This list makes no pretense to completeness, especially since many works termed "artificioso" are found in theoretical and practical treatises on counterpoint,[4] or in works not dealing primarily with musical matters.[5] At this stage, however, it will be sufficient to use information drawn from the most specific and extensive witnesses as the basis for sketching a general picture of this kind of composition.

The list contains works of several rather different types, which can be classified according to three main categories. A first category is formed by the polymorphous canons (canons admitting more than one solution) and canons on words (in which the subjects are determined by solmization syllables based on the vowels of these words); this category includes enigmatic canons, the solutions of which are hinted at in a short epigram.[6] A second category is composed of didactic or illustrative works, exem-

Table 1   *Artificioso* compositions from the time of Frescobaldi

Date	Composer	Title	Place of publication	Publisher
c. 1592	G. M. Nanino	*Cento cinquantasette contrapunti sopra del Canto fermo intitolato la Base di Costanzo Festa*		Manuscript
1610	F. Soriano*	*Canoni et oblighi di cento, et dieci sorte sopra l'Ave maris stella*	Rome	G. B. Robletti
1611	F. Valesi	*Canoni di più sorti fatti sopra doi canti fermi del primo tuono*	Milan	Tini & Lomazzo
1612	A. Brunelli	*Canoni varii sopra un soggetto solo*	Venice	G. Vincenti
1615	R. Micheli	*Musica vaga et artificiosa*	Venice	G. Vincenti
1618	R. Micheli	*Canoni di A. Willaert . . . con 4 parti in canone aumentate da R. Micheli da cantarsi a 12 voci*	Venice	G. Vincenti
1621	R. Micheli	*Certezza d'artificii musicali non più fatti*	Venice	G. B. Bonfadino
1625	(L. Zacconi)	*Resoluzioni et partiture di cento e dieci canoni . . . di Francesco Soriani . . . con le considerazioni in fine*		Manuscript
c. 1625 (?)	(L. Zacconi)	*Partiture e risoluzioni di 100 contrappunti di Don Fernando de Las Infantas Hispano*		Manuscript (lost)
c. 1625 (?)	(L. Zacconi)	*Lo scrigno musicale contenente e pieno di diverse dotte ed arteficiose musiche*		Manuscript (lost)

Table 1 (continued)

Date	Composer	Title	Place of publication	Publisher
1627	P. Agostini	*Spartitura della messa et motetto Benedicam Dominus ad canones, a quattro voci. E la resoluzione delle ligature a 4 di Gio. Maria Nanino; accomodata per un motetto*	Rome	G. B. Robletti
1627	P. Agostini	*Spartitura delle messe del primo libro* (on canons and *obblighi*)	Rome	G. B. Robletti
1627	P. Agostino	*Spartitura del secondo libro delle messe e motetti a quattro voci con alcuni oblighi de canoni*	Rome	G. B. Robletti
1627	P. Agostini	*Partitura del terzo libro della messa sine nomine, a quattro* (with different *obblighi*)	Rome	G. B. Robletti
1627	P. Agostini	*Libro quarto delle messe in spartitura* (with different *obblighi*)	Rome	G. B. Robletti
1629	P. F. Valentini	*Illos tuos misericordes oculos ad nos converte. Canone . . . con le sue resolutioni in più di duemila modi*	Rome	P. Masotti
1631	P. F. Valentini	*Canone nel nodo di Salamone a novantasei voci con le sue resolutioni*	Rome	P. Masotti
1631	P. F. Valentini	*Resolutione seconda del canone nel nodo di Salamone*	Rome	P. Masotti

Table 1   (continued)

Date	Composer	Title	Place of publication	Publisher
1632	G. Briccio	*Canoni enigmatici musicali*	Rome	P. Masotti
1633	R. Micheli	*Specimina musices magis reconditae*	Rome	P. Masotti
1641	G. P. Del Buono	*Canoni, Oblighi et Sonate in varie maniere sopra l'Ave maris stella*	Palermo	Martarello e D'Angelo
1644 (repr. 1649)	R. Micheli	*Vivit Deus. Canones super plurium verborum vocalibus*	Rome	Grignani
1645	P. F. Valentini	*Canon denis altis super vocalibus*	Rome	no publ.
1645	P. F. Valentini	*In animas purgatorij propriae et novae inventionis canon quatuor compositus subiectis*	Rome	Fei
1645	R. Micheli	*Canoni musicali sopra le vocali di più parole*	Rome	Grignani
1650	R. Micheli	*Canone musicale a quattro voci . . . composto sopra le vocali di nuovo, e curioso artificio*	Rome	Grignani
1652 (?)	R. Micheli	*In honore del nome di Giesù e di Maria canone musicale a 5 voci composto sopra le vocali*	Rome	Mascardi
1655	R. Micheli	*Hic finis: non plus ultra. Hic deum adora. Selecta artificia musicalia*	Rome	Balmonti

*See also 1625, *Resoluzioni* by L. Zacconi

plified by canons and *obblighi* ("obligations"—to be explained further on) on a cantus firmus. A third category consists of works composed for a specific liturgical or secular use and written on rigorous *obblighi*, for example, the *Madrigale in canone* of Romano Micheli, the *Sonate* of Del Buono, and the Masses by Agostini.

This classification incorporates a certain gradation: the more a composer concentrated exclusively on the study of the artifice, the less his works were connected with any practical function. The third category has the least rigid boundaries; it could be widened to include various compositions of Frescobaldi.[7] I have limited myself here to a discussion of the first two categories, since these can be related to certain cultural phenomena that may provide insight into the musical language of the early seventeenth century, in particular that of Frescobaldi.[8]

Musical historiography has, on the whole, not paid much attention to these works, whether because of their apparent backwardness or because of their curious but sterile eccentricity. At a time when the most obvious innovations on the musical horizon seem to have been the rise of the *seconda prattica* and of opera, those phenomena not destined for a similar fortune may seem in retrospect rather opaque and unconnected with evolving currents, and therefore tend to be neglected by a conception of history concerned with "determining" events. Furthermore, the rather minimal aesthetic and practical value of these pieces has not helped in arousing interest today; they were in fact composed more to be looked at and studied than to be performed.

But these are explanations of an existing situation, rather than arguments against the study of the subject, and are the consequence of a teleological vision of history which takes into account only those elements that relate to future "progress."[9] If we reject this perspective, we shall perceive elements of considerable interest in this group of *artificioso* works. The canon, for example, can point to the proper direction for this inquiry: obviously the canon is not in itself an innovation of the seventeenth century. It is a procedure rooted in tradition; but precisely because it is a phenomenon present through centuries of music history, we cannot overlook elements that changed significantly. The problem is not to find something absolutely new but to understand how new concepts can be expressed even by aspects of culture inherited from the past, and to determine the various forms these aspects can take in a changing cultural context. On the other hand, the fact that most of this music was not intended primarily for performance but designed for other composers —composers capable of recognizing the artifices—is almost without precedent.[10] Thus, the point is not to initiate a re-evaluation of this or that composer or genre, but rather to reconstruct an aspect of musical mentality that has been long neglected.

Our traditional view of *artificioso* composition notwithstanding, Romano Micheli—stubborn polemicist in addition to *artificiosissimo* composer —never missed an opportunity to vaunt his own practices as musically superior. From the many passages in his works that emphasize his self-awareness and professional pride, I have chosen one of the earliest:

> It is true that those who compose skilled and graceful composi-tions are considered worthy men, but because this is a skill which is acquired in a few years, they are considered ordinary musicians; the most excellent are instead those who, being not satisfied to com-pose perfect music, also want to understand the most profound studies of music, that is, canons of different kinds and other special abilities, which are not to be acquired so easily or in such a short period of time as some claim; thus, the belief that men of such excellence do exist must not seem strange. And if this could be said by anyone, it could be said by me, because I have been curious to meet most of the principal composers in Italy.[11]

Micheli sanctions the primacy of the most learned (*i più dotti*)[12] studies of music over skilled and graceful compositions (*composizioni studiose, e vaghe*). Whether or not Micheli's ideas were universally shared among musicians,[13] he brings to music a concept that informs the early seven-teenth century as a whole: the supremacy of intellectual culture, as so clearly expressed by Fernand Braudel: "Never as in that time was the primacy of culture so officially accepted."[14] Micheli is, no doubt, any-thing but modest; but his claims may have been legitimate in a climate still completely permeated by a faith in the power of intellect, a power that was applied almost frantically in the most diverse directions.

At the same time that foundations of experimental and quantitative methods of inquiry were being laid in philosophy and science, another branch of knowledge flourished, based on the acceptance of number as a

Pythagorean concept.[15] The Lullist tradition[16] and, above all, the Hermetical tradition, cultivated in Rome particularly by the Jesuits, were much in vogue at this time. In the countries most affected by the Reformation, these years saw the birth of great enthusiasm for the philanthropic ideals of that elusive sect, the Rosicrucians, itself largely inspired by Hermetic culture.

Hermetic doctrines were based on a belief in the numerous works attributed to the Egyptian Hermes Trismegistos. This personage, now known never to have existed, was considered the first and greatest of all philosophers; he was supposed to have drawn on the ultimate occult truths, transmitting them, in equally occult form, in his own works. According to this tradition — accepted by the church, with some reservations, from the time of Pope Alexander VI — Hermes had anticipated some of the themes of Christianity, since he had possessed, among other things, "foreknowledge of the Trinity." Furthermore, Egyptian hieroglyphics were interpreted as symbols containing hidden divine truths.[17] Although within the church the evil and perverse magical practices transmitted by the Hermetic writings were rejected, the so-called natural magic — a distinction introduced during the Renaissance — was admitted and recognized as effective. "By numbers, a way is had, to the searching out, and understanding of every thyng, hable to be knowen," Pico della Mirandola had said,[18] and his message was accepted, although in different ways, not only by Galileo and Bacon, but also by John Dee and Athanasius Kircher; the historically confirmed distinction between true and false science was not entirely clear at that time. If it is true that in some ways the early seventeenth century was a period in which Hermetic influence reached its apex,[19] one should at least consider whether it can be documented that there was an interplay between the theory and practice of music, on one side, and, on the other, the tradition that for brevity's sake I shall call "magical-hermetic"; further, one should try to establish the levels at which a real interaction was at work.

Frances Yates has convincingly described the cultural connections of the Rosicrucians with the court of Frederick V, Elector Palatine of the Rhine, and his English wife Elizabeth Stuart. In that "Golden Age" of Hermetic culture, music had a prominent role, being considered the most important of the sciences based on number.[20] In utopian politics, too, music makes its appearance as an institution: in the Rosicrucian

Christianopolis, the longed-for city of the future, music receives the highest praise, and "in order to enter the school of music one must pass through those of arithmetic and geometry."[21] Apart from allusions to the mathematical basis of music, this evidence is rather general. Something more precise appears in one of the central documents of the Rosicrucian tradition, the description of the tomb of the presumed founder of the order, Brother Rosen-kreutz. The mythical sepulchre was illuminated by a sun within; the outside sun never penetrated its walls. There were geometric figures on the walls and it contained many treasures: among these were some works by Paracelsus, wonderful bells, and "chiefly wonderful artificial songs."[22] These fictitious musical treasures might have been similar in conception to the "alchemistic musical emblems" published by the Rosicrucian Michael Majer in his *Atalanta fugiens* (1618) and described on the title page as "musical fugues for three voices."[23]

For Italy, and for Rome in particular, the convergence of interests of the Jesuits and the cultivators of artifice were already noted twenty-five years ago by Walter Blankenburg,[24] but that scholar's complaint of a lack of research in this area is still valid today. In this light, the need remains to investigate the intellectual and personal relationships among Athanasius Kircher, Pier Francesco Valentini, Romano Micheli, and others who gravitated toward that sphere of interest. If Kircher's *Musurgia universalis* contains the most explicit evidence of enthusiasm for the *artificioso* genre,[25] Micheli in turn exploits the authority of the Jesuit scholar in his polemics:

> In this respect I approve of the *artificiose* modulations contained in the work . . . *Musurgia sive ars magna consoni et dissoni.* . . . Athanasius Kircher of the Company of the Jesuits has made illustrious the profession of music together with other sciences . . . and the city of Rome, having used, among others, examples taken from the works of some worthy, skillful, and not vulgar musicians of Rome.[26]

This apology occurs in a notice sent by Micheli to "the famous and most skillful musicians of Italy and of all other kingdoms and states"— implying that it is addressed *only* to those excellent men—in which he defends a canon on the words "Pater, et Filius, et Spiritus Sanctus, et hi tres sunt." Micheli casts aside the accusations of an unnamed critic, showing that the latter had not even understood the hidden and unexpressed meaning of it, because he did not understand the occult mystery of that canon, which symbolizes the Holy Trinity; to that aim it was necessary to know that which by the sacred theologians is taught, that is, in God are three relative existences, through which the three divine persons have a perfect existence, that is, they exist incommunicably; and the three persons have an undivided essence; and this essence has its own absolute existence, which is different from the three relative existences of the [three] persons; but this essence lacks incommunicability, and thus it is improper existence, because it is not incommunicable. Given this, I wanted my canon to represent the Holy Trinity, under obscure symbols, and hieroglyphics, so that it is not understood, except by the intelligent musician.[27]

I have given this long quotation in its entirety as much for its language as for its contents. The Trinity of which the mythical Hermes had fore-knowledge is the same as that which Micheli symbolized obscurely in his canon, for the benefit of only those who could understand it. Micheli's claim to pre-eminence in his field, and his high-sounding call to the "musicians of Italy and of all other kingdoms and states," become less ridiculous if one keeps in mind the theological aspect of the subjects treated in that work and the prominence of theology in the culture of the period.

At this point it should come as no surprise to learn that the same Kircher, the author of the *Musurgia*, published in Rome in 1652 a vast treatise of Hermetic pseudo-Egyptology, entitled *Oedipus Egiptiacus*. This kind of interest should not be ascribed to eclecticism but to an encyclopedic-scientific attitude of a unifying nature. Kircher coolly ignores the rejection of the historical existence of Trismegistos based on the dating of some of the Hermetical writings, and he reaffirms the interpre-tation of the Egyptian hieroglyphics as symbols of hidden truths. Truth lies in the occult and, moreover, only insofar as it remains occult are its existence and its possession guaranteed.[28]

One should resist the temptation to make fanciful hypotheses when examining the way in which Hermetic culture was applied to music. Although experiments of a magical or incantatorial sort were probably made,[29] it is more urgent to understand how the premises of Hermetic thinking affected the musical thinking of Micheli, Valentini, and other, less extreme, composers. The taste for intellectual games and virtuosity is merely the common ground, rather than the full explanation of such widespread and diverse phenomena as enigmatic composition (one recalls Frescobaldi's "intendami chi può che m'intend'io"[30]), canons on vowels of words, and finally the compositional research on polymorphous canons or on *obblighi*, so significantly exemplified by many of Frescobaldi's works.

Interest in the possible applications of contrapuntal devices seemed to have been extraordinary, just as the possibilities of their extension seemed infinite. For example, Nanino's *157 Contrappunti* or Soriano's *110 Canoni et obblighi*, all on the same cantus firmus, did not exhaust the material; Zacconi in 1625 advised students of Soriano's work to compose six hundred more canons or *obblighi* in different forms on the same hymn.[31] And in 1641 Del Buono returned to the same point:

> I publish these works of mine: canons, *obblighi* and sonatas on the cantus firmus *Ave maris stella*, even if that famous man Francesco Soriano composed on the same cantus many years ago in such an excellent and *artificioso* manner. Nonetheless, I wanted to use the same cantus firmus, so that everybody may see how infinite this science is, that although Soriano made so many works on it with such variety, I could compose one hundred more.[32]

The polemical and didactical production of the time offers a cross-section of the musical republic, where everything leads in the direction of learned study and investigation, lively epistolary exchanges, public experiences, *virtuose accademie*,[33] pronouncements destined to cross borders, challenges, and acrimonious controversies—but also reciprocal and gallant homage between musicians.

In the same years and within this cultural framework, Romano Micheli dedicated one of his works to Francesco Soriano and Girolamo Frescobaldi, in order to honor the singular virtues of the two composers (see plate 1). The print consists of two pages only, containing an introduction and the solution of an enigmatic canon by Gian Paolo Cima, one of the devotees of the genre.[34] Micheli claims to have found a more fitting solution to the enigma and selects an appropriate text for the occasion: the Gospel address of Christ to Thomas, "Quia vidisti, Thoma, credidisti. Beatii qui non viderunt et crediderunt."

The text of the dedication is interesting because Micheli takes his distance from those who practice artifice in a common way; that is, with little rigor.[35] Such criticism underlines his aristocratic disdain for the "musicians of little knowledge in these studies, who think to show their understanding of the matter with their fancy tricks [*chimere*],"[36] and reveals to what extent the practice of artifice had taken on the character of an intellectual status symbol. That Frescobaldi is paired with Soriano in the only dedication by Micheli to two individual composers lends credibility to the idea that Frescobaldi fits into the intellectual climate outlined here.

Can the study of the *artificioso* tradition help to solve problems concerning Frescobaldi's works—in particular, the problem of the sources of his musical language? It is too soon to give a final answer to this question, because a systematic and complete study of the *artificioso* repertory has yet to be made. This is evident from the prevalent misunderstanding of these works, which, when not completely ignored, are described as exercises in "strict counterpoint."[37]

A comparative analysis of these compositions with works by Frescobaldi would miss the point, since the idiomatic nature of keyboard compositions or, in any case, compositions destined for a particular performance medium, cannot easily be fitted to the abstract formulation of works such as canons and *obblighi* on a cantus firmus. In other words, the sources for a keyboard language must be sought in works written for a similar purpose. But one can use the didactic works for another purpose: for example, to establish the relationship, and also the distance, between didactic tools and compositional practice, or to arrive at a clearer understanding, in either conceptual or technical terms, of the differences between seventeenth-century practice and the tradition that preceded it.

As was shown by Zacconi, the 110 *Canoni et oblighi* of Soriano had an eminently didactic purpose (it remains to be determined whether the traditional claim that they were composed to answer a challenge by Sebastiano Raval is accurate)[38] and were meant to provide an example to the student,[39] who was expected to use a single cantus firmus as the basis for his canons and *obblighi*. Thus the cantus firmus was a fixed point of reference[40] and the canons and *obblighi* were not so much *one* of various ways of composing, as *the* generative rule for writing the different voices. This exercise does not exhaust the possible kinds of composition, not even of didactic composition; nevertheless it is, accord-

All'Illuſtri , & Eccellentiſſimi Signori Muſici li Signori

FRANCESCO SORIANO
MAESTRO DI CAPPELLA, ET
GIRONIMO FRESCOBALDO
ORGANISTA IN S. PIETRO DI ROMA

Età tutti li altri Signori Eccellentiſſimi Muſici Romani

Miei patroni Oſſeruandiſſimi,

On l'occaſione datami dal R. D. Giouanni Riſeghino Organiſta nella Cathedrale di Concordia, donando-mi la ſequente Cantilena a Quattro voci in dui Canoni, ſtampata, come iui ſi vede ſenza li tempi, & li ſoliti ſegni, con quell'Enigma in dechiaratione, acciò li moſtraſſe il modo di cantarla; onde vi ſendo io quel verſo, che dice, E l'Aria fà ondeggiar l'Acqua d'intorno, ilquale ſignifica, che l'Alto ſia guida, & faccia mouere il Tenore, coſa, che per certo tui non è, & vedendo parimente la punta di quel Canone, doue cantano dui Alti all'uniſono vno dopo l'altro vna minima, io gli diſſi come quella ſi doueua cantare, e che la Cantilena, erà di bello ſtudio, mà non conforme al ſignificato dell'Enig-ma, ilquale richiede altro artificio, e di molto maggior ſtudio: & il detto R. D. Giouanni moſtran-doſi incredulo alle mie parole, li ſoggionſi, che di queſto li hauerei fatto vedere la propria eſperienza, & perciò ho volu-to fare l'altra Cantilena, con laquale ſi cantano quelle parole Euangeliche. Qui vidutu ... ch nua creduto, dando io nelle ſue proprie mani la Cantilena, come in ſi vede, acciò egli vedeſſe maggiormente ſatisfatto.

Dico dunque , che molte ſono le Cantilene , che io hò veduto, nelle quali ſono ſcritte le maſſime per le ſemicrome , & altre coſe ſimili; ò ſenza li ſegni, & le chiaui, ouero con li Enigmi , che non hanno il ſignificato conforme le Cantilene; & in fine molte altre chimere , lequali ſono infinite , e ſenza ritegno di ſtudio alcuno ſono fatte da Muſici. Et quando vn Mu-ſico non ritrouaſſe il modo di far cantare dette Cantilene , che ſe hauerebbe à dir di lui? che fuſſe poco accorto? Io per certo non ſono di queſto parere , perche li Muſici non profeſſano d'Aſtrologia ; anzi dico , che quelle Cantilene ſono fatte da Muſici di poca pratica in queſti ſtudij , poiche con quelle loro chiaure credono moſtrarli di ciò intelligenti; mà quando poi ſi viene alla partitura di eſſe , ſi vedono componimenti di poca periria. Hò veduto ancora Canti ene artificioſe fatte da Muſici più Eccellenti , nelle quali vi è ſcritto con quante voci quelle ſi cantino , & con li ſoliti ſegni di ſuoi luoghi doue le parti comin-ciano, acciò agenolmente li poſſa ritrouare il modo di cantare, & quando vn ...ſiſno l'adoua ritrovate non è di così merauig-lia , come molti ſi reputano, perche li ſegni ſono poſti à queſti ſi è il potere ritrovare, e cantare: Mà ben farebbe coſi ſingola-re quando ſi faceſſe vn'altra Cantilena differente da quella con li medeſimi ſuti. Et ſo ricouerò per faſore che li Signori Muſi-ci, tanto dentro, quanto fuori d'Italia ſi ſegnaſſero farmi parte di qualche Cantilena con ſuo artificio non più fatto , che ſe bene di quello io non haueſſe cognitione alcuna, ad ogni modo procurarei di fa' altrettato à cente Cantilena col medeſimo artif io.

Mi ricordo della promeſſa da me fatta nella ſtampa dell' anno paſſato per il acquato fiores che di cò di M ...
... la di N. S. la quale non hò potuto metter in eſſecutione, perche ... ...
ilquale mi aſtrinſe à non douermi allontanare da quelle ... ...
do io fare humiliſſimo dono alla Santità di N. S. N ...
obligi, laquale per quanto hò veduto, & in Roma, & per molti altri habi principi ...
tificio qual fin'hora non ſia più ſtato fatto, mà in oa ... ...
rappreſentato in figura in ſtampa di rame ; & ciò à l'imitatione di quel ... ...
nino Muſico Eccellentiſſimo nella Cappella di N. S. rappreſentato in vna Croce in figura ... dedicata All'Illu-
ſtriſſimo Signor Cardinal Faneſel à nno 1592, ... l'occaſione perciò datami dal Signor D. Gironimo Giacobbo Maeſtro di
Cappella Meritiſſimo in S. Petronio di Bologna, moſtrandomi la detta Croce in figura, & ſignificandomi quello eſſere vn belliſ-
ſimo artificio, & io per moſtrar d'intendere qual forte di ſtudio foſſe, volli fare vn'altra Cantilena in quella ſimilitudine
di ſtudio, ma differente da quello di detta Croce, & ... tre giorni feci vedere il componimento de' detto Dialogo al ſpradetto Signor D. Gironimo, ilquale poi ſi degnò di farlo cantare, & a moltiſſi … coſi parimente le VV. SS. potranno il tutto vedere,
e ſentire quando ſi vorranno degnare. Fra tanto per moſtrare al mond a la molta memoria, & oſſeruanza, ch'io tengo al loro ſin-
golar valore, le faccio corteſe dono di queſta eſperienza inuſuale, benche picciola ſia. Accettino dunque volunta ſi queſto poco,
con la molta prontezza dell'animo mio, ilquale ſtarà ſempre vigilante alli ſeruitij delle VV. SS. all'qui di pregandoli ogni maggior
contento riuerente bacio le mani. Di Venetia li 16. Nouembre 1619.

Delle VV. SS. Illuſtri.

Affettionatiſſimo Scrittore

Romano Micheli

Di Paolo Cima Organiſta nella Chieſa della Madonna appreſo S. Celſo in Milano.

BASSO	CANTO	ALTO	TENORE
La Terra ora ſi regge ſotto il Foco, Lontan dodici gradi (per tre colpi,)		E l'Aria ſà ondeggiar l'Acqua d'intorno, Perche s'unil con loi in queſti fuoco.	

Plate 1 Romano Micheli, *Solution to a Canon by Gian Paolo Cima* (Rome, 1619)

A prefente Cantilena à 4. voci in Partitura da cantarfi in dui Canoni, è ftata compofta ad'imitatio: re del proprio fignificato del fopradetto Enigma, il quale applica li quattro Elementi alle quattro parti della Mufica, cioè la Terra al Baffo, l'Acqua al Tenore, l'Aria all'Alto, & il Foco al Canto, Onde fi come li Elementi fono perpetui, cosi le parti deuono cantare vna Cantilena perpetua, cioè con li foliti Ritornelli, li quali non folo moftrano il cantare infinito, ma anco obligano in quefta forte di ftudio, che l'Armonia dell'ultimo fi vnifca con quella del principio come in quefta fi vede, confiderandofi tanto all'aumentatione fatta nel Baffo delli trè vltimi tempi conforme la parte che guida, quanto all'obligo che li dui Canoni cantano fopra le modulationi delle note le parole duplicate fenza far barbareimo alcuno.

Di Romano Micheli Romano. Manfionario nella Metropoli d'Aquilea.

ing to Zacconi, "the doorway of any good music."[41] How does this "doorway" conform to the already codified rules of counterpoint? There is an indication of a discrepancy even in the terminological distinction between counterpoint and composition, clearly defined, for example, by Silverio Picerli:

> Counterpoint and composition are quite different, because all counterpoint is composition, while the contrary is not true. Counterpoint, strictly speaking, must use very few leaps, and all of them appropriate to singing; it must contain fine inventions and scales repeated in different ways, with ornaments, dissonances and imitations. One should not use octaves or unisons at the beginning of a measure, nor breves, nor dotted semibreves, nor, probably, simple semibreves but only syncopated ones, nor perfect cadences of the mode, except when one wants to repeat the subject or the imitations, or begin new ones; but in general, cadences are avoided. Lacking some of these elements, the music cannot properly be called counterpoint, but rather composition, which does not observe such strict rules.[42]

In examining these didactic works, one soon discovers that they are not always formulated according to "strict rules." Whenever possible they adhere to the conventions, but, as Soriano remarks in his preface, "If you find things that may seem harsh or exceptional, blame it on the *obblighi*."[43] Del Buono takes up the same argument:

> You will find canons with some oddities, and even compositions with *obblighi* in all parts; these are things that, on a cantus firmus, are of no little difficulty. Be indulgent then, if you will find some mistakes, either in the printing or in the composition, because *obblighi* and especially canons require some licenses.[44]

One can find among Soriano's *obblighi* examples of such liberties; for example, in no. 69, note the unresolved chromaticism and the resulting false relation between mm. 3 and 4 (see example 1). In no. 74, the awkward melodic lines derive from the *obbligo* of different, constant rhythmic values in each voice (see example 2). In no. 80, the syncopated dissonance in m. 2 resolves upward (see example 3).

Example 1 Soriano, *110 Canoni et oblighi*, no. 69

Example 2 Soriano, *110 Canoni et oblighi*, no. 74

More examples could be given; but rather than being amazed at the inclusion of such liberties in one of the most respected didactic works of the time, one must attempt to understand the underlying mentality: an attitude open to new possibilities and very flexible in matters of compositional practice. Contrapuntal difficulties resulting from the decision to use a certain type of canon are met pragmatically, since the norms of counterpoint are no longer—if they ever were—absolute. The chosen

Example 3　Soriano, *110 Canoni et oblighi*, no. 80

obbligo was considered the prevailing necessity, and thus constituted the needed tool for the expansion of compositional possibilities. Once again, the "scientific" attitude was in no way confined to traditional positions, even if it did not necessarily transgress them.[45]

In the first half of the seventeenth century the idea of having surpassed the achievements of the ancients is vividly portrayed by the image of the dwarf who can see further when he climbs onto the shoulders of a giant. According to Bartolomeo Grassi, Frescobaldi too "has surpassed not only the modern masters of this most noble art of music, but even the most excellent of the past."[46] Similar considerations, from those regarding the larger cultural environment to those regarding the smallest technical details, should dissuade the scholar from falling back on the traditional interpretative categories. I refer in particular to the notions of *stile antico* and *stile palestriniano*, whose validity is still too often taken for granted. The mythical nature of these categories emerges both from historical research and from musical analysis.[47]

Giovanni Maria Nanino, who long worked with Palestrina and who had a great influence on composers of the following generation, stated that he considered Palestrina to be an "expert and excellent man in music, but not the first, nor the second, and neither the third."[48] But the idea that in Rome one had to conform reverently to his style is so persistent that, even where a direct stylistic relationship is denied, this idea tends to be readmitted in a different form. Yet the persistence of the use of Palestrina's music and this composer's true significance as normative ideal are altogether different problems.[49] It should go without saying that the study of Frescobaldi's works can only profit from the removal or correction of these historiographical preconceptions.

My point of departure, *artificioso* compositions, has led me to the investigation of a variety of problems—probably too many. This variety is perhaps the consequence of working in almost virgin territory. But even if my research has not yet yielded definitive results, I hope at least to have shown why it is necessary. For those who believe that even for music a history of mentality—a history based on the examination of the musical language and not only of musical grammars—is of importance, *artificioso* music, in spite of the traditional neglect, must be counted as an indispensable source.

Notes

I would like to thank all friends and colleagues who helped with discussions or suggestions in the preparation of this paper, in particular Frederick Hammond, Lorenzo Bianconi, Pierluigi Petrobelli, and Raffaella Comaschi. I am also grateful to Barbara Walker for the translation of the text.

1. With regard to this problem, the activity of the *Lessico intellettuale europeo* of the University of Rome, a group of scholars collecting and studying intellectual terminology throughout history, should be of particular interest to the musicologist.

2. The "artifice" in this case refers to ability or craftsmanship, as in the dedication of Gian Paolo Cima, *Concerti ecclesiastici* (Milan: Eredi di Tini e Lomazzo, 1610): "Therefore I present these *concertini* to you, as to a person who will perfectly understand their value and the graceful movements, full of affects, which are introduced in them with so much artifice [A lei dunque presento io questi concertini, come a quello che conoscerà benissimo il valore di essi, et gli gratiosi e affettuosi movimenti, che con tanto artificio posti vi sono]." Athanasius Kircher uses the term with various meanings; the adjective stands for "artificial" in *Musurgia universalis* (Rome: Corbelletti, 1650), 1:43: "De sono artificioso sive Musica eiusque prima institutione, aetate, vicissitudine, propagatione"; but sometimes, instead, for the style of a composition, as in *Musurgia* 1:581: "De vario stylorum harmonicorum artificio." The use of the term is generally more specific in music than, for instance, in literature or philosophy. I wish to thank Dr. Gianni Adamo, who kindly allowed me to examine the preparatory materials for the entry "Artificio" of the *Lessico intellettuale europeo*.

3. See, for instance, the *Avviso inviato da me Romano Micheli insieme col foglio reale del canone musicale Fons Signatus* (Rome: Grignani, 1650), in which the composer speaks of "experiences of musical compositions, both free, and with the artifices [experienze di componimenti musicali tanto sciolti, quanto con gl'artifici]," p. 1; "to that musician I will not answer, because he did not understand the inner aspects of artifices [al detto musico io non rispondo, poiché non ha penetrato gl'intimi degl'artifici]," p. 4; "such artifice is to be used only by the most learned musicians [tal artificio non è se non da musici dottissimi]," p. 4, and so on.

4. For instance, in Camillo Angleria, *Regola del contrapunto, e della musical compositione . . . con due ricercari l'uno a 4 e l'altro a 5 dell'autore, e un ricercare, e canoni a 2, 3 e 4 da cantarsi in varii modi del signor Gio. Paolo Cima . . .* (Milan: Giorgio Rolla, 1622). See also Kircher, *Musurgia* 1:583 ff., where examples of *artificioso* works of Pier Francesco Valentini are presented.

5. See Michael Majer, *Atalanta fugiens* (Oppenheim: G. Gallero, 1617) to which I shall refer later on.

6. The canons on the vowels of words (which Micheli claimed to have invented) differ from the older canons *super voces musicales* in the relatively large number of words—often a complete sentence—from which the subject was drawn. Also, the text was usually created by the composer in such a way that the vowels provided a subject appropriate to contrapuntal treatment, including statements in retrograde or inverted form.

7. I refer in particular to the *Capriccio cromatico con ligature al contrario*, the *Ricercare con obligo di non uscir di grado*, the two *Capricci* with *obligo di cantare la quinta parte senza toccarla*. Similar in conception, although not specifically *obbligati* are the capriccios and ricercars on solmization-syllable subjects.

8. It is only for brevity's sake that I shall refer to these compositions as a genre; their characteristics are, in fact, not homogeneous enough to be considered such. Rather one ought to talk about a common intellectual attitude applied to different genres. It should be noted that many of the composers were pupils of Giovanni Maria Nanino (Brunelli, Agostini, Micheli, and Valentini), and two were colleagues of Frescobaldi during his period as organist at St. Peter's (Soriano for twelve years, from the beginning of Frescobaldi's service until his retirement in 1620; Agostini from 1626 when he was appointed maestro di cappella in St. Peter's to December 1628 when Frescobaldi left for Florence).

9. This has not yet been fully recognized for music, as it has been in other historical fields, as clearly expressed, for example, by Frances A. Yates: "It is now considered normal to study the great thinkers of the past, not only through an analysis of the ways in which their work looked towards the future but also taking into account the elements of their thought previously neglected as lacking historical interest." My translation from the preface to the Italian edition of *The Rosicrucian Enlightenment* (London and Boston: Routledge and Kegan Paul, 1972): *L'illuminismo dei Rosa-Croce* (Turin: Einaudi, 1976), xxii (the statement does not appear in the original English edition).

10. An aristocratic model of behavior was evidently alive in the musical world and the musical aristocracy was determined to gain supremacy over the "ordinary musicians." See the quotation from Romano Micheli on p. 200.

11. From the preface to *Musica vaga ed artificiosa* (Venice: Giacomo Vincenti, 1615), p. [iii]: "Vero è, che sono valentuomini quelli, che fanno composizioni studiose, e vaghe, il che si acquista in pochi anni, oltre [ben]ché sono tenuti valent'uomini, ma ordenari: eccellentissimi sono poi quelli, che non contenti di fare perfettissimi componimenti, ma anco vogliono intendere li più intimi studi della musica, cioè canoni in più modi, e altre particolari abilità, il che non si acquista in sì breve tempo, né così facilmente come alcuni dicono e perciò non gli deve parere cosa strana il credere, che si trovino uomini di tanta eccellenza: e se ciò da alcuno si può dire, può esser detto da me, poiché sono stato curioso di praticare con la maggior parte delli principali musici d'Italia."

12. The same expression appears in other writings of his, such as *Virtuoso manifesto sopra li più dotti studi della musica* (Rome: Grignani, 1624); or *Virtuoso avviso sopra li più dotti studi della musica, e del modo d'accrescere il numero de' cantori di bellissime voci* (Rome: Grignani, 1633).

13. I do not suppose that the attitude toward *artificioso* practices was unanimously positive; it is significant that both of the most *artificioso* composers were professional anomalies: Valentini, being a nobleman, was not dedicated to music for need; and Micheli, a priest, set up his career as a continuous musical pilgrimage between the principal Italian cities. But those who had to deal with day-to-day musical life, with the problems of running a *cappella*, showed a looser attitude toward *artifici*. Francesco Soriano, in the preface to *Canoni et oblighi*, remarks, "because my friends asked me to publish some of my canons and other musical inventions that I had composed for my own pleasure . . . to be used until some other, more elegant and graceful works, with a more successful result and artifice are published [Essendomi diverse volte fatta istanza d'amici, di dovere pubblicare alcuni miei canoni, et altre invenzioni musicali, fatte già per mio diporto . . . mi son risoluto a mandare fuori le presenti cento dieci diversità . . . da servirsene fin tanto, che con piu eleganza, et soavità: con più felice successo et artificio eschino fuori altre opere]." Giovanni Briccio ends his preface to *Canoni enigmatici musicali* by stating that this work "at the end is nothing but a musical joke [alfine non è altro che un scherzo musicale]."

14. Fernand Braudel, "Tre Italie in due secoli" in *Storia d'Italia* (Turin: Einaudi, n.d.), 2:2173 (my translation).

15. Frances A. Yates, *Giordano Bruno and the Hermetic Tradition* (London: Routledge and Kegan Paul, 1964), 151: "But the Pythagorean medieval tradition, Hermetism and Cabalism added immense richness and complexity, swelling out the universal harmonies into a new symphony . . . One of the most characteristic aspects from Giorgi onwards, though it used number in a Pythagorean or qualitative sense and not as mathematics proper, yet by so forcefully directing attention on number as the key to all nature it may be said to have prepared the way for a genuine mathematical thinking about the universe."

16. Derived from the numerological and symbolic works of Raymond Lull.

17. See Yates, *Giordano Bruno*, 416 ff.

18. Cf. Pico della Mirandola, *Opera omnia* (Basel, 1572), 1:101, as translated by John Dee in the preface to H. Billingley, *The Elements of . . . Euclide* (London, 1570). Quoted in Yates, *Giordano Bruno*, 148 and n. 3.

19. *The Rosicrucian Enlightenment*, xii:

[The Hermetic tradition was] far from losing its power in the early seventeenth century . . . or losing its influence over cultural movements of major importance. . . . There was actually a renaissance of it in the early seventeenth century, fresh manifestations of it in new forms which had absorbed alchemical influences, and which were particularly important in relation to the development of the mathematical approach to nature.

20. See Yates, *The Rosicrucian Enlightenment*, 12.

21. See ibid., 148: "Of immense importance in the city is music, and to enter the school of music one must pass through those of arithmetic and geometry; musical instruments hang in the theatre of mathematics. Religious choral singing is taught and practised. They do this in imitation of the angelic choir whose services they value so highly." For a complete description of Christianopolis see F. E. Held, *Christianopolis: An Ideal State of the Seventeenth Century* (Oxford, 1916).

22. See Yates, *The Rosicrucian Enlightenment*, 247. The matter is also discussed on p. 44. The document translated by Yates in the appendix is the *Fama fraternitatis* (Kassel, 1614). The function of the Rosicrucian treasures was to preserve in a concealed form the secrets of the sect so that "if it should happen after many hundred years the Order of fraternity should come to nothing, they might by this only vault be restored again" (*ibid.*, 247).

23. Michael Majer, *Atalanta fugiens, hoc est, Emblemata nova de secretis naturae chymica, accommodata partim oculis et intellectui, figuris cuproincisis, adiectisque sententii, epigrammatis auribus & recreationi animi plus minus 50 fugis musicalibus trium vocum, quarum duae ad unam simplicem melodiam distichis anendis peraptam, correspondeant, non absq. singulari iucunditate videnda, legenda, meditanda, intelligenda, dejudicanda, canenda & audienda* (Oppenheim: Gallero, 1617). Concerning the characteristics of this work—which deserves further research, from a musical point of view—I refer the reader to its preface. For a general discussion of the emblem, the fundamental text remains Mario Praz, *Studies in Seventeenth-Century Imagery* (Rome: Edizioni di Storia e Letteratura, 1964). On Majer see J. B. Craven, *Count Michael Majer* (Kirkwall, 1910).

24. See Walther Blankenburg, "Kanon," *Die Musik in Geschichte und Gegenwart*, vol. 7 (1958), in particular cols. 527–28. With regard to the Hermetic tradition cultivated in Rome, it must be kept in mind that the most important work on Hermetic Egyptology, the *Oedipus Egiptiacus* by Athanasius Kircher (Rome: Mascardi, 1652), was promoted by Cardinal Francesco Barberini, who obtained permission from the General of the Jesuits to have Kircher come to Rome. This is referred to by the author himself in tomo 1, caput 4 of this work.

25. Kircher, *Musurgia* (libro 7, caput 5, "De vario stylorum harmonicorum artificio"), 1:583–84.

26. R. Micheli, *Avviso inviato*, p. [11]:

Non mi essendo in contrario in questo le modulationi artificiose quali si contengono nell'opere . . . Musurgia sive ars magna consoni et dissoni, del molto R. P. Athanasio Kircherio della Compagnia del Giesù, il quale anco con altre scienze maggiormente ha illustrato la professione della musica, e . . . quest'alma città di Roma, con essersi valuto in dette sue opere fra gl'altri, de molte cantilene di alcuni degni, peritissimi, e non vulgari signori musici di Roma.

27. R. Micheli, *Avviso inviato*, p. [4]:

Il nascosto, e non espresso significato di essa, per non intendere peritamente l'occulto mistero del predetto canone, simbolo della santissima Trinità, essendo che era necessario di sapere quel tanto, che insegnano i sacri teologi, cioè, che in Dio sono tre sussistenze relative, per le quali le tre persone divine perfettamente sussistono, cioè, incomunicabilmente, e tutte le tre persone hanno una essenza indivisa, qual essenza ha la sua sussistenza assoluta distinta dalle tre sussistenze relative delle Persone; alla quale però manca l'incomunicabilità, e così viene ad essere sussistenza impropria, in quanto che non è incomunicabile. Supposto questo, io ho voluto, che il mio canone rappresenti la Santissima Trinità, sotto oscuri simboli, e geroglifici, acciò non sia inteso, se non dal musico intelligente.

28. Michel Foucault observes acutely that "quand il était enoncé, le savoir du XVIe siècle était un secret mais partagé. Quand il est caché, celui du XVIIe et du XVIIIe siècle est un discours au-dessus duquel on a ménage un voile." Michel Foucault, *Les Mots et les choses* (Paris: Gallimard, 1966), 103.

29. Frances Yates, for instance, thought that the *Ballet comique de la Reine* (1581) must have been shaped as a sort of "extended and complicated talisman, an arrangement of the planetary gods in a favourable order, invoked by favourable incantations, resulting not only in a marvellous work of art, but in a magical action by which something was done, by which the favour of the heavens was actually drawn down in aid of the French Monarchy" (see Yates, *Giordano Bruno*, 176). On a similar problem see Yates, "Poésie et musique au mariage du Duc de Joyeuse" in *Musique et poésie au XVIe siecle* (Paris: CNRS, 1954), 241 ff.

30. The motto, borrowed from Petrarch, prefaces the second ricercar of the *Messa della Madonna* in the *Fiori musicali*. The motto referred to the addition of the *quinta parte* to be sung by the player, who had to guess where it was to be inserted.

31. See Ludovico Zacconi, "Resolutioni et partiture di cento, e dieci canoni musical sopra l'Ave maris stella di Francesco Soriani . . . con le cosiderazioni in fine ad'uno per uno . . .," I-Bc Ms. C. 36, a miscellaneous codex entitled "Io. M. Nanini / Franc. Soriani / Opera advers. / Sebast. Ravalle / cum notis / Ludovici Zacconi," fol. 143 ff.

32. From the preface to *Canoni, oblighi, et sonate in varie maniere sopra l'Ave maris stella* (Palermo: A. Martarello and S. d'Angelo, 1641): "Mando in luce queste mie opere di canoni, oblighi e sonate sopra il canto fermo dell'*Ave maris stella*, ove benché così eminentemente e con tanto artificio molt'anni sono vi fabricò quel sì celebre uomo Francesco Soriano, nulladimeno ho voluto far sempre l'istesso canto fermo, acciò ciaschedun curioso conosca quanto sia infinita questa scienza, che avendo il Soriano con tanta varietà fattovi sopra tante opere, ancor io ne abbi fatte altre cento."

33. Antonio Maria Abbatini, for instance, held a monthly academy at his home. The texts of some of his lectures are preserved in a manuscript at the Civico museo bibliografico musicale at Bologna (see Gaetano Gaspari, *Catalogo della biblioteca del Liceo musicale di Bolo-*

gna [Bologna: Romagnoli Dall'Acqua, 1890], 1:188). The same Abbatini wrote about his education by the Jesuits, and his activity as a learned musician in an autobiography in verse (published in Lorenzo Bianconi, *Il Seicento* [Turin: Edizioni di Torino, 1982], 280–87).

34. As appears from Camillo Angleria, *Regola del contrappunto* (Milan: G. Rolla, 1622), dedication and p. 84. Angleria publishes a canon by Cima for two, three, and four voices, to be sung "in fifty different ways, with different harmony [in cinquanta modi con differente armonia]."

35. Micheli declares in the dedication, "There are many pieces, which I have seen, in which *maximae* are used instead of sixteenth notes, and similar things; or without the [tempo] signatures and the clefs; or with enigmas that are not appropriate to the piece; and finally many other fancy tricks which are infinite and are used by musicians although they bear no relevance as studies. And, if a musician could not find the way to have such pieces sung, what could one say about him? Perhaps that he is not clever enough? I am certainly not of this opinion, because musicians are not astrologers." This may also suggest some kind of polemic between Micheli and Cima.

36. See the complete text in plate 1.

37. See S. Philip Kniseley, "Soriano, Francesco," *The New Grove Dictionary of Music and Musicians* (London: Macmillan, 1980), 17:538, where, furthermore, the *Canoni et oblighi* are incorrectly classified as "secular works," along with madrigals.

38. This claim may have come from a misinterpretation of Micheli's preface to *Musica vaga ed artificiosa*, where the episode of the challenge is reported but without any explicit reference to particular works. Besides, Soriano does not mention the challenge at all in his preface to *Canoni et oblighi*.

39. Zacconi, "Resolutioni et Partiture"; at fol. 142v the following notice is found: "Those who want to become perfect musicians should study this book and practice what it indicates, demonstrates, and explains [Chi vuol esser perfetto musico, studij questo libro; e ponghi in effetto, quanto ch'egli t'adita, mostra e dice]."

40. We must keep in mind the clear conceptual analogy between these kinds of compositions, whose length is determined by the cantus firmus, and the formal unit of most instrumental compositions, that is, the section. In each section a particular compositional process, a countersubject or an *obbligo* is treated. A further analogy is determined by the necessity to treat in different ways a basic material (i.e., the cantus firmus) that imposes clearly defined tonal limits. Such exercises would seem to form an ideal training for compositions of the kind of Frescobaldi's capriccios on solmization-syllable subjects or with the *obbligo* to sing the *quinta parte*.

41. Zacconi, "Risoluzioni et partiture," fol. 143: "La porte di ogni buona musica."

42. Silverio Picerli, *Specchio secondo di musica* (Naples: Nucci, 1631), chap. 2, p. 10:

> Il contrapunto, e compositione sono alquanto differenti, poiché ogni contrapunto si può dir compositione, ma non è converso. Onde il contrapunto propriamente detto, deve procedere con pochissimi salti tutti cantabili, con bell'inventioni, e tirate, diversamente replicate, con fiori, legature, e fughe. Non vi si devon fare ottave, overo unisoni, in principio di misura, né brevi, né semibrevi co'l punto, né forsi semplici, ma

solo sincopate, né le cadenze perfette, e proprie del tono, eccetto quando si vuol replicar il soggetto, o fughe, e dar principio all'altre, ma in generale si sfuggono. Mancandogli alcune di dette cose non si potrà dire propriamente contrapunto, ma compositione, quale non procede con sì rigorose osservationi.

43. Soriano, *Canoni et oblighi*, p. [3]: "se . . . vi trovassero cose da stimarle forse dure o licentiose; quest s'attribuischino agli oblighi."

44. Del Buono, *Canoni oblighi et sonate*, p. [3].

45. The *artificioso* experiments of Frescobaldi should also be considered within this cultural framework. The value of such compositions is determined not only by the originality of the self-imposed *obbligo*, but especially by the mastery of its treatment. One probably should not overemphasize the weight of the *inventio*, because the originality of the artifice is a feature common to the genre by definition. In other words, the surprising fact that Frescobaldi chose, for instance, to resolve dissonances upward, should not cause us to ignore his personal stylistic use of that particular technique.

46. Preface to Frescobaldi's *Canzoni* (Masotti, 1628): "ha non solo superato li moderni maestri di quest'arte tanto nobile della musica, ma ogni più eccellente dei passati."

47. On this problem, see Gino Stefani, "Miti barocchi: Palestrina 'Princeps musicae,'" in *Nuova rivista musicale italiana* 8 (1974): 347–55; Helmut Hucke, "Palestrina als Autorität und Vorbild im 17. Jahrhundert," in *Claudio Monteverdi e il suo tempo: Atti del congresso internazionale*, ed. Raffaello Monterosso (Verona: Valdonega, 1969), 253–61; Sergio Durante, "La *Guida Armonica* di Giuseppe Ottavio Pitoni: Un documento sugli stili musicali in uso a Roma al tempo di Corelli," in *Nuovissimi studi corelliani*, ed. Sergio Durante and Pierluigi Petrobelli (Florence: Olschki, 1982), 285–327.

48. See Raphael Molitor, *Die Nach-tridentinische Choral-Reform* (Leipzig: Leuckart, 1901), 2:48 n. 1 (my translation).

49. See Bianconi, *Il Seicento*, 107–9.

The Influence and Tradition of Frescobaldi's Works in the Transalpine Countries

FRIEDRICH W. RIEDEL

F RESCOBALDI WAS THE most important teacher of the German keyboard masters in the baroque era. The influence and dissemination of Frescobaldi's works north of the Alps can be traced from the early seventeenth century to the age of Haydn and Beethoven. This is all the more astonishing when one realizes that there was only one German organist who can with certainty be shown to have been a pupil of Frescobaldi: Johann Jakob Froberger. It seems likely that Emperor Ferdinand III had sent Froberger to Rome in 1637 to study with Frescobaldi. We know nothing more about his four years there. But there is no doubt that Froberger was familiar with several of Frescobaldi's compositions and brought them back to Vienna, where he was Imperial Court Organist until 1657 or 1658.[1]

It is not clear whether Johann Kaspar Kerll, who later became Leopold I's Imperial Court Organist, had also been a pupil of Frescobaldi. Kerll, born in 1627, was sent to Rome by his later patron in Brussels, Archduke Leopold Wilhelm, to study with Giacomo Carissimi.[2] Some of Kerll's biographers have conjectured that he also studied with Frescobaldi.[3] Although the dates of Kerll's stay in Rome are not known, they probably correspond to a time when Frescobaldi was very old or had already died. Nevertheless, Kerll certainly studied Frescobaldi's works and used them as models for his own compositions. Such was also the case with his colleague in Vienna, Alessandro Poglietti, although we are equally uncertain whether Poglietti was a pupil of Frescobaldi.[4] Neither has evidence been produced thus far to support the assertion by earlier writers that two North German organists, Franz Tunder from Lübeck and Johann Heckelauer from Gottorf, had personal contact with Frescobaldi.[5]

The dissemination of Frescobaldi's printed works north of the Alps was far more important as a source of influence than any private students he may have had.[6] Here one must distinguish between two groups of works: those in strict imitative style (fantasias, ricercars, canzonas, and capriccios) printed by movable type in full score; and those in free-voiced keyboard styles (toccatas, partitas, and dances) engraved in keyboard tablature. In the first group, the *Fantasie*, printed in Milan in 1608, apparently came out in a small edition, which saw no wide distribution. Nevertheless, transcriptions of individual works from this edition survive from about 1625. Codex 714 of the Minorite archives in Vienna contains four fantasias.[7] There also exists a collection of keyboard works in Berlin containing eight fantasias.[8] In the first manuscript the pieces have been transcribed in full score. The second manuscript, copied in Brussels, uses German keyboard tablature.

After 1626 the imitative works were printed in Venice by Alessandro Vincenti. Even after Frescobaldi's death, all of them were still listed in Vincenti's *Indice di tutte le opera di musica* (Venice, 1649).[9] There is no doubt that this catalogue was known north of the Alps, since Vincenti had trading links with German booksellers. Four years later the Munich bookseller Paul Parstorffer published a volume using the same title as Vincenti, in which the same works by Frescobaldi were offered for sale.[10] Parstorffer had extensive business contacts and principally sold Italian printed music in Austria.[11] Copies of the 1628 and 1642 editions of the *Capricci, canzon francese e recercari* and the *Fiori musicali* (1635) can be found in the Benedictine and Cistercian monasteries of Switzerland (Einsiedeln and St. Gall), Bavaria, Austria, Moravia, and Silesia.[12] Around 1680 Franz Xaver Anton Murschhauser, organist in Munich and a pupil of Kerll, purchased the stock of Parstorffer's Munich publishing house.[13]

In addition, there exist numerous complete transcriptions of these collections. The earliest rendering of the ricercars and capriccios in German tablature appears in a manuscript from the Minorite monastery in Asparn an der Zaya (Lower Austria),[14] copied during the first half of the seventeenth century—that is, probably during Frescobaldi's lifetime. Another seventeenth-century transcription of the *Recercari* and the *Capricci* has been preserved in Vienna.[15] Around 1720 Alexander Giesel, a Viennese Minorite, made a complete transcription of the *Capricci, canzon francese e recercari*.[16] Transcriptions of these cycles of imitative works continued into the second half of the eighteenth century. For example, Angelus Widmann, a Benedictine from Wessobrunn, transcribed the cycle in 1775,[17] as did Bach's pupil Johann Philipp Kirnberger, his son C. P. E. Bach, and his first biographer, Johann Nikolaus Forkel.[18]

The *Fiori musicali* seems to have been even more frequently copied, either completely or partially, particularly at the beginning of the eighteenth century. We know of copies made by two pupils of Johann Joseph Fux, Alexander Giessel in Vienna and Johann Dismas Zelenka in Dresden.[19] Even J. S. Bach copied the *Fiori musicali* in 1714,[20] although his sons and pupils, specifically C. P. E. Bach, Kirnberger, and Forkel, were content to copy only the ricercars. The aforementioned Angelus Widmann made a complete transcription in 1775.[21] Individual pieces from the *Fiori musicali* appear in many manuscript collections of the seventeenth century. For example, in 1670 Poglietti transcribed the *Bergamasca* into his sketchbook.[22] The Minoritenkonvent in Vienna has an organ book from the late seventeenth century containing the "Ricercare con obligo di Basso."[23] A manuscript from central Germany, dated 1695, contains the *Bergamasca*, as well as a ricercar and a canzona in German keyboard tablature.[24]

The second group of keyboard works is represented by the two books of toccatas printed in Rome. We do not know whether the printer, Nicola Borbone, had contacts in Germany, as Vincenti had with Parstorffer. In any case, the *Toccate*, particularly the last editions of 1637, can be found in many of the same places as the *Capricci, canzon francese e recercari* and the *Fiori musicali*, either in their original printed form, or in seventeenth- and eighteenth-century manuscript transcriptions.[25] Copies of *Toccate I* and *II* even found their way to northern Germany. The famous organist at St. Katherine's Church in Hamburg, Johann Adam Reincken, possessed a copy of the *Toccate II*,[26] and a copy of each book has been discovered in Rostock.[27]

Individual toccatas, canzonas, and versets, especially from the *Toccate II*, are found in manuscript collections from the seventeenth and eighteenth centuries. The aforementioned Minorite organ book in Vienna contains Toccatas VIII and XI from *Toccate II*;[28] Codex E.B. 1688, now found at Yale University and supposedly compiled by Vincenzo Albrici (1631–96), contains Toccata III from the same collection (with an erroneous attribution to Poglietti).[29] Individual excerpts from the toccatas are included in several "Versette" books, found, for example, in the Viennese Minoritenkonvent.[30]

A study of the sources shows that Frescobaldi's keyboard compositions were disseminated into almost all the German-speaking territories, and continued to be transcribed up to the end of the eighteenth century. How were Frescobaldi's works used during the long period of 150 years after his death? Of course, they were played on the organ or the harpsichord, but they also served, especially later, as models for compositional techniques.

At this point we should consider the various genres of Frescobaldi's works and arrange them according to style and form of notation. According to baroque theories of style, they fall into four distinct categories:

1. *Stilus fantasticus*, that is, a free style with elements of virtuosity, harmonic tension, and rhythmically contrasting sections, exemplified by the twenty-three toccatas in Frescobaldi's *Toccate I* and *Toccate II*.

2. *Stilus choraicus* or *stilus hyporchematicus*, that is, the dances, to which belong *balletti, correnti, gagliarde, passacagli, ciaccone,* and extending to the *pastorale* and the *battaglia*. The latter belongs, at the same time, to descriptive or program music.

3. *Stilus melismaticus* or "song style," to which I would assign the *partite* and *arie variate*.

4. *Stilus moteticus* or *stilus gravis*, that is, all works in the strict or fugal style, such as ricercars, canzonas, and capriccios and the organ Masses of the *Fiori musicali*.[31]

In the original versions and in most transcriptions, pieces belonging to the first three genres are mostly found in Italian keyboard tablature with two staves—the upper having six lines, the lower, eight. In contrast, compositions of the fourth genre are scored so that each voice has its own staff. Playing from a score was quite familiar to seventeenth- and eighteenth-century organists; however, the *spartitura* was used at the same time "per qualunque studiosi di contrapunti," as is stated in the score edition of Cypriano de Rore's madrigals (1577).[32]

The individual toccatas, partitas, canzonas, fantasias, ricercars, and capriccios surviving in manuscript collections were used mostly for keyboard performance. They appear written either in the original Italian *intavolatura,* with six and eight lines, or in French keyboard tablature, i.e., the modern system with two staves of five lines each. Imitative pieces were also transcribed on two systems, for example in the aforementioned seventeenth-century codices of the Viennese Minorite monastery.[33] Farther north in Germany, organists transcribed the imitative pieces into the German letter tablature, which they found easier to read than the mensural notation of Italian tablature.

In the preface to his edition of toccatas, Frescobaldi states that one can play the different parts of the toccatas separately, and that the player may conclude a toccata at will, without finishing the entire piece. This practice is reflected in several handwritten organ books of the seventeenth and early eighteenth century: one transcribed only those parts that one intended to play as a prelude or interlude during the Mass or Vespers. Consequently, complete toccatas or canzonas were broken apart, and the separate parts appear in different places in the manuscript.[34]

Frescobaldi's high reputation among organists into the early nineteenth century is proven by compositions that erroneously were attributed to him but actually came from a much later time: for example, a cycle of Versetti in all the church modes,[35] or a fugue by Gottlieb Muffat that Muzio Clementi published under the name Frescobaldi.[36] The inclusion of Frescobaldi's *toccatae majores* in professional organists' repertoires throughout the seventeenth century is mentioned in two representative publications. In the preface to the *Wegweiser . . . die Orgel zu schlagen,* an organ book originally printed in Augsburg in 1668 and reprinted many times well into the eighteenth century, one reads, "Anfangenden gleich des Frescobaldi oder andere schwere Toccaten vorzulegen wird kein Vernünftiger gut sprechen."[37] Hence Frescobaldi's toccatas were still considered standard works in the art of organ playing. Georg Muffat, in the preface to his *Apparatus Musico-Organisticus* (1690), a collection including twelve large toccatas, remarks that no editions of large toccatas had appeared since those of Frescobaldi.

However, as the eighteenth century progressed, interest in the performance of toccatas seemed to fade. Instead, there was more interest in compositions in the *stilus gravis,* particularly among Johann Joseph Fux in Vienna, J. S. Bach in Leipzig, and their pupils. Frescobaldi's imitative compositions in particular served as models for an exact contrapuntal style.[38] Excerpts from these compositions were entered as examples in printed pedagogical works, from Wolfgang Schonsleder's *Architectonice Musices Universalis* (1631) and François Roberday's collection *Fugues et Caprices* (1660),[39] to Friedrich Wilhelm Marpurg's *Abhandlungen von der Fuge nach den Grundsätzen und Exempeln der besten deutschen und ausländischen Meister* (1753), and the *Dreissig Fugen für das Piano-Forte, verfasst nach einem neuen System von Anton Reicha*, printed in Vienna in 1804 and dedicated to none other than Joseph Haydn.[40]

Meanwhile, pieces in the *stilus gravis* took on another function: as movements for string quartet. Specifically, fugues for string quartet came into fashion in Vienna after the middle of the eighteenth century. Composers such as Matthias Georg Monn, Carlo Ordoñez, and Johann Georg Albrechtsberger come to mind.[41] One also looked back to the compositions of older masters, for instance, Mozart's arrangements of fugues from the *Wohltemperiertes Clavier* for string quartet.[42] Ricercars and capriccios by Frescobaldi, arranged in this manner, appear in a 1793 manuscript from Vienna[43] and in a collection published by Trautwein in Berlin about 1830.[44] Hence many works by Frescobaldi were still in practical musical use two hundred years after his death.

We now come to the question of Frescobaldi's influence on the composition of keyboard music in the transalpine countries during the seventeenth and eighteenth centuries. This influence manifests itself mainly in the *stilus gravis* and in the *stilus fantasticus*, but also to some extent in the *stilus melismaticus* and the *stilus hyporchematicus*.

With respect to the *stilus gravis*, we need to distinguish the two types of Frescobaldi's imitative compositions:

1. Imitative compositions without changes of meter and without variation of the subject. In these pieces, one or more subjects are elaborated, with or without fixed countersubjects.
2. Imitative variation-pieces. These compositions consist of several sections with different meters. A single subject is varied rhythmically and melodically in each new section, by itself, or with a distinct countersubject.[45]

The first type of fugue appears in Frescobaldi's *Recercari* from 1615 and in his *Fiori musicali* from 1635. The ricercars have up to four separate sections and up to four subjects. In certain cases, Frescobaldi combined three or four subjects in three- or four-part counterpoint.

Frescobaldi's pupil Froberger apparently was less fond of this type of fugue. In his ricercars from 1656 and 1658, he invariably employs only one subject which is augmented, diminished, or rhythmically varied. Frescobaldi's technique, the fugue that combines one or more subjects without variation, we find mostly in the ricercars of the Viennese court organists, Alessandro Poglietti and Gottlieb Muffat—the latter a pupil of Johann Joseph Fux. This technique was also used in the ricercars by Nikolaus Adam Strunck, who came from Hamburg but composed in Vienna and Venice.[46] All three composers' works were dominated by a contrapuntal technique of intensification; augmentation, diminution, inversion, stretto, and the combination of several subjects lead to an increasingly dense texture.

It is striking that simple subjects of Frescobaldi's imitative compositions were practically ignored by later composers. An exception is an anonymous fugue in a manuscript from the Franciscan Pantaleon Roskovsky written in Budapest around 1750 (*H-Bn* Ms. mus. 749).[47] The anonymous author took the subject of the *Recercar cromaticho* from the *Fiori musicali*, but worked it out in a completely different way (see example 1).[48] In addition, the subject of the Fantasia III by Frescobaldi was used in slightly altered form by Gottlieb Muffat in his Ricercar IV (see example 2).

Example 1 Anon., fugue (*H-Bn* Ms. mus. 749)

Example 2 Subjects from Girolamo Frescobaldi, Fantasia III, and Gottlieb Muffat, Ricercar IV.

But the influence of Frescobaldi's ricercars does not appear to be limited to the keyboard music of his successors. One also finds some of his stylistic traits in eighteenth-century vocal compositions, especially in those of Johann Joseph Fux. It is evident that Fux used the *Fiori musicali* as a model for composition in the strict style,[49] since in some of his own *Offertoria pro Dominicis Adventus*,[50] the subjects and the technique of counterpoint show a certain relationship to Frescobaldi's ricercars and Kyrie versets. Thus we find in Fux's *a cappella* compositions more influences of Frescobaldi than of Palestrina's vocal style. A comparison between Palestrina's and Fux's *offertoria* on the one hand, and Fux's *offertoria* and Frescobaldi's imitative keyboard compositions on the other, will prove this thesis. While in Palestrina's settings the polyphonic and homophonic structures change, Fux prefers a strict imitation of subjects, which are similar to the subjects of Frescobaldi's ricercars (see example 3).[51]

The imitative piece of the second type, which consists of one single subject that is varied in several sections of the composition, is represented especially in Frescobaldi's *Capricci* of 1624. The number of sections, which differ markedly in meter and in compositional form, is considerable. The compositional technique is less strict than in the ricercars. Almost every section ends with a free, toccata-like interlude. There is more rhythmic difference among the subjects than among those of the

Example 3 Johann Joseph Fux, openings of offertories "Ad te Domine levavi" and "Benedixisti"

ricercars. Several subjects are based on melodies from popular songs or dances, as in the bassa fiamenga, spagnoletta, ruggiero, "or che mai rimena," girolmeta, or bergamasca, and these melodies, as well as those based on traditional hexachords or on simple cuckoo calls, are treated in very artistic ways.

The influence of Frescobaldi's capriccios is manifested in various ways in the works of later composers. The subjects were taken over and reworked; for example, the subject *"ut re mi fa sol la"* of Frescobaldi's first capriccio was employed by Froberger for the first of his fantasias.[52] Froberger also used one of the subjects from Frescobaldi's Capriccio VIII in his Capriccio VI (1658),[53] and Gottlieb Muffat used this same subject in his Ricercar XXXII.[54] The subject from Frescobaldi's Capriccio X we encounter in Froberger's Ricercar V (1658).[55] Several thematic affinities to Frescobaldi can be established in the works of Gottlieb Muffat. The motif of the *Cuccho* is reworked by Johann Kaspar Kerll in a capriccio,[56] and the theme of the Bergamasca was used not only by Buxtehude,[57] but also in the Quodlibet from the *Goldberg Variations* by J. S. Bach.

The manner of composition in the multisectioned capriccio, with variations of the subject and toccata-like interludes, is developed further, above all by Froberger, but also in a few programmatic pieces by Poglietti, and finally in the Canzona IX by Muffat, composed around 1730.[58] At the same time, one finds a strong affinity to this form of composition in northern Germany, in the works of Buxtehude, for instance in his Praeludium in G minor (BuxWV 150), which is in reality a capriccio with a toccata-like introduction. The last section, with the second variation of the subject, almost could have been composed by Frescobaldi. It is probably no coincidence that one can dispense almost completely with the pedal in this section of the composition. In this same way, Johann Sebastian Bach's *manualiter* toccatas show an affinity to Frescobaldi's capriccios.

Frescobaldi's influence on the keyboard music of North German composers, especially on Buxtehude and Reincken, proceeds in the first place from his capriccios, and less so from his toccatas.[59] The type of Frescobaldi toccata in the *stilus fantasticus* (without elaborate imitative sections) was developed further only in southern Germany. This type appears mostly in the compositions by Froberger, Kerll, Poglietti, Speth, Johann Krieger, Georg Muffat, and his son Gottlieb Muffat. The use of Frescobaldi as a model is particularly apparent in Gottlieb Muffat's music.

The tendency toward a more formal arrangement in larger sections and toward expansion of the imitative sections can be observed in the compositions of Froberger, Kerll, and Georg Muffat.[60] Although a French influence is also apparent in Georg Muffat's music, his son returned to Frescobaldi's idea of the fantasy-toccata. In the second half of the eighteenth century, we encounter similar pieces written by the Bohemian organists around Joseph Seger.[61]

Frescobaldi's works were evidently also used as models in the technique of variation, even though Frescobaldi certainly should not be considered the father of all baroque variation cycles, passacaglias, and ciacconas. His variations are related in their fantastic form to his toccatas. Differentiated and often bizarre rhythms; the avoidance of frequent, stereotyped musical changes; and a richly varying harmony are his particular characteristics. In this respect, one composer above all followed and further developed Frescobaldi's style: Alessandro Poglietti. I have already mentioned his ricercars, capriccios, and toccatas. Here let me add two variation works in which direct references to Frescobaldi are made: (1) the passacaglia in the "partita Ribellione d'Ungheria,"[62] in which Poglietti adopts Frescobaldi's Passacaglia in E minor from *Toccate I* (1637)[63] and develops it into a larger cycle of variations; (2) the "Aria Allemagna con alcuni Variazioni" from the cycle "Rossignolo" (1677)[64] in which there is not only dense contrapuntal movement but also diverse rhythmic forms and harmonic tension, such as were found during the seventeenth century only in Frescobaldi's variation sets.

In summary, Frescobaldi's printed works for keyboard instruments were known and disseminated north of the Alps, particularly in the German-speaking countries, as far as the Baltic Sea. They were used for pedagogical purposes well into the eighteenth century. Frescobaldi's compositions also served as models for the further development of certain genres of keyboard music. This was especially true of the toccatas in the *stilus fantasticus* and the ricercars in the *stilus gravis*, which were cherished in South German and Hapsburg territories until the late eighteenth century. It also was the case for the capriccios, which not only were further developed in the southern regions, but evidently were also used by North German organists as models for their toccatas with variation fugues. Finally, this special technique of variation was further pursued particularly at the Viennese court.

Froberger, Kerll, and especially Alessandro Poglietti and Gottlieb Muffat in Vienna were among those masters who carried on Frescobaldi's stylistic traditions. But the music of Dietrich Buxtehude from Lübeck also suggests stylistic influences from Frescobaldi. Finally, the compositions of Johann Sebastian Bach, especially the earlier toccatas, as well as the later works in the *stilus gravis*—i.e., the *Musical Offering* and the *Art of the Fugue*, may be considered the culmination of this tradition. Quite correctly, then, Ernst Ludwig Gerber, in his *Lexikon der Tonkünstler*, called Frescobaldi the "father of the true style of organ music."[65]

Notes

1. See Margarete Reimann, "Froberger," *Die Musik in Geschichte und Gegenwart*, vol. 4 (Kassel: Bärenreiter, 1955), cols. 982–93; Anthony Newcomb, "Frescobaldi," *The New Grove Dictionary of Music and Musicians* (London: Macmillan, 1980), 6:824–35.

2. See Friedrich W. Riedel, "Neue Mitteilungen zur Lebensgeschichte von Alessandro Poglietti und Johann Kaspar Kerll," *Archiv für Musikwissenschaft* 19–20 (1962–63): 124–42.

3. See Johann Kaspar Kerll, *Ausgewählte Werke des kurfürstlich bayerischen Hofkapellmeisters*, ed. Adolf Sandberger, Denkmäler der Tonkunst in Bayern, vol. 3 (Leipzig: Breitkopf und Härtel, 1901), xii; Albert C. Giebler, "Kerll," *The New Grove Dictionary* 9:874–76.

4. See Friedrich W. Riedel, "Poglietti," *MGG* 10 (1962), cols. 1368–72; and idem, "Poglietti," *The New Grove Dictionary* 15:19.

5. See Margarete Reimann, "Frescobaldi," *MGG* 4 (1955), cols. 912–26; George J. Buelow, "Froberger," *The New Grove Dictionary* 6:858–62.

6. See Friedrich W. Riedel, *Quellenkundliche Beiträge zur Geschichte der Musik für Tasteninstrumente in der zweiten Hälfte des 17. Jahrhunderts* (Kassel: Bärenreiter, 1960), 119 n. 18.

7. See Friedrich W. Riedel, *Das Musikarchiv im Minoritenkonvent zu Wien (Katalog des älteren Bestandes vor 1784)* (Kassel: International Association of Music Libraries, 1963), 56.

8. D-Bs Mus. Ms. 40316 (now in Krakow, Biblioteka Jaglielońska); see Lydia Schierning, *Die Überlieferung der deutschen Orgel- und Klaviermusik aus der ersten Hälfte des 17. Jahrhunderts* (Kassel: Bärenreiter, 1961), 55.

9. Robert Eitner and F. X. Haberl, Beilage to *Monatshefte für Musikgeschichte* 14–15 (1882–83); Riedel, *Quellenkundliche Beiträge*, 50–51.

10. Riedel, *Quellenkundliche Beiträge*, 51.

11. See Friedrich W. Riedel, "Das Musikalienrepertoire des Benediktinerstiftes Göttweig (Niederösterreich) um die Mitte des 17. Jahrhunderts," in *Translatio Studii: Manuscript and Library Studies Honoring Oliver L. Kapsner, O.S.B.*, ed. Julian G. Plante (Collegeville, Minnesota: St. John's University Press, 1973), 149–55.

12. See Riedel, *Quellenkundliche Beiträge*, 120.

13. See Johann Gottfried Walther, *Musicalisches Lexikon* (Leipzig: Wolffgang Deer, 1732), fol. 5v (Vorbericht).

14. *D-B* Mus. Ms. 40615.

15. *A-Wn* Cod. 19231.

16. *A-Wm* Musikarchiv XIV 694.

17. *D-B* Mus. Ms. 6611.

18. *D-B* Mus. Ms. 6615.

19. See Riedel, *Quellenkundliche Beiträge*, 55 n. 66.

20. The manuscript, formerly in the library of the Hochschule für Musik in Berlin, has been lost since World War II; see Christoph Wolff, *Der Stile antico in der Musik Johann Sebastian Bachs: Studien zu Bachs Spätwerk* (Wiesbaden: Steiner, 1968), 26–27.

21. *D-B* Mus. Ms. 6610.

22. See Friedrich W. Riedel, "Ein Skizzenbuch von Alessandro Poglietti," in *Essays in Musicology: A Birthday Offering for Willi Apel*, ed. Hans Tischler (Bloomington: School of Music, Indiana University, 1968), 145–52.

23. *A-Wm* Musikarchiv XIV 725 (see Riedel, *Das Musikarchiv*, 80).

24. *D-LEm* II.2.51.

25. See Riedel, *Quellenkundliche Beiträge*, 120.

26. The copy in Hamburg, Staats- und Universitätsbibliothek, was destroyed during World War II.

27. See *RISM A/I/3: Einzeldrücke vor 1800* (Kassel: Bärenreiter, 1972), 3:115.

28. *A-Wm*, Musikarchiv XIV 714 (see Riedel, *Das Musikarchiv*, 80). The manuscript also contains Toccata VI from *Toccate I*.

29. See Riedel, *Quellenkundliche Beiträge*, 106; and idem, "Musikalische Darstellungen der Türkenbelagerung Wiens im Jahre 1683," in *Festschrift Othmar Wessely zum 60. Geburtstag* (Tutzing: Schneider, 1982), 457–83.

30. See Riedel, *Quellenkundliche Beiträge*, 91; and Hans Schmid, "Una nuova fonte di musica organistica del secolo XVII," *L'Organo* 1 (1960): 107–13 (manuscript from the Benedictine Abbey at Neresheim).

31. See Emil Katz, "Die Stilbegriffe des 17. Jahrhunderts" (Ph.D. diss., Freiburg, 1926); and Riedel, *Quellenkundliche Beiträge*, 23–26.

32. Riedel, *Quellenkundliche Beiträge*, 34.

33. *A-Wm* Musikarchiv XIV 725 (see Riedel, *Das Musikarchiv*, 77–80).

34. *A-Wm* Musikarchiv XIV 717–22 (see Riedel, *Das Musikarchiv*, 73–75).

35. *A-Wm* Musikarchiv XIV 723 (see Riedel, *Das Musikarchiv*, 76).

36. Muzio Clementi, *Selection of Practical Harmony* (London: Clementi, 1811–15); see Giacomo Benvenuti, "Noterella circa tre fughe, attribuite al Frescobaldi," *Rivista musicale italiana* 27 (1920): 139; and Josef Hedar, *Dietrich Buxtehudes Orgelwerke* (Stockholm: Nordiska Musikförlaget, 1951), 141–42 n. 28.

37. See Riedel, *Quellenkundliche Beiträge*, 58–72.

38. See Friedrich W. Riedel, "Der Einfluss der italienischen Klaviermusik des 17. Jahrhunderts auf die Entwicklung der Musik für Tasteninstrumente in Deutschland während der ersten Hälfte des 18. Jahrhunderts," *Analecta Musicologica* 5 (1968): 18–33.

39. In his "Advertissement" Roberday says that one fugue in his collection was composed by "Frescobaldy," but it is impossible to identify this piece; see François Roberday, *Fugues et Caprices pour orgue*, ed. Jean Ferrard, Le Pûpitre 44 (Paris: Heugel, 1972).

40. Contains the *Recercar Cromaticho post il Credo* from the *Messa delli Apostoli* in *Fiori musicali* (1635).

41. See Warren Kirkendale, *Fuge und Fugato in der Kammermusik des Rokoko und der Klassik* (Tutzing: Schneider, 1966); 2d ed., trans. Margaret Bent and the author, *Fugue and Fugato in Rococo and Classical Chamber Music* (Durham, N.C.: Duke University Press, 1979).

42. K. 404a, 405.

43. *D-B* Mus. Ms. 6616.

44. *5 Fugen für 2 Violinen, Viola und Violoncello. Entnommen aus der 'Auswahl vorzüglicher Musik-Werke in gebundener Schreibart von Meistern alter und neuer Zeit,"* Nr. V. Frescobaldi, 14. Lieferung (Berlin: T. Trautwein, ca. 1830), no. 42.

45. See Friedrich W. Riedel, "Die zyklische Fugenkomposition von Froberger bis Albrechtsberger," *Die süddeutsch-österreichische Orgelmusik im 17. und 18. Jahrhundert*, ed. Walter Salmen (Innsbruck: Musikverlag Helbling, 1980), 151–67.

46. See Fritz Berend, "Nikolaus Adam Strunck 1640–1700: Sein Leben und seine Werke" (Ph.D. diss., Munich, 1913); Riedel, *Quellenkundliche Beiträge*, 184–88.

47. See Johann Joseph Fux, *Werke für Tasteninstrumente*, ed. Friedrich W. Riedel, Fux-Gesamtausgabe VI/I (Kassel: Bärenreiter, 1964), 67–69.

48. I wish to thank Prof. Peter Widensky, of Vienna, who sent me a transcription of this fugue.

49. See Friedrich W. Riedel, "Johann Joseph Fux und die römische Palestrina-Tradition," *Die Musikforschung* 14 (1961): 14–22.

50. Johann Joseph Fux, *Motetten*, ed. Johannes Evangelist Habert, Denkmäler der Tonkunst in Österreich, vol. 3 (Vienna: Breitkopf und Härtel, 1895).

51. See Karl Gustav Fellerer, *Der Palastrinastil und seine Bedeutung in der vokalen Kirchenmusik des 18. Jahrhunderts* (Augsburg: Filser, 1929), 121–25.

52. Johann Jakob Froberger, *Orgel- und Klavierwerke I*, ed. Guido Adler, Denkmäler der Tonkunst in Österreich, vol. 8 (Vienna: Breitkopf und Härtel, 1897), 33–37.

53. Johann Jakob Froberger, *Orgel- und Klavierwerke III*, ed. Guido Adler, Denkmaler der Tonkunst in Österreich, vol. 21 (Vienna: Breitkopf und Härtel, 1903), 74–76 (Capriccio XVII).

54. *A-Wm* Musikarchiv XIV 712, p. 111.

55. Froberger, *Orgel- und Klavierwerke III*, 92–94 (Ricercar XI).

56. Kerll, *Ausgewählte Werke*, 38–46.

57. Dietrich Buxtehude, *Sämtliche Suiten und Variationen für Klavier/Cembalo*, ed. Klaus Beckmann (Wiesbaden: Breitkopf und Härtel, 1980), 88–101 (Aria: "La Capricciosa").

58. Gottlieb Muffat, *Toccata, Fuge und Capriccio*, ed. Friedrich W. Riedel, Die Orgel II/8 (Lippstadt: Kistner und Siegel, 1958), 5–13.

59. Therefore, I cannot agree with Josef Hedar's opinion about the fundamental importance of Frescobaldi's toccatas for the development of the North German baroque toccata (*Dietrich Buxtehudes Orgelwerke*, 132).

60. See Riedel, "Einfluss der italienischen Klaviermusik," 23–26.

61. Josef Ferdinand Norbert Seger, *Composizioni per organo*, ed. Jan Racek, Musica Antiqua Bohemica, vol. 51 (Prague: Státní Hudební Vydavatelství, 1961).

62. Hugo Botstiber, ed., *Wiener Klavier- und Orgelwerke*, Denkmäler der Tonkunst in Österreich, vol. 27 (Vienna: Breitkopf und Härtel, 1906), 35–36.

63. Girolamo Frescobaldi, *Il primo libro di toccate d'intavolatura di cembalo e organo 1615–1637*, ed. Etienne Darbellay (Milan: Zerboni, 1977), 89; see Hedar, *Dietrich Buxtehudes Orgelwerke*, 67–68.

64. Botstiber, *Wiener Klavier- und Orgelwerke*, 13–22.

65. Ernst Ludwig Gerber, *Neues historisch-biographisches Lexikon der Tonkünstler, I. Theil (1812)* (reprint, Graz: Akademische Druck- u. Verlagsanstalt, 1966), col. 193.

Frescobaldi's Instrumental Music: Compositional Procedures and Rhetoric

U NDOUBTEDLY THE MOST interesting but also in some ways the most difficult issues for the Frescobaldi student concern the composer's own music. James Ladewig combines historical and analytical approaches in his study of the canzona—a genre that played a large role in Frescobaldi's work and occupied him throughout his life. From a survey of the early canzona repertory he observes that the composer's sophisticated treatment of the variation canzona is almost without precedent, but he then proceeds to demonstrate by means of a detailed analysis that a clear model can be found in a canzona by Ercole Pasquini.

There is perhaps no better laboratory to study the development of a composer's musical thinking than his revisions of his own earlier works, especially when such revisions involve substantial recomposition. For earlier composers, such revisions rarely have survived; we are therefore fortunate to possess successive versions of unquestionable authenticity of some of Frescobaldi's works. John Harper guides us through the complex reorganizations and recompositions in the several editions of the ensemble canzonas; he is able to trace one canzona through four different guises (including an early keyboard version), spanning a period of nearly twenty years. He demonstrates the composer's increasing concern with the cohesion and integrity of the entire composition, and also the increasing sophistication of the tonal planning.

Emilia Fadini points to the significance of rhetorical traditions in

Frescobaldi's compositional approach, and emphasizes the value of understanding these traditions to the performer of his works. She illustrates her ideas with an analysis of a segment of one of the toccatas in terms of rhetorical concepts, and brings to this analysis her insights as one of Italy's foremost interpreters of his music.

The Origins of Frescobaldi's Variation
Canzonas Reappraised

JAMES LADEWIG

RESCOBALDI'S VARIATION CANZONAS for keyboard represent a high point of his art and one of his most significant contributions to the emerging baroque style. Yet we know little of the impulses that inspired Frescobaldi to create the finest masterpieces in this genre. Nearly half a century ago, Willi Apel set forth the theory that two Neapolitans, Giovanni Maria Trabaci and Ascanio Mayone, directly influenced Frescobaldi.[1] One of Apel's crucial pieces of evidence was their cultivation of the variation canzona during the first decade of the seventeenth century, just prior to Frescobaldi's first essays in the form. Apel, however, was unaware of a number of composers whose keyboard variation canzonas predate those of Trabaci and Mayone. We may now identify not only an earlier generation of Neapolitans, including Fabrizio Filomarino, Carlo Gesualdo, Rinaldo dall'Arpa, Scipione Stella, and their *caposcuola* from Flanders via Rome, Giovanni de Macque, but also two important masters of the Ferrarese keyboard style, Ercole Pasquini and "Giaches" (either Giaches de Wert or Jacques Brumel; see p. 244, below), all of whom composed variation canzonas.[2] Thus we have a much wider circle of composers among whom to search for the roots of Frescobaldi's variation canzonas, and besides Neapolitans, this circle includes musicians associated with his native Ferrara, where Frescobaldi spent his crucial student years and first gained renown as a keyboard prodigy.

At the end of the sixteenth century, Ferrara was celebrated not only for its madrigals and singing ladies,[3] but also as an important center of keyboard composition. Even as late as 1669, Ferrarese organists such as Luigi Battiferri looked back nostalgically upon this period as the golden age of keyboard music in Ferrara.[4] Our understanding of this facet of the city's musical life had long been hampered by the loss of nearly the entire corpus of Ferrarese keyboard music, with the exception of a canzona by Pasquini and two ricercars and a toccata by Luzzasco Luzzaschi,[5] the leading composer at court and Frescobaldi's teacher. But the recovery over the last two-and-a-half decades of nearly sixty keyboard works by Luzzaschi,[6] Pasquini, and "Giaches" allows us to appraise the influence of Ferrarese music, versus that of Neapolitan music, on the development of Frescobaldi's style in general and on his variation canzonas in particular.

It is no coincidence that virtually all the composers of keyboard variation canzonas before Frescobaldi were associated with either Naples or Ferrara,[7] for at the end of the century these two cities enjoyed close musical ties. The most famous meeting of Neapolitan and Ferrarese musicians occurred during 1594–96, when Carlo Gesualdo traveled to Ferrara to marry Leonora d'Este, cousin of Duke Alfonso II, and remained in residence there for two years. The musical significance of the coming-together of the courts of the two most melomaniacal noblemen in all Italy had been virtually unexplored until the appearance in 1968 of Anthony Newcomb's documentary study on Gesualdo in Ferrara.[8] Newcomb translates and examines a series of eight letters written to Duke Alfonso from the Ferrarese madrigal composer Alfonso Fontanelli, whom the former had assigned to accompany Gesualdo on his travels during 1594.[9]

The most important discovery that arises from these letters regarding the musical relationship between Naples and Ferrara is that Gesualdo greatly admired Ferrarese music, particularly that of Luzzaschi. In one letter Fontanelli tells the Duke, "[Gesualdo] exalts Ferrara and things Ferrarese incessantly. This morning especially, he spoke extremely enthusiastically about the music-making of your ladies."[10] In another letter he relates that "[Gesualdo] says that he has abandoned his first style and has begun to imitate Luzzaschi, whom he admires greatly and praises constantly."[11] In a third letter we catch a glimpse of the belligerent side of Gesualdo's personality: "Meanwhile, the Prince has been composing continually and, just having put together two new madrigals, he says that he intends to come to Ferrara surrounded by such thick fortifications of works (these were the terms he used) that he will be able to defend himself against Luzzaschi. This latter is the only enemy he fears, he says; the others he laughs at."[12] Luzzaschi was apparently undaunted by the pugnacious overtones in Gesualdo's admiration, for he reciprocated by dedicating to the prince his fourth book of madrigals in five voices (1594).[13]

Gesualdo's respect for Luzzaschi was felt, furthermore, by Neapolitan musicians in general. Fontanelli writes in two letters,

> Meanwhile I find that the fame of your ladies is very great [in Naples] and that the name of Luzzaschi has such great renown that everyone who is trying to glorify his own position declares himself his imitator. He is truly of universal fame.[14]

> I had forgotten to say that Luzzaschi has such a reputation here that, as much as I beg to hear new works, everyone wants to hear things by him, whom they name as the master.[15]

Newcomb points out that Luzzaschi's fame had been high in Naples as early as 1582, as is shown by a letter to Duke Alfonso from Count Ercole Estense Tassone, Jr., the son of a Ferrarese nobleman who was then visiting Naples: "[The Neapolitans] say they have no worthy musicians, and hold Signor Luzzaschi in such esteem and venerate him so that no other musician, I suspect, has ever had such a reputation as he in this state. Being Ferrarese, it has been very difficult for me to get people to sing at all, since they feel that anyone who has heard the compositions of Luzzaschi must hold all others in contempt."[16]

From Fontanelli's correspondence we learn that Gesualdo did not visit Ferrara alone, but came with an entourage of Neapolitan musicians who shared his reverence for Ferrara and for Luzzaschi. Fontanelli relates that one of these men, Fabrizio Filomarino, "says that he would not die content if he had not spent at least six months under the discipline of Luzzaschi."[17] Two other musicians are also mentioned as members of Gesualdo's retinue: Scipione Stella and Rinaldo [dall'Arpa].[18]

The variation canzonas of these Neapolitans who visited Ferrara typify the early stage of the genre in that they apply rhythmic but not melodic variation to the subjects. (A variation canzona may be defined as one that exhibits a sectional form with passages in contrasting duple and triple meters and that presents rhythmic and/or melodic variants of one or more subjects in at least two of the sections.)[19] One variation canzona each for Filomarino, Rinaldo dall'Arpa, and Gesualdo survives in *GB-Lbl* Add. Ms. 30491.[20] Although the problems concerning the dating and authorship of this manuscript are very complex, the most recent research holds that it was probably compiled by Luigi Rossi over a long period beginning sometime after 1610.[21] A poem inscribed in cipher code at the beginning seems to suggest that Rossi compiled the manuscript as an homage to his teacher, Giovanni de Macque, the most eminent composer employed at the court of Gesualdo. Of the eight composers represented in the keyboard portion of the manuscript—Filomarino, Gesualdo, Francesco Lambardo, Macque, Rinaldo dall'Arpa, Stella, Ippolito Tartaglino, and Trabaci—all worked in Naples, and many are known to have been connected with Gesualdo. Although Rossi probably began the manuscript sometime during the second decade of the seventeenth century, the variation canzonas, as well as many of the other keyboard pieces, were likely composed a number of years earlier.[22]

Filomarino's "Canzon Cromatica"[23] makes only a trial attempt at the variation canzona. It exhibits one of the two most common formal patterns of the genre: it is divided into five sections, of which the second and fourth are in triple meter. (The other pattern consists of three sections, with the second in triple meter.) But no single subject unifies all the sections as in many other variation canzonas (see example 1). The opening two sections rhythmically vary the popular chromatic fourth in its ascending form, which is here distinctively contorted by an *inganno*.[24] In

Example 1   Filomarino, "Canzon Cromatica," subjects

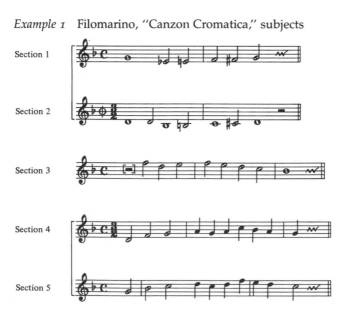

an *inganno* (deception or trick), the solmization syllables of a subject are retained, but a portion of the subject mutates to a different hexachord, thus altering its melodic shape.[25] The first note should be d' (*re* in the natural hexachord), but it has been replaced by g' (*re* in the soft hexachord). This subject points forward to other chromatic subjects contorted by *inganni* such as that of Frescobaldi's "Recercar cromaticho" in the *Fiori musicali*.[26] A more conventional subject unifies the last two sections.

The "Canzon"[27] by Rinaldo dall'Arpa displays, in contrast, a consistent application of variation. A single subject in various rhythmic guises unifies all sections of the canzona (example 2).[28] In the homophonic, triple-meter opening,[29] the subject is at first intentionally hidden away in the alto, but the soprano takes it over immediately and openly states it twice. The three sections of the canzona exhibit an unconventional triple-duple-triple pattern. Rinaldo makes an important attempt at formal expansion by dividing both the first and second sections into two subsections, each of which presents its own rhythmic variation of the subject. Thus the main subject appears in five different versions.

The most remarkable composition in the manuscript is without doubt the "Canzon francese del Principe."[30] If Rossi indeed compiled the entire

Example 2 Rinaldo dall'Arpa, "Canzon," variants

manuscript, the author of this canzona must certainly be Gesualdo. This piece—the only surviving keyboard work attributable to Gesualdo—is famous chiefly for the virtuosic, cadenza-like embellishments which function as alternative versions of the cadences. It is equally notable for the subtlety and playful diversity of the rhythmic variants of its main subject (see example 3). Gesualdo's work is unusual among variation canzonas in that it is in duple meter throughout, and it seems not to have served as a model for any later variation canzonas. (It may be included in the present study because the quasi-cadenzas divide it into a series of discrete sections, each presenting a new variant.) Many of the scholars who have discussed this piece suggest that it may be based on a vocal model, though none gives evidence to support such a hypothesis.[31] It seems to me, however, to be entirely instrumental in conception. Indeed, this piece resembles a ricercar more than a canzona, as is seen in the melodic character of the subject, the moderate tempo necessitated by the florid ornamentation, and the lack of a triple-meter section. Could the unornamented version of this composition be one of Gesualdo's three ensemble ricercars which Macque included in his 1586 publication of *Ricercate et canzoni francesi*? Verification of this hypothesis must wait until the sole surviving tenor partbook of Macque's publication becomes available to scholars.[32]

Rossi's inclusion of so many variation canzonas in *GB-Lbl* Add. Ms. 30491 suggests that his teacher Macque, in whose honor he apparently

Example 3   Gesualdo, "Canzon francese del Principe," rhythmic variants

compiled the manuscript, played an important role in the development of the genre. Indeed, three of Macque's keyboard works employ variation, and much documentary evidence connects him intimately with the musical establishments of both Ferrara and Naples in which the variation canzona was being cultivated. Although he worked mainly in Rome prior to 1585, Macque had also achieved a reputation in Ferrara and contributed to the two Ferrarese madrigal anthologies in honor of the famous soprano Laura Peverara, *Il lauro secco* (1582) and *Il lauro verde* (1583). He was not soon forgotten at the Este court; as late as 1597 the ducal printer Baldini issued his third book of madrigals for five voices. In 1585 Macque moved from Rome to Naples and entered the service of Fabrizio Gesualdo, Carlo's father. During that same year Macque made public his musical respect for his patron's son, not only by dedicating the above-mentioned book of *Ricercate et canzoni francesi* to Carlo Gesualdo, but also by including in it three of the prince's ricercars. Subsequent dedications by Macque include the second book of madrigals for five voices (1587) to Don Cesare d'Avalos, father of Gesualdo's ill-fated first wife Maria d'Avalos, and the second book of madrigals for six voices (1589) to Fabrizio Gesualdo.

Compared to the handful of known compositions by other keyboard composers active in Naples during the 1580s and 1590s (largely those surviving in *GB-Lbl* Add. Ms. 30491), Macque's music has fared well over the centuries. Thirty-five of his keyboard pieces are extant in one printed anthology and five manuscripts.[33] The three pieces that exhibit variation are the "Capriccio sopra un sogetto" in *I-Nc* Ms. 73,[34] the *Seconda parte* of the "Canzon chiamate le due Sorelle" in *GB-Lbl* Add. Ms. 30491,[35] and the eleventh ricercar ("Undecimo tono") from *I-Fn* Ms. 106bis.[36] The "Capriccio sopra un sogetto" displays a variation technique more exhaustive than that of any other composer in Gesualdo's circle. In addition to introducing a new variant with each change of meter, Macque continues to transform the subject within the sections, as is strikingly seen in the opening duple-meter passage (example 4). Despite the great diversity of rhythmic variations—ranging from strict diminution and augmentation to a multitude of free transformations—Macque alters the melodic shape of the subject only in two brief passages of strict inversion. He further demonstrates his mastery of the form by spinning out the entire four-voiced texture with virtually nothing but these varied state-

Example 4   Macque, "Capriccio sopra un sogetto," variants

ments of the subject, so that free counterpoint hardly appears at all. The piece thus abounds with presentations of the subject in stretto and in parallel thirds and tenths. The "Canzon chiamate le due Sorelle" is unusual in that it is actually a pair of adjoining but separate canzonas, presumably intended to represent two sisters. Yet its treatment of variation remains rudimentary and occurs only within the *Seconda parte*. The subject appears in the most naive rhythmic variations in each of the three sections, which are in the typical duple-triple-duple form. In contrast to the "Capriccio sopra un sogetto," this piece rarely presents the subject in counterpoint with itself, and Macque leaves the task of providing musical interest to the accompanying voices with their thematically unrelated and trite division-style ornamentation. Macque's "[Ricercar] Undecimo tono" belongs to a small group of ricercars that contain a middle section in triple meter in the manner of a canzona. It presents not one but three subjects, each of which is varied rhythmically in the triple-meter section and then returns in its original form in the concluding section (example 5). This piece is closely akin to the "Capriccio sopra un sogetto"; the subjects appear in the greatest possible variety of contrapuntal combinations, and nearly the entire four-voiced texture derives from thematic material, so that free counterpoint is all but absent. Indeed, many of the twelve ricercars in *I-Fn* Ms. 106bis resemble the capriccio in their great diversity of rhythmic variations.[37] But the eleventh ricercar is the only one that transforms the subjects into triple meter in the manner of a variation canzona. Macque shows in each of these three variation pieces little interest in altering the melodic shape of his subjects. In this respect, he reveals his affinity with Gesualdo and his fellow Neapolitan composers who traveled to Ferrara in 1594–96.

Scipione Stella, the other Neapolitan composer who visited Ferrara with Gesualdo, Filomarino, and Rinaldo dall'Arpa, is represented in *GB-Lbl* Add. Ms. 30491 by two polythematic keyboard canzonas.[38] Four little-known canzonas also survive in *I-Nc* Ms. 55, and the second of these employs variation.[39] This manuscript comprises a set of four partbooks for ensemble. Stella's fame as an organist and harpsichordist is well documented,[40] and at least the second canzona may have been originally intended for keyboard, because near the beginning of the

Example 5 Macque, "[Ricercar] Undecimo tono," subjects and variants

Subject 1

Subject 2

Subject 3

third section a rising scalar line passes in turn through the four voices in a manner typical of keyboard writing (example 6).[41] This canzona employs four subjects, which are stated in order by every voice in the opening point of imitation (example 7). In unifying the three sections, Stella restricts himself to rhythmic variations of the subjects (except for a few necessary tonal adjustments in their answers). Toward the end of the last section, each of the four subjects returns in its original form. The piece bears an unmistakable resemblance to Macque's "Capriccio sopra un sogetto" and "[Ricercar] Undecimo tono" by deriving virtually all its material from the subjects.

In Ferrara, Ercole Pasquini and a certain "Giaches" were also pursuing the variation canzona. Four fantasias[42] for keyboard attributed merely to "Giaches" in *I-Rvat* Ms. Chigi Q.VIII.206, fasc. 41, fols. 156r–167r, came to light in the 1960s.[43] Scholars had generally come to agree that they were by Giaches de Wert[44] rather than the midcentury Ferrarese organist Jacques Brumel, but Anthony Newcomb's essay in the present volume

Example 6　Stella, "[Canzona] seconda," excerpt

Example 7　Stella, subjects and variants

raises the controversy anew by favoring Brumel and by attributing to the same composer ten similar ricercars in *F-Pn* Rés. Vma. Ms. 851. No matter which composer may be the author, the musical style of these pieces strongly suggests a close connection with Ferrarese keyboard music, since the works share with Luzzaschi's ricercars many salient characteristics: a strict, vocally conceived contrapuntal texture, an absence of idiomatic keyboard figuration, subtle thematic interrelationships among the subjects, and fondness for the inversion ricercar.[45]

Of the four fantasias specifically attributed to "Giaches" in *I-Rvat* Ms. Chigi 206, the one on *la sol fa re mi*[46] includes a triple-meter passage in which this solmization subject is treated in the manner of a variation canzona. It thus represents another hybrid piece along the lines of Macque's eleventh ricercar. Like the composers of Gesualdo's circle, "Giaches" virtually ignores melodic variation in this piece with the exception of some *inganni* of the subject, which are especially prominent in the triple-meter section. But he surpasses all the Neapolitan variation canzonas, even Macque's "Capriccio sopra un sogetto," with the endless variety of rhythmic configurations—over forty in all—which he applies to this venerable subject (see example 8). Straightaway in the opening point of imitation, each voice enters with a different rhythmic variant, starting with a boldly syncopated statement in the tenor.[47] "Giaches" achieves a sense of long-range direction in this lengthy and ever-changing piece by introducing augmentation in breves one-third of the way through, and then in longas at the two-thirds mark (see example 9). Like the cresting of a wave, the augmentations break into a flurry of rhythmic activity in the triple-meter passage. This is followed by a brief, subdued duple-meter conclusion in which most statements of the subject appear in a single, broadly paced variant.[48]

If "Giaches's" fantasia-ricercars provide a tantalizing glimpse of the role variation played in the keyboard music of Ferrara during the generation or two before Frescobaldi, the compositions of Ercole Pasquini afford a broader vantage point from which to assess more clearly the direct influence of the Ferrarese variation canzona on the young composer. Nine canzonas by Pasquini survive, and six of them employ variation. In mere numbers, these nearly equal the surviving variation pieces by all the previously discussed Neapolitans.

Pasquini had long been known as the composer of only a handful of

Example 8 "Giaches," "Fantasia" [sopra *la sol fa re mi*], selected rhythmic variants

Example 9   "Giaches," formal outline

madrigals and motets in contemporary anthologies and a single key-board canzona reprinted by Torchi.[49] There has been growing interest in him since the discovery during the early 1960s of about thirty keyboard pieces in manuscripts.[50] Alexander Silbiger, in his study of seventeenth-century Italian keyboard manuscripts, concludes that "although Fresco-baldi's dominating role in 17th-century keyboard music remains uncon-tested, a second composer, Ercole Pasquini, emerges from the manu-scripts as having generated much interest among musicians of the period."[51]

Pasquini is doubly important because his career almost mirrored that of Frescobaldi, even though he was at least a generation older.[52] Battiferri includes Pasquini's name among those of Luzzaschi, [Alessandro] Milleville, and Frescobaldi as the great organists of Ferrara (see n. 4), and posthumous accounts attest to the brilliance of his organ playing. Superbi said of him, "He had a most delicate and quick hand; he played so excellently sometimes, that he enraptured the audience and truly amazed them."[53] Pietro Della Valle's statement, "Was not there an Ercole of great fame in St. Peter's? a Frescobaldi who is alive today . . . ?"[54] has been mistakenly interpreted as calling Frescobaldi a "Hercules,"[55] but the "Ercole of great fame" is certainly none other than Pasquini.

Of Pasquini's six variation canzonas, one stands out because of the thoroughness and subtlety with which it develops its thematic material: no. 16 in Shindle's edition[56] (example 10). Not surprisingly, this canzona appears to have been Pasquini's most widely disseminated keyboard composition, surviving in six manuscript sources.[57] This is extraordinary not only for Pasquini, but for any Italian composer of the time. As Silbiger has noted, no other Italian sixteenth- or seventeenth-century keyboard work comes down to us solely in so many manuscript concordances.[58] Amazingly, the renown of this canzona lasted well into the eighteenth century, as its presence in *I-Rsc* Ms. A/400 indicates. Considering the work's extraordinary popularity and that Frescobaldi obviously knew Pasquini personally, the conclusion is inescapable that Frescobaldi was well acquainted with this canzona.

This piece deserves close examination, for in it there begin to appear the truly flexible techniques for achieving thematic unity that are the hallmarks of the mature variation canzona as practiced by Frescobaldi. Melodic variation at last assumes a role on a par with rhythmic variation,

Example 10   Ercole Pasquini, "Canzona franzese" (*I-Nc* Ms. 48)

1. Mm. 3–5, left hand is notated a third higher in manuscript.

2. g′ in manuscript.

3. a' in manuscript.

4. b′ and c″ are semifusae in manuscript.

Editorial lines have been added between the staves to clarify the voice-leading of the inner parts.

Example 11   Pasquini, variants

and the melodic transformations are now imaginative and free rather than restricted to rigid devices such as inversion and *inganni*. Most important, the variations unfold from beginning to end in a carefully calculated, progressive manner which endows the piece with a new, more elevated sense of musical unity.

Pasquini's concise canzona is divided into three sections, each of which presents a variation of the subject (see example 11). In spinning out these variants, Pasquini gives each of the three sections its own coherent internal shape, an important element in achieving the above-mentioned sense of unity. The first section itself divides into three subsections (mm. 1–16, 16–22, and 23–29). It opens with a spacious exposition in which the subject enters every two or three measures. In m. 16, the pace quickens with entries in stretto every one or two measures. In the third, coda-like subsection, a short motive from the middle of the countersubject (the second through fifth eighth notes in the right hand of m. 4) enters every half-measure, often in parallel tenths. The entire passage closes as the tenor and soprano present, over a dominant pedal, a compressed version of the main subject in stretto at the quarter note. The methodical shortening of the interval between subject entries, from two- and three-measure intervals at the beginning down to a quarter note in the last stretto, imparts a clear sense of forward motion and unity to the opening section. A similar cumulative design binds together the triple- meter section, but here it is achieved by increasing complexity in the contrapuntal texture. While the entries are spaced consistently one mea- sure apart within the points of imitation, more voices enter in each successive point, thus producing increasingly dense textures. The first and second points contain two entries each (mm. 30–31 and 34–35); the third, three (mm. 39–41); and the last, five (mm. 43–47). The height- ened intricacy of the last two points derives as well from entrances on pitches other than A and E (*la* in the natural and hard hexachords). The growing energy of this section is expended in a broad, homophonic half-cadence in duple time (mm. 48–50) which should be arpeggiated by the performer following Frescobaldi's advice, "non lasciar v[u]oto l'Istromento."[59] In the short but intense concluding duple-meter section (which begins with the last three eighth notes of m. 50), Pasquini again effectively builds and releases tension. A short motive outlining in skele- tal fashion the shape of the subject enters in stretto every half-measure (mm. 50–55).[60] The rhythmic pace quickens at m. 55 as a free diminution of the motive appears in pseudo-stretto, first in the left hand and then in parallel tenths between the hands, before dissolving into a rapid flurry of nonthematic sixteenth notes over an elaborated dominant harmony. Rather than being an extraneous bit of virtuosity, this closing toccata-like flourish culminates and resolves the rhythmic energy which has built up steadily throughout the canzona.

Just as each individual section builds to its own climax, so the canzona from beginning to end is propelled forward by the contracting shape of the subject. The passing notes that fill in the diminished fourth are omitted in the triple-meter variation, creating a more compact and boldly angular version of the subject. In the last section, the initial repeated notes disappear, and the subject's underlying contour of two interlock- ing fourths is condensed into the span of four eighth notes. Thus through- out the canzona the variants approach a quicker, ever more telegraphic shape. This new principle of melodic variation through simplification and compression distinguishes Pasquini's piece from other variation canzonas of the time and will play an important role in the canzonas of Frescobaldi.

The two Neapolitans who continued to pursue the variation canzona throughout the first decade-and-a-half of the seventeenth century were Giovanni Maria Trabaci and Ascanio Mayone. They are today the best-known Neapolitan keyboard composers, principally because their keyboard music was printed.[61] The first volume of each composer appeared just five years before Frescobaldi's *Fantasie* of 1608. Mayone's second book dates from 1609, and Trabaci's from 1615. All except the 1615 book of Trabaci contain variation canzonas, as well as a cross-section of the important Italian keyboard genres of the day.[62] Trabaci and Mayone were pupils and protégés of Macque, and their keyboard output shows many stylistic similarities to that of their teacher.[63] Especially Trabaci in his first book seems to model a number of works directly after pieces by Macque.[64] Although there remains no documented connection between Trabaci or Mayone and the Gesualdo court, both young composers were certainly well acquainted with Gesualdo, Rinaldo, Filomarino, Stella, and their music.[65]

Half of Mayone's eight canzonas employ variation.[66] Trabaci uses it in four of his seven canzonas,[67] and, like Macque, he extends the principle to related contrapuntal genres such as the ricercar and capriccio.[68] As with Pasquini, we shall single out the most intensive essay of these two composers in the genre: Trabaci's "Canzona franzesa sesta" of 1603.[69]

This piece is the earliest example of a canzona in five sections in which one subject is consistently varied throughout. It thus holds an important position as the forerunner of a number of Frescobaldi's variation canzonas. Here, as in all his variation canzonas, Trabaci follows the earlier Neapolitans in changing only the rhythm of the subject. But he surpasses them by striving to create the maximum rhythmic variety possible among the sections. After the initial downbeat of the subject and first variant (S_1 and S_2 respectively; see example 12), he precisely reverses the notes on which the strong and weak beats fall. S_3 likewise tends to turn the weak notes of S_1 into strong ones, though not quite so meticulously as did S_2.[70] This duple-meter variation is quicker and rhythmically more "square" than the original. The long, accented F resolving to E, one of the main subject's most expressive characteristics, becomes a short, unaccented note in both S_2 and S_3 to avoid its association with the Phrygian cadence so much exploited in the opening section.

Example 12 Trabaci, "Canzona franzesa sesta" (1603), subjects and counter-subjects

Example 13 Trabaci, formal outline

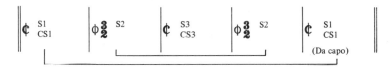

The five sections of this piece follow an arch-form unusual in the canzona repertoire (see example 13). The final section is a literal *da capo* of the opening, except for a short, toccata-like flourish added over the dominant harmony of the final cadence. Similar repetitions occur in a few other canzonas of Trabaci and Mayone[71] and are perhaps a vestige of the genre's derivation from the French chanson. Trabaci extends the symmetry by using a common variant in the flanking triple-meter sections, though he completely recomposes the accompanying material. He further highlights the arch-form by adding countersubjects to the opening, central, and closing duple-meter sections.[72] This technique of employing quick, motivic countersubjects that contrast with the expansive subject would later be exploited by Frescobaldi in his canzonas. Despite his innovations in this canzona, Trabaci looks backward to the previous generation in the avoidance of melodic variation and in his restatement of the opening section at the end,[73] which seems quaintly anticlimactic in comparison to Pasquini's progressive view of the variation canzona.

The variation canzona reached its artistic high point in the works of Frescobaldi. More than any other genre, the canzona absorbed Frescobaldi's energies throughout his entire career. The variation canzona in particular must have kindled his highest creative skills with the basic compositional problem it poses: to create an abstract musical form with a perfect balance of variety on the surface and unity underneath. The epitome of his work in the genre is the "Canzon seconda" from the *Recercari, et canzoni franzese* (1615). In both the ricercars and the canzonas of this volume, Frescobaldi seems consciously to pull together and bring to consummation all the earlier achievements of his Neapolitan and Ferrarese predecessors in these two contrapuntal genres. The "Recercar secondo" is an homage to Luzzaschi, his teacher, modeled directly upon the master's opening ricercar in *Il secondo libro de ricercari a quattro voci* (1578).[74] Four others follow in the Neapolitan tradition of the ricercar "sopra tre soggetti" (nos. 1, 3, and 5) and "sopra quattro soggetti" (no. 9) as practiced by Macque, Trabaci, and Mayone.[75] Frescobaldi's five canzonas, like the canzonas of all his Neapolitan and Ferrarese precursors, run the gamut of variation techniques. The "Canzon quinta" displays no variation whatsoever. The opening subject of the "Canzon quarta" returns, though unvaried, in the final section in the manner of a French chanson. The "Canzon prima" exhibits variation only between the last two sections. The "Canzon terza" employs variants of two distinct subjects to tie together all five sections, though neither appears in every section.[76] And the most exhaustive of all, the "Canzon seconda," presents variations of one main subject in all five sections. In no other canzona, capriccio, or fantasia—neither for keyboard nor for ensemble—does Frescobaldi surpass the number and diversity of the rhythmic and melodic variants presented in this canzona.[77]

The "Canzon seconda" follows in the thoroughgoing spirit of the Pasquini and Trabaci canzonas discussed above. Within it, Frescobaldi expands upon Pasquini's flexible style of melodic variation and the idea of unfolding the variants with an ever increasing dramatic intensity. He also incorporates Trabaci's use of countersubjects and the unification of all five sections with variants of a single subject. But Frescobaldi endows

Example 14   Frescobaldi, "Canzon seconda" (1615), formal outline

his canzona with a more highly sophisticated form than had Trabaci (example 14). He divides the opening and middle duple-meter passages into two and three sections respectively, each with its own version of the subject, so that the canzona now comprises eight main sections.[78] He furthermore adds a different countersubject to each of the three sections of the middle passage and does Trabaci one better by deriving them all from the main subject. This raises the total number of variants to eleven.

The shape of the main subject is a deceptively simple arch-like gesture, rising and falling a fourth, symmetrically arranged around a leap back down to the opening d' in the middle (see example 15). Melodic tension and resolution within this extremely compact and perfectly balanced subject is obtained through the f♯' in the ascending tetrachord which reverts to f♮' in the latter half of the subject. Frescobaldi surpasses Pasquini in the variety of techniques with which he transforms the melody of his subject. Not only does he simplify it, but he adds notes to it and at times divides it into shorter motives. Frescobaldi also refines Pasquini's principle of unity through a rising level of dramatic intensity. Whereas the sections of Pasquini's canzona may be compared to three separate cresting waves, Frescobaldi ties together all eight sections of his canzona into a single, unbroken surge of rising rhythmic and melodic complexity.

Even within the first section (mm. 1–11), Frescobaldi is not content to present the subject always in the same shape. As soon as all four voices have entered with the subject, he begins to vary it by changing the canzona's traditional dactylic opening rhythm of a half note and two quarter notes to a quarter rest and three quarter notes (m. 6). Although such a change from a downbeat to an upbeat entry had been common in canzonas and ricercars for decades, Frescobaldi gives this convention expressive significance here as the first step toward the increased rhythmic excitement that will continue throughout the canzona and bind the variations into a unified whole. In the opening section, Frescobaldi also

Example 15   Frescobaldi, subjects and countersubjects

Example 16   Frescobaldi, mm. 9–10, bass

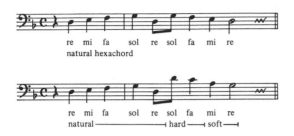

begins to vary the melodic shape of the subject. In one instance, two *inganni* carry the subject through all three hexachords (example 16).

The variation in the second section, S_2, modifies only the rhythm of the original, but, as in the opening section, the changes are significant since they continue the trend toward increased rhythmic activity. Furthermore, while S_1 always enters in its opening point of imitation on the downbeat at one- or two-measure intervals, S_2 (mm. 12–14) fluctuates between strong- and weak-beat entrances and enters in stretto at half-measure intervals.

The resulting rise in rhythmic and metric excitement continues in the following variations. The triple meter of S_3 increases the rhythmic verve, and this is enhanced as the subject enters in a series of close strettos (mm. 22–24 and 27–30). All statements begin on the downbeat except that of the alto in m. 28, which is displaced one whole note to rhythmically prepare the hemiola cadence in mm. 30–31. This entry also deviates from the norm by entering on C rather than G or D so as to stress the subdominant before the cadence. In this section, Frescobaldi begins to vary the melody of the subject with more imaginative techniques than *inganni*, transferring the leap, g′-d′, from the middle to the beginning.

The long central duple-meter passage begins with S_4 in stretto at the interval of a half note, the shortest interval of imitation thus far. Melodically this subject is identical to S_3 except that the f♯′ has been omitted. CS_4 begins with a lively three-note pickup figure which will dominate the rest of the central duple-meter passage and continue to heighten the rhythmic excitement of the canzona. (This upbeat pattern had first appeared in the statement of S_1 in m. 6.) CS_4 represents only the first half of the original subject, concluding with a strong cadence on the high point, g'. With S_5 and CS_5, the pace of the upbeat rhythm quickens to eighth notes. CS_5 is similar in melodic contour to the last half of S_5, but at the same time incorporates the three eighth-note upbeats from the first half of S_5. The last subject of the central duple-meter passage, S_6, presents the three upbeats in augmentation. As a foil to this slow-moving subject, CS_6 is the most disjunct and rhythmically active of all eleven variants. It seems at first glance hardly related to the original subject. But even though the pitch content of CS_6 deviates sharply from that of S_1, this countersubject presents an identical series of gestures: three conjunct pickup notes, a descending and an ascending leap, and part of a descending scale. The rhythm of CS_6 is, furthermore, an exact diminution of the upbeat version of S_1 that entered in m. 6. The contrast between the animated motion of CS_6 and the ponderousness of S_6 provides the entire middle passage of the canzona with a sense of climax.

The variants of the last two sections return to the downbeat opening of S_1, but at the same time continue to heighten the rhythmic excitement. The tempo of S_7 in minor hemiola is faster than that of the earlier triple-meter variation, according to Frescobaldi's instructions in the preface to the *Capricci*.[79] In both S_7 and S_8, Frescobaldi adopts Pasquini's technique of simplified and compressed melodic variations, an ideal means for achieving a brilliant climax. S_7 strips the rising and falling fourth to the barest bones possible that still make sense as a melody. With S_8, he purges the leap to d' in the middle, smooths over the fluctuation between f♯' and f♮', and often breaks off the subject before it reaches the final d'. The rhythm of S_8 is extremely terse, and the variant first enters in stretto at the tight interval of a half note, bringing to a culmination the canzona's crescendo of rhythmic excitement.

By the turn of the seventeenth century, the musicians of Naples and Ferrara had forged a common keyboard style. This is illustrated by their monopoly on the keyboard variation canzona and by the many stylistic similarities in the rest of their keyboard music.[80] But which of these cities initiated this new style which Frescobaldi was to inherit? The line of development of the variation canzona before Frescobaldi is clouded, since all the examples, other than those of Trabaci and Mayone, survive in manuscripts and are thus difficult to date precisely. There are three good reasons to suppose, however, that the Ferrarese led the way.[81] First,

Ercole Pasquini developed a more sophisticated variation technique than any of the Neapolitans. Second, the idolization of Luzzaschi by the Neapolitans indicates their eagerness to ape the Ferrarese style, whereas little evidence suggests that the Ferrarese were similarly infatuated with Neapolitan music. Third, Macque could have helped to carry the variation canzona from Ferrara to Naples long before Gesualdo's sojourn in 1594–96. He must have come in contact with Ferrarese keyboard music at least by 1582, when he had gained sufficient reputation in the city to be asked to contribute to *Il lauro secco*. After going to Naples in 1585, he became the leading musical figure at court and exerted a strong influence on Gesualdo[82] and certainly on the other composers in the prince's circle as well. With the residence of the Neapolitans in Ferrara in the mid-1590s, the influence of Ferrarese music reached its apex. In this light, the relationship of Trabaci and Mayone to Frescobaldi emerges not as that of precursors and follower, as hitherto believed, but as two separate offshoots of a common Ferrarese source.[83] Frescobaldi's compatriot Ercole Pasquini, rather than the Neapolitans, showed him the way to link a chain of imaginative rhythmic and melodic variants together into a dramatic progression. In perfecting Pasquini's example, Frescobaldi raised the variation canzona to its highest peak of expressive power.

Notes

This article is based in part on portions of my dissertation, "Frescobaldi's *Recercari, et canzoni franzese* (1615): A Study of the Contrapuntal Keyboard Idiom in Ferrara, Naples, and Rome, 1580–1620" (Ph.D. diss., University of California, Berkeley, 1978). Research for the present study was supported by a fellowship from the American Council of Learned Societies.

1. Willi Apel, "Neapolitan Links between Cabezon and Frescobaldi," *Musical Quarterly* 24 (1938): 419–37. A number of scholars have expanded upon this widely accepted viewpoint; see Joseph A. Burns, "Neapolitan Keyboard Music from Valente to Frescobaldi" (Ph.D. diss., Harvard University, 1953); Raymond H. Kelton, "The Instrumental Music of Ascanio Mayone" (Ph.D. diss., North Texas State College, 1961); Roland Jackson, "The Keyboard Music of Giovanni Maria Trabaci" (Ph.D. diss., University of California, Berkeley, 1964); Domenico Celada, "L'opera organistica di Giovanni Maria Trabaci," *Quaderni della Rassegna Musicale* 2 (1965): 159–69; and Roland Jackson, "On Frescobaldi's Chromaticism and Its Background," *Musical Quarterly* 57 (1971): 255–69.

2. In his more recent *History of Keyboard Music to 1700*, trans. and revised by Hans Tischler (Bloomington: Indiana University Press, 1972), 423, 427–28, Willi Apel refers to

some of the newly recovered canzonas by these composers, but only regarding Pasquini does he say a few words about variation. Even John Caldwell, "Canzona," *The New Grove Dictionary of Music and Musicians*, (London: Macmillan, 1980), 3:742–45, and Kurt von Fischer, "Variations," *The New Grove Dictionary* 19:540–45, mention no variation canzonas prior to Frescobaldi other than those of Trabaci and Mayone.

3. See Anthony Newcomb, *The Madrigal at Ferrara: 1579–97* (Princeton: Princeton University Press, 1980).

4. In the preface to his *Ricercari* (1669), Battiferri singles out Luzzaschi, Ercole Pasquini, [Alessandro] Milleville, and Frescobaldi as the great organists in Ferrara's history. Claudio Sartori, *Bibliografia della musica strumentale italiana stampata in Italia fino al 1700* (Florence: Olschki, 1952, 1968), 1:456–57, reprints the preface.

5. These four compositions first appeared in modern edition in Luigi Torchi, ed., *L'arte musicale in Italia* (Milan: Ricordi, n.d.), 3:149–52, 257–60. Torchi's version of the Pasquini canzona is corrupt; see n. 57 below. Luzzaschi's pieces are from Diruta, *Il transilvano* (1593_3 and 1609–10).

(Throughout this article, a music publication's date followed by a subscript numeral refers to its listing in Howard M. Brown, *Instrumental Music Printed before 1600: A Bibliography* [Cambridge, Mass.: Harvard University Press, 1965]. A date followed by a lower-case letter [and occasionally without a letter] refers to Sartori, *Bibliografia della musica strumentale*.)

6. Only one canzona by Luzzaschi survives. It is for ensemble and makes no significant use of variation. Luzzaschi might, however, have composed variation canzonas, for contemporary accounts refer to a number of keyboard works by him which are now lost. For a discussion of Luzzaschi's keyboard music, see Ladewig, "Frescobaldi's *Recercari, et canzoni franzese*," 1:9–27, and idem, "Luzzaschi as Frescobaldi's Teacher: A Little-Known Ricercare," *Studi musicali* 10 (1981): 241–64.

7. Only two sixteenth-century composers from outside this circle, Vincenzo Pellegrini and Andrea Gabrieli, tried their hands at the variation canzona for keyboard, and they were clearly dabbling in unfamiliar waters. They employ the technique in only one and two pieces respectively: Pellegrini's "Canzon detta la Capricciosa" from the *Canzoni: de intavolatura d'organo* (1599_9) and Gabrieli's first and second "Ricercari Ariosi" published posthumously in his *Canzoni alla francese* (1605f). Despite their titles, Gabrieli's pieces are in the style of the canzona; see Apel, *History of Keyboard Music*, 199–200. Each of these pieces applies variation technique much more primitively than do any of the Neapolitan or Ferrarese examples. They use the most rudimentary type of rhythmic variation to unify at most two sections (the first and second and the first and third sections of Gabrieli's two works, respectively; and the first two sections of Pellegrini's canzona). Related to these canzonas is the only true ricercar for keyboard from the sixteenth century that employs variation and that is by a composer not associated with Naples or Ferrara: Andrea Gabrieli's "Ricercar del Primo Tuono" in his *Ricercari* (1595_3). This ricercar displays a variation technique no more advanced than that of the Pellegrini and Gabrieli pieces just mentioned. (Jacques Buus's "Recercar primo" from the *Intabolatura d'organo* [1549_4] need not be included here since it is certainly a transcription of the ensemble version of this piece which appeared in the same year.)

Among the vast amount of ensemble music printed in Italy in the sixteenth and early seventeenth centuries, there is a very small group of ricercars and canzonas that exhibit variation. The approximately two dozen such pieces published before the appearance of Frescobaldi's first works in 1608 include Buus, 1549₅, ricercar no. 1; Padovano, 1556₉, ricercar no. 4; Conforti, 1558₁, ricercar no. 3; Malvezzi, 1577₄, ricercars nos. 4 and 8; Peetrino, 1583₅, aria francese; A. Gabrieli, 1589₃, ricercar no. 2; Vecchi, 1590₈, fantasia; Bariolla, 1594₁, canzona no. 20; Mazzi, 1596₉, ricercars nos. 1, 4, and 6; Cavaccio, 1597₂, no. 18 "La Pasti"; Stivori, 1599₁₀, ricercar no. 12 and canzonas nos. 1 and 2; Canale, 1600d, canzonas nos. 4, 9, 15, and 16; Quagliati, 1601b, nos. 9 and 18; G. Guami, 1601e, no. 16 "La Chiarina"; and Bonelli, 1602b, ricercar no. 7 and canzonas nos. 2 and 6. None of these ensemble pieces approaches the sophistication of the keyboard variation canzonas of the Neapolitans and Ferrarese. They restrict themselves to the simplest sort of rhythmic variation, avoid melodic variation entirely, often fail to unify all the sections of a piece, and display no more than one internal triple-meter section. Perhaps an elaborate variation technique evolved only in keyboard music because the practice of improvising a piece based on a single subject had long been an integral part of an organist's training. See, for example, the well-known audition requirements for organists at St. Mark's in Venice, given in James Moore's article in the present volume (p. 369).

8. Anthony Newcomb, "Carlo Gesualdo and a Musical Correspondence of 1594," *Musical Quarterly* 54 (1968): 409–36.

9. For more information on Fontanelli, see Newcomb, "Carlo Gesualdo," 412–13. Fontanelli's letters have also been examined and translated in Glenn Watkins, *Gesualdo: The Man and His Music* (Chapel Hill: University of North Carolina Press, 1973), 43–70. Their complete Italian texts appear in Nino Pirrotta, "Gesualdo, Ferrara e Venezia," in *Studi sul teatro veneto fra rinascimento ed età barocca*, ed. Maria Teresa Muraro (Florence, 1971), 305–19, as well as in Newcomb's article.

10. Letter of 21 May 1594 from Venice. Translation from Newcomb, "Carlo Gesualdo," 419.

11. Letter of 18 February 1594 from Argenta. Newcomb, "Carlo Gesualdo," 414.

12. Letter of 23 May 1594 from Venice. Newcomb, "Carlo Gesualdo," 424. Fontanelli's accounts of Gesualdo's veneration of Luzzaschi are corroborated by the Ferrarese chronicler Faustini, who says, "Among all [the Ferrarese musicians] that [Gesualdo] heard, he particularly praised the organist Luzzasco de' Luzzaschi for his exquisite manner of playing, and for a certain enharmonic instrument which [Luzzaschi] played for him [frà tutti, ch'egli udì, lodò particolarmente il Sig. Luzzascho de' Lazzaschi {sic} Organista, per l'esquisita sua maniera di suonare, et per certo strumento Inarmonico, che suonando gli fè udire]." See Agostino Faustini, *Aggiunta* to Gasparo Sardi, *Libro delle historie ferraresi* (Ferrara, 1646; reprint, Bologna: Forni, 1967), 90.

13. A partial translation of the dedication appears in Alfred Einstein, *The Italian Madrigal*, trans. A. H. Krapp, R. H. Sessions, and O. Strunck (Princeton: Princeton University Press, 1949), 2:698–99. Gesualdo's presence in Ferrara seems to have renewed Luzzaschi's interest in publishing madrigals. Whereas his first three books had come out in 1571, 1576, and 1582, the fourth through sixth books appeared one each year from 1594 to 1596.

14. Letter of 9 September 1594 from Naples. Newcomb, "Carlo Gesualdo," 427–28.

15. Letter of 16 September 1594 from Naples. Newcomb, "Carlo Gesualdo," 433.

16. Ibid., 428–29. Luzzaschi's repute in Naples extended well into the seventeenth century, as is shown by Trabaci's "[Ricercare] Settimo Tono" from his *Ricercate* (1615c), in which he proudly points out a subject borrowed from Luzzaschi's now lost third book of ricercars. See Ladewig, "Frescobaldi's *Recercari, et canzoni franzese*," 1:14, or idem, "Luzzaschi as Frescobaldi's Teacher," 243.

17. Letter of 16 September 1594 from Naples. Newcomb, "Carlo Gesualdo," 433.

18. Ibid., 414–15. P. 415 n. 8, and Roland Jackson, ed., *Neapolitan Keyboard Composers circa 1600*, Corpus of Early Keyboard Music, vol. 24 (n.p.: American Institute of Musicology, 1967), ix, identify this musician as Rinaldo dall'Arpa.

19. This excludes many ricercars—especially those by Neapolitan and Ferrarese composers such as "Giaches," Macque, Trabaci, and Mayone—that are in duple meter throughout and exhibit a more amorphous, evolving type of variation. Such a variation technique is quite distinct from that of a typical canzona, which progresses in a series of discrete formal units.

20. For further information on this manuscript see Alexander Silbiger, *Italian Manuscript Sources of Seventeenth-Century Keyboard Music* (Ann Arbor: UMI Research Press, 1980), 86–92; Newcomb, "Carlo Gesualdo," 414 n. 8; Apel, *History of Keyboard Music*, 424–28; and Augustus Hughes-Hughes, *Catalogue of Manuscript Music in the British Museum* (London: British Museum, 1909), 3:204. There is no complete modern edition, but nearly all the keyboard music appears in Jackson, *Neapolitan Composers*, and Joseph Watelet, ed., *Charles Guillet, Giovanni (de) Macque, Carolus Luython: Werken voor Orgel of voor vier Speeltuigen*, Monumenta Musicae Belgicae 4 (Antwerp: Vereniging voor Muziekgeschiedenis te Antwerpen, 1938), 33–35, 50–69.

21. See Silbiger, *Italian Manuscript Sources*, 86–92.

22. The Ms. appears to be a retrospective collection of Neapolitan keyboard music composed over three or four decades. The oldest composer represented, Ippolito Tartaglino, died in 1582. (See Jackson, *Neapolitan Composers*, ix, regarding the identification of the Ippolito mentioned in the Ms. at Tartaglino.)

Jackson (ibid., ix–x) attempts a chronology of the keyboard pieces based on "stylistic evidence or on the little that is known of the composers' lives." Such a chronology is, at best, tenuous. In particular, his belief that Gesualdo composed this canzona after the residence in Ferrara has no factual support.

23. *GB-Lbl* Add. Ms. 30491, fols. 15v–16v. Modern edition in Jackson, *Neapolitan Composers*, 23–26.

24. This subject also appears in Trabaci's "Canzona franzesa settima Cromatica" from his *Ricercate* (1603c).

25. For more information on the *inganno*, see Roland Jackson, "The *Inganni* and the Keyboard Music of Trabaci," *Journal of the American Musicological Society* 21 (1968): 204–8, and John Harper, "Frescobaldi's Early *Inganni* and Their Background," *Proceedings of the Royal Musical Association* 105 (1978–79): 1–12.

26. Regarding the use of *inganni* in this and other pieces by Frescobaldi, see Jackson, "Frescobaldi's Chromaticism," 259–67.

27. *GB-Lbl* Add. Ms. 30491, fols. 27v–28v. Modern edition in Jackson, *Neapolitan Composers*, 17–19.

28. Only in mm. 7–13 does Rinaldo slightly and insignificantly alter the melody of the subject by expanding the interval between the second and third notes from a third to a fourth.

29. Such a beginning to a canzona is a Neapolitan idiosyncrasy; see Silbiger, *Italian Manuscript Sources*, 35.

30. *GB-Lbl* Add. Ms. 30491, fols. 34v–38v. Modern edition in Jackson, *Neapolitan Composers*, 37–45.

31. Jackson, *Neapolitan Composers*, x; Apel, *History of Keyboard Music*, 428; and Watkins, *Gesualdo*, 291.

32. The partbook is owned by Signor Graglia, an engineer in Turin. For information on it, and for transcriptions of the dedication to Gesualdo in which Macque states that he is including three ricercars by his fellow composer, see Claudio Sartori, "Madrigali del Passerini e ricercari di de Macque e Gesualdo," in *Testimonianze, studi, e ricerche in onore di Guido M. Gatti*, Quadrivium 14 (Bologna: Università degli studi di Bologna, 1973), 184–86; Ruth I. DeFord, "Ruggiero Giovanelli and the Madrigal in Rome, 1572–1599" (Ph.D. diss., Harvard University, 1975), 1:281–85 and 293–94; and Friedrich Lippmann, "Giovanni de Macque fra Roma e Napoli: Nuovi documenti," *Rivista italiana di musicologia* 13 (1978): 243–44.

33. Woltz, ed., *Nova Musices Organicae Tabulatura* (1617e); *GB-Lbl* Add. Ms. 30491; *I-Nc* Ms. Mus. str. 48; *I-Nc* Ms. Mus. str. 73; *I-Fn* Ms. Magl. XIX 106bis; and *D-Bds* Ms. 13320. For lists of these pieces, see Silbiger, *Italian Manuscript Sources*, 169, and Ladewig, "Frescobaldi's *Recercari, et canzoni franzese*," 1:79.

34. Fols. 112v–125r; modern edition in Watelet, *Werken voor Orgel*, 39–41.

35. Fol. 18; modern edition in Watelet, *Werken voor Orgel*, 58–59. Burns, "Neapolitan Keyboard Music," 194, mistakenly states that the *Prima parte* of this canzona and Macque's third canzona in Woltz, ed., *Nova Musices* (1617e) exhibit variation technique.

36. Fols. 29v–32r; modern edition in Ladewig, "Frescobaldi's *Recercari, et canzoni franzese*," 2:49–51. The series of twelve ricercars in this Ms. may represent Macque's first book of ricercars, for the nineteenth-century copyist of the two ricercars in *D-Bds* Ms. 13320 alleges that his are taken from Macque's second book. The original publications of both books are now lost, but an inventory dated 1665 of the instruments and music left by Archduke Siegmund Franz of Innsbruck cites "Il secondo libro delle Recercari a 4 Voci di Giovanni Macque"; see Franz Waldner, "Zwei Inventorien aus dem 16. und 17. Jahrhundert über hinterlassene Musikinstrumente und Musikalien am Innsbrucker Hofe," *Studien zur Musikwissenschaft* 4 (1916): 136.

37. Ladewig, Frescobaldi's *Recercari, et canzoni franzese*," 1:84. See also the discussion of evolving variation in Anthony Newcomb's essay in the present volume.

38. Fols. 14r–15r and 19v–20r. Modern edition in Jackson, *Neapolitan Composers*, 9–14.

39. The Ms. contains works by Neapolitan composers including Gesualdo, Macque, Giovanni Maria Sabini, and Trabaci. See Roland Jackson, ed., *A Neapolitan Festa a ballo "Delizie di Posilipo Boscarecce, e Maritime" and Selected Instrumental Ensemble Pieces from Naples Conservatory MS 4.6.3.*, Recent Researches in the Music of the Baroque Era, vol. 25 (Madison:

A-R Editions, 1978), ix–x, and Richard L. Manner, "Naples, Biblioteca del Conservatorio di musica San Pietro a Maiella, MS 55: The Naples Gagliarde Manuscript" (M.A. thesis, Kent State University, 1975), the latter of which includes a complete modern edition of the manuscript.

40. See Newcomb, "Gesualdo, Carlo," 414, 418, and Keith Larson, "Stella, Scipione," The New Grove Dictionary 18:113–14.

Giovanni Pietro Bellori includes in his Le vite de' pittori scultori et architetti moderni (Rome, 1672), 358, a transcription of a letter written by Domenichino to Francesco Albani in which the painter mentions Stella (along with Luzzaschi and Gesualdo) in connection with an enharmonic harp he had built:

> In questi ultimi tempi, per necessità non havendo alcuna conversatione, ne divertimento, casualmente mi diedi un poco di diletto alla musica, e per udirne, mi posi à fare istrumenti, et ho fatto un liuto, et un cembalo, et hora faccio fare un'arpa con tutti li suoi generi Diatonico, Cromatico, et enarmonico: cosa non più stata fatta, nè inventata. Mà perche è cosa nuova alli musici del secolo nostro, non hò potuto per anco farlo sonare. Mi rincresce non sia vivo il Signor Alessandro, il quale disse ch'io non haverei fatto cosa alcuna, mentre il Luzzasco ne haveva fatto prova. Quì in Napoli vi è stato il Principe di Venosa, e lo Stella de' primi musici, e non l'hanno potuto ritrovare: se verrò alla patria, voglio far fare un'organo in questa maniera. Napoli li 7. Decembre 1638.

An English translation appears in Richard E. Spear, Domenichino (New Haven: Yale University Press, 1982), 1:40–41. In this letter, Domenichino must be speaking of events that occurred at least three decades earlier, since Luzzaschi had died in 1607 and Gesualdo in 1613. The Signor Alessandro to whom Domenichino refers could well be his Bolognese compatriot Alessandro Piccinini, since it seems from the wording of the letter that Signor Alessandro had only recently died at the time of the letter, and we know that Piccinini died somewhat before 1639.

41. Similar figuration occurs in a number of keyboard canzonas in GB-Lbl Add. Ms. 30491: Gesualdo, "Canzon francese del Principe"; Macque, "P[rim]a Canzon"; Stella, "P[rim]a Canzon"; and Tartaglino, "Canzon."

The possibility of Stella's second canzona in Naples, Cons. Ms. 55, being a keyboard work is strengthened by the presence in the Ms. of two gagliarde from Trabaci's first book of keyboard music (Ricercate, 1603c). (Naples, Cons. Ms. 55 also contains a gagliarda by Macque which appears for keyboard in GB-Lbl Add. Ms. 30491.) Regarding the rather common survival of pieces in both keyboard and ensemble sources, see Ladewig, "Frescobaldi's Recercari, et canzoni franzese," 1:294–301.

42. The handful of other keyboard fantasias that survive from the sixteenth century (in Rodio, Libro di ricercate, 1575₅; Valente, Intavolatura de cimbalo, 1576₃; and A. Gabrieli, Ricercari, 1596₇) have few characteristics in common. Thus, little can be said of the keyboard fantasia other than that it is a sort of ricercar.

43. Edward E. Lowinsky, "Early Scores in Manuscript," Journal of the American Musicological Society 13 (1960): 135–36, and Carol MacClintock, "The 'Giaches Fantasias' in MS Chigi

Q VIII 206: A Problem in Identification," *Journal of the American Musicological Society* 19 (1966): 370–82. Modern edition in Ladewig, "Frescobaldi's *Recercari, et canzoni franzese*," 2:15–42.

44. Wert was a regular visitor to Ferrara from nearby Mantua where he served as maestro di cappella for the Gonzagas; see Newcomb, *The Madrigal at Ferrara* 1:210.

45. See Ladewig, "Luzzaschi as Frescobaldi's Teacher"; idem, "Frescobaldi's *Recercari, et canzoni franzese*," 1:16–21; Anthony Newcomb, "*Il modo di far la fantasia*: An Appreciation of Luzzaschi's Instrumental Style," *Early Music* 7 (1979): 34–38; and Anthony Newcomb, "Form and Fantasia in Wert's Instrumental Polyphony," *Studi Musicali* 7 (1978): 85–102, which contains a detailed analysis of one of the "Giaches" fantasias.

46. I-Rvat Ms. Chigi 206, fols. 163r–167r; F-Pn Ms. 851, pp. 415–16. For a study of compositions based on this subject, beloved by composers from Josquin to Frescobaldi and Froberger, see James Haar, "Some Remarks on the 'Missa La sol fa re mi,'" in *Josquin des Prez: Proceedings of the International Josquin Festival-Conference*, ed. Edward E. Lowinsky (London: Oxford University Press, 1976), 564–88.

47. The opening point of this fantasia is given in MacClintock, "Giaches Fantasias," 372.

48. Five of the anonymous ricercars in *F-Pn* Ms. 851 (Mischiati, "Antologia manoscritta," nos. 295, 306, 308, and 310–11) that Newcomb attributes to "Giaches" also have an internal triple-meter section. Like the fantasia on *la sol fa re mi*, these pieces employ rhythmic transformation and *inganni*, demonstrating that variation is a regular feature of this composer's instrumental style.

49. Torchi, *L'arte musicale* 3:257–60. For a study of the vocal works, see W. Richard Shindle's essay in the present volume.

50. See Oscar Mischiati, "Pasquini, Ercole," *Die Musik in Geschichte und Gegenwart*, 10 (1962), col. 868, and W. Richard Shindle, "The Keyboard Works of Ercole Pasquini" (M.A. thesis, Indiana University, 1963). Modern editions appear in W. Richard Shindle, ed., *Ercole Pasquini: Collected Keyboard Works*, Corpus of Early Keyboard Music, vol. 12 (n.p.: American Institute of Musicology, 1966). A brief overview of Pasquini's keyboard music appears in Apel, *History of Keyboard Music*, 421–23.

51. Silbiger, *Italian Manuscript Sources*, 3. Pp. 178–86 of this study contain a discussion of the manuscript sources for Pasquini's keyboard works.

52. Already in 1593 Giovanni Battista Aleotti referred to Pasquini as a "buon vecchio," and nothing is known of his activities after 1608. For more biographical information on Pasquini, see Ladewig, "Frescobaldi's *Recercari, et canzoni franzese*," 1:44–49, and W. Richard Shindle, this volume.

53. "Aveva una mano delicatissima, et velocissima; suonava alle volte tanto eggregiamente, che rapiva le persone, e faceva stupire veramente." Agostino Superbi, *Apparato de gli huomini illustri della Città di Ferrara* (Ferrara, 1620), 132.

54. "Non ci è stato di gran fama un Ercole in S. Pietro? un Frescobaldi, che oggi vive . . . ?" Pietro Della Valle, "Della musica dell'età nostra" (1640); reprinted in Angelo Solerti, *Le origini del melodramma* (Turin: Fratelli Bocca, 1903), 158.

55. See Ernest Thoinan [Antoine Ernest Roquet], ed., *Maugars, célèbre joueur de viole . . . sa biographie suivie de sa response* (Paris, 1865), 30 n. 2.

56. See n. 50 above. In three of Pasquini's canzonas (Shindle, *Ercole Pasquini: Collected Keyboard Works,* nos. 11, 12, and 15), only the outer sections are related by variation. He unifies all the sections in the other three (Shindle, nos. 10, 13, and 16). For a general discussion of these pieces, see Ladewig, "Frescobaldi's *Recercari, et canzoni franzese,*" 1:50–61.

57. See Ladewig, "Frescobaldi's *Recercari, et canzoni franzese,*" 1:53, and Silbiger, *Italian Manuscript Sources,* 182–84. Of the six manuscripts, *I-Nc* Ms. Mus. str. 48, contains the earliest and musically the best text for the canzona. This version has long been known in a corrupt modern edition in Torchi, *L'arte musicale* 3:257–60 (see Silbiger, 184–86). Example 10 represents a corrected modern edition.

58. Silbiger, *Italian Manuscript Sources,* 55.

59. See the preface to his first book of *Toccate* (1615a).

60. The likeness between this motive and that which closed the first section signals a rounding off of the entire piece.

61. For further information on their keyboard music, see Apel, "Neapolitan Links"; Apel, *History of Keyboard Music,* 429–47 (a more concise and up-to-date examination of their keyboard music); Celada, "L'opera organistica"; Jackson, "Trabaci"; Jackson, "Inganni"; Kelton, "Mayone"; and Ulisse Prota-Giurleo, "Giovanni Maria Trabaci e gli organisti della Cappella di Palazzo di Napoli," *L'Organo* 1 (1960): 185–96.

62. For the contents of their publications, see Sartori, *Bibliografia della musica strumentale* 1 (1603b, 1603c, 1609f, and 1615c); or Apel, *History of Keyboard Music,* 429, 439.

The complete keyboard works of Mayone and Trabaci are available in modern edition as appendixes to two doctoral dissertations: Kelton, "Mayone," and Jackson, "Trabaci." Mayone's canzonas from 1603b and 1609f are also available in Christopher Stembridge, ed., *Ascanio Mayone: Diversi capricci per sonare, Libro I, Napoli 1603* (Padua, 1981), and Macario Santiago Kastner, ed., *Ascanio Mayone: Secondo Libro di Diversi Capricci Per Sonare (Napoli 1609),* Orgue et Liturgie, vol. 63 (Paris: Éditions musicales de la Schola cantorum et de la Procure générale de musique, 1964), respectively; and Trabaci's canzonas from 1603c in Domenico Celada, ed., *Giovanni Maria Trabaci (1575?–1647): Ricercate e canzone per organo dal primo libro* (Rome, 1963), and Oscar Mischiati, ed., *Giovanni Maria Trabaci: Composizioni per organo e cembalo (7 Canzoni francesi, 2 Capricci, 4 Canti fermi dal Libro I, 1603),* Monumenti di Musica Italiana, ser. 1, vol. 3, fasc. 2 (Brescia: Paideia, 1969).

63. Ladewig, "Frescobaldi's *Recercari, et canzoni franzese,*" 1:91–93.

64. See ibid., 1:90, and Silbiger, *Italian Manuscript Sources,* 167–70. Thus, many of Macque's works, including the "Capriccio sopra un sogetto" and "[Ricercar] Undecimo tono" discussed above, almost certainly date before 1603.

65. Two gagliards by Trabaci are included by Luigi Rossi in *GB-Lbl* Add. Ms. 30491, along with the canzonas by Gesualdo and his entourage of composers.

66. 1603b, nos. 3 and 4; and 1609f, nos. 2 and 4.

67. 1603c, nos. 1, 5, 6, and 7.

68. See ricercars nos. 8 and 10, "Capriccio sopra un soggetto solo," and "Capriccio sopra la, fa, sol, la" (1603c); and Ricercar 6 (1615c).

69. This canzona is discussed briefly in Apel, "Neapolitan Links," 430–31, and Apel, *History of Keyboard Music,* 441. It is readily available in Archibald T. Davison and Willi Apel,

eds., *Historical Anthology of Music* (Cambridge, Mass.: Harvard University Press, 1946–50), 2:16–17, though better modern editions appear in Jackson, "Trabaci," 2:53–56, and Mischiati, *Trabaci Composizioni*, 16–19.

70. Pasquini employs similar rhythmic techniques in the canzona discussed above, but not so rigorously as Trabaci.

71. Trabaci, 1603c, no. 1, and Mayone, 1609f, nos. 1 and 2.

72. Countersubjects will be designated by CS plus the numeral of the variant of the subject they accompany.

73. This trait recalls such quintessentially sixteenth-century works as Andrea Gabrieli's canzona-like "Ricercar del Duodecimo Tuono" in his *Madrigali et ricercari* (1589₃).

74. This book of ricercars, which has recently come to light, is available in modern edition in Michelangelo Pascale, ed., *Luzzasco Luzzaschi: Il secundo libro de ricercari a quattro voci*, Musica Rinascimentale in Italia, vol. 6 (Rome: Pro Musica Studium, 1981). Ladewig, "Luzzaschi as Frescobaldi's Teacher," discusses the influence of the "Ricercar primo" from this volume on Frescobaldi's "Recercar secondo" of 1615.

75. For a discussion of these pieces, see Ladewig, "Frescobaldi's *Recercari, et canzoni franzese*," 1:110–19.

76. See ibid., 1:130–37, for a fuller discussion of these canzonas.

77. The only pieces to approach the variation technique of the "Canzon seconda" are the "Capriccio sopra un sogetto" from the *Capricci* (1624b) and the "Canzona seconda" in the second book of *Toccate* (1627b). But even they fall short with eight and six versions of their subjects, respectively. In his other capriccios, Frescobaldi restricts himself largely to rhythmic variation, perhaps because most are based on well-known tunes and solmization subjects. While the *Fantasie* (1608i) intensely exploit rhythmic variation, they limit melodic variation to inflexible techniques such as inversion and *inganni*.

78. Such formal expansion had appeared earlier in Rinaldo's "Canzon" and in some of Pasquini's canzonas. Regarding its use by Pasquini, see Ladewig, "Frescobaldi's *Recercari, et canzoni franzese*," 1:58–61.

Frescobaldi signifies that all eight sections and their variants are of equal structural importance by closing each section with a complete cadence on a chord of a minim or longer and with a major third above the root. This is his customary manner of signaling the ends of major formal divisions in all his canzonas of 1615.

79. "Nelle trippole, ò sesquialtere, se saranno maggiori, si portino adagio, se minori alquanto piu allegre, se di tre semiminime, più allegre se saranno sei per quattro si dia illor tempo con far caminare la battuta allegra," p. [3].

For more information regarding tempi in the music of Frescobaldi, see the article by Etienne Darbellay in the present volume.

80. Regarding the resemblances among the Ferrarese and Neapolitans in their ricercars, toccatas, variation sets, dances, and so forth, see Ladewig, "Frescobaldi's *Recercari, et canzoni franzese*," 1:92–93. Most of the traits listed in Apel, "Neapolitan Links," 437, as being passed from Trabaci and Mayone to Frescobaldi are actually common to the keyboard music of Ferrara and Naples in general. Anthony Newcomb reaches the same conclusion in his essay in the present volume and in "Frescobaldi's Toccatas and Their Stylistic Ancestry,"

in *Proceedings of the Royal Musical Association* 111 (1984–85), 28–44.

81. I believe this hypothesis will be confirmed as we learn even more about the keyboard music of Ferrara during the late sixteenth century—for example, from the newly discovered Luzzaschi ricercars (see n. 74).

82. See Watkins, *Gesualdo*, 226–27, and Lorenzo Bianconi, "Gesualdo, Carlo," *The New Grove Dictionary* 7:316.

83. As late as 1615, Trabaci himself tellingly calls attention to his emulation of Luzzaschi (see n. 16).

Frescobaldi's Reworked Ensemble Canzonas

JOHN HARPER

T HE THREE EDITIONS of ensemble canzonas belong to the mature period of Frescobaldi's output. The first two prints appeared after a spate of publishing activity that included the *Capricci* (1626), the *Toccate II* (1627), and the surviving volume of motets (*Liber secundus*, 1627), and came just before the *Arie musicali* (1630). The third print was published only a few months before *Fiori musicali* (1635). As a collection they straddle Frescobaldi's Florentine sojourn.

The two earlier editions of the *Canzoni* both appeared in 1628 in Rome, one in partbooks (Robletti), the other in score (Masotti).[1] Both made use of movable type. The former has prefatory material by Frescobaldi; the latter, in score, was prepared and seen through the press by his Luccan pupil Bartolomeo Grassi. Unlike a number of Milanese publications including ensemble music, three Venetian prints, and Cifra's Roman publications of 1619, the partbooks and score were not prepared together.[2] The edition dated 1634 (published in Venice in the spring of 1635, new style) is again in partbooks and printed with movable type. It was prepared by Frescobaldi but—on internal evidence—seems not to have been proofread by him.

There has been a general tendency for scholars to consult Grassi's score edition: it is, after all, splendidly and accurately presented. This has nevertheless meant that the substantial differences between the three editions have been slow to emerge and to be precisely evaluated. The overall organization of all three issues is the same. Each includes canzonas scored for one to four instruments, arranged in groups that systematically explore every combination of treble and bass instruments up to CCBB as well as some scored for CATB.[3] As such this represents the most

systematically comprehensive collection of canzonas in the period
—indeed of any ensemble music published by that date, and by a single
composer.[4] Furthermore, the collection includes the first published works
for B, and the most substantial groups of pieces scored for BB, CBB, and
CCBB.

The Contents

The contents of no two of the three sources correspond exactly (see table
1). However, the two editions of 1628 do correlate to a large extent. The
canzonas for two and three instruments appear in the same order and
with only occasional differences of musical detail. The canzonas for solo
instrument are presented in a different internal sequence, and the group
for C solo in each source includes a canzona not found in the other
source. The editions also differ in the presentation of canzonas for four
instruments. Grassi's collection separates the pieces for CCBB from those
for CATB, presented as a composite group in the partbooks, and two
pieces have a shortened text. Grassi also includes two additional canzonas (one of them unique to this source) and an appendix of pieces
scored for spinettina and for spinettina and violin.

The contents of the third edition of 1634 correspond to neither of the
1628 editions (see table 2). In only one group of canzonas, those for CB,
does it retain the same contents presented in the same order as the
other sources. The canzonas for C solo correspond with those of Grassi's
scorebook, but with the second and third pieces reversed. Of the other
canzonas for one and two instruments, two canzonas are omitted and
the remainder include some reordering. However, in each group for
three and four instruments there are new pieces included in the edition
of 1634: two for CBB, two for CCB, one for CCBB, and (perhaps surprisingly)
five for CATB. Except in the group for CCB there are also omissions: one
for CBB and two each for CCBB and CATB.

Overall, eight canzonas from the 1628 editions are omitted from the
1634 edition; ten new canzonas are introduced (all for three or four
instruments) and thirty are transferred from the earlier editions (twenty-
eight found in both sources, two exclusive to the scorebook). None of
these canzonas is transferred without some alteration, though in thirteen cases the changes are limited to small revisions of minor details. In

Table 1 The three editions: summary of contents and orderings
(for explanation of abbreviations, see note 3)

Scoring	1628-S	1628-P	1634	Scoring	1628-S	1628-P	1634
C	1	—	1	CBB	24	1	1R
	2	1	3		25	2	2R
	3	4	2		26	3	—
	4	3	4		—	—	3
	—	2	—		—	—	4
B	5	1	1 R	CCB	27	4	4 R
	6	3	2 R		28	5	3 [R]
	7	4	—		29	6	2
	8	2	3 R		—	—	1
CC	9	1	1 R		—	—	5
	10	2	2 R	CCBB	30	1	4
	11	3	4		31[a]	2	—
	12	4	—		32	4	—
	13	5	3 R		33	5	2 R
BB	14	1	1 R		34	—	1 R
	15	2	3 R		—	—	3
	16	3	2 R	CATB	35	3	—
	17	4	4 R		36[a]	6	3 R
CB	18	1	1		37	—	—
	19	2	2		—	—	1
	20	3	3		—	—	2
	21	4	4		—	—	4
	22	5	5		—	—	5
	23	6	6		—	—	6

a. shorter version in 1628-S.

another (the third canzona for CCB) a single section is rewritten, but the remainder of the piece is unchanged.

In the remaining sixteen canzonas, the transferral from the 1628 to the 1634 edition involves substantial reworking of the original materials. These revisions are concentrated in particular areas of the collection: none of the canzonas for C solo or CB is altered in substance, whereas all of the transferred pieces for B solo, BB, and CBB and the sole transferred canzona for CATB are changed radically, as are three of the four canzonas

Table 2   The three editions: additions, deletions, transfers, and revisions

Scoring	1628-S				1628-P				1634				Total	
	1628-S only	1628-S+P	1628-S+1634	1628-S,P+1634	1628-P only	1628-S+P	1628-P+1634	1628-S,P+1634	1634 only	1628-P+1634	1628-S+1634	1628-S,P+1634	1628-S,P+1634	Overall totals
C	—	—	1	3	1	—	—	3	—	—	1		3	5
B	—	1	—	3	—	1	—	3	—	—	—	—	3R	4 + 3R
CC	—	1	—	4	—	1	—	4	—	—	—		1 3R	5 + 3R
BB	—	—	—	4	—	—	—	4	—	—	—	—	4R	4 + 4R
CB	—	—	—	6	—	—	—	6	—	—	—		6	6
CBB	—	1	—	2	—	1	—	2	2	—	—		2R	5 + 2R
CCB	—	—	—	3	—	—	—	3	2	—	—		2 1R	5 + 1R
CCBB	—	2	1	2	—	2	—	2	1	—	—	1R	1 1R	6 + 2R
CATB	1	1	—	1	—	1	—	1	5	—	—	—	1R	8 + 1R
Totals	1	6	2	28	1	6	—	28	10	—	1	1R	13 15R	48 + 16R
			(37)				(35)				(40)			

1634–   8 rejected
10 new
14 transferred
16 reworked

for CC, one of the three canzonas for CCB, and two of the three canzonas for CCBB. Consequently, one third of Frescobaldi's published ensemble canzonas (sixteen of forty-eight) survives with two substantially differing texts.

The Revisions

The limited changes of detail made in the thirteen straightforwardly transferred canzonas are indicative of Frescobaldi's general practice.

1. The basso continuo. This part shows the most frequent differences of detail among the three sources. As a rule, the revisions in the 1634 edition, though small, serve to simplify the part (by removing passing

notes and figurative detail), to make it more suitable for harmonic realization, and on occasion to strengthen the harmonic substructure, particularly at sectional transitions. As might be expected, there are more bass figures in the later print, though the figures remain sparse (see example 1).

2. Sectional delineation. There are no verbal tempo indications in the 1628 partbooks; there are some in the scorebook, but rather more in the edition of 1634. They serve to articulate the sections of the canzonas as separate units and to undermine any idea of a constant tactus.[5] A similar tendency may be discerned in the notation of a number of triple-meter sections with shorter note values. At sectional transitions in the earlier editions, the mensuration sign of a solo line may have changed from C to 12/8 or 6/4, while the continuo remained in an unaltered C; in the 1634 versions both solo and continuo parts change from simple to compound meter, as in Canzon IV for c solo (example 2).[6]

Nevertheless, when one examines the c solo and cв canzonas that dominate the transferred group, one is struck by the conservative nature of their conception. Their roots lie in the polyphonic canzona and, as for instance in Cima's early solo sonatas of 1610,[7] it is possible to reconstruct a four-part imitative texture from the given treble and bass, especially in the opening duple-meter allegros. (Canzon IV for c solo is typical: each of the four main sections can be analyzed as a series of imitative points, the last using a double counterpoint. The exceptions are the short triple-

Example 1a

Example 1b

Example 2

meter section and the two brief adagios.) Second, as with all Frescobaldi's canzonas, they depend on variation techniques as a means of unification, although not as overtly as some of the earlier keyboard canzonas. Third, they are retrospective—that is, reminiscent of sixteenth-century techniques, not only in their polyphonic substructure but in the contour of

Table 3   Summary of reworked canzonas

Canzona (1634 number)	B/1	B/2	B/3	CC/1	CC/2	CC/3	BB/1	BB/2
Overall length								
Extended (E) or Abbreviated (A)	E		E			A		
Sections								
Unchanged	4	3	—	1	1	1	1	2
Revised	—	1	1	3	3	—	—	1
Reordered	—	—	1	—	—	—	1	—
Rewritten	2	4	—	1	1	2	2	2
Reordered & rewritten	—	—	1	—	—	2	2	—
Replaced	1	1	3	1	1	—	—	1
Added	2	1	3	1	—	4	—	2
Omitted	—	—	—	—	1	2	2	—
Total								
1628	7	9	6	6	7	7	8	6
1634	9	10	9	7	6	9	6	8

a. 6 in 1628-P, 5 in 1628-S.

lines, in their decorative figurations, and in the predominant modality of their harmonic syntax. There are modernisms: echo sections; contrasts of meter, tempo, and expressiveness; chromaticisms; and glimmers of the rhetorical language of the toccatas—but they are subservient.

The Reworked Canzonas

The earlier versions of the reworked canzonas reflect these same traits (see table 3). But for the most part they are scored for combinations for which polyphonic and imitative techniques are less apposite: those for bass instruments, or where bass instruments predominate, and those with two equal treble instruments. The nature of the reworking is of two kinds. First, there is internal revision, rewriting or replacement of material within an individual section of a canzona; then there is the overall reorganization of a canzona affected by the reordering, addition, or omission of sections. An examination of table 3 shows just how extensive this

BB/3	BB/4	CBB/1	CBB/2	[CCB/3]	CCB/4	CCBB/1	CCBB/2	CATB/3
E	A	F	E		E	E	E	A
3	—	1	—	4	1	1	—	—
2	1	—	—	—	—	—	—	2
—	—	—	—	—	—	—	2	—
1	1	2	3	1	—	—	1	—
—	4	—	—	—	—	—	1	1
1	1	2	2	—	2	2	—	1
—	3	2	2	—	—	1	2	2
1	2	1	—	—	1	1	—	1
8	9	6	5	5	4	4	4	6[a]
7	10	7	7	5	3	4	6	6

process of recomposition was. The summary of sections gives an indication of the nature of the changes. (And it is worth explaining that by a
section one may refer to a unit as short as three semibreves or as long as
thirty, but in every instance identifiable by independence of material,
texture, articulation, or treatment.) Those sections listed as "unchanged"
are unaltered in substance, but are subject to the amendment of detail
observed in the transferred canzonas. The same is true of the reordered
sections: only their placement has substantially changed. "Revised" sections are unaltered in length and general substance, but include some
alteration of the material—often for a new opening or closing cadence,
or involving revision of details of the part-writing. The "rewritten" sections retain the meter and some vestige of the original material, but may
be totally transformed with regard to length, substance, phrasing, texture,
harmony, and figuration. "Replaced" sections retain the basic meter and
structural function of an earlier section but otherwise contain new
material.

Even from this rough summary it should be clear that in the 1634
versions of the reworked canzonas, the transformation is extensive. Only
about a third of the material has been transferred without substantial
and substantive alteration of content, and slightly less than a third retains
a comparable position in the ordering of each piece. Nearly half of the
sections are rewritten or replaced; the remaining fifth is entirely new.
Most often the new material consists of adagio sections, introduced to
articulate transitions between faster sections by contrast and/or transition.
Triple-meter sections frequently survive without alteration or substantial
revision, but the longer, quasi-imitatively fashioned sections, with their
modal stability, are often candidates for radical remodeling.

In the detailed reworking of sections there is a stylistic shift from a
dependence on the polyphonic model for structure and continuity to a
more plastic conception, growing from the control of phrasing, cadence,
and basic tonal planning; motive interchange; and textural control. This
control leads to a more sophisticated treatment of such "modern" devices
as echo and chromaticism, more telling use of passagework for climactic
and rhetorical effect, and more affective exploitation of adagio lines.
Increasingly the writing shows a greater understanding of and response
to violin technique in motives, figuration, and articulation. By far the
most striking group of concerted ensemble canzonas are those for CCBB,

with their bold display of the varieties of scorings and textures offered by the ensemble. But even here, Frescobaldi remains far short of the bravura, virtuosity, and experiment of contemporary violinist-composers. Nevertheless, in these canzonas for CCBB, Frescobaldi exhibits, in linearly conceived music, a sculptural grasp of the malleable sound resource that had long been a feature of his improvisatory keyboard music.

This may be seen more widely: in his reorganization and recomposition of the complete group of sixteen reworked canzonas he seems to move from a successive system of composition, reliant on techniques of imitation and variation, toward a more cohesive concept, concerned not only with the articulation and integrity of an individual section but with its relation and contribution to the whole. This pattern of independence and interdependence is to some extent evident in the 1628 collections, but an examination of the reworkings underlines its development.

All seven canzonas for bass instruments are recast in the edition of 1634; no doubt this is indicative of the novelty of the scoring and the composer's uncertainty in handling it. They are in themselves a testament to Frescobaldi's commitment to explore, revise, and improve. An examination of the overall reordering of the four canzonas for BB illustrates something of his process of recomposition (see table 4). At first sight, the reworking of the second and third canzonas seems straightforward: the former simply separates fast and triple sections by introducing two new adagios, and replaces an allegro section; the latter omits one section and replaces another. But this is only part of the process. There are significant revisions in the third canzona; and in the second, about half of the rest of the material is remodeled. In the first canzona the reorganization is far more extensive: the opening section is greatly expanded, and is followed by a clutch of three sections previously placed at the end of the work; two other (independent) sections are moved to the end, while two others are omitted. Again there is considerable internal rewriting.

By far the most radical transformation takes place in the fourth canzona for BB. The long, imitative allegro is whittled down and melodically reconceived as a brief but expressive solo line whose contours recur in succeeding adagio sections (see example 3). It is followed by an entirely new triple-meter section: three crisp three-bar phrases, each with a clear cadence, moving the piece on straightaway. None of the sections is long,

Table 4   Sections in canzonas for *due bassi*

BB/1 1628	BB/1 1634		BB/2 1628	BB/2 1634	
A (11 ○)[a]	A (33 ○)	Rewritten	A (23 ○)	A (27 ○)	Rewritten
B (10 ○)	F (13 ○·)			X (14 ○) Adagio	
C (15 ○)	D¹ (6 ○) Adagio	Rewritten	B (20 ○·)	B (22 ○·)	Rewritten
D (20 ○)	G (19 ○) Allegro		C (17 ○)	C (17 ○) Allegro	
E (12 ○)	D (19 ○) Adagio	Rewritten	D (12 ♩♩)	D (12 ♩♩)	
F (13 ○·)	B (23 ○) Allegro	Rewritten		Y (15 ○) Adagio	
D¹ (5 ○)			E (19 ○)	Z (18 ○) Allegro	Replaced
G (19 ○)			F (4 ○)	F (4 ○) Adagio	Revised

a. Length of section

and this contributes to an episodic, exploratory structure, in which the return of the adagio as an implicit if not exact refrain is critical. Again, the concluding section is moved forward and the original second section (which had formed a conclusion to the opening sections) now forms a frame to conclude the canzona.

But here, as in most of the canzonas, Frescobaldi is unwilling to write homophonically for the solo instruments as a pair. Only in the canzonas scored for three and four instruments are there brief homophonic passages. The canzona remained pre-eminently a contrapuntal genre for him. Nevertheless, one four-part canzona, the third for CATB in the edition of 1634, provides a striking insight into his changing and changeable attitude over the years, for it exists in four different forms (see table

BB/3 1628	1634		BB/4 1628	1634	
A (19 o)	A (19 o)		A (28 o)	V (A¹) (8 o)	Replaced
B (22 ♩.)			B (19 o)	W (9 ⋈·)	
C (15 o)	C (15 o) Adagio		C (19 ⋈·)		
D (29 o)	D (29 o) Allegro	Revised	D (6 o) Adagio	X (A²) (6 o) Adagio	Rewritten
E (15 ⋈·)	E (15⋈·)		E (21 o) Allegro	E (12 o) Allegro	Rewritten
F (9 o)	F (9 o) Adagio		E¹ (8 o)	E¹ (8 o)	Revised
G (7 ¹²₈)	G (13 ⁶₄)	Revised	F (11 o·)	D¹(A³) (9 o) Adagio	Rewritten
H (14 o)	Z (28 o)	Replaced	D¹ (8 o)	G (12 o)	Rewritten
			G (26 o)	Y (13 ⋈·)	
				Z (A⁴) (8 o) Adagio	
			→B	B (16 o) Allegro	Rewritten

Example 3

1628-S,-P: BB/4, 1–8

B1.

B2.

1634: BB/4, 1–8

B1.

Table 5   Sections in the four texts of catb/3 (1634)

1615 (Canzon III)	1628-P	1628-S	1634	
			W	
			(8 ♮·) F	
A	A	A	→X (V¹)	Rewritten
(33 ○)ᵃgᵇ	(33 ○) g	(33 ○) g	(13 ○) FB♭C	
B———	S	S	S	Revised
(13 ♮·) g	(3 ○) B♭	(3 ○) B♭	(4 ○) B♭	
C	T	T	T	Revised
(14 ○) gD	(22 ♩·) B♭	(22 ♩·) B♭	(22 ○·) B♭	
D	E¹	E¹	Y	
(11 ○·) DB♭g	(27 ○) gD-Dg	(27 ○) gD-Dg	(5 ○) B♭C(G)	
E————′	B	V——————′	Z	
(26 ○) gB♭g	(13 ♮·) g	(6 ○) g	(21 ○) CFB♭F	
	V			
	(6 ○) g			

a. Length of section.
b. Principal cadences and tonal orientation.

Example 4

1615:
Canzona 3

5 and example 4). In its earliest form it appears as Canzon III in the *Recercari* (1615).[8] There it is presented as a straightforward variation canzona: five sections with alternating duple and triple meters, their material all derived from the opening subject, and all firmly set in the transposed G-dorian mode (see table 5 and example 4A-E). The canzona manages an easy transition from keyboard to ensemble scoring, and exists in two different forms in the 1628 editions. Both preserve the opening section of the 1615 print (*A*) unaltered; both include a totally recomposed section related to *E*; but only the partbooks' text has the triple-meter section *B* as the penultimate unit. In both versions there are three new sections: the first, a short tailpiece to the opening, establishes a pitch center of B-flat (*S*); the second follows it, still centered on

B-flat, and emphasizes the interval of the rising fourth in its motives (*T*); and finally a new conclusion is added to the canzona, again exploiting the rising fourth, but here in a closeknit consort texture, with overlapping imitation and interlocking partwriting (*V*).

The transformation in the edition of 1634 is complete: all the material from the 1615 version is eliminated. There is a new opening in triple meter (*W*), and then follows a section derived and expanded from *V*, which had appeared at the end of the 1628 versions. Thereafter comes the tailpiece *S* and the triple-meter section *T*: the latter is altered first by doubled note values, but more particularly by the introduction of dotted rhythms that bring a new lyricism. To these are added two new sections to conclude the piece: a short homophonic passage of two modulating phrases, and a leisurely imitative section with four motives (*Z*).

The motivic characteristics of the 1634 text bear no direct aural relationship to that of 1615, though they can be linked through the 1628 texts and by intellectual musical processes by such transformations as *inganni*. But the fundamental and most startling contrast emerges with an examination of harmonic features and pitch centers. Whereas the 1615 version was rooted in transposed dorian and the 1628 texts moved in the second and third parts to B-flat, the 1634 text is in a different mode. Its final is F, the mode is major, and the canzona has a very clear pattern of tonal reference to B-flat, as also to C. The material transferred from the 1628 edition has a new orientation. In this instance the process of recomposition in the ensemble canzonas is quite unique. On the other hand, the transformation provides a touchstone to our understanding of a stylistic development spanning twenty years.

Notes

1. For bibliographical citations of the three editions of the *Canzoni*, see the "Bibliography of Frescobaldi's Printed Collections," this volume.

2. Claudio Sartori, *Bibliografia della musica strumentale italiana* (Florence: Olschki, 1952, 1966) lists references to scores (frequently identified as the organist's part) in the following publications before 1628: Milan—1610d, 1610e, 1611f, 1613i, 1614h, 1617d, 1627d, 1627e; Venice—1613a, 1614a, 1614e; Rome (Cifra)—1619b (and by inference, 1619d).

3. The following abbreviations will be used here for the scorings: c = *canto*, a = *alto*, t = *tenore*, b = *basso*, bc = *basso generale* or *bassus ad organum* (bc is generally omitted in indications of scoring). In addition, the following abbreviations are used in the musical

examples and tables: 1628-P = *Canzoni* (Robletti, 1628), partbooks; 1628-S = *Canzoni* (Masotti, 1628), score (compiled by Grassi); 1634 = (Vincenti, 1634 [= 1635 new style]), partbooks; R = reworked.

4. P. F. Bartolomeo's volume of *Canzoni Fantasie et Correnti* (Venice: Magni, 1638) appears to be the only other publication of the period to attempt a similar organization (but see Silbiger, this volume, regarding analogous organizational principles in some of Frescobaldi's vocal collections).

5. See Darbellay, this volume, regarding Frescobaldi and the constant tactus principle.

6. The new sign in 1634 is related to Frescobaldi's rhythmic alterations of the continuo part. Nevertheless, the findings of Etienne Darbellay and Margaret Murata recorded elsewhere in this volume raise broader questions regarding Frescobaldi's changes of mensuration/tempo signs in his revised canzonas.

7. Giovanni P. Cima, *Concerti Ecclesiastici . . . & sei sonate, per instrumenti* (Milan: Herede di Tini et Lomazzo, 1610).

8. Regarding this canzona, see also Ladewig, this volume.

The Rhetorical Aspect of Frescobaldi's Musical Language

EMILIA FADINI

THE NEED TO ANALYZE the rhetorical aspect of Frescobaldi's language arises out of the performer's experience. The intuition of a performer may be adequate to grasp the expressive intensity of the instrumental language of the early 1600s; but this does not exclude or diminish the importance of an analysis designed to clarify and define the semantic value of those melodic, rhythmic, and harmonic details (the rhetorical-musical "figures") that were inspired by the technique of oratory. These figures were used by baroque composers to strengthen musical expression and to assure the communication of specific emotional feelings to the listener. This type of analysis may not be difficult to apply to vocal music, where the text is an infallible guide to the recognition of the musical figures, their significance, and consequently, their necessary interpretative pronunciation; but such an analysis is not so easy to perform on instrumental music. Too often the manual ability and technique of the performer threaten to overshadow the communicative aspect of the musical language and obscure its semantic value. The present analytical attempt is aimed at penetrating the aspect of rhetorical *elocutio* in the first section of the "Toccata terza per l'organo da sonarsi all'Elevatione" from Frescobaldi's *Toccate II.*

There are two ways to approach the art of a distant epoch: either one abandons oneself to personal feelings and emotions in subjective response to the work of art, or one attempts to penetrate and comprehend through the surviving documentation the goals pursued by people of the time. The performer, like the historian, is called upon to accomplish this second type of cultural operation.

The responsibility of a performer is therefore to decipher a complex code (signals, rules of the musical language) with which to reach the thought of the composer one intends to study. The operation is very difficult, because the cultural and ideological world of the scholar tends inevitably to superimpose itself upon the epoch being studied. This implies that the scholar must force himself to abandon the linguistic code of his own period and immerse himself in a different reality.

The first thing to be considered when approaching the musical language of the late 1500s and early 1600s is its principal objective: the transmission and communication of human sentiments and passions. This aim required a precise system of symbols; and for their organization, musicians turned to the models of literary language and oratory, principally rhetoric. From the art of rhetoric they obtained not only the model for the organization of musical discourse but, in particular, the practical devices of its language.

Already during the Middle Ages theorists had borrowed literary concepts for the analysis of liturgical melodies.[1] John Cotton, in *De musica*, distinguishes the *principius, medius*, and *finis* of a chant in analogy to the three parts of rhetorical discourse. The rhythmic modes and the mensural system of note values derived from metric feet show the profound analogy that existed between the linguistic and the musical systems. If one keeps in mind the close connection between grammar and music in ancient Greece[2]—the source from which medieval culture constantly drew—it should come as no surprise that the School of Notre Dame, or such theorists and musicians as Guido of Arrezzo, Franco of Cologne, Johannes de Grocheo, and Guillaume de Machaut, took metric and poetical literary forms as models for the structuring of musical discourse, and often adopted a common terminology.[3]

Also from Greek culture derived the theory regarding the influence on the human soul of the various modes, which were capable of arousing moderate (*ethos*) as well as more violent (*pathos*) emotions. During the Middle Ages music was similarly regarded as a force of nature, exerting its influences on man. As late as the end of the fifteenth century, Johannes Tinctoris listed twenty different effects that music could produce upon man: it could elevate the spirit, subdue sadness, put the devil to flight, enrapture, cure sickness, gladden, give relief to the laborer, excite sensuality and lust, soothe suffering, communicate astral influences, and so forth. Recognizing that music had the power to produce specific effects upon man meant submitting to it; on the other hand, subjecting it to the domination of words meant bending it to the will of man. The dominance of the text over music guaranteed the control of the effects that music could produce.

But let us return to the close ties between rhetoric and music, and observe how they proceeded unseparated from the Middle Ages to the Renaissance. The rediscovery of the "Institutio oratoria" by M. F. Quintilian in 1416 had a great influence on the development of the links between music and rhetoric. It was printed in Rome in 1468 and saw over a hundred editions in the sixteenth century. The study of rhetoric was one of the pillars of cultural education in Europe; this had significant consequences for both sacred and secular vocal music, for the late sixteenth-century madrigal as well as for seventeenth-century opera. Most musicians and theoreticians of the sixteenth century used oratory as a model to show how musical composition should be structured after speech and how its performance should arouse specific feelings in the listener. It is sufficient in this regard to recall the testimonies of Silvestro Ganassi, Nicola Vicentino, and Gioseffo Zarlino. Ganassi, for example in *Regola Rubertina* (1542),[4] urged the viol player to express by physical movements, facial expressions, and the position of the head the moods suggested by the words that are being sung, and to draw inspiration for his interpretation from the rules of oratorical declamation (*actio*).

Similarly, Nicola Vicentino, in the *Antica musica ridotta alla moderna pratica* (1555), urged the musician to use emphasis (*accenti*) according to the affects (*affetti*) of the words:

> The observation of an orator will teach one by watching the way he acts during an oration; the way he now speaks loudly, now softly, and slower and faster, and in this manner strongly moves his audience. This way of moving the beat has a great effect on the spirit, and for this reason the music is sung with the thought of imitating the accents and effects of the parts of an oration. What effect would an orator produce, who recites a beautiful speech without putting in place his accents and pronunciations, the quicker and slower movements, and speaking softly or loudly? That would not move the audience. Thus it should be in music.[5]

Gioseffo Zarlino, in *Istitioni harmoniche* (first published in 1558) poses the affects (*affetti*) contained in speech (*oratione*) as the primary reference on which to base musical decisions. In the chapter entitled "How the Intervals [*harmonie*] Are Adapted to the Words Placed beneath Them," Zarlino affirms that with regard to intervals and melodic motion, speech is the primary consideration (*la cosa principale*).[6]

Going deeper into the argument, Zarlino stresses that, although for the purpose of the representation of the affective content of the speech the choice of the mode is important, that of the intervals, of the accidentals to be introduced in the melody (*movimento accidentale*), and of the rhythmic figuration corresponding to the poetic rhythm (*i numeri*) is nevertheless no less decisive:

> It is necessary that we choose intervals and rhythms corresponding to the nature of the subject contained in the speech. . . . We must use joyful intervals and fast rhythms for joyful subjects, and mournful intervals and slow rhythms for mournful subjects; so that everything is done in proper relationship . . . and I must stress that, insofar as possible, one must accompany each word in such a way that, when it denotes harshness, hardness, cruelty, bitterness, and similar things, the intervals will be likewise, that is, somewhat hard and harsh, but in a manner that is not offensive. Similarly, when some of the words express laments, pain, grief, sighs, tears, and similar things, the harmony must be full of sadness.[7]

Thus, Zarlino suggests the employment of melodic motion that proceeds mainly through intervals of the whole tone and the major third, and the avoidance of semitones, wherever the words

> denote harshness, hardness, cruelty, bitterness, and similar things . . . allowing the major sixth or thirteenth—which by nature are somewhat harsh—to be heard over the lowest tone of the harmony; and these should be accompanied by the suspension of the fourth or of the eleventh over this same tone, with somewhat slow resolutions [*movimenti*]; among these one may also use the suspension of the seventh.[8]

On the other hand, to express "laments, pain, grief, sighs, tears, and similar things," one has recourse to "movements that proceed through semitones, minor thirds, and similar intervals, and make frequent use of minor sixths and thirteenths—which by their nature are soft and sweet—over the lowest tones of the composition."[9]

But the choice of intervals does not suffice for expressing the affects; it must correspond to proper choices in the melodic range: "The natural movements (that is, without altered notes) have more virility than those made by means of notes that have accidentals." Melodies that touch upon altered notes, on the other hand, "are somewhat languid." And finally we read, "With regard to the employment of rhythm, consider above all the subject treated in the speech: if it is joyful, one must proceed with vigorous and fast movements, that is, with figurations that result in a fast tempo, such as half notes and quarter notes; but when the subject is plaintive one must proceed with slow and lingering movements."[10]

The importance that humanistic culture attributed to the renewed study of rhetoric had, therefore, a profound influence upon musical language in the Renaissance and the Baroque. Rhetorical discourse, like musical discourse, required the combination of diverse capacities: the possession of ideas (*inventio*); the ability to put them in order and support them with appropriate arguments and demonstrations (*dispositio*—in music, elaboration of the subjects); the application of all the devices of language, the rhetorical figures necessary to reinforce the concepts (*elocutio*); the delivery of oration with the correct tone of voice and gestures (*actio* or *pronuntiatio*[11]—in music, with similarly appropriate dynamics, rhythmic fluctuations, and phrasings); and, finally, the cultivation of memory, whether for learning the oration or for making opportune use of quotations, maxims, and anecdotes.

This originally formed the whole of rhetorical art. But during the sixteenth century (specifically with the humanists Agricola, Vives, and Ramus) the notion appeared of a separation between *inventio* and *dispositio* on one hand and *elocutio* on the other. Rhetoric became identified with *elocutio*, and concentrated on the figures of ornate oratory; the ideas, arguments, and structuring of discourse were transferred, so to speak, from rhetoric to dialectic. The "ornamental" aspect of discourse began to overshadow dialectic considerations. It is no coincidence that in a century of profound and lacerating ideological conflict between religious and secular culture, between Protestant Reformation and Catholic Counter-Reformation, the ornamental aspect of discourse took on such exaggerated importance. The ideological war was waged with greatly intensified emphasis, from church pulpits and in town squares.

The end of the century witnessed the liberation of the artist's imagination, which attempted to bend language to the expression of feelings. To cite Guido Morpurgo in "Aristotelismo e barocco":

> The crisis in rhetoric coincides with the cultural crisis of the Renaissance, with the collapse of its equilibrium, and with the antagonism between two modes of living—the edifying and the libertine, or education [*docere*] and enjoyment [*delectare*]—that the Counter-Reformation had provoked. These were the two voices with which the humanistic Renaissance closed and the Counter-Reformation opened; and they offer us two themes whose dialectic would constitute the meaning of the Baroque.[12]

The musical repercussion of all this is more than evident: one needs only to think of the madrigals of Gesualdo, D'India, Luzzaschi, the Camerata of Bardi, and finally of the entire oeuvre of Monteverdi. The overwhelming importance of musical elocution with respect to the *dispositio* (the structure of the composition) fits into this reality and gradually leads, through the tormented path of mannerism, to a new equilibrium: the Baroque. Vincenzo Galilei, more than any other theoretician, helps us understand the delicate passage from the expressivity of the Renaissance to that of the Baroque. The polemic fury that inspired Galilei's lengthy treatise *Dialogo della musica antica et della moderna* (1581) provides a key to the interpretation of the musical Baroque. Galilei made a clear distinction between "states of the soul" (the affects) expressed through the descriptive character and the onomatopoeia of madrigalisms—which he criticized and derided in a sharp and entertaining manner—and states of the soul expressed according to the rules of the arts or oratory and declamation—that is, by using rhetorical *actio* and theatrical recitation as models.[13] He encouraged musicians to observe the most famous orators and actors of tragedy and comedy:

> the manner in which he speaks, with what voice with regard to highness and lowness, with what volume of sound, with what kind of emphases and gestures, how they are employed with respect to speed or slowness of movement . . . , how he acts infuriated or

excited, as a married woman, as a young girl, as a simple child, as a clever harlot, as one in love . . . , as those who lament, as those who scream; as the frightened, and as those who rejoice in happiness. . . .[14]

Further on one reads,

Before singing any poem, the ancient musician examined with extreme diligence the character of the person who was speaking, his age, his sex, toward whom and toward what end he acted; conceptions that the poet had earlier prepared with carefully chosen words . . . were then expressed by the musician in such a tone, with such accents and gestures, with such quantity and quality of sound, and with such rhythm as fitted the action and the person.[15]

According to Galilei, music should not serve the words through a pictorial melody, but rather by musically reproducing the proper pronunciation and accents of the words according to the *actio*, or rhetorical delivery. This, in fact, provides inspiration to musicians for the shape and placement of ornaments and the choice of rhythms, or range, of harmonic elaboration, and of all those devices of musical language that seventeenth-century musicians called "rhetorical figures"; these, by themselves, "speak" and express moods like the text, but do so independently.

In the preface to the *Nuove musiche* of 1602, Caccini writes, "To compose well in this manner and sing in this style serves much more the comprehension of the idea and the flavor of the text, and, similarly, its imitation in affective sounds when expressing it by affective singing, than it serves counterpoint."[16]

This is the key that allows one to understand how between the end of the sixteenth and beginning of the seventeenth centuries musical language, like that of literature, painting, and sculpture, passed from the Renaissance rhetoric based upon *inventio, dispositio,* and *elocutio* to a baroque rhetoric in which *elocutio* overcame the others and became *dispositio*. In other words, ornament became structure, and the structure of composition arose from the expressive potential of the ornament.

Based on the preceding, the second thesis of Galilei's treatise is of particular interest here. Galilei maintained—contradicting even his own teacher Gioseffo Zarlino—that instruments could express the *affetti*, independently of the words. A few lines after the previously cited passage, we read, "Do not doubt, even if Zarlino appears to say the opposite in chapter seven of the second part of his *Istitutioni*, that the sound of an instrument created art without the use of words, since it had, as I mentioned to you before and as Aristotle has stated, the nature to imitate custom, having in itself a great ability to effect in the souls of the listeners most of the affects that pleased the expert player."[17]

The expressivity of instrumental language in fact began moving toward extremes. From the keyboard literature alone, I might mention the Neapolitan experiments of Mayone and Trabaci, the fragmentation of Frescobaldi's toccatas into strongly contrasting episodes, the free improvisational linking of rhetorical-musical figures, from which sprang the allemandes of Froberger and the nonmeasured preludes of Louis Couperin; and—again of Froberger—the powerful expressivity of sarabandes, comparable to the most touching moments of the *toccate per l'Elevazione* of Frescobaldi. These last examples bring to mind the words with which Girolamo Diruta, when advising on the most suitable modes for the liturgical moment of the Elevation, urges the performer to imitate "in his playing the bitter torments of the Passion."[18]

The figures as expressed in harmony, melody, and rhythm thus began to compromise, and sometimes to distort, the ethos of the modes. Although, for example, in 1609 Girolamo Diruta attributed a single character to each mode, Athanasius Kircher, approximately forty years later, made it clear that a particular manner of treatment could modify the affects of the different modes.

Regarding the first two tones, for example, Diruta states that "the first tone renders the harmony grave and modest,"[19] but according to Kircher "the first tone, when it is more lively and nimble, is naturally suited to dances, to ballets, and to jubilant festivities; but when it is calm it is appropriate to the expression of devotion, of divine love, and of the desire for heavenly things."[20] Similarly, according to Diruta, "the second tone renders the harmony sad and distressing,"[21] but for Kircher "the second tone is suitable to express feelings of tenderness and compassion, but when it is more lively it can also serve to express feelings of joy."[22]

Why is it important for a performer to be concerned with rhetorical-musical figures? Because I believe that the identification of these figures will help the performer to understand the details of the musical discourse. It will encourage a careful reading, which gives much attention to the breath, the expectant pause, the emphases, the decay of sound. Let me examine the first section—just the first twelve measures—of Frescobaldi's *Toccata III* from *Toccate II*, and consider the figures that appear therein (see example 1).

After the prolongation of the first chords, one observes in the second measure three figures: the *prolongatio* (the first dissonant suspension), the *cromatismo*, and the *anaphora*. The *prolongatio*, whether as a suspension, as the first note tied to a group of short note values, or as suspended over a passing tone or neighbor tone, expresses moral and physical pain and requires a sighing pronunciation, lightly prolonging the note in question. The same applies to the *cromatismo*, concerning which Mersenne in his *Harmonie universelle* (1636) stated, "Semitones or sharps represent tears, moans, because of their small intervals which express weakness, since small intervals as they ascend and descend are like children, old people, and those recovered from a long illness."[23] And finally, he provides this interesting performance suggestion: "Stopping upon the notes after the semitone accentuates this character of weakness." The *anaphora*, the third of the indicated figures, expresses anxiety; but the anapestic rhythm of the melodic beginning, which is repeated three times in succession in different voices of the polyphonic framework, dampens the agitated character of the figure and makes it sighing and sorrowful.

In the next (third) measure there are two other harmonic dissonances: the false relation at the octave and the tritone (*parrhesia*). The fourth measure brings the tension of the rising *anabasis*. The tenor line introduces two *prolongationes*, to be echoed by the soprano in the next measure.

In addition there are prolongations of passing or neighboring tones. The iambic rhythm of these prolongations brings out the accent, the breath that every sustained note requires. The dotted note is a note contained in itself: in the dot it must diminish, thin out, die—it is an accent.

The fifth measure presents the *exclamatio*, f♯" to a'. The close succession of trochaic and iambic rhythms, together with the large falling interval of a major sixth, makes this one of the most pregnant of musical figures. In the sixth measure, the chain of the various *exclamationes* is interrupted by two eighth notes, or an *antitheton*—a figure which unexpectedly introduces an element of contrast. In this case it expresses

Example 1 Toccata terza per l'organo da sonarsi all'Elevazione

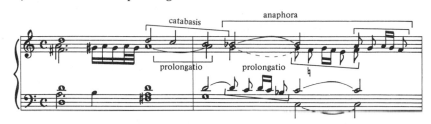

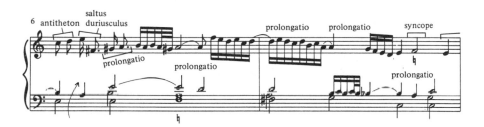

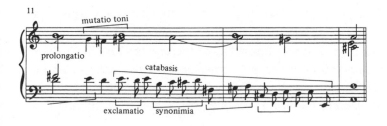

a moment of repose that precedes the last sorrowful *exclamatio*, the interval of a seventh, e" to f♯' before the cadence.

In the seventh measure the breath of the *prolongatio*, repeated three times in succession, is interrupted by the *syncope*, whose accent prepares the long and slow *anabasis* in the soprano (covering mm. 8 and 9). In m. 10, the *anabasis* proceeds in the bass; after reaching its apex, the *antitheton*, represented by the *mutatio toni* moving from a minor to a major chord, prepares the following *catabasis*. The precipitating *catabasis* dissolves the tension accumulated by the long ascent of the *anabasis*. It is interesting to observe how accurately Frescobaldi indicates the dynamism of this *catabasis*: an initial *exclamatio* followed by a triple *synonimia*, whose first element, composed of four chromatic notes, initially checks the downfall, which, through the following two elements—each composed of only three notes—leads to the concluding cadence of the first section of the toccata. The notation of the eighth notes, each flagged separately, unambiguously indicates the weight, the emphasis of each note.

I have chosen the first section of this toccata because it presents a particular concentration of figures. In the successive sections of the same toccata, the figures appear much more diluted. In other compositions, for example in Toccata IV, often a single figure (*prolongatio*, *anaphora*, or *exclamatio*) characterizes an entire section. Evidently these are two different ways to elaborate a musical discourse; the result of the first manner is much more agonizing than that of the second.

The rhetorical-musical figures became defined over the centuries with the evolution and maturation of the musical language. Their identification within the confines of instrumental composition means—in the absence of words—reading the music in a semantic manner, and thus recognizing therein the process of connotation that characterizes musical as well as literary discourse.

Music is by nature a figurative, that is, a rhetorical language. To express affects through sound necessarily means translating actual expression into rhetorical-poetic expression. This means that between sign and significance there cannot be a direct connection, but only a connection marked by ambiguity. Musical figures, like literary figures, have their roots in ambiguity, and both the performer and the listener should be aware of this. The figure, whether a brief pause or exclamation, or even a more extended element like the *anabasis* or the *anaphora*, is intended to emphasize and reinforce the inspirational meaning of a musical discourse. Gérard Genette, when discussing literary analysis in the Baroque, writes in *Figures I*, "Thus, the existence and character of figures are absolutely determined by the existence and character of fictitious signs, which I compare to real signs by positing their semantic equivalence."[24] The search for such equivalences, in fact, forms the basis for the technique of the musical language of figures through which the *affetti* are expressed. The baroque musician was not interested in the novelty or originality of the figures; on the contrary, he drew, in large part, from a code in common possession, as if integrating his own expressions into a language, without compromising the originality of his inventive process.

The early seventeenth-century theorists (especially the Germans —Burmeister, Lippius, Kircher, Bernhard, Walther, and many others) concerned themselves with this subject. By taking the principal figures of the musical literature and giving them labels derived from rhetoric, they ended up by inventing a considerable number, which were classified according to their expressive meaning or, in modern terms, according to their specific connotative value.

I conclude with another quotation from Vincenzo Galilei. After describing the origin and characteristics of the principal instruments, he lists the qualities and defects of the instrumentalists of his time: "Much more reputable," he writes, "are those who teach us the virtues (that is, transmit the sentiments), and especially since they are so much more rare and excellent than those who simply entertain us."[25] These words were echoed for centuries by the best musicians. François Couperin remarked, "I love what moves me much more than what surprises me,"[26] and C. P. E. Bach expressed himself in much the same manner.[27] Clearly, the composer's communication of affective emotions through the performance to the listener formed the principal aim of music.[28]

Notes

1. Regarding the relationships between poetical and musical language in the Middle Ages, see F. Alberto Gallo, *Il medioevo*, Storia della musica, vol. 2 (Turin: EDT, 1977), 3–12.

2. In this connection, see Donatella Restani, "Il *Chirone* di Ferecrate e la 'nuove' musica greca: Ricerca sul lessico retorico-musicale," *Rivista italiana di musicologia* 18 (1983): 139–92.

3. On musical-rhetorical terminology in medieval treatises, see F. Alberto Gallo, "Beziehungen zwischen grammatischer, rhetorischer und musikalischer Terminologie im

Mittelalter," in International Musicological Society, *Report of the Twelfth Congress, Berkeley 1977*, ed. Daniel Heartz and Bonnie Wade (Kassel: Bärenreiter, 1981), 787–90.

4. Silvestro Ganassi, *Regola Rubertina* (Venice, 1542; reprint, Bologna: Forni, 1970), 6.

5. Nicola Vicentino, *L'antica musica ridotta alla moderna pratica* (Rome, 1555; reprint, Kassel: Bärenreiter, 1959), fol. 94v (misprinted as fol. 88v).

6. Gioseffo Zarlino, *Istitutioni harmoniche* (Venice, 1573; reprint, New Jersey: Gregg Press, 1966), 419 (misprinted as 319).

7. Ibid.

8. Ibid., 420.

9. Ibid.

10. Ibid.

11. On the relationships between rhetoric and music in the Graeco-Roman tradition with respect to *pronuntiatio*, see F. Alberto Gallo, "Pronuntiatio: Ricerche sulla storia di un termine retorico-musicale," *Acta musicologica* 35 (1963): 38–46. On expression in musical performance in Italy during the sixteenth century, see Frederico Mompellio, "Un certo ordine di procedere che non si può scrivere," in *Scritti in onore di Luigi Ronga* (Milan: Ricciardi, 1973), 367–88.

12. Guido Morpurgo Tagliabue, "Aristotelismo e barocco," in *Atti del Congresso internazionale di studi umanistici* (Rome: Fratelli Bocca, 1955).

13. Vincenzo Galilei, *Dialogo della musica antica et della moderna* (Florence, 1581; reprint, New York: Broude Bros., 1967), 88.

14. Ibid., 89.

15. Ibid., 90.

16. Giulio Caccini, *Le nuove musiche* (Florence, 1602; reprint, Rome: Accademia d'Italia, 1939), prefazione.

17. Galilei, *Dialogo*, 90.

18. Girolamo Diruta, *Il transilvano: Dialogo sopra il vero modo di sonar organi, et istromenti da penna* (Venice: Alessandro Vincenti, 1622; reprint, Bologna: Forni, 1969), 22.

19. Ibid., libro 3, p. 4.

20. Athanasius Kircher, *Musurgia universalis* (Rome, 1650; reprint, Hildesheim: Olms, 1970), 2:142.

21. Diruta, *Il transilvano*, libro 3, p. 4.

22. Kircher, *Musurgia universalis*, 2:142.

23. Marin Mersenne, *Harmonie universelle* (Paris, 1636; reprint, Paris: CNRS, 1963), 2:173.

24. Gérard Genette, *Figures I* (Paris: Édition du Seuil, 1966), 210.

25. Galilei, *Dialogo*, 148.

26. François Couperin, *Pièces de clavecin* (Paris, 1713), 1: preface.

27. Carl Philip Emanuel Bach, *Versuch über die wahre Art das Clavier zu spielen* (Berlin, 1753; reprint, Leipzig: Breitkopf & Härtel, 1957), chap. 3, in particular pp. 115–25.

28. For a bibliography on musical rhetoric, see George J. Buelow, "Rhetoric," *The New Grove Dictionary of Music and Musicians* (London: Macmillan, 1980), 15:793–803. Since this bibliography covers only material published through 1980, I shall take the opportunity to supplement it with the following items (in addition to those by Gallo and Restani cited in

notes 1, 2, and 3 above): Warren Kirkendale, "Ciceronians versus Aristotelians on the Ricercar as Exordium from Bembo to Bach," *Journal of the American Musicological Society*, 32 (1979): 1–44; Ursula Kirkendale, "The Source for Bach's Musical Offering: The Institutio Oratoria of Quintilian," *Journal of the American Musicological Society* 33 (1980): 88–141; Catherine Renoult, "De la déclamation musicale à l'âge classique, Lully ou l'émergence d'un style," *Musique ancienne* 8–9 (1980): 4–33; idem, "Rameau et l'héritage lulliste: Les problèmes esthétiques de l'âge classique: Les accents pathétiques dans la déclamation du récitatif à l'âge classique," *Musique ancienne* 10 (1981): 4–17; L. F. Tagliavini, "Notentext und Ausführung einer Toccata von Frescobaldi," in *Kongressbericht Bayreuth 1981*, 218–21; Dalmonte Sartini, *Musica-Retorica-Teoria degli affetti*, distributed by Università di Bologna, Facoltà di Lettere, Dipartimento di Musica e Spettacolo, 1983–84.

Performance Practices and Original Performance Conditions

EW ASPECTS OF THE performance of Frescobaldi's music are as troubling as those involving meter and tempo relationships. In the prefaces to his publications, as well as in his use of a large variety of metric and rhythmic notational devices, the composer shows his great concern with communicating the proper tempos to the player, but the precise meaning of his comments and special notational practices have thus far remained elusive. Etienne Darbellay and Margaret Murata tackle the problem from different angles but their conclusions are substantially in agreement. Darbellay confines himself to Frescobaldi's *Capricci*, in which the composer's concern with tempo is especially evident; he shows that Frescobaldi ingeniously adapted traditional practices to create a consistent system for prescribing complex and musically effective tempo relationships. Murata bases her discussion on the concrete and highly practical advice given in a little-known treatise by a Roman contemporary, Pier Francesco Valentini. She draws from this treatise some startling conclusions regarding the rhythmic interpretation of music of the time —conclusions often at variance with current performance practices.

We are still much in the dark regarding the specific purposes for which many of Frescobaldi's works were composed and the contexts in which they were meant to be performed. James Moore, in a study of newly discovered documents regarding the liturgical traditions at St. Mark's in Venice, is able to provide a detailed picture of the use of organ music in elaborate ritual at that church. He concludes that Frescobaldi's collection of organ Masses, the *Fiori musicali*, is ideally suited to the practices at St. Mark's, and may have been written specifically for Venice (where it was published), rather than—as was believed in the past—for the general use of small parish churches.

Tempo Relationships in Frescobaldi's
Primo Libro di Capricci

ETIENNE DARBELLAY

O NE OF THE MAIN differences between Frescobaldi's capriccios of 1624 and his ricercars of nine years earlier is the liveliness of the capriccios—the result of the contrasting tempos and characters of their successive variation sections. The composer's preface to the *Capricci* is devoted largely to these "different tempos and variations," and explains how to deal with the difficulties that may arise from them. The preface shows, in short, that he was aware of departing in some ways from the common practice of his time.[1] Since this document forms the basis of much that follows here, I shall quote it in full:

> To the students of this work:
>
> Since for some [players] the performance of these pieces might prove difficult, in view of the different tempos and variations, and, further, since it appears that many [players] have abandoned the practice of studying from a score [i.e., a full score], I wish to point out that in those places that seem not to be governed by contrapuntal practice, one should first search for the affect of the passage, and the composer's intention for pleasing the ear, and [thus] discover the manner of playing it. In those compositions entitled *Capriccio* I did not maintain as easy a style as in my ricercars, but their difficulty should not be judged before trying them out adequately at the keyboard, where one will discover through study which affect must prevail. Furthermore, since my purpose is ease of performance as well as beauty, it seems appropriate that the performer to whom the playing of a piece from the beginning to the end seems too difficult, shall feel free to play whichever passages he likes best, as long as he ends with those that conclude in the key [of the piece].

The beginnings should be taken adagio, in order to give more spirit and beauty to the following passage, and the cadences should be held back somewhat before the next passage is begun. In the *trippole* [patterns in triple proportion] or *sequialtere* [patterns in $\frac{3}{2}$ proportion]: if they are major [i.e., a three-semibreve pattern], one must play adagio; if they are minor [a three-minim pattern], somewhat more allegro; if [the patterns consist of] three semiminims, more allegro; if there are six [semiminims] against four, one must take their tempo by an allegro beat. It is appropriate to hold back at certain dissonances and arpeggiate them, in order to make the following passage more lively.

This is said in all modesty, and I entrust myself to the good judgment of the students [of these works].

Frescobaldi expresses three basic ideas pertaining specifically to his tempos:

1. a contrast principle between sections: he alludes to "different tempos," to slowing down on cadences between passages, and to arpeggiating certain dissonances "in order to make the following passage more lively";
2. an acceleration principle: he asks the performer to begin adagio in order to "give more spirit and beauty to the following passage";
3. a variable tactus speed: for triple-meter sections he stipulates a tactus speed that varies according to the time signature and the range of predominant note values (the *Notenbild*).

The third point is of utmost importance. This principle departs unmistakably from the late Renaissance theories of an invariable tactus whose fixed speed governs the note values irrespective of the Notenbild.[2] Had it not been applied to a collection of contrapuntal works, this stipulation would not be as far-reaching, since a variable tactus must be assumed in any case for the large range of new *galanterie* associated with the *seconda prattica*. I shall come back later to the specific problems of tempos in triple-meter sections, but must first turn to the basic question of whether a variable tactus still allows for traditional proportional relationships between the meters of successive sections.

The Proportion Principle and Its Limitations

I shall first consider some constraints on the tactus principle itself. The concepts of meter, proportion, and tactus in the music of the period are not related in the same way as their modern counterparts, the time signature and the (conductor's) beat. Meter corresponds essentially to the division of the breve "measure," as indicated by the *tempus* and the *prolatio*, proportion corresponds to the augmentation or diminution of the duration of note values by a specified factor or ratio; and tactus corresponds to the gestural indication (usually a downward motion of the hand) of the semibreve in *integer valor* (that is, without proportion).[3] According to the tactus principle, the rate of the underlying *integer valor* semibreve must remain constant, even when proportions are applied.

The proportions indicated by Frescobaldi frequently relate the meter defined by the mensuration sign to the semibreve tactus, as in the commonly employed *tempus perfectum* with *proportio tripla* (see example 1).

Example 1

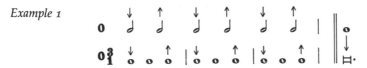

(In these examples, downward arrows correspond to the tactus; the following upward gesture falls on the second subdivision in duple meters and on the third subdivision in triple meters; the note values to the right of these examples show the equivalency relationships.)

Equally common is the expression of a relationship between contrasting meters governed by a shared tactus (see example 2).

Example 2

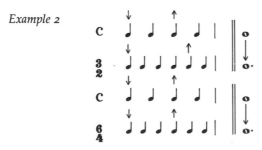

In these examples the proportion serves both to create the actual meter and to diminish the note values so as to make the metric pattern agree

with the reference semibreve tactus in common time. For example, the
$\frac{6}{4}$ proportion creates a pattern of six semiminims, but also reduces the
duration of each semiminim by one-third, so that the length of the
pattern corresponds to that of a semibreve in *integer valor* (see example
2). For certain proportions, however, the tactus principle will result in a
conflict between the tactus and the actual meter. Such a conflict arises,
for example, at the opening of Frescobaldi's *Partite sopra Follia (Toccate I)*
(example 3).

Example 3

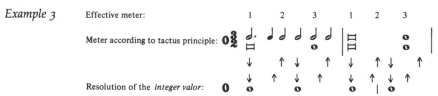

The sesquialtera ($\frac{3}{2}$) proportion reduces the duration of each semibreve
by one-third, and since the rate of the tactus remains fixed, the measure
becomes equivalent to two ternary semibreve tactus units, the second of
which contradicts the actual meter of three semibreve units.

The "tempo tyranny" of the tactus principle of the late Renaissance,
that is, the subjugation of the tempo and the metric organization of a
composition to the invariable tactus, eventually came into conflict with
the freedom required by the metric patterns and tempos of the new
baroque practices. Since under the tactus principle a proportion will
generate simultaneously a change of meter and a change of the speed of
the note values, a proportional signature generally cannot be used to
change one without changing the other. For example, the hypothetical
proportion $\frac{5}{4}$ following a section in common time will result in both a
speeding up of the quarter notes (with the durational equivalence of five
quarter notes of the new section to four quarter notes of the previous
section) and in setting up a new meter of five quarter notes to the tactus[4]
(see example 4).

Example 4

A proportion is not capable of specifying a change of meter, say from c
to $\frac{5}{4}$, with an equivalence of the surface pulse, such as quarter note

equals quarter note, because this would slow down the tactus and thus violate the tactus principle (see example 5).

Example 5

Conversely, a proportion is not capable of specifying a change of tempo, say of five quarter notes of the new tempo equivalent in duration to four quarter notes of the old tempo, and yet maintain the same meter (see example 6),

Example 6

because this results in a speeding up of the tactus, and hence, again, a violation of the tactus principle. To be sure, there are cases in which the proportion merely effects a redistribution of the grouping of the same number of pulses, as with a change from $\frac{3}{2}$ to $\frac{6}{4}$ (example 7).

Example 7

Only in such cases do the proportions effect a change of meter without a change in the speed of the surface pulses, since for both proportions the relationships to the reference values in *integer valor* are the same.

Some meter changes cannot even be expressed as proportions. For example, an important problem facing Frescobaldi was the specification of a fast simple triple meter, as when moving from common time to the metric pattern expressed today by $\frac{3}{4}$, with a relationship of three quarter notes in the new tempo equivalent to two quarter notes in the old tempo (see example 8).

Example 8

If one were to use the proportion $\frac{3}{4}$, the quarter notes would slow down rather than speed up (example 9).

Example 9

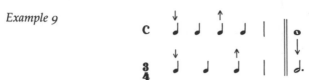

If one uses the proportion $\frac{6}{4}$, the quarter notes would indeed speed up by the desired amount, but the resulting meter is a compound triple rather than a simple triple meter (example 10).

Example 10

Finally, if one were to use the proportion $\frac{3}{2}$ applied to a group of two quarter notes, the ratio no longer acts on the semibreve reference value, and hence, the proportion is not legitimate; in other words, the desired combination of meter and tempo change cannot be effected without a speeding up of the tactus itself (example 11).

Example 11

Since a proportion cannot change the tempo without changing the metric organization, no proportions are likely to appear between two successive duple-meter sections. In fact, all duple-meter sections in the *Capricci* are marked by the common-time signature C; not even the *alla-breve* signature ¢ is used in this collection.[5] In practice, a true proportion can be realized only when a triple meter is involved—that is, either between a duple-meter and a triple-meter section, or between two triple-meter sections involving different patterns, as between $\frac{6}{4}$ and $\frac{3}{2}$. In both cases a tactus of the same duration can be maintained, but with a change of subdivision: from a division into an equal (*aequalis*) number of subunits between the downbeat and the upbeat to one into an unequal (*inaequalis*) number of subunits.

Frescobaldi's preface stipulates that the speed of the tactus in triple-meter sections is a function of the Notenbild. To what extent is this prescription compatible with the tactus principle and the system of proportions? We have seen that a true proportion between successive sections requires that the meters of both can be related through the common-time interval of the tactus. I shall consider the implications of two different situations. The first is that of the existence of a proportion between a section in duple meter and a section in triple meter, implying that both sections are governed by proportions to an *integer valor* with the same tactus rate. The dependence of the tactus rate on the Notenbild in the triple-meter section will by necessity also affect the tempo of the duple-meter section that is related to it by a proportion, and hence the sections in duple meter must also have different tactus rates. The second situation, that of two different triple-meter sections conceivably related by a proportion, occurs infrequently in the *Capricci*; I shall consider this case further on.

Tactus in Duple-Meter Sections

Are there any indications of possible changes in the speed of the tactus in duple-meter sections? The capriccios that include different meters generally show a progression of the Notenbild from a predominance of white note values (whole and half notes) to a predominance of black note values (quarter to sixteenth notes).[6] A parallel progression can be observed in the compositional style, which moves from more or less old-fashioned Renaissance counterpoint to a canzona texture of lively motives in eighth and sixteenth notes. If the tactus were held constant throughout the composition, an unreasonably slow tempo would be required for the beginning in order to arrive at a realistic speed for the final sixteenth notes. And yet, Frescobaldi prescribes that the beginnings should be taken adagio—a prescription that within the framework of a constant tactus speed makes little sense. It is more reasonable to assume that Frescobaldi's prescription served merely to prevent a contemporary performer from being induced by the white Notenbild into beginning with too lively a tempo, and, furthermore, that he expected shifts in the tactus speed for subsequent duple-meter sections similar to those he stipulated for triple-meter sections.

A discussion of the placement of bar lines will prove enlightening here. In Frescobaldi's time bar lines were introduced in score notation to serve as points of reference that facilitated the visual perception of the simultaneous progression of different voices. According to Diruta, the bar lines ordinarily are spaced at the interval of a breve.[7] In most editions of the time, however, this interval often is reduced or enlarged, seemingly at random or dependent on the layout of the music on the page. But in the *Capricci* a consistent policy is followed: within a section, the metric unit chosen for the interval of barring usually remains the same. The few irregularities in the 1624 edition of the *Capricci* can be explained by a comparison with the later (1626, 1628, and 1642) versions. Where in an earlier edition a barred unit is not completed at the end of a system due to lack of space but spills over into the next system, a bar line has sometimes been inserted in a subsequent edition—presumably by a printer who failed to notice the consistency in the bar line spacing in the earlier edition (compare plate 1, which shows m. 61 of Capriccio IV in the 1624 edition divided between two systems, and plate 2, which shows that in the 1626 edition a superfluous bar line had been added within that measure).[8] Most likely, the irregular extra bar lines in the first (1624) edition were similarly the result of units broken between successive staves in the lost manuscript exemplar.

The interesting fact about Frescobaldi's barring practice in the *Capricci* is that in duple-meter sections in which a Notenbild focused on the half note prevails (the *prima-prattica* scale of note values), a breve-unit measure is used, but that in those duple-meter sections in which an eighth- to sixteenth-note surface pulse prevails (the *seconda-prattica* scale) the bar lines correspond to semibreve-unit measures. On the other hand, in the triple-meter sections, including the compound-meter sections in $\frac{6}{4}$, the barring unit always corresponds to a single tactus (as determined by the proportion to the semibreve reference unit).[9]

Common Time and Cut Time

In order to understand how Frescobaldi uses notation to suggest tempo in his duple-meter sections, it is necessary to review some aspects of the notational practice of his time—in particular, the relationships between the signatures C and ¢, the Notenbild, and the tactus. For this purpose I shall turn to the writings of three representative composers and theorists: *Della prattica musica* (1601) by the Neapolitan Scipione Cerretto; *Cartella musicale* (1614) by the Bolognese Adriano Banchieri; and *Syntagma musicum* (1619) by the German Michael Praetorius.[10]

All three authors agree on two points: (1) Cut time, indicated by ¢, is no longer beaten *alla breve* (i.e., on a fixed breve tactus)—a new practice, which these authors criticize; (2) cut time is associated with a prevailing Notenbild of white notes (according to Praetorius, the "motet style"), and common time with a prevailing Notenbild of black notes (i.e., short note values—Praetorius's "madrigal style"). But there seem to be disagreements between their comparisons of the resulting tempos in cut time and common time. Praetorius and Banchieri describe cut time as *celerior* or *presto*, compared to *tardior* or *adagio* for common time, while Cerretto states that "cut time is the appropriate sign for *cantilene* which must proceed *grave*." The explanation for this contradiction is not that Cerretto is still thinking of the old alla-breve practice and expects a slow breve tactus.[11] Rather, he is referring to the speed of the surface motion of the piece—that is, the tempo conveyed by the predominant note values at the appropriate tactus rate—while Praetorius and Banchieri are referring to the speed of the tactus itself. In fact, Cerretto goes on to criticize the use of cut time in pieces containing a large number of sixteenth notes and states that if this time signature were taken literally, the progression of diminutions would be so fast as "to give the listeners nausea."

With the earlier practice of beating cut time alla breve, the whole-note to quarter-note Notenbild of cut time is equivalent to the half-note to eighth-note Notenbild of common time (assuming a common tactus rate) (see example 12 and table 1, a and b).

Example 12   *Table 1*

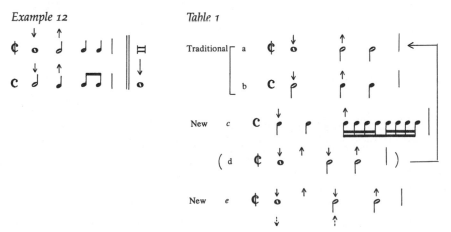

Plate 1   Capriccio IV in *Capricci* (1624)

Plate 2   Capriccio IV in *Capricci* (1626)

In the early seventeenth-century *seconda prattica*, the scale of commonly used note values in common time was effectively displaced one unit toward smaller values, since sixteenth notes had become widely used as an integral part of the new compositional style (see example 13).

Example 13

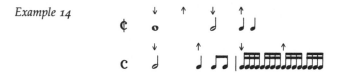

On the other hand, analogous long runs of eighth notes are rarely found in the cut-time *prima prattica* style; within the older practice they belonged to the realm of *alla mente* improvisation.

The increasing presence of sixteenth-note diminutions eventually forced the use of a slower tempo in common time. However, no equivalent slowing down of the tactus in cut time was necessary, and as a result, the tactus of cut time, now generally taken at the semibreve, became faster than the semibreve tactus of common time (see example 14 and table 1c and d).

Example 14

Eventually a point might have been reached at which the semibreve tactus of cut time would move more than twice as fast as the tactus in common time, but in actual practice the movement in a white Notenbild was also slowed down somewhat (table 1e).

Table 1 shows that this new tactus in cut time (1e), if beaten alla breve (indicated by dotted arrows), would be slower than the traditional tactus (1a), and barely faster than the tactus of common time (1c). But when beaten *alla semibreve*, it is notably faster than either one, in spite of the effective slowing down of the earlier tempo associated with the corresponding Renaissance Notenbild. This explains why contemporary theorists speak of a fast tactus for pieces proceeding by a relatively moderate movement. Banchieri, for example, states that cut time is now "beaten at a fast motion [*presto*], because it governs white notes, whereas common time is slow [*adagio*] because it governs black notes."[12]

Tempo in the Duple-Meter Sections

Having shown that in general early seventeenth-century practice the speed of the tactus in duple-meter sections was subject to variation depending on the Notenbild, I shall now return to Frescobaldi's personal system. By dispensing with the cut-time signature, Frescobaldi eliminated any uncertainty regarding the reference value (breve or semibreve) of the tactus. Starting always from a semibreve tactus, Frescobaldi worked out a notational system for the communication of tempos—a system based on both Notenbild and barring.

To indicate the style formerly governed by cut time, he uses a predominantly white Notenbild with bar lines spaced at the interval of a breve. This notation implies a comparatively fast semibreve tactus, but, in effect, a slow tempo, due to the predominant motion of half notes. This style is most often found at the beginning of the capriccios, and hence is in accordance with his prescription to begin these pieces *adagio*. On the other hand, new-style canzona-like passages—especially common in the final sections of the capriccios—ordinarily are represented by a black Notenbild that includes many sixteenth notes, and in such sections the bar lines are spaced at the interval of the semibreve. The effective tempo, especially of the sixteenth notes, will be fast, but the semibreve tactus will be slower than that of the old-style sections.

Between these extreme scales of note values (prevailing half notes and prevailing sixteenth notes) almost all capriccios include sections showing two intermediate Notenbilder, in which either quarter notes or eighth notes are predominant. The quarter-note pattern is usually barred in breve units and the eighth-note pattern in semibreve units. Both intermediate patterns are most often found in middle sections and are consistently employed in all chromatic sections—possibly reflecting the expressive character of such sections. If one assumes that the breve-unit barring is generally associated with a faster tactus, and the semibreve-unit barring with a slower tactus, four relative levels of tactus speed, corresponding to the four well-defined scales of note values, can be postulated. The result is that as one progresses from the half-note to sixteenth-note patterns, the tactus becomes slower but the predominant note values become faster.

Some guidelines for the magnitudes of these changes in tactus speed can be arrived at by the following considerations. They must be bounded by the limiting cases of, at one extreme, no change at a transition between sections, and at the other extreme, a halving of the tactus speed at a transition. The latter would merely result in a doubling of the speed of identical note values, and thus no longer represents a true change of tactus speed, since the same result could be obtained by notating the section in double note values. Table 2 illustrates the comparative speeds for the four patterns under the assumption that they are more or less evenly distributed within this range; the accompanying hypothetical met-ronome indications merely suggest a set of possible values for the tem-pos of these patterns.[13]

Incidentally, a similar relationship between the Notenbild and bar-line spacing is observed in the examples provided by Banchieri and Praetorius for their discussions of C and ¢: the bar lines are spaced by a breve in their examples in cut time, with a whole-note to quarter-note scale, and by a semibreve in the examples in common time, with a half-note to eighth-note scale.[14]

Frescobaldi's Prescriptions for Sections with Triple-Meter Groupings

I shall now examine the conditions under which true proportions (i.e., proportions that preserve the speed of a common tactus) can be real-ized between sections in duple meter and in triple meter, taking into account both the different levels for the tactus speed in duple meter and the prescriptions given in Frescobaldi's preface for the tempo in triple-

Table 2

meter sections. In the latter, Frescobaldi distinguishes four possible patterns:

[A]   In the *trippole* [patterns in triple proportion] or *sesquialtere* [patterns in $\frac{3}{2}$ proportion]: if they are major [i.e., a three-semibreve pattern] one must play adagio;

[B]   if they are minor [a three-minim pattern], somewhat more allegro;

[C]   if [the pattern consists of] three semiminims, more allegro;

[D]   if there are six [semiminims] against four one must take their tempo with an allegro beat [*battuta*].

Of the four patterns described here, the first, second, and fourth correspond to well-defined traditional proportions ($\frac{3}{1}$, $\frac{3}{2}$, $\frac{6}{4}$). But such is not the case for the pattern of three semiminims, the tempo of which, according to Frescobaldi's prescription, seems to fall somewhere between that of a sesquialtera pattern of half notes and a pattern of triplet quarter notes.[15] With the exception of this three-semiminim pattern, the tactus rates attributed to these proportional time signatures agree closely with those stipulated by Praetorius. The slower tactus (*tactus tardior*) governs both common-time ($\mathbf{C}$) and triple meters of three whole notes (*proportio tripla*); the faster tactus (*tactus celerior*) governs both cut-time ($\mathbf{\mathbb{C}}$) and triple meters of three half notes (sesquialtera); and a *tactus mediocris* (meaning here "smaller," that is, faster tactus) is reserved for divisions that are more or less equivalent to Frescobaldi's $\frac{6}{4}$ pattern.[16]

As a result of the different prescribed tactus speeds in both duple and triple meter, a true proportion can be realized only between certain types of sections—specifically between those sections that can have a common tactus speed. An examination of the capriccios shows that at transitions in which no proportion is possible, the earlier section frequently concludes with an extended cadence, or its beat is dissolved by passages of free gestures in a toccata style. Free sections of this type are usually attached to the end of triple-meter sections, especially if followed by a duple-meter section whose bar-line spacing is not equivalent to that of the preceding duple-meter section, and hence—according to the above theory—whose tactus speed would be different. In the capriccios, proportions are generally possible only in transitions from duple-meter sections to triple-meter sections; the few transitions from triple meter to

duple meter that do allow proportions, in fact, lack toccata-like interme-
diary sections; see, for example, Capriccio VII ("Or che noi rimena"),
mm. 11–12, 45–46, 64–65.

Proportions: Duple-Meter Sections Versus
Triple-Meter Sections

I shall now turn to the crucial question regarding the tempo relationships in the *Capricci*: are there transitions between sections at which
proportions must be observed?

To begin with, there are a few sections in which different metric
patterns, specifically those governed by C and by $\frac{6}{4}$, appear simultaneously in different voices. In these situations there can of course be no
doubt regarding the need for observing an exact proportion. For example,
in Capriccio II, mm. 49–62, the different voices exchange their time
signatures during the course of the section. Moreover, at m. 49 the $\frac{6}{4}$
signature is introduced in the lower three voices but not in the upper
voice, which evidently continues to be governed by the earlier C
signature. Since there is no indication in the part for the upper voice that
the tactus speed should be changed at this point, clearly a common
tactus is shared by the two contiguous sections.

If my theory regarding the dependence of tactus speed on bar-line
spacing and Notenbild is correct, then for all transitions between duple-
meter and triple-meter sections (or vice versa) at which a proportion is
intended, the tactus speed implied by the pattern of the duple-meter
section should correspond to the tactus rate prescribed by Frescobaldi
for the triple-meter section. Thus, a section in duple meter with bar-line
spacing at the breve should be followed or preceded by a section in
sesquialtera ($\frac{3}{2}$) or in $\frac{6}{4}$, since both require a comparatively fast tactus.
(Frescobaldi's case of the three-semiminim pattern must be ruled out
here, since, as explained earlier, it does not represent a proportion.)
Similarly, duple meter with semibreve bar-line spacing should be associated with *proportio tripla* ($\frac{3}{1}$), since both require a slower tactus. These
are exactly the correspondences found in the *Capricci*—with a few exceptions to be explained shortly.

These proportional relationships between duple and triple meters, as
well as a few other relationships to be discussed below, are illustrated in

table 3, in which models a and b represent the slower tactus, and models c and d the faster tactus patterns. Note that each case allows for some variation of the tactus speed, depending on whether the Notenbild corresponds to model a or model b of table 2 for the slower tactus case, or to model c or model d for the faster tactus case.

The relationships described thus far do not allow for a proportional relationship between a compound triple ⁶₄ pattern and a duple meter with a slow tactus. The fact that Frescobaldi does not use the ⁶₄ signature —associated with a fast tactus—for that situation but resorts to other notational means, provides additional support for the theory. He either introduces quarter-note triplets within a duple meter, as in Capriccio I, mm. 133–47, or uses the black notation of *hemiola minor*, as in Capriccio V ("sopra la bassa fiamenga"), mm. 57–71; both methods are illustrated in table 3 below pattern A. The groups of six black minims resulting from

Table 3

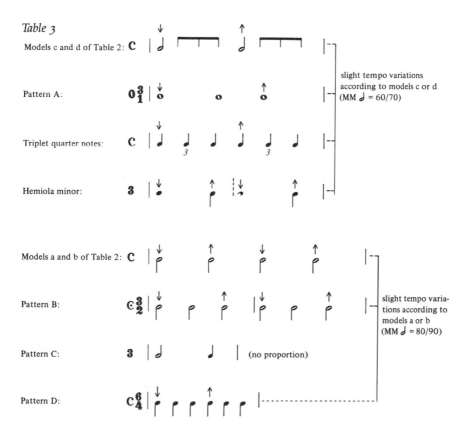

this last notation are visually identical to the groups of quarter notes in the triplet notation, or, for that matter, to the groups of quarter notes under the $\frac{6}{4}$ signature, although the latter proceed at a faster pace. The slower tempo of the *hemiola minor* is corroborated by the contemporary practice of beating this pattern with a downward stroke corresponding to groups of three rather than to six black minims (see table 3). Furthermore, Praetorius states that if the tactus is taken according to groups of six ("tactus trochaicus diminutus"), the rate should be somewhat slower than that for the corresponding $\frac{6}{4}$ signature.[17]

Ordinarily, in passages preceding or following a duple meter with a fast tactus pattern (table 2, models a and b), the $\frac{6}{4}$ signature is used, but in Capriccio II, mm. 24–31, black *hemiola minor* notation is employed in spite of the fast tactus clearly implied by the preceding tactus. Two alternate explanations can be offered. First, the section contains an odd number of triple units, and since as a rule each section must conclude with a downbeat,[18] the passage could not be beaten according to tactus associated with the $\frac{6}{4}$ notation (since this would result in an upstroke at m. 32). Second, the $\frac{6}{4}$ notation would have obscured the cross-rhythms between the ternary and binary divisions of the breve at mm. 24, 27, and 28, which is more clearly represented by the hemiola notation. Most sections notated by Frescobaldi in $\frac{6}{4}$ maintain a rhythmically straightforward binary division of the pattern.

Relationships between Successive Triple-Meter Sections

Frescobaldi's specific choices among the available notations for both duple and triple meters provide persuasive evidence that he intended traditional proportions to be observed. This hypothesis is further supported by an examination of the relationships between successive sections that are both in some form of triple meter. Furthermore, a number of seemingly anomalous or ambiguous situations, far from endangering my theory, in fact serve to confirm it.

There are cases in which a section in the sesquialtera pattern is immediately followed by a section in the $\frac{6}{4}$ pattern. Since Frescobaldi in his preface appears to attribute different tactus speeds to these two patterns, it would seem that a proportion—requiring the preservation of the tactus rate—is not possible between those sections. But in fact, Frescobaldi does not really compare the tactus speeds of the four patterns. The first three patterns are described only in terms of their relative performance tempo ("si portino adagio . . . alquanto più allegre . . . più allegre"), and only for the $\frac{6}{4}$ pattern does he make explicit reference to a beat ("far caminar la battuta allegra"). I believe this "fast beat" is not the tactus governing the entire pattern but the beat corresponding to groups of three semiminims. Indeed, if this beat referred to the entire tactus, an unreasonably fast tempo would result for the $\frac{6}{4}$ patterns. Besides, the simultaneous use of $\frac{6}{4}$ and $\mathbf{C}$ in different parts in Capriccio II (see above) gives an indication of the tempo implied by Frescobaldi's "battuta allegra." Hence, although the beat corresponding to three semiminims of the $\frac{6}{4}$ patterns is somewhat faster than the tactus corresponding to the three-semiminim pattern, the tactus governing the entire pattern is slower, and may well be equal to that of the next slower pattern, the sesquialtera. If such is the case, the sesquialtera pattern ($\mathbf{C}_2^3$) and the $\frac{6}{4}$ pattern can in fact be combined as proportions governed by a common tactus. Although the quarter-note surface pulse remains constant at the transition, its rhythmic distribution changes from three binary units to two ternary units (see example 15).

Example 15

An example of this proportional relationship can be found in Capriccio VI ("sopra la spagnoletta"), between the sections given by mm. 32–43 and mm. 44–52. The context of these sections provides further insight into Frescobaldi's use of notation to achieve sophisticated rhythmic relationships. The $\frac{6}{4}$ pattern continues from m. 53 to m. 60, but in this section there is a superimposed pattern of eighth notes, set off in groups of three. These groups of eighth notes are accompanied by the numeral 3 as if they were triplets, but the metric context clearly shows that no triple subdivision of the quarter note is involved. Rather, the notation clarifies a rhythmic redistribution of the eighth notes within the $\frac{6}{4}$ pattern: from six groups of two eighth notes to four groups of three eighth notes (hence equivalent to the modern $\frac{12}{8}$ signature).[19] As a result, the rhythmic redistribution of the earlier transition at m. 44 is repeated in m. 53 at the next higher level of the metric hierarchy. The opening motive of the spagnoletta tune, originally spread over two measures (mm. 32–33), is transformed at m. 44 to a version that occupies only one measure and then, at m. 53, to a version occupying only half a measure. If a fixed tactus is maintained throughout these transitions, the listener perceives a kind of "zoom" effect, in which twice in succession the motive is foreshortened to half its duration. The relationship at the second transition —which is not marked by a proportion, but takes place automatically —suggests strongly that a similar relationship is intended at the first transition, and that proportion between the sesquialtera and the $\frac{6}{4}$ patterns described earlier should be observed here.

Actually, the section preceding the sesquialtera section is in duple meter (C), with semibreve barring and eighth-note Notenbild, and thus with a slow tactus (table 2, model c). Therefore, one would have expected at m. 32 the tripla pattern, corresponding to a slow tactus, rather than the sesquialtera pattern with the faster tactus. I presume that Frescobaldi introduced the sesquialtera notation because this would allow him to establish the proportional relationship with the subsequent $\frac{6}{4}$ section. Nevertheless, the earlier slow duple section will result in a somewhat restrained tempo for the sesquialtera section, which, in turn, will keep the speed of the eighth-note surface pulse at m. 53 within reasonable bounds.

A second example of such a zoom effect is provided by Capriccio II ("la, sol, fa, mi, re, ut"); in this case the reduction is even carried to a fourth stage. At m. 78 the alto part introduces within a sesquialtera a motive of alternating ascending seconds and descending thirds. The following section, commencing at m. 92, is notated in C, with semibreve barring and a Notenbild of eighth notes; the implied slow tactus seems in character with the expressive chromatic variant of the descending hexachord. The idea of the ascending seconds and descending thirds from the preceding sections reappears, but stated in eighth notes; under an exact proportion between the two sections the motive will be speeded up by a factor of four (eighth notes) to three (quarter notes).

At m. 114 a section commences in black hemiola notation, but with a bar-line spacing corresponding to three black minims, rather than to six black minims as encountered with this notation in the cases discussed earlier (at m. 24 in this capriccio and in m. 57 in Capriccio V). For those cases I proposed that the black minims should be read as quarter notes (to which they are visually identical), with six quarter notes being equivalent to four quarter notes of the preceding duple section. In another case, not yet discussed, mm. 92–107 of Capriccio VI ("sopra la spagnoletta"), *hemiola minor* notation is associated with bar-line spacing according to groups of three black minims, but introduced by the signature ₵₃. In this case the black minims probably should be read as equivalent to the white minims of the preceding section (mm. 86–90), which has the same signature and bar-line spacing, although the reason for introducing coloration is different. Returning to the situation in Capriccio II, m. 114, the signature there is ₃ (*tripla vulgaris*), which is usually associated with the fast triple-meter patterns, such as the three-semiminim model described by Frescobaldi, or with the minor hemiola with equivalence of the black minims to semiminims. As a matter of fact, this is the only notation available to Frescobaldi when he wishes to indicate a type of would-be proportion between a pattern involving an entire tactus (the hemiola pattern), and one minim—that is, half a tactus—of the preceding section. Although using a system of notation that was no longer appropriate to his new ideas, Frescobaldi, by means of this ingenious technical device, expresses his rhythmic intention in a manner that would be understood by his contemporaries.

Two further anomalous cases remain to be discussed. At m. 85 of Capriccio VI ("sopra la bassa fiamenga") a section commences in *tripla maggiore* (O_1^3, with three semibreves to the measure)—the slowest of Frescobaldi's triple-meter patterns. A slow tempo indeed seems appropriate, in view of the counterpoint of running quarter notes—the only case in the *Capricci* of a continuous flow of short note values (or quadruple division of the triple beat). The preceding section, however, is notated in duple meter with barring at the breve and a quarter-note Notenbild (table 2, model b—rather fast tactus). This suggests either that no proportion is observed at the transition (m. 85), or that appropriate tempos must be taken for both sections to make the proportion feasible: not too fast for the duple-meter section and not too slow for the triple-meter section. Indeed, Frescobaldi may have deliberately used breve barring for the duple-meter section (rather than semibreve barring, which would have made the proportion less problematic) to warn the player against setting too slow a tempo, which otherwise might have been suggested by the chromaticism of the countersubject.

A rather different explanation can be given for the anomaly in Capriccio III ("sopra il Cucho"), in which at m. 24 a section with breve barring and a half-note Notenbild (table 2, model a—fast tactus) is followed by a section in *proportio tripla maggiore* (three breves per measure—slow tactus). I have shown elsewhere that the triple-meter section commencing at m. 24 was originally intended as the concluding section of the entire capriccio, where it would have been preceded by a duple-meter section with a slow tactus (semibreve barring with an eighth-note Notenbild), in accordance with the theory.[20] The plate for the triple-meter section had already been engraved when it was decided to move the section to its present location, and no adjustments were made in the notation. In the light of this last-minute revision, what at first sight appears to be an exception in fact provides further confirmation of the consistency of Frescobaldi's system.

Conclusion

The objective of this inquiry was to explore the limitations of the available contemporary notation for expressing the tempos and the metric and rhythmic relationships required by the *seconda prattica*. Frescobaldi was faced with the problem of how to use the customary notational symbols, but depart from their traditional meaning in a manner that would be unequivocally understood by his contemporaries. The replacement of the ambiguous cut-time signature, ₵, by a combination of Notenbild and bar-line spacing (modeled on the system of triple meter explained in his preface) was a clever solution—fascinating both for its psychological pertinence to the performer's instinct for tempo and for its efficiency in representing visually the inner content of the contrapuntal textures. The validity of this system is demonstrated by the consistency of the relationships between the duple-meter and triple-meter models of successive sections as well as by the correlation between these models and the expressive characters of those sections. No other publication of Frescobaldi exhibits such a consistency of notational means.

My conclusions regarding tempo relationships in the *Capricci* can be summarized as follows. The four tempo levels in duple meter illustrated in table 2, a, b, c, and d, correspond to two main levels in triple meter, depending on the bar-line spacing, as illustrated in table 3. Of the four triple-meter patterns described by Frescobaldi in his preface only three are available for true proportions: patterns A, B, and D. Since patterns B and D are distinguished only by their rhythmic distribution and not by the speed of the tactus, they can be related through a proportion, and together represent only a single tactus speed level. When Frescobaldi wants to establish a similar correspondence within his A (slow) level, he uses notational substitutes for the fast $\frac{6}{4}$ pattern: either quarter-note triplets within common time or *hemiola minor* (see table 3). Thus, with the proportional triple-meter patterns he employs two distinct tactus rates, although for each he provides a certain latitude, depending on the Notenbild of the preceding duple-meter section (as determined by the alternatives represented by table 2, a and b in one case, and table 2, c and d in the other).

Notes

I wish to express my gratitude to my colleague, Professor Arthur B. Wenk, for his assistance with the translation of my text.

1. The capriccios first appeared in *Capricci* (1624), the ricercars in *Recercari* (1615); the entire contents of *Recercari* was appended to the subsequent editions of the *Capricci* (1626, 1628, and 1642). Frescobaldi alludes to the difference between his ricercars of 1615 and his capriccios of 1624 in the preface to his *Capricci*: "In those compositions entitled *Capriccio* I did not maintain as easy a style as in my ricercars." For the original Italian text of the preface, see Claudio Sartori, *Bibliografia della musica strumentale italiana stampata in Italia fino al 1700* (Florence: Olschki, 1952), 295–96. A detailed account of the original editions of the *Capricci* and their publication history is given in my forthcoming *Le toccate e i capricci di Girolamo Frescobaldi: genesi delle edizioni e apparato critico* (Milan: Suvini Zerboni, in press), companion volume to vols. 2, 3, and 4 of Frescobaldi's *Opere complete*. In this essay the numbering and titles of individual pieces as well as measure-number references correspond to those in the *Opere complete*.

2. Of the many statements of this doctrine, I shall quote the one by Angelo Pisa, who, as late as 1611, devoted an entire treatise to the subject of the *battuta*: "Confirmando, che questa *Misura* è stata ritrovata per reggere il Canto, e però il Canto deve accomodarsi alla Misura, e non la misura al canto. . . . Et che si canta nel progresso del moto, e non nella quiete ò stare fermo della mano. . . . Et così il canto ancora. Tanto delle Proportioni. Quanto alla Breve. Et Semibreve. Et che non è altro, che una sola Battuta, ò Misura, con la quale si reggono tutte le tre sorti del Canto sudetto" (I confirm that this "Measure" was invented in order to govern the song [i.e., the music] and therefore the music should

comply to the measure and not the measure to the music. . . . [I say also] that one sings during the progressive movement of the hand, and not while it stops or holds still [cf. Murata, this volume]. The same holds true either for music in proportion, or music *alla breve* or *alla semibreve*. And [I state] that there is but a single beat or measure, which governs all three kinds of music mentioned above). *Battuta della musica* (Rome: Zannetti, 1611; reprint as *Breve dichiriazione della battuta musicale*, Bologna: Forni, 1969), 130–31.

3. For a detailed discussion by a contemporary writer of the movement of the hand to indicate the tactus, see Murata, this volume.

4. Some theorists provide examples that show the possibility of slightly speeding up or slowing down the surface pulse by the use of a proportion; see, for example Franchinus Gaffurius, *Practica musicae* (1496), trans. Clement Miller (n.p.: American Institute of Musicology, 1968), 186, ex. 83. However, these altered values are essentially surface diminutions, equivalent to, say, quintuplet eighth notes in a modern ⁴₄ measure; the underlying meter, as given by the mensural signature, and the corresponding reference tactus rate are not affected.

5. An isolated case of the signature ₵, coupled with a ³, appears in Capriccio IX, at m. 78; this case is equivalent to Frescobaldi's *sesquialtera maggiore*; see Darbellay, *Toccate*.

6. Capriccio VII ("Cromatico con ligature al contrario") and Capriccio VIII ("di durezze") do not contain any triple-meter sections. They are harmonic experiments in the Neapolitan tradition, similar to Toccata XII in *Toccate I* and Toccata VIII in *Toccate II*.

7. "A due battute per casella"; see Girolamo Diruta, *Il transilvano: Dialogo sopra il vero modo di sonar organi, et istromenti da penna* (Venice: Alessandro Vincenti, 1622; reprint, Bologna: Forni, 1969), Seconda parte, Libro primo, 1–2. Incidentally, in Diruta's musical examples no distinction is made between cut-time and common-time signatures with regard to bar-line spacing.

8. This question is fully explained in Darbellay, *Toccate*.

9. In this essay triple-meter will be understood as referring to both simple triple meter and compound triple meter (such as the meter indicated by ⁹₄).

10. Cerretto: "poiche si vede apertamente, che molti moderni Compositori commettono uno si fatto errore, che segnano ne i loro Madrigali, & Canzoni, i circoli, & semicircoli corrotti [◐ ₵], mentre con quelli procedono al spesso con figure di semicrome, non considerando questi tali che sotto tali segni di circoli, & semicircoli corrotti si canta la Breve à Battuta, posciache tali diminutioni convengano più tosto à circoli, & semicircoli senza correttione [O C], si come hanno osservato, cossi gli Antichi, come Moderni Musici Periti, benche loro non si ne advedono di simili sciochi, & insensati osservationi, che quando tali componimenti si cantassero del modo come da loro sono stati scritti non se porriano cantare senza grandissima difficultà, & disgusto del Cantore, delche ne nascerebbe, che più presto darrebbe nausia a gl'ascoltanti, che dolcezza, & soavità. Siche il segnare i circoli, & semicircoli corrotti, cioè tempi mediati, convengono di segnarse in quelle Cantilene, che haveranno dello caminare, & procedere grave. . . . Et si bene al tempo d'hoggi parche non si osserva il Cantare per medio [i.e. the alla-breve practice], non per questo sarà osservatione laudabile, mentre vi sono segni proportionati à simili componimenti diminuiti, quali sono i

circoli, & semicircoli senza correttione." Scipione Cerretto *Della prattica musica* (Naples: Carlino, 1601; reprint, Bologna: Forni, 1969) 264.

Banchieri: "sotto il [Tempo] perfetto maggiore [₵] si mandano dui Semibrevi (che fanno una breve per battuta, & sotto il perfetto minore [C] si mandano dui Minime) che sono una Semibreve per battuta, tanto di note nell'uno & l'altro come di Pause. Vero è che al giorno d'oggi, per modo d'abuso convertito in uso, vengono amendui praticati l'istesso cantando, & pausando sott'il valore della Semibreve, & battendo il perfetto maggiore presto (per essere di note bianche) & il minor perfetto adagio essendo di note negre, l'uno & il secondo riescono il medesimo . . ." Adriano Banchieri, *Cartella musicale* (Venice: 1614, G. Vincenti; reprint, Bologna: Forni, 1968) 29.

Praetorius: "[Tactus] aequalis seu spondaicus est vel tardior, vel celerior pro variatione signorum. Tardioris signum est C, quo signantur Madrigalia; celerioris ₵, quo signantur Motetae. . . . Jetziger Zeit aber werden diese beyde Signa meistentheils also observiret, dass das C fürnemlich in Madrigalien, das ₵ aber in Motetten gebraucht wird. Quia Madrigalia & aliae Cantiones, quae sub signo C, Semiminimis & Fusis abundant, celeriori progrediuntur motu; Motectae autem, quae sub signo ₵ Brevibus & Semibrevibus abundant, tardiori: Ideo hic celeriori illic tardiori opus est Tactu. . . . Darumb deuchtet mich nicht übel gethan seyn wenn man die Motecten, und andere geistliche Gesänge welche mit vielen schwarzen Noten gesetzt seyn mit diesem signo C zeichnet; anzuzeigen dass alsdann der Tact etwas langsamer und gravitetischer müsse gehalten werden. . . ." After which Praetorius comments on the many discrepancies and incongruities found in contemporary Italian music with regard to the use of these signs. Michael Praetorius, *Syntagma musicum* (Wolfenbüttel: E. Holwein, 1619; reprint, Kassel: Bärenreiter, 1958) 3:48, 50.

11. Praetorius, in his explanation of the tactus practice of the "old musicians," interprets the *alla breve* tactus as a real doubling in duration of the *alla semibreve* tactus. He first mentions some contemporary terminology—*tempus perfectum minus* or *signum minoris tactus* for C and *tempus perfectum majus* or *signum majoris vel totalis tactus* for ₵—and continues: "Dieweil sie in denen Cantionibus, so mit diesem Signo, ₵ bezeichnet zwo Semibreves und also zweene Tactus minores auff einen doch gar langsamen Tact, den die Itali allá Breve genennet also mensuriret haben dass ein o oder ♩♩ in depressione, die ander o oder beyde Minimae in elevatione tactus sind gesungen worden" (Praetorius, *Syntagma musicum*, 3:49). For a given Notenbild this practice would not result in any difference in tempo, and relates to the so-called *pro indoctis tactus* (with which the faster minor tactus provides an easier rhythmical understanding of the music). Praetorius may have been confused by the terminology. In his text, *minor* and *major* are understood as referring to the duration of the tactus, whereas the musical example that follows (and which clearly establishes the equivalence of |₵ o· ♩ |and| C ♩ ♩ |) those terms appear to refer to the Notenbild: *major* for a breve unit and *minor* for a semibreve unit, with a common tactus. See Praetorius, *Syntagma musicum* 3:49 and Darbellay, *Toccate.*

12. See n. 8, above.

13. The estimate given by Praetorius for a "moderate" (*mittelmässigen*) tactus, "80 tempora

in half of a quarter-hour," is equivalent to a rather slow MM $\mathbf{\downarrow}$ = 42.5; however, his suggestion concerns the performance of choral works within a church service.

14. See Banchieri, *Cartella musicale*, 35 (although in scored examples that do not pertain specifically to the *battuta* question, Banchieri, like Diruta, spaces the bar lines at the breve); and Praetorius, *Syntagma musicum* 3:57–69 and 70–72 (at least in those passages in which all parts are in common time or in cut time).

15. Except for a special case discussed below (Capriccio II, m. 114), there is only one example of this meter in the *Capricci*: Capriccio III, m. 87. Later in the century, Bismantova described this meter as a proportion of ⅜, which in theory would imply an augmentation; see Bartolomeo Bismantova, *Compendio musicale* (Ferrara: 1677; reprint, Florence: Studio per edizione scelte, 1978), [17]–[20]. Frescobaldi, on the other hand, uses a ³ as time signature, presumably to avoid suggesting such an augmentation. Actually, this meter may have originated from hemiola minor notation | ● ♩ |, with a reinterpretation of the black minim as a semiminim. Praetorius, for example, speaks of "sechs minimae, oder minimae denigratae" (six quarter notes or black half notes) (*Syntagma musicum* 3:73). See Darbellay, *Toccate*, and my preface to the *Opere complete* 4:xiv for a discussion of this matter and of the unusual manner of notating the rests with this practice.

16. See the tables in Praetorius, *Syntagma musicum* 3:49 and 79.

17. Praetorius, *Syntagma musicum* 3:73.

18. Many theoreticians of the time insist on this principle; see, for example, Praetorius, *Syntagma musicum* 3:50, or Cerretto, *Prattica musica*, 264.

19. Note that here Frescobaldi provides only a single 3 for each group of six eighth notes, whereas in Capriccio XII ("Or che noi rimena"), mm. 96–97, which involves actual eighth-note triplets (in the modern sense), a 3 is provided for each group of three eighth notes.

20. See Darbellay, *Toccate*, and Darbellay, "L'énigme de la 1e édition (1624) des Capricci de G. Frescobaldi," *Canadian University Music Review* 3 (1983): 123–57.

Pier Francesco Valentini on Tactus and Proportion

T
HE ROMAN NOBLEMAN Pier Francesco Valentini (1586–1654) was a composer of learned canons, motets, and madrigals, as well as theatrical music. Many of his compositions were published posthumously from his estate. In addition, seven of his treatises on music have been preserved in manuscript in the Barberini collection of the Vatican Library.[1] Five of these deal extensively with temperament, transposition on the lute, and the classification of modes. Two concern the notation and performance of musical rhythm. In all these, Valentini writes as a scholarly pedagogue. Each treatise is organized in a highly schematic fashion, demonstrating by a series of examples a few basic ideas that illuminate each subject. The demonstrations reveal, however, Valentini's knowledge of earlier music theorists,[2] his recognition of the complexity and contradictions of the musical system, and his ability to argue a position drawing on current practice and beliefs. For although he mentions few contemporaries by name, Valentini's observations and comments clearly derive from firsthand, practical experience. His intent is never to present music as a science, a body of knowledge, as Kircher and Mersenne did. Valentini is more creative, more an experimental than a historical theorist, while he retains the foundation of traditional knowledge. The purpose of the method and detail in his treatises is to change or correct performance practice, whether to advocate equal-tempered tuning or to teach how to beat time.[3]

Both the "Treatise on Tempus, Modus, and Prolation" and the "Treatise on Musical Tactus" were written around 1643, but in response to controversies and "dispareri" or differences about rhythmic practice that Valentini dates from 1611, the year of publication of Agostino Pisa's

Explanation of Musical Tactus.[4] Thus the terms as well as the period of the discussions come from Frescobaldi's Rome. Although neither Frescobaldi nor any contemporary instrumental music figures in the treatises, Valentini gives a detailed picture of how rhythm could be thought about in the earlier seventeenth century. He has sifted through the problems of Renaissance theory, and he shows what by his time had been discarded as wrong, inapplicable, or obsolete. Valentini's rejections, his acceptances, and his extensions of traditional theories provide a contemporary scale by which to interpret or evaluate the strictness or freedom in Frescobaldi's notation of rhythm.[5]

Etienne Darbellay has focused the questions about rhythm in Frescobaldi in the preface to his edition of *Toccate II:*

1   to establish the correct metric division of the "measure"
2   to fix the tempo and then to determine whether any "proportions" occur between consecutive sections.[6]

Another question associated with Darbellay's first point, and which Valentini's treatises help answer, asks how meter was felt in performance —that is, whether understanding the correct metric divisions can affect the way the performer will sing or play the score.

The rhythmic concept that relates all three questions to one another is that of *tactus*, called *battuta* in Italian. A tactus is a grouping of either an even or an odd number of equal durations—what we now call beats —and was generally described by the physical action of the hand that coordinated the performance of polyphonic music. Each group defines what we now call a measure.[7] From Adam von Fulda in 1490 to Valentini in 1643, only two beat patterns were required. In the first, the hand moved down, then up, defining one equal tactus divided into two units, which Valentini called half beats. In the second beat pattern, the hand moved down for two counts and rose on the third, defining the unequal tactus of three parts.[8] Writers discuss beating time and musical meter together and use terms, such as "beat," that suggest both; one should keep in mind that the context for most written explanations is vocal music, and hence music performed by singers who have their hands free to beat time. As with current practice, we must assume that keyboard performers or lutenists learned to realize rhythmic notation in the same context, and that any one time signature suggested the same patterns of stress or

Example 1a   Valentini: How to beat an equally divided tactus

Example 1b   Valentini: How to beat an unequally divided tactus

duration to an organist as to a tenor. Whether the tactus was a constant, unstressed pulse—as is assumed characteristic of Renaissance music— or whether it was perceived as a distinct metric "foot," we have to assume that well-trained instrumental players as well as solo singers internalized its image, and thought of rhythm in terms of beating time. Valentini, most helpfully, gives precise descriptions for the location of the hand in beating the tactus, and thus enables us to reconstruct how rhythm could "look."

Examples 1a and 1b conflate illustrations from Barb. lat. 4417 and summarize the motions of the hand in measures increasingly subdivided. Valentini uses capital *M* to represent the initial downward motion and lower case *m* for the subsequent rise of the hand; both are *motions*. *Q* and *q* denote *quiete*, or times when the hand does not move. His description can be summarized as follows: The first part of the tactus is the descent. This equals one-eighth of a tactus in equal time, or one-fourth of half a measure. In triple time, the descent of the hand takes a twelfth of the tactus. The second part of the tactus is waiting to fill out either the first half of the tactus in equal time, or the first two-thirds of a tactus in triple time. The third part is the ascent of the hand. Like the first part it equals one-eighth or a twelfth of the tactus. The fourth part is waiting to fill out the remainder of the tactus.[9] Valentini represents these geometrically (see plates 1 and 2; they do not show beat patterns). In the treatise, Valentini carefully marks all *M*'s and *Q*'s in his illustrations of varying subdivisions and notational situations, such as ties, syncopated entries, rests, long values. All the illustrations result in equal or unequal simple beat patterns. Examples 2a and 2b apply the patterns to two passages from Frescobaldi, in a straightforward manner.

Valentini's method of beating tactus yields several insights into the

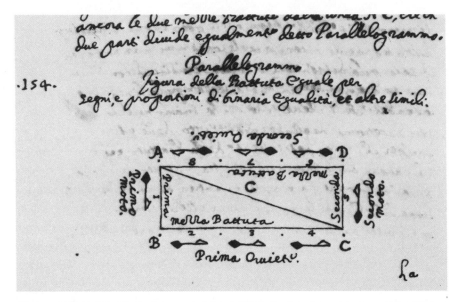

Plate 1   I-Rvat Ms. Barb. lat. 4417, fol. 76. With the kind permission of the Biblioteca Apostolica Vaticana.

organization of rhythm. The first is that the beat itself is unaccentual, because it begins as the hand starts to move; there is no beginning to hit and no rebound. Second, the duple division of the equal tactus must remain duple, because although there are four parts to the tactus (M-Q-m-q), the four parts are not equal in duration. Indeed, the semiminim level cannot be conveyed.[10] And finally, the meter is apparent, because the movement of the hand, resting so long between fall and rise, is quite discontinuous. One further effect of Valentini's asymmetrical division of the half beats is the freeing of all the notes that are performed while the hand is quiet. They are free not only from the control of the smaller subdivisions, but also from distortions that can be caused by motion at the ends of beats, such as in the modern upbeat. Melismas of subdivisions, for instance, do not get pushed or rushed toward the metric beat.

The quiet parts of the beats also restrict the use of agogic pauses to locations before metric subdivisions: you cannot articulate what is not moving. The pauses noted by commas in the right hand of example 3 can be conducted if the hand delays its moving. The slurs in the left hand, however, show notes performed while the "hand" is quiet. Valentini does mention the special effect of lengthening the initial portion of the downbeat, before the *quiete*, which is done at the whim of the person beating time as one of the refinements of madrigal singing.

Valentini also acknowledges the cadential convention of lengthening the penultimate note in a cadence when it is ornamented.[11] The rhythmic flexibility that we associate with the music of Monteverdi and Frescobaldi may indeed be associated with the increased layer of ornament in divisions far smaller than the standard tactus unit. In fact for *passaggi* of *semicrome* and *semibiscrome*, Valentini shows how they fit into

Plate 2   I-Rvat Ms. Barb. lat. 4417, fol. 79. With the kind permission of the Biblioteca Apostolica Vaticana.

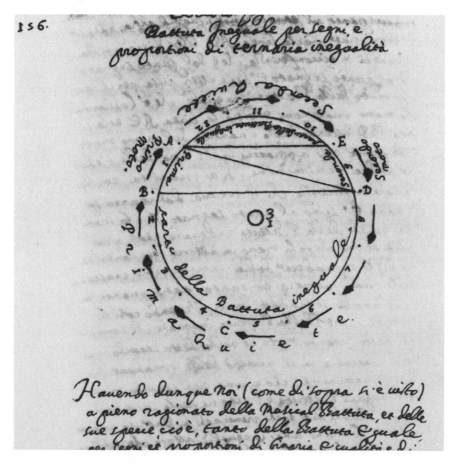

Example 2a   Frescobaldi, Canzona IV, *Toccate II* (ed. Darbellay), mm. 1–5; tactus markings after Valentini

Example 2b   Frescobaldi, Canzona VI, *Toccate II*, mm. 41–45; tactus markings after Valentini

Example 3   Frescobaldi, Toccata VII, *Toccate II*, mm. 55–57; tactus and articulation markings after Valentini

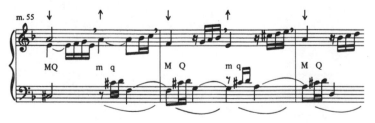

the tactus, but notes that it is usual in airs to sing them out of time ("si sogliono nell'arie cantare senza battuta"). He confirms the desirability of this freedom in his discussion of the length of the quiet parts of the *battuta*. He says that first of all, the tongue is more agile than the hand "in proferire le crome e semicrome," and goes on to state that a *battuta velocissima* (one that would reflect the smaller subdivisions) would be "tiring to the musician, strange to the singer, hateful to the viewer, and in practice disproportionate, violent, insupportable and impossible." He specifically objects to showing subdivisions within a broad beat.[12]

In compositions where the note values predominate at half or a quarter of the tactus length, the hand moves syllabically, as it were—that is, on almost every note. In much of the "modern" music of Valentini's time, the tactus unit is instead highly subdivided, with motion eight or sixteen times faster than the tactus. In these cases, the hand is perceived as moving more slowly. This is an important stylistic point for all florid music of the early seicento: the quick notes are moving within semibreves and breves. The music may seem to speed up by becoming highly subdivided, but the meter, the rhythmic framework trying to contain the subdivisions, will actually slow down, become a *tactus tardior*, and make the contrast between the metric frame and actual motion all the more pronounced.[13] Frescobaldi uses no mensuration signs that specify *tactus alla minima*, that is, rhythm that groups semiminims into the equivalent of $\frac{2}{4}$ or $\frac{3}{4}$.[14] To shift the meter to smaller rhythmic units in performance is to lose the flexibility between metric frame and ornament as well as the contrast between syllabic and florid styles.

Tempo, however, was not just a perception of the relation between the tactus unit and the number of subdivisions. Valentini supports the recent conclusions of Dahlhaus and Bank that, despite the writings and influence of the Renaissance theorist Sebald Heyden, the tactus of invariable speed is not a permanent aspect of the mensural system.[15] Tempo does not concern Valentini—that is, to him mensuration signs seem to have no fixed connotations of speed. (He argues that there are as many pulse rates as people.) He states that the tactus, which can be represented by breves, semibreves, or "qualunque altre note," can have different tempos, sometimes *adagio*, sometimes *presto*, and sometimes in between *presto* and *adagio*, according, he says, to the style of the composition, or the sense of the words.[16] He includes a *battuta veloce* of short little motions.[17] Frescobaldi illustrates this free choice of basic tempo when he advises that a just and moderate tempo, a *battuta commoda*, should be chosen for his partitas, as it is unseemly to start quickly and then have to slow down for the fast passages. It is noteworthy that even for this genre of composition, the sense of basic tempo should remain steady throughout.[18] Valentini seems to agree, since he also observed that "passi affettuosi" in motets and madrigals were sung with a *battuta larga*—a broad beat that presumably differs from the surrounding context—and he notes that in certain modern pieces, tempos fluctuate "accidentally," *accidentalmente*, being *adagiata* or *affrettata*, or *alterata*.[19] These "accidents" suggest, however, that for any one composition, there still will be a normative tactus rate. An illustration of this is the *affetti* Frescobaldi described for performing the toccatas in his first book, which have no changes of mensuration sign within them.[20] It is in his *Capricci* of 1624 that Frescobaldi associates specific tempo designations with types of meters.[21] The question is whether these associations imply free-standing tempos relatively consistent from piece to piece and unrelated by proportion to what precedes or follows, or whether Frescobaldi's notation is strictly proportional and his verbal associations of certain tempos with certain meters redundant, or whether the tempo words are perhaps an aid to understanding his use of proportional signs in a somewhat new way.

Valentini, who does not associate note values with tempo, nevertheless understands successive mensuration signs proportionally. He spends half of his "Treatise on Modus, Tempus, and Prolation" on proportions, using as examples works by composers such as Josquin, Compère, Palestrina, and Metallo. The interpretation of Frescobaldi's proportional signs according to Valentini seems to confirm that Frescobaldi's practice is rational, not very arcane, proportional, and playable.

The dupla proportions in Frescobaldi's music are infrequent and present no difficulties. The signs for triple meters, however, are many and frequent, and at times pose problems of differences among the sources. Most of the time they create sesquialtera ($\frac{3}{2}$) relationships, sometimes they offer an opening of a piece in triple meter, and rarely do they suggest a tripla proportion ($\frac{3}{1}$). Table 1 gives a working chart of many of Frescobaldi's proportional signs and Valentini's interpretation of these signs in terms of a *battuta* or tactus unit. Not all of Frescobaldi's works

Table 1 Proportional Mensuration Signs

In Frescobaldi		Valentini's interpretation			
Sign		Multiple	Tactus	Subdivision	Proportion
Equal battute	¢	⊨	⊨ = o o		*proportione dupla*
	C	⊨ or |o o|	o = ♩ ♩		cancels previous proportion
	6/4 (4/6)	–	o· = ♩· ♩·		*sesquialtera di semiminime*
	12/8 (8/12)	–	o· = ♪· ♪· ♪· ♪·		*sesquialtera di crome*
Unequal battute	O3	–	⊨· = o o o		_____ a
	C3	–	⊨· = o· o·		_____ b
	O 3/1	–	⊨· = o o o		*tripla maggiore*
	¢3 (▬ •)c	⊨·	⊨·	—	*tempo diminuito*
	3/2	–	–	—	*sesquialtera*
	C 3/2	–	o· = ♩ ♩ ♩		*sesquialtera minore di minime*
	₵	–	o·/o = ♩ ♩ ♩/♩ ♩		_____ b
	₵3	|o· o·|	o· = ♩ ♩ ♩		_____ b
	₵ 3/2	–	o· = ♩ ♩ ♩		*sesquialtera di minime* d
	3	–	–	▬▬▬	*moliola*
	[3] ▬ •	–	◄· = • • •		*emiola maggiore*
	[3] • ♩	◄·	•· = ♩ ♩ ♩		*emiola minore*

Note: Perfection in the breve and semibreve are denoted by the modern dot of addition.

a. In Frescobaldi, effectively a *sesquialtera maggiore*.

b. In Frescobaldi, effectively a *sesquialtera minore*.

c. Only in the "Capriccio sopra un soggetto" with *emiola maggiore* notation. Despite the vertical line through the half-circle, the breve equals two semibreves *integer valor*. See Darbellay's edition of the *Capricci*, xxiv–xxv.

d. In Frescobaldi, this sign appears in conjunction with other triple mensurations, rearranging the metric accent.

have been surveyed for this chart; for example, the instrumental canzonas are not included. A list that at first might have suggested a host of
tempo relationships or metric schemes turns out, with Valentini's tactus
equivalents, to represent only two levels of triply divided tactus. Some
signs establish a perfect semibreve, others, the perfect breve. On the
whole, when the ratio is 2:3, a shift to perfect prolation ($\s'=\'\'\'$) speeds
the tempo up, and a shift to perfect tempus ($\circ\circ=\circ\circ\circ$) slows the
tempo down.

Example 4 shows speeding up with the substitution of three minims
for two. This is the standard *sesquialtera minore* that Frescobaldi designated "alquanto più allegre" in the 1624 preface (example 4a). The *emiola
minore*, indicated by coloration, belongs in this category. It is often given
a redundant proportional mensuration sign, as in example 4b. According to Valentini, example 4c does not have a proper sign for proportion,
as ₵3 does not express a ratio. As a sign for a semibreve of three minims,
it can follow equal *battute* as it does here. Frescobaldi also used it to
follow triple meters.[22] A commonly found sign for a sesquialtera of
minims is one also not recognized by Valentini as a true proportion,
namely the number 3 without denominator. In the keyboard music, as
stated above, it often appears before sections in coloration, and is probably related to the convention of marking black minim triplets that Valentini

Example 4   (Model) *Sesquialtera minore* with increase in tempo. (Metronome markings here and subsequently are chosen for illustration only.)

Example 4a   Frescobaldi, Canzona IV, *Canzone* (1645) (ed. Pidoux), mm. 36–39

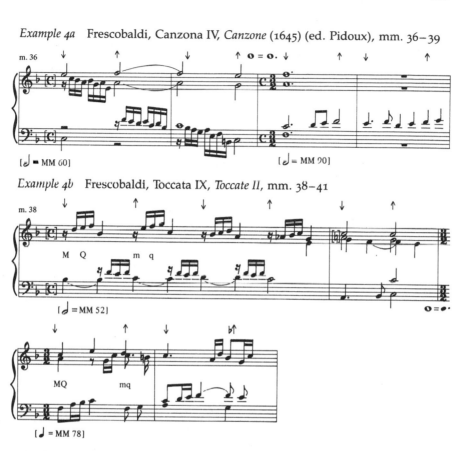

Example 4b   Frescobaldi, Toccata IX, *Toccate II*, mm. 38–41

Example 4c   Frescobaldi, Canzona I, *Toccate II*, mm. 22–25

Example 4d   Frescobaldi, Canzona "O dolore, o ferita," *Arie II*, mm. 20–23

Example 4e   Frescobaldi, "Capriccio sopra la bassa fiamenga," *Capricci* (1624), mm. 17b–21

identifies as *meliola*.[23] With regular, uncolored notation, the floating 3 appears in the *Arie musicali* (1630) and in the *Toccate II* (1627) following equal *battute*, in passages of six or three minims (example 4d).

Sesquialtera proportions do not always shift the meter from an equal to an unequal tactus. The $\frac{6}{4}$ ratio, which in practice replaces four semiminims with six in a sesquialtera of semiminims, is, according to Valentini, divided as an equal tactus.[24] This yields effectively two sets of modern triplets (see example 4e). Thus the six semiminims of a $\mathbf{C}_2^3$ measure are metrically different from the six in a $\mathbf{C}_4^6$ measure (see also example 9 below).

Frescobaldi also achieved a shift from a duple tactus to a slow, triply divided tactus in more than one way (see example 5). With the simple proportional sign $\frac{3}{2}$ he indicated three semibreves replacing two (see example 5a). The value of the new breve equals that of the old breve. In his 1624 preface, Frescobaldi defined this level of sesquialtera as *adagio*. The notation alone gives the impression of looking white and therefore slower; strict proportional meters result in an actual slowing down by 4:3 from the minim in equal time to the semibreve in unequal time (e.g., $\mathbf{C}$ $\downarrow$=M.M. 90 slows to $\circ$=M.M. 68). In examples 5b and 5c, the new tactus of a ternary breve is twice as long as the previous tactus of a ternary

Example 5 (Model) *Sesquialtera maggiore*. The tempo decreases in moving from semibreve tactus to breve tactus.

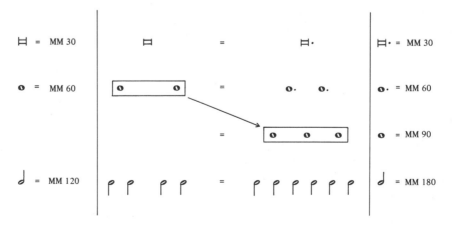

Example 5a   Frescobaldi, Fantasia I, *Fantasie* (ed. Pidoux), mm. 37–40

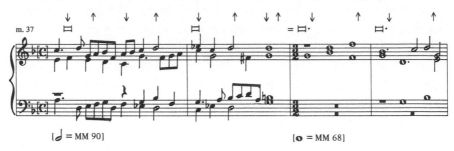

[♩ = MM 90]   [𝗈 = MM 68]

Example 5b   Frescobaldi, Canzona V, *Toccate II*, mm. 24–28

[♩. = MM 48]   ♩.= ♩.   [𝗁. = MM 24]

semibreve. Example 5b indicates a perfect breve with a mensuration sign;[25] 5c uses *emiola maggiore* notation. In all three cases, according to Valentini, not only would the music in ternary breves sound slower, but also the visible tactus would broaden:

> Concerning the ternary proportions, that is about those that have the 3 above the lower number, as for instance $\frac{3}{1}$, $\frac{3}{2}$, $\frac{3}{4}$, in their own right . . . [they] should be sung with an unequal beat, performing the three notes which equal the one.[26]

Frescobaldi's use of the open circle *non diminutum*, as in example 5b, suggests this.[27] Another indication that Frescobaldi imagined a visible tactus shift from semibreve to breve levels lies in his avoidance of the mensuration sign $\mathbf{O}_1^3$, which Darbellay's meticulous bibliographic research has revealed as a sign used by Frescobaldi's copyists and editors, but not by Frescobaldi in exemplars edited by himself. Valentini defines $\mathbf{O}_1^3$ as three minims per *battuta*. This yields a *sesquialtera maggiore*, as three

Example 5c   Frescobaldi, Canzona VI, *Toccate II*, mm. 24–30

Example 5d   Frescobaldi, *Missa sopra l'Aria della Monica* (ed. Mischiati and Tagliavini), Gloria, mm. 36–40 (organ and choir II omitted).

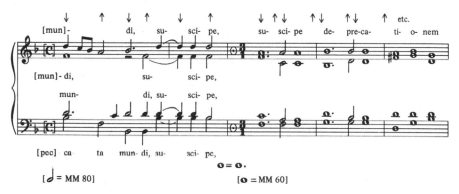

minims of a perfect breve replace one imperfect semibreve, and four fussy hand motions establish the new breve (see example 5d and note 25).

In general, Frescobaldi's melodic motives define the desired tactus level of semibreve or breve. The prevailing barring of a duple section often visually establishes a breve and makes the shift up to a *tactus alla breve* smooth and logical, as in examples 5a and 6.

Frescobaldi's puzzle in reading triple proportions is Canzona V from the second book of toccatas. It has the series of mensuration signs:

O_1^3 - C - 3 (*emiola minore*) - O3 - C3 - C - O3 - C - 3 (*emiola minore*)

The three duple signs, however, are only for three single, semibreve measures that link passages in different ternary meters. These are ter-

Example 6   Frescobaldi, Canzona II, *Recercari, et Canzoni* (1615), mm. 20–24

nary meters with both *tactus alla breve* and *alla semibreve* (see example 7a). The duple measures *alla semibreve* in all three instances signal the change from a *tactus alla breve* to *alla semibreve* or vice versa, as in example 7b. The initial mensuration sign, then, indicates a *sesquialtera maggiore* proportion with respect to a semibreve standard. The actual perception of the tempo relationships depends on the initial speed chosen. If the opening tripla is too stately, the first passage in *emiola minore* has no vivacity. If the opening tripla is too fast, the *tempus imperfectum, prolatio perfecta* (**₵3**) passage is too quick. Each of the ternary sections settles nicely somewhere around an *integer valor* of ○=M.M.48, that is, an opening ○= M.M. 72 in *tempus perfectum* (see example 8). Because in duple time there

Example 7a Frescobaldi, Canzona V, *Toccate II*. The ternary mensurations.

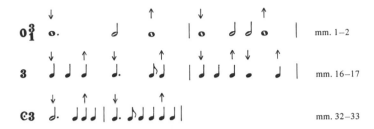

Example 7b Frescobaldi, Canzona V, *Toccate II*. Changes between *tactus alla breve* and *alla semibreve*, mm. 14–16 and mm. 41–43.

are no values smaller than the semibreve, Canzona V is unusual in that the minim retains a constant pulse throughout.

The tempo significance of proportional notation is completely lost in modern editions that reduce note values and then alter mensuration signs. The madrigal "Bella tiranna" from Frescobaldi's 1630 print has three ternary sections, an opening and closing section in C3—or $\frac{6}{2}$— and a quick middle passage in $\frac{6}{4}$. If the semibreve tactus is M.M. 36, the minim subdivision will move at M.M.108. In the $\frac{6}{4}$ passage, the semi-minims of "dardi pungenti" flash by at M.M. 216. The slower tempo returns at m. 23 for the petulant ending (see example 9).

There are numerous conclusions to be drawn from examining Fresco-

Example 8   Frescobaldi, Canzona V, *Toccate II*. Comparative tempi for the ternary meters.

Example 9   Frescobaldi, Madrigal "Bella tiranna infida," *Arie II*, the ternary meters compared.

baldi's rhythm and its notation. One, which is brought out further in Etienne Darbellay's study in this volume, is Frescobaldi's apparent restriction of white notation to slower tempos, almost eliminating the Renaissance category of *tempus diminutum, tactus celerior*.[28] A second conclusion is the presence of both breve length and semibreve length tactus units. These characteristics suggest leanings toward the modern notation of accentual groups in different speeds denominated by varying note values. Nevertheless, the relative durations of those note values are not precompositionally, externally fixed. Within any composition, their values are determined by the system of proportions, which appears to be traditionally based on equalities of perfect and imperfect semibreves. Dahlhaus has already observed that the proportional system retained its validity late into the seventeenth century.[29] A Roman opera score of 1668 uses $\mathۧ{C}_1^3$, $\mathۧ{C}_4^3$, $\mathۧ{C}_4^3$, $\mathۧ{C}_8^6$, and $\mathۧ{C}_8^3$ as mensuration signs, and $\mathۧ{C}_1^3$ and $\mathۧ{O}_1^3$ as proportional signs. The retention of the half-circle and the half-circle with dot indicates that the unit of the beat was still defined in terms of the semibreve and its subdivisions.[30] To ignore the tempo relationships of the proportions, as occurs in Helga Spohr's edition of Frescobaldi's *Arie*, is to lose an essential aspect of both form and interpretation. To ignore the meter of the tactus units in favor of an undifferentiated pulse is to lose the matrix within which Frescobaldi's polyphony creates cross accents, syncopations, and super-metric gestures. Frescobaldi's rhythm is not the product of a confused transitional period, during which music was abandoning a steady, unaccented pulse in favor of a hierarchy of metric groups defined by stress or accent. In Frescobaldi there are three orderly streams of rhythm going on simultaneously. First, there are successive shifts in the metric framework from equal to unequal tactus units. Second, the metric framework is made elastic by changes in tempo, which are determined by the proportional system. Finally, the changes are unified by the value of the semibreve, which at times cannot be perceived in either the tempo of the meter or of its divisions, but which nevertheless provides the cohesive source from which spring the changes in meter and tempo. One of the attractive features of Frescobaldi's music is that these controlled changes proceed from a spirit of spontaneity and exuberance. The logical metric constructions serve as broader parallels to the playful *passaggi* and other expressive *affetti* which shape the whole and make it flexible.

Notes

1. The most comprehensive bibliography for Valentini until recently, and the only extended discussion concerning him and his theories, is Lucas Kunz, *Die Tonartenlehre des römischen Theoretikers und Komponisten Pier Francesco Valentini*, Münsterische Beiträge zur Musikwissenschaft, Heft 8 (Kassel: Bärenreiter, 1937). A new extended bibliography and biographical essay is Mariella Casini Cortesi, "Pier Francesco Valentini: Profilo di un musicista barocco," *Nuova rivista musicale italiana* 3–4 (1983): 529–62.

2. Aside from ancient Greek and Latin writers, in the treatises on rhythm, Valentini cites such Renaissance theorists as Ramis, Sebald Heyden, Zarlino, Lanfranco, Dentice, Tigrino, Spataro, Vanneo, and Nicholas Wollick (Vuollico).

3. In a letter-treatise of 1646, Valentini criticizes a motet printed three years earlier for its indecipherable proportional signs, and pities the "povero cantore" (*I-Rvat* Barb. lat. 4418, part 3, "La mortificata presontione, epistola," p. 26). Equal temperament is derived and described by Valentini in *I-Rvat* Barb. lat. 4330, "Monochordo et nova costitutione di musica et accordatura di cimbalo, d'arpa, d'organo, e di simili istrumenti, con toni, semitoni, e con tutti gli altri intervalli eguali"; see also P. Barbieri, "Il temperamento equabile nel periodo frescobaldiano," in Sergio Durante and Dinko Fabris, eds., *Girolamo Frescobaldi: Nel quarto centenario della nascita*, Quaderni della Rivista italiana di musicologia 10 (Florence: Olschki, 1986). Two earlier drafts of this treatise are *I-Rvat* Barb. lat. 4338 and *I-Ras* Biblioteca, Ms. 368, fols. 85–97. The treatises on rhythm are discussed below.

4. *I-Rvat* Barb. lat. 4419, "Trattato del tempo, del modo, e della prolatione di Pier Francesco Valentini romano," and Barb. lat. 4417, "Trattato della Battuta musicale di Pier Francesco Valentini romano, opera utilissima per quelli che imparano di cantare . . . ," for which a date of 1643 is given on p. 3. The previous treatise is referred to in the treatise on tactus. Pisa, called Asip by Valentini, published his *Battuta della musica dichiarata* in Rome in 1611; for a discussion of this treatise and the surrounding controversies, see Walther Dürr, "Auftakt und Taktschlag in der Musik um 1600," in *Festschrift Walter Gerstenberg zum 60. Geburtstag* (Wolfenbüttel: Möseler, 1964), 26–36. Valentini accuses Pisa of not knowing how to sing and traces many of his "false opinions," especially the notion of a tactus of invariable speed, to Sebald Heyden (*I-Rvat* Barb. lat. 4417, §§55, 58, pp. 29, 31); see also Darbellay, this volume.

5. No attempt can be made here, however, to summarize the topics or arguments in either of Valentini's treatises, which go beyond the points brought forward for this inquiry. The relationship between Valentini and Frescobaldi in the area of learned contrapuntal practice is explored in the study by Sergio Durante, this volume.

6. G. Frescobaldi, *Il secondo libro di toccate . . .* , ed. Etienne Darbellay (Milan: Suvini Zerboni, 1979), xix. The word "measure" appears in the English version of the preface; in the French version Darbellay uses the Italian term *battuta*. See also his essay in this volume and his preface to Frescobaldi's *Capricci* (Milan: Suvini Zerboni, 1984).

7. "La Battuta con la quale si regge il Canto figurato altro non è che la debita et conveniente misura della quantità di qualsivoglia figura e pausa musicale" (*I-Rvat* Barb. lat. 4417, §2, p. 7). Valentini cites Stefano Vanneo and agrees with him that *misura* is a most appropriate

synonym for *battuta* (the *tactus-mensura*). For a survey of terms and references to the beating of musical time, see J. A. Bank, *Tactus, Tempo and Notation in Mensural Music from the 13th to the 17th Century* (Amsterdam: Annie Bank, 1972), especially pp. 113–23. Many of these earlier terms are discussed by Valentini in *I-Rvat* Barb. lat. 4417, §§72–86, pp. 37–43.

8. Thus all meters, duple or triple, no matter how slow or quick, are what we today call "in one." Valentini illustrates unequal measures with $\mathbf{\Phi}_2^3$ (*sesquialtera maggiore*), $\mathbf{O}_1^3$ (*tripla maggiore*), and also $\mathbf{C}_4^5$ (*sesquiquarta proportione*), $\mathbf{C}_4^7$ (*supertripartiente quarta*), $\mathbf{C}_8^9$ (*sesquiottava proportione*). In §62, Valentini describes the preparatory upbeat, stressing that it is not the beginning of the tactus (*I-Rvat* Barb. lat. 4417, p. 33).

9. *I-Rvat* Barb. lat. 4417, fols. 76 and 79.

10. Valentini describes the duply divided measure as having a "moderato e non vehemente caminar de' moti" (*I-Rvat* Barb. lat. 4417, §42, p. 23). Carl Dahlhaus analyzed two Italian descriptions from 1627 and 1679 of the M-Q-m-q type of discontinuous motion. Thinking that the four parts were of equal duration, he concluded that this way of beating time symptomized the change from tactus as a mensural sign to tactus as a marker of musical metric feet. See his "Zur Geschichte des Taktschlagens im frühen 17. Jahrhundert," in *Studies in Renaissance and Baroque Music in Honor of Arthur Mendel*, ed. R. Marshall (Kassel: Bärenreiter, 1974), 117–21. Valentini cites G. B. Rossi (*Organo de Cantori*, Venice, 1618), who does specifically divide a semibreve into four semiminims. Valentini refutes Rossi and says that in practice one can see that Rossi is wrong (*I-Rvat* Barb. lat. 4417, §141, pp. 68–69). Valentini's method may not even be modern: the *continua motio* (Adam von Fulda, *De Musica*, ca. 1490) of the hand certainly refers to the fact that the hand beats throughout a composition, not obviously that it is in constant motion through every tactus (which is an unstable way to beat time). In modern practice, the beat begins at the bottom, and normally the remainder of the beat-subdivision is in the rebound, keeping the hand up—except for the last beats of measures, when the duration of the last beat is the duration of the stroke of the upbeat. In modern theory, at least in America, the time elapsed in moving from the upbeat to the bottom of the beat does not seem to exist.

11. "Il cantare nella quiete appare anco manifestissimamente da questo, che nella penultima nota della compositione usandosi tenere la mano alquanto ferma e sollevata in aria avanti che cali con la battuta nella nota finale"; §115, p. 56: "nella detta penultima nota più che altrove da cantanti è sostenuto, allungato, et ornato di passaggi" (*I-Rvat* Barb. lat. 4417, §134, pp. 64–65).

12. *I-Rvat* Barb. lat. 4417, §§103–15, pp. 50–56; §144, pp. 74–75; §188, p. 105.

13. This is the effect illustrated by Etienne Darbellay in the present volume in his table 2; the metronome markings show hypothetical increases in the duration of the tactus as the number of subdivisions increases. Theoretical references to this effect are clearly presented in Bank, *Tactus*, 241–45, 251–53. See also Carl Dahlhaus, "Zur Entstehung des modernen Taktsystems im 17. Jahrhundert," *Archiv für Musikwissenschaft* 18 (1961): 229–30.

14. These were certainly available to him. A problem with the sign $_4^3$ is that in the proportional system a semiminim in $_4^3$ is longer than a semiminim in $\mathbf{C}$, because there are only three notes where before there were four. An interesting parallel is the florid music of the earlier fifteenth century, which J. A. Bank sees organized to the semibreve and

breve, refuting Charles Hamm's notion that, for example in Dufay, the tactus is the minim (Bank, *Tactus*, 117–19).

15. Bank, *Tactus*, passim; Dahlhaus, "Zur Theorie des Tactus im 16. Jahrhundert," *Archiv für Musikwissenschaft* 17 (1960): 22–39; idem, "Entstehung"; also n. 4 above.

16. *I-Rvat* Barb. lat. 4417, §229, p. 137; cf. §33, p. 19; §51, p. 27: "oltre la Breve et oltre la Semibreve, sì nella eguale come anco nella inegual Battuta, qualsivoglia nota musicale, per mezzo delle date proportioni può esser misurata, et abbracciata dal tempo et intervallo di una battuta." In sections 47–51 he refutes Vanneo, Heyden, and Pisa.

17. *I-Rvat* Barb. lat. 4417, §230, p. 138; cf. §90, pp. 44–45: "Ma se ad alcuni poco pratici paresse nel cantarsi le messe e simili opere con la battuta veloce (i cui moti si sogliono fare piccioli e corti), che la nota che cade nel principio della Battuta, venga proferita quando il dito o la mano tocca et è calato a basso . . . sappiamo questi tali che s'ingannano."

18. "Nelle partite si pigli il tempo giusto et proportionato, et perchè in alcune son passi veloci si cominci con battuta commoda, non convenendo da principio far presto et seguir languidamente; ma vogliono esser portate intere col medesimo tempo," given in G. Frescobaldi, *Il primo libro di toccate . . . 1615–1637*, ed. Etienne Darbellay (Milan: Suvini Zerboni, 1977), p. xxvi.

19. "Eased," "hastened," or "modified" (*I-Rvat* Barb. lat. 4417, §143, p. 69). Beating altered subdivisions is described in §148–49, pp. 72–73; the *battuta adagio* §64, p. 34 and §129, p. 62.

20. These instructions have been quoted with great frequency, and include cadential *ritardandi*, slow arpeggiated openings, unmeasured trills, lombard inequalities in *semicrome* against *crome*, little pauses before or after certain ornaments. See Frescobaldi, *Primo libro di toccate*, ed. Darbellay, p. xxvii.

21. This is quoted in this volume in Darbellay's study. The passage is carefully discussed by Alexander Silbiger in his unpublished study "Meter and Tempo in the Keyboard Music of Frescobaldi" (Brandeis University, 1971, typescript), which he generously placed at my disposal.

22. See example 8, m. 32. The half circle with dot by itself means the same thing. The only instances I have found as a proportion are in conjunction with the $\frac{6}{8}$ proportion: "Aria detta Balletto," part six (*Toccate* II); "Balletto III," closing section (1637 "Aggiunta"). Valentini mentions $\mathbb{C}^3_2$ as a sesquialtera of minims or semiminims, depending on what mensuration it follows. In Frescobaldi, this too appears following other sesquialteras: "Partite sopra Follia" (*Toccate* II); "Cento partite" ("Aggiunta"). See Darbellay, this volume.

23. Valentini uses the lone 3 in a section entitled "Of a certain proportion called by some with the name Meliola, which according to the quality of the signs under which it appears, can be of different sorts of proportions." It is an unequal tactus of three black minims with the number three placed somewhere in each tactus (*I-Rvat* Barb. lat. 4419, §1002, p. 370). We would call them triplets. In §1006, p. 373, Valentini states that in effect, the *meliola* notation creates an *emiola minore* when it follows the mensuration $\mathbb{C}$. This is clearly the notation of Monteverdi's much-examined ritornello from *Orfeo*. F. J. Machatius, *Die Tempi in der Musik um 1600* (n.p.: Laaber-Verlag, 1977), 147–51 and Dahlhaus, "Geschichte," 121–23 summarize and discuss various solutions. Dahlhaus's transcription is correctly propor-

tional only if the first two and last two semiminim values are in C *integer valor* and the intervening notes are sped up at the rate ♩ = ♩.. The relationship is a normal sesquialtera. Monteverdi's original bar lines mark the divisions of semibreve tactus.

24. "anco per la battuta eguale intendiamo quella battuta che . . . sotto questa sesquialtera C_4^6. . . mandasse a battuta sei semiminime in luogo delle quattro, che ve ne andavano prima, cio è le prime tre nella prima parte, e l'altre tre nella seconda parte della Battuta" (*I-Rvat* Barb. lat. 4417, §44, p. 24). Other duply divided *battute*, according to Valentini, are C_8^{10} and C_4^{12} (ibid.).

25. A sesquialtera resulting from a tripla mensuration sign was recognized in the sixteenth-century literature as the *tactus proportionatus*, apparently beaten two against three. Valentini only allows this in performing simultaneous proportions, when the equal beat takes precedence.

26. *I-Rvat* Barb. lat. 4419, §1049, p. 388.

27. Silbiger, "Meter and Tempo," 26–27, approached this conclusion when he related the sign O³ and minor hemiola (which often, as in example 5b above, appears barred in groups of two tactus) with a tempo associated with *tactus alla breve* but *diminutum* (₵). This would have required, however, that the performer adjust his tempo orientation when different classes of signs appeared in the same piece. The same effect can be achieved through proportions. Dahlhaus reads shifts down to beat patterns in *tactus alla minima* in his examples 1 and 2 in "Entstehung," 236–40, with a corresponding change in the tempo perception to *allegro*. Altering of the beat without change of mensuration sign occurs in the *Fiori musicali* by means of tempo words, for example, in the "Canzon Quarti Toni dopo il post comune."

28. See Dahlhaus, "Entstehung," 229–30 and the survey in Bank, *Tactus*, especially 226–30.

29. Dahlhaus, "Entstehung," 234–36.

30. In *La comica del cielo*, music by Antonio Maria Abbatini, *I-Rvat* Chigi Q.VII.100–102.

The Liturgical Use of the Organ in Seventeenth-Century Italy: New Documents, New Hypotheses

JAMES H. MOORE

O N 31 DECEMBER 1647 the young German composer Paul Hainlein, studying in Venice, wrote the following report to his patron in Nuremberg: "As far as organists are concerned, Frescobaldi's equal is met no more; and such a performer is not to be heard today except in the person of Signor Cavalli in St. Mark's."[1] The letter is an ironic document; for while Hainlein dubbed Cavalli the nearest Venetian heir to Frescobaldi, not one of Cavalli's compositions for organ is known, and we must consider his keyboard skill as one more example of the "ephemeral baroque," like those pieces of occasional art whose descriptions are so tantalizing yet so frustrating.

The two organs of St. Mark's, in the lofts above the altars of St. Peter and St. Clement, had obtained a near-mythic reputation even in the early seventeenth century, as one can see from Giovanni Stringa's reverent discussion of them in his 1604 description of the basilica.[2] And if the myth that their lofts were tied up with the early history of *cori spezzati* has recently been shattered,[3] the importance of the organs themselves remains intact. The chain of organists at St. Mark's is no less renowned than that of the *maestri di cappella* and contains some of the most brilliant figures attached to the basilica: Andrea and Giovanni Gabrieli, Claudio Merulo, Annibale Padovano, and for most of his career, Francesco Cavalli. Moreover, the sixteenth-century organists have bequeathed us a repertoire of music that is one of the glories of the late Venetian Renaissance.

Just how the organs of St. Mark's were used within the ceremonies of the basilica, however, is a problematic question. The organists of the mid-seventeenth century have left us no equivalent of the *Fiori musicali*, Frescobaldi's unusual organ Masses in which isolated Kyrie *versetti* are followed by compositions designed as substitutes for items of the Proper.[4] Nor do we have a Venetian equivalent from midcentury of Frescobaldi's *versetti* for hymns and the Magnificat or for his independent Elevation toccatas.[5] To be sure, we have a fairly clear idea of how the two major organs of St. Mark's as well as the two portable *organetti* were used to accompany vocal works;[6] but how solo organ music was used in the basilica is a question that has not yet been addressed in detail. The sixteenth-century prints by the organists of St. Mark's contain no explanation of how their contents were to be used, and most seventeenth-century organists' manuals, such as those by Adriano Banchieri and Giovanni Battista Fasolo, were designed for small parish churches and monastic churches rather than such major centers as St. Mark's or St. Peter's.[7] Thus the liturgical books from St. Mark's are particularly important, for they reveal how a church with a major musical establishment used the organ in its ceremonies.

The principal liturgical source from St. Mark's is preserved in a complicated series of manuscripts. In 1564, master of ceremonies Bartolomeo Bonifacio finished composing his huge *ceremoniale*, which described the services of the basilica in detail.[8] Bonifacio's original copy became almost a sacred text, and it was handed down from one master of ceremonies to another throughout the late sixteenth and seventeenth centuries. Each *maestro* added his own annotations, glosses, and marginalia so that the volume eventually became somewhat chaotic, as one can see from the page reproduced as plate 1. Indeed, by the end of the seventeenth century, the manuscript was no longer usable, and in 1695 master of ceremonies Bartolomeo Duramano had a fair copy made of the text, incorporating the annotations and adding new marginal notes to show which ceremonies had changed between 1564 and 1695 (see plate 2). Thus, Bonifacio's original manuscript and Duramano's revision are our principal guides to the ceremonies of the basilica in the late sixteenth and the seventeenth centuries.

To Bonifacio's *ceremoniale* we can add a number of other sources: Giovanni Pace's *Ceremoniale magnum*, assembled between the 1640s and 1678;[9] special prints for Christmas Matins and for the Blessing of the Water on the eve of Epiphany;[10] a long series of Holy Week prints that stretches from Giovanni Stringa's annotated edition of 1597 through the

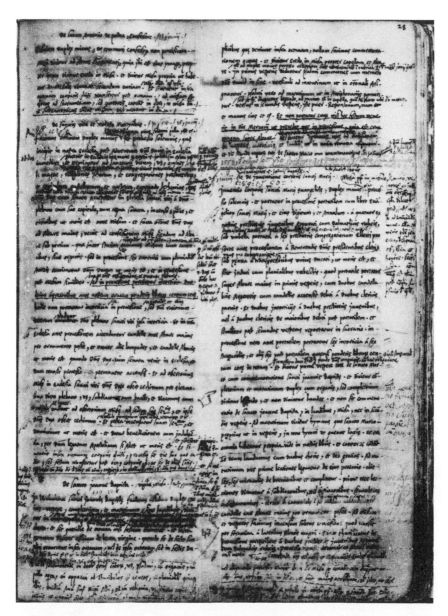

Plate 1. A page from Bartolomeo Bonifacio's *Rituum ecclesiasticorum ceremoniale*, with descriptions of the ceremonies for the feasts of St. Anthony of Padua, Ss. Vitus and Modestus, St. John the Baptist, and the Apparition of the Body of St. Mark. (Venice, Biblioteca nazionale marciana, Cod. lat. III-172 [= 2276], fol. 47r).

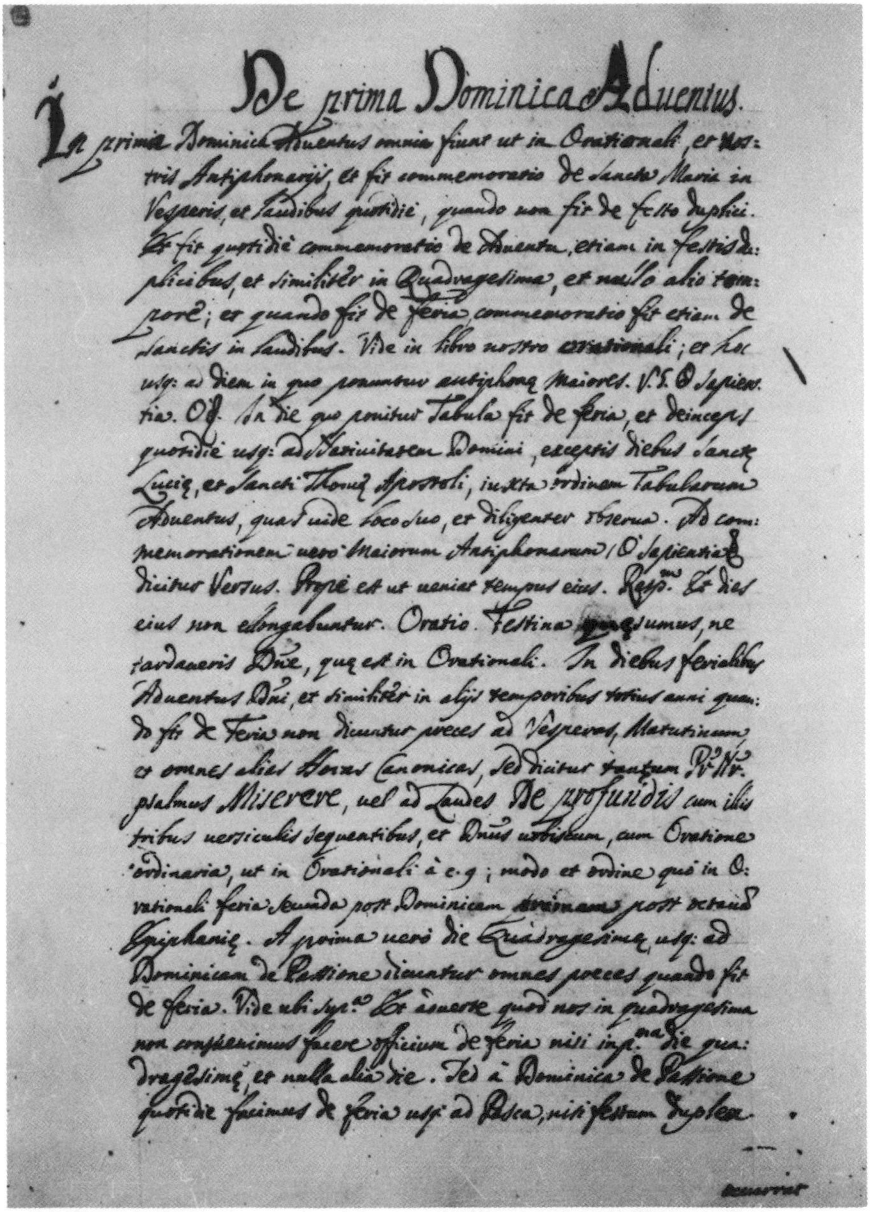

De prima Dominica Adventus.

In prima Dominica Adventus omnia fiunt ut in Orationali, et nos-
tris Antiphonarijs, et fit commemoratio de Sancta Maria in
Vesperis, et Laudibus quotidie, quando non fit de festo duplici.
Et fit quotidie commemoratio de Adventu, etiam in festis du-
plicibus, et similiter in Quadragesima, et nullo alio tempore; et quando fit de feria commemoratio fit etiam de
Sanctis in Laudibus. Vide in libro nostro Orationali; et hoc
usq: ad diem in quo ponuntur antiphonę maiores. V.S. O Sapientia. O. In die quo ponitur Tabula fit de feria, et deinceps
quotidie usq: ad Natiuitatem Domini, exceptis diebus Sanctę
Lucię, et Sancti Thomę Apostoli, iuxta ordinem Tabularum
Adventus, quas uide loco suo, et diligenter obserua. Ad com-
memorationem uero Maiorum Antiphonarum (O Sapientia &c.)
dicitur Versus. Prope est ut ueniat tempus eius. Resp.m Et dies
eius non elongabuntur. Oratio. Festina quęsumus, ne
tardaueris Dne, quę est in Orationali. In diebus ferialibus
Adventus Dni, et similiter in alijs temporibus totius anni quando fit de Feria non dicuntur preces ad Vesperas, Matutinum,
et omnes alias Horas Canonicas, sed dicitur tantum Pr. Nr.
psalmus Miserere, uel ad Laudes De profundis cum illis
tribus uersiculis sequentibus, et Dnus uobiscum, cum Oratione
ordinaria, ut in Orationali à c. 9; modo et ordine quo in O-
rationali feria secunda post Dominicam primam post octauã
Epiphanię. A prima uero die Quadragesimę usq: ad
Dominicam de Passione dicuntur omnes preces quando fit
de feria. Vide ubi sup.a Et auerte quod nos in Quadragesima
non consueuimus facere officium de feria nisi in p.ma die quadragesimę, et nulla alia die. Sed à Dominica de Passione
quotidie facimus de feria usq: ad Pascha, nisi festum duplex

occurrat

Plate 2. A page from Bartolomeo Duramano's 1695 revision of Bonifacio's *Rituum ecclesiasticorum ceremoniale*, describing ceremonies for Advent and for Christmas Eve. (Venice, Archivio della Curia Patriarcale, Archivio capitolare di Venezia, item 53, fols. 3v–4r).

occurrat, quamuis p̄ nostros libros appareat špius in Qua:
dragesima de feria fieri debere. In his etiam temporibus
Aduentus Domini, uidelicet, feria quarta, et feria sexta non
cantantur duæ Missæ, sicut in alijs quatuor temporibus anni,
sed una tantum Missa de feria, in sabbato uero duæ Missæ
cantantur. pᵃ de Domina, 2ᵈᵃ de feria. Sed si Vigilia Na:
tiuitatis uenerit in sabbato Missa dicitur sola de Vigilia.

¶ Feria quarta, et sexta Missa cantatur hora solita, dilicet
mediarum tertiarum; per cantores ueniunt ad Missam feriæ
quartæ, et ad Missam de Domina in die sabbati.

1559. feria 4 quatuor temporum cum uigilia s.ti Thomæ Aſli
dicuntur duæ Missæ. Prima de temporibus; 2ᵈᵃ de uigilia.
In quarta feria Prophetia ante Epistolam dicitur in tono
prophetiæ, sed Epistola dicitur in tono Epistolæ ferialis, ut
in ferijs quatuor temporum p̄ annum. Et nota quod à
primo sabbato de Aduentu usq̄ ad natiuitatem Domini
post Salue Regina dicitur ℣ Angelus D͞n͞i nun-
ciauit M.ᵃ R̴ Et concepit &c. O̅r̅o Deus qui
B.ᵃ M.ᵃ Et in processione p̄ᵐ Dominicæ Decembris in medio
Ecclesiæ dicitur ℣ Laus honor, Virtus gloria; loco glo:
ria tibi D͞n͞e quod dicitur eundo in Choro post processio:
nem in tono hymni Conditor alme Sydexum.

De Vigilia Natiuitatis Domini.

In uigilia Natiuitatis D͞n͞i cantatur sola Missa de Vigilia, et ha:
bet unam Prophetiam ante Epistolam, pulsata media
tertia de more; et Cantores non interuenti, nisi hæc Vigi:
lia uenerit in Dominica; et Subcanonicus cantat Missam
et dicitur cum paramentis albis sine In principijs, Kyrie

et gloria

late eighteenth century;[11] and special manuscript descriptions of individual feasts.[12]

The rule of thumb for the organists' presence in the basilica was a simple one: they were required every time the singers of the *cappella* appeared, with a few exceptions such as the last part of Holy Week, the Sundays of Advent, and Lent. Both organists played on major feasts, and they alternated week by week for those lesser feasts on which only one player was required.[13] This linking of the organists and the professional singers was quite strict, and Masses are generally described by Bonifacio as being either "in cantu plano sine organis" or "cum cantoribus et organis."[14] The organists also played for a few services in which the professional singers did not participate, such as the Blessing of the Water on Epiphany, and at Matins for Corpus Christi, St. John the Baptist, Ss. Peter and Paul, and the Apparition of the Body of St. Mark.[15] Indeed, the documents for these ceremonies are far more extensive than those for some of the major feasts of the church year, a fact that brings up a general idiosyncrasy in the manuscript sources. In some ways, the *ceremoniali* provide the opposite of what we might hope. We have few statements of general practice; for a normal service the organists knew what to do and did not need to be informed. Instead, the documents concentrate on certain specific ceremonies that were particularly complex: Matins for Christmas, the Blessing of the Water for Epiphany, Mass and Vespers for Holy Saturday, Vespers for Easter Sunday, Mass for the Vigil of Pentecost, for the feasts of St. Isidore and St. Nicholas, and for Carnival Thursday. Thus, any discussion of the ritual use of the organ in St. Mark's must begin with those special ceremonies for which we have the most complete documentation.

The first twenty-one documents in the appendix are concerned with the Office (Matins and Vespers) and with the ceremony of the Blessing of the Water on the eve of Epiphany.[16] The participation of the organ is extensive, and it fills the three roles we would expect from the published organists' manuals of the early seventeenth century: *alternatim* performance with either the singers of the *cappella* or the plainchant choir; playing at the place of antiphons and responsories; and playing for the *Deo gratias* at the end of the Office.

The items that received *alternatim* performance at St. Mark's are the very ones described in published sources: the psalms, the Magnificat, the Te Deum, and the hymn.[17] Contrary to the printed material, however, there is no specification of *alternatim* performance for Marian antiphons.[18] The most extended use of *alternatim* performance was surely for Vespers psalms. While double-choir *salmi spezzati* and modern *concertato* psalms dominated the Venetian repertoire in the early seventeenth century, *alternatim* psalmody between a polyphonic choir and the organ seems to have been the most common medium in the sixteenth; for in 1624, the organists Carlo Filago and Gian Pietro Berti were asked to come to the basilica on Sundays and certain feasts and to revive the "uso antico di chiesa di San Marco" by playing responses to individual psalm verses, certainly an archaic custom by that date (document 15).[19] Thus, *alternatim* performance between the organ and the singers was certainly intended for Willaert's *I sacri e santi salmi* (Venice: Gardane, 1555) as well as for works such as the *salmi a versi senza risposte* in Willaert and Jachet of Mantua's famous print of *I salmi appertinenti alli vesperi per tutte le feste dell'anno* (Venice: Gardane, 1550), rather than an *alternatim* performance in plainchant and polyphony as is suggested in Walter Gerstenberg's preface to his edition of the 1550 print.[20]

Other types of *alternatim* psalmody occurred in St. Mark's on certain occasions. For the special "split" Vespers service on Easter Sunday (document 20), two different forms of *alternatim* psalmody were used within the same service.[21] The first three psalms were divided between the professional singers and the organ. After the Magnificat and the procession to the baptismal font, the final two psalms were sung in plainchant by the choir of priests, divided into two groups. If, however, the doge decided to remain in St. Mark's and not make his usual *andata* to San Zaccaria (document 21), all five Vespers psalms were sung in *canto figurato* by two choirs of singers, and the organ merely played for the antiphon after each psalm.

Alternatim performance of the Magnificat between the singers and the organs is specified for Holy Saturday (documents 17 and 18), where Vespers is connected with Mass, a service for which Banchieri also specifies an *alternatim* Magnificat.[22] However, in view of the decree of 1624 to re-establish the "uso antico" of *alternatim* psalmody, it is likely that *alternatim* performances of the Magnificat may have been liberally sprinkled throughout the church year.[23]

Alternatim performance of the Te Deum is specified at Matins for Christmas (document 3) and Corpus Christi (document 5) as well as for the Blessing of the Water (documents 8, 9, and 13). For certain ceremonies, the manner of performance was flexible, for document 8 states that the Te Deum can be performed either by two choirs or *alternatim* between a choir and the organs. Document 9 explains that the missing text in such performances was supplied in St. Mark's by a *zago* (cleric) who read the missing verses from the choir of the church. For Matins of Christmas, this sort of performance was evidently not festive enough (document 3). Bonifacio states that at one time the deacon and subdeacon had intoned the Te Deum, which was performed *alternatim* by the singers with the organs. However, Willaert later set all the verses of the Te Deum so that the entire text could be sung by the singers, and they took over the intonation as well.

The only mention of the hymn in these documents is in the description of Matins for Corpus Christi (document 5), in which Bonifacio says that everything from the chapter onward is sung in plainchant, and that the organ plays at the hymn, the Benedictus, after the Benedictus, and at the *Benedicamus Domino*. The hymn is clearly to be sung *alternatim* with organ *versetti* similar to those which Frescobaldi published in the second book of toccatas,[24] although an annotated copy of the Venetian rite for Matins of Christmas shows that there might be some surprising leeway in the roles of choir and organ[25] (see plate 3). This is a much later document, not necessarily indicative of *seicento* practice. However, if one can trust the annotations, the first four stanzas were performed *alternatim* by the choir and the organ; the fifth was omitted entirely; the sixth was divided between the choir and the organ; and the final stanza was performed by the choir, with the organ playing at the Amen.[26]

The second use of the organ in the Office at St. Mark's was to play at the place of certain liturgical items whose texts would be recited quietly rather than sung. At Christmas Matins, Bonifacio states that the organ is played at the end of every psalm, i.e., in place of the antiphon, and similarly at the place of the responsory (documents 1 and 2). Both practices are illustrated in the annotated print of 1759.[27] Moreover, in the case of the antiphons, the marginalia confirm that the organ is to be played for the antiphon following the psalm, while the antiphon preceding the psalm is to be sung in full, a practice that agrees with the *Caeremoniale episcoporum* of Clement VIII, a volume St. Mark's belatedly purchased in 1620.[28] At any rate, the use of organ music in place of the repetition of an antiphon was clearly the practice at St. Mark's on every important occasion. Of all the services described in documents 1–21, only that for the "split" Vespers on Easter Sunday prescribes the reiteration of an antiphon after the psalm; in every other case, the text of the antiphon is merely recited under the organ. Moreover, in the ceremony for the Blessing of the Water, large portions of the text were recited quietly while the organ played[29] (see plate 4).

The organ also played regularly for one other item in the Office, the versicle and response, *Benedicamus Domino—Deo gratias*. This practice is recorded by Banchieri as well.[30] There seem to have been several ways to handle this liturgical item in St. Mark's. Often, the text *Benedicamus Domino* was sung, and the organ played at the place of the *Deo gratias*, as one sees in documents 17 and 18. In other cases, however, Bonifacio clearly states that the opposite is to take place; that is, the organ plays at the *Benedicamus Domino*, and the singers perform the *Deo gratias* (see documents 3, 4, 8, and 14).

While there is copious documentation for the role of the organs of St. Mark's at Matins and Vespers, the *ceremoniali* are strangely silent on the very topic on which Banchieri and Fasolo lavish most of their attention: the use of the organ at Mass, either participating in an *alternatim* performance of the Ordinary or playing independent compositions as substitutes for items of the Proper. Although a number of Masses are described in detail from a liturgical point of view, the organ is mentioned prominently in only two cases, both exceptional ones: the Mass on Holy Saturday and the parallel Mass on the Vigil of Pentecost (see documents 22–32). Indeed, many of the same rubrics occur in both services.

For each Mass, Bonifacio states that the Kyrie is begun by the organs and continued by the singers (documents 22, 23, 24, 29, and 30). These are the only records we have of an *alternatim* performance of the Ordinary at St. Mark's. Moreover, there is an important parallel with the *Fiori musicali* in this case, since in the *Fiori* as well, the Kyrie is the only item of the Ordinary to be set in versets for *alternatim* performance. Slightly odd, however, is the statement in document 30 that the singers answer the organ in *canto figurato*, which suggests that Bonifacio is describing not a

4   Offic. in Noɛe Nat. Domini,

Titolati Quóniam Deus magnus Dóminus, & Rex magnus fuper omnes deos : quóniam non repéllet Dóminus plebem fuam , quia in manu ejus funt omnes fines terræ , & altitúdines móntium ipfe cónfpicit .

Coro Veníte adorémus .

Titolati Quóniam ipsíus eft mare , & ipfe fecit illud , & áridam fundavérunt manus ejus : veníte , adorémus , & procidámus ante Deum : plorémus coràm Dómino , qui fecit nos , quia ipfe eft Dóminus Deus nofter : nos autem pópulus ejus , & oves páfcuæ ejus .

Coro Chriftus natus eft nobis , veníte adorémus .

Titolati Hódie fi vocem ejus audiéritis , nolíte obduráre corda veftra , ficut in exacerbazióne fecúndùm diem tentatiónis in desérto : ubi tentavérunt me patres veftri , probavérunt , & vidérunt ópera mea .

Coro Veníte adorémus .

Titolati Quadragínta annis próximus fui generatióni huic , & dixi , Semper hi errant corde : ipfi verò non cognovérunt vias meas , quibus jurávi in ira mea , fi introíbunt in réquiem meam .

Coro Chriftus natus eft nobis , veníte adorémus .

Titolati Glória Patri , & Fílio , & Spirítui fanɛo .

Coro Sicut erat , &c. Veníte adorémus .

Titolati Chriftus natus eft nobis , veníte adorémus .

Coro   Hy-

Organo

Plate 3.   Venice, Biblioteca del Civico Museo Correr, Codice Cicogna 1151. *Officium in nocte nativitatis domini ad matutinum, secundum consuetudinem ducalis ecclesiae Sancti Marci Venetiarum* (Venice: Pinelli, 1759).

Ad Matutinum. 5

Hymnus.

CHriſte Redémptor ómnium, Coro
Ex Patre Patris únice,
Solus ante princípium,
Natus ineffabiliter.
Tu lumen, tu ſplendor Patris, Organo
Tu ſpes perénnis ómnium:
Inténde quas fundunt preces
Tui per orbem fámuli.
Meménto ſalútis auctor, Coro
Quod noſtri quondam córporis,
Ex illibáta Vírgine,
Naſcéndo formam súmpſeris. Organo
Sic præſens teſtátur dies
Currens per anni círculum:
Quod ſolus à ſede Patris
Mundi ſalus advéneris.
Hunc cœlum, terra, hunc mare,
Hunc omne quod in eis eſt,
Auctórem advéntus tui,
Láudans exúltat cántico.
Nos quoque qui ſancto tuo Coro
Redémpti sánguine ſumus:
Ob diem natális tui, Organo
Hymnum novum concínimus.
Glória tibi Dómine, Coro
Qui natus es de Vírgine:
Cum Patre, & ſancto Spíritu,
In ſempitérna ſæcula. Amen. Organo

A 3 IN

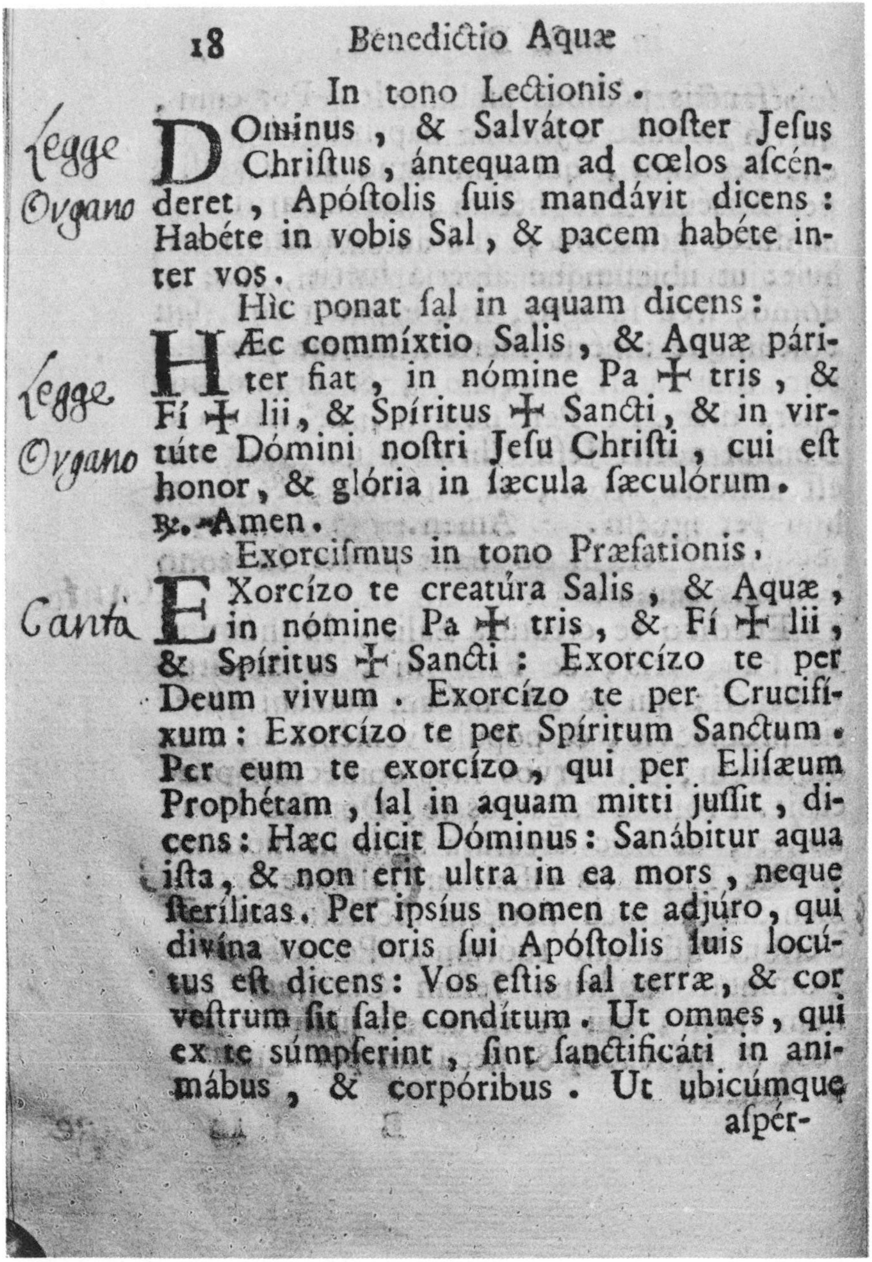

18　　　Benedictio Aquæ

In tono Lectionis .

legge

Organo

Dominus , & Salvátor noſter Jeſus Chriſtus , ántequam ad cœlos aſcénderet , Apóſtolis ſuis mandávit dicens : Habéte in vobis Sal , & pacem habéte inter vos .

Hìc ponat ſal in aquam dicens :

legge

Organo

Hæc commíxtio Salis , & Aquæ páriter fiat , in nómine Pa ✠ tris , & Fí ✠ lii , & Spíritus ✠ Sancti , & in virtúte Dómini noſtri Jeſu Chriſti , cui eſt honor , & glória in ſæcula ſæculórum . ℞. Amen .

Exorciſmus in tono Præfationis .

Canta

Exorcízo te creatúra Salis , & Aquæ , in nómine Pa ✠ tris , & Fí ✠ lii , & Spíritus ✠ Sancti : Exorcízo te per Deum vivum . Exorcízo te per Crucifíxum : Exorcízo te per Spíritum Sanctum . Per eum te exorcízo , qui per Eliſæum Prophétam , ſal in aquam mitti juſſit , dicens : Hæc dicit Dóminus : Sanábitur aqua iſta , & non erit ultra in ea mors , neque ſterílitas . Per ipſius nomen te adjúro , qui divína voce oris ſui Apóſtolis ſuis locútus eſt dicens : Vos eſtis ſal terræ , & cor veſtrum ſit ſale condítum . Ut omnes , qui ex te súmpſerint , ſint ſanctificáti in animábus , & corpóribus . Ut ubicúmque aſper-

Plate 4.　Venice, Biblioteca del Civico Museo Correr, Codice Cicogna 1151. *Benedictio aquae quae fit in nocte Epiphaniae, juxta consuetudinem ecclesiae ducalis Sancti Marci Venetiarum* (Venice: Pinelli, 1759).

In nocte Epiphaniæ: 19

aspérsa fúeris, effúges inimícum, & præstes ómnibus remissiónem peccatórum, sanitátem mentis, & protectiónem salútis? expéllas insídias, & exclúdas omnes dæmonum tentatiónes. Te autem, Dómine, cónditor, & restaurátor ómnium elementórum, qui hæc fluénta, nómine tuo sanctificáta, ad purgatiónem locórum profícere jussísti, déprecor, ut nóminis tui invocáta majestáte, grátiam Spíritus Sancti hæc aqua accípiat, atque ad expelléndas diabólicas artes, per manus servórum tuórum aspérsa, profíciat. Quam tu Dómine sanctificándo, sancti ✝ fices, & benedicéndo bene ✝ dícas: Ut omnis immúndus spíritus, aspersióne hujus áquæ, repúlsus, & confúsus discédat: Omnísque incúrsus sáthanæ, & omne phantásma, omnísque immundítia, & putrédo inimicórum longè recédat: Nullámque prorsus aut consisténdi, aut resisténdi, vel in eódem loco standi, seu commorándi hábeat potestátem: sed victus, atque destrúctus abscédat diábolus cum omni pompa sua: Per virtútem, & glóriam Dómini nostri Jesu Christi: qui cum Deo Patre, & Spíritu Sancto vivit, & regnat Deus per ómnia sæcula sæculórum.
℟. Amen.

Item

typical organ Mass but rather an alternation of organ versets and polyphonic sections of the Kyrie. Another use of the organ in both Masses occurs in the special Alleluia (documents 25, 26, 27, 31, and 32). The word *Alleluia* is sung thrice, each time at a higher pitch; then the organ plays in place of the verse, after which two singers begin the Tract and the rest complete it.

There is one further crucial document for Mass on Holy Saturday. Bonifacio notes that certain items are left out of the Mass, and he warns the organists not to play in their place (document 28): "The Offertory is not said, nor is the organ played for the Offertory; The Agnus Dei is not said, nor is the organ played for the Agnus Dei; The Communion is not said, nor is the organ played for said Communion." The document is an important one, for if the organists had to be warned not to play for missing liturgical items, the implication is that they did play for those items on other occasions.

The pattern of organ music prescribed for Holy Saturday at St. Mark's differs entirely from that which Banchieri gives for the same day.[31] According to Banchieri, the Gloria should be performed *alternatim*. He warns the organist not to play anything after the Epistle, and he gives no instructions for the playing of the verse of the Alleluia. The Credo is not sung, and the organist plays at the place of the Offertory, at the Sanctus, and after the Agnus Dei—points that vary from the rubrics of St. Mark's. In the Vespers service annexed to the Mass, however, Banchieri's instructions correspond exactly to those for St. Mark's.

These minimal data on the use of the organ at Mass in the basilica suggest two major questions: first, the extent to which the organ Masses of such figures as Claudio Merulo or Andrea Gabrieli found a place in the performance of the Ordinary at St. Mark's; and second, the extent to which the principle of Proper substitutes given by Banchieri and Fasolo was followed. The answers to these questions are complex, however, and I should like to consider them a bit later in this discussion.

Numerous exceptional ceremonies call for special rubrics regarding the use of the organs. Bonifacio says the organist should play for the singing of the greater litanies on the Vigil of the feast of St. Mark (document 33), a duty that recalls Frescobaldi's obligation to play for Marian litanies every Saturday during his tenure at Santa Maria in Sassia in 1620–21.[32] The organist plays on Low Sunday as the singers approach the main door of St. Mark's after earlier ceremonies in San Geminiano, the church of Jacopo Sansovino which stood across the piazza from St. Mark's until the end of the eighteenth century (document 34). On the feast of St. Isidore, some complex staging was necessary, since Mass was celebrated in the chapel of St. Isidore on the north side of the church, the singers sang in the *pulpito magno* at the south end of the iconostasis, and the organists played above in their lofts. The master of ceremonies was charged with coordinating these widely dispersed forces (document 35).

A special Mass took place on Carnival Thursday (document 42); as the document reads, a lively Mass, composed by a "Todesco" for the victory of the French king over the Swiss and called the *Messa della Battaglia*, was performed over "ricercate dell'organo." In fact, the "Todesco" was Janequin; the Mass was his *Missa super la Bataille*, which exists in manuscript in Venice without ascription, but with the designation "Mass for Carnival Thursday."[33] The reference to *ricercate dell'organo* is obscure; read literally, the document would seem to refer to a Mass based on what was originally instrumental material; but elsewhere Giovanni Pace, the author of this *ceremoniale*, does not show himself to be very knowledgeable about music. In fact, the "ricercate dell'organo" may be merely keyboard *battaglie* played during the celebration of Mass, compositions that would certainly have been appropriate on this day when Venice celebrated her victory over the twelfth-century patriarch of Aquileia; moreover, as one can see in document 43, independent organ compositions were used on this day in certain years.[34]

One additional use of the organs in St. Mark's was to fill what otherwise would have been "gaps in sound" in the services, or to accompany liturgical actions. In the ceremony for the Blessing of the Water, the text of the service breaks off at one point for a procession: "Here the canon makes a pause; meanwhile, the organ is played until the procession with the cross has reached the altar with the water" (document 11). On the feast of St. Isidore, whose elaborate procession included the six *scuole grandi* and the nine congregations of Venetian clergy, we are told that the *scuole* pass without singing while the organs are played, although later when the nine congregations of clerics pass, the chapter of St. Mark's sings litanies in two choirs (document 36). At the investiture of the Primicerius, the service ended with the singers performing a double-choir Te Deum from the hexagonal pergola, and then the organs played while everyone went up to shake the hand of the new Primicerius and to celebrate the occasion (document 37). And at one point in the ceremony for the entrance of the new dogaressa into the *palazzo ducale*, the ducal chronicler reported a pause in the ceremony while the organs of St. Mark's were played (document 38).

As might be expected when supreme virtuosi were asked to fill a temporal gap in the service, *Spielfreude* seems to have overtaken the organists on more than one occasion. It was, no doubt, during a ceremony like one of the above that Diruta witnessed the famous "duello di due Organi" between Claudio Merulo and Andrea Gabrieli.[35] In 1556 Annibale Padovano had been suspended for six months for continuing to play the organ while the priests were trying to celebrate Mass for the Queen of Poland (document 40). In 1564 the Procurators warned the priests to wait until the organists had finished playing before proceeding with the service.[36] And Bonifacio singles out First Vespers of the feast of the Ascension as a service at which the organists must be warned not to play too long (document 41).

Thus the ceremonial books and prints from St. Mark's give us a fair amount of detail about the use of the organ in specific services. Large lacunae exist, however, and certainly the most important are connected with the two questions I raised earlier about the celebration of Mass: the use of organ Masses at St. Mark's for the Ordinary and the use of independent organ compositions to substitute for items of the Proper.

In determining the extent to which the famous organ Masses of Claudio Merulo[37] or the manuscript organ Masses of Andrea Gabrieli[38] could have been used in the basilica, several points are pertinent. First of all, Bonifacio's rubrics almost always equate Mass in *canto figurato* with the singers of the *cappella* and plainchant with the choir of *giovani di coro* and other priests. Indeed, in a description of the services for the death of the pope, Bonifacio emphasizes that Mass is to be sung in plainchant "even though the singers are in church," a negative indication of this usual pairing, although he adds that the singers will sing at the Offertory and the Communion (document 46). The organists were to attend only those services at which the professional singers were present plus a few other special ceremonies. And as mentioned earlier, the most common rubrics for Mass describe its celebration "cum cantoribus et organis" or "in cantu plano sine organis."[39] Thus, there seem to be no days on the calendar when merely the organists and a plainchant choir would assemble for an *alternatim* Mass. In fact, by the early seventeenth century, polyphony seems to have infiltrated nearly the entire church calendar, for when Monteverdi made his famous purchase of Roman polyphony in 1614, he specified that it would be used on ferial days.[40] Thus, although Merulo published his *Messe d'intavolatura d'organo* during his tenure at St. Mark's, proclaimed his position on the title page, and encouraged other organists to aim for such a prestigious position themselves, the three organ Masses in his print might seldom if ever have been used in the basilica.

It is difficult to tell how extensively organ music was used to substitute for items of the Proper, for the silence of the *ceremoniali* may mean either that no substitution took place, or that the substitution was taken for granted. A fair amount of evidence can be gathered for the latter interpretation. From other sources, we know that motets were sanctioned at the start of Mass, at the Gradual, the Offertory, the Elevation, the Communion, and at the very end of Mass before the singers left. For example, on an occasion in 1619, we are told that "the musicians, who were placed in the organ lofts, sang and played a motet while [the clergy] took their places in the choir."[41] And later on, the Primicerius "read the *Missa dello Spirito Santo* while the singers and players in the lofts made music from the Offertory onward"[42]—that is, they performed compositions as liturgical substitutes in the latter part of the Mass. We also have Ignazio Donati's famous statement that the Venetian Sanctus and Agnus Dei were brief to provide time for a *concerto* at the Elevation and a *sinfonia* at the Communion.[43] Indeed, we have Masses by Alessandro Grandi and Giovanni Rovetta, Monteverdi's *vice maestri* at St. Mark's, that have no Sanctus or Agnus Dei at all.[44] Moreover, we have seventeenth-century payments to violinists for playing sonatas at the Elevation,[45] and wind music was played at the Gradual and the Elevation during the Mass for a ducal coronation (document 39).

In other words, we have documents sanctioning other para-liturgical music at the spots that Banchieri and Fasolo reserve for organ music; and there are documents that suggest that music for organ, music for instrumental ensemble, and motets had analogous functions in St. Mark's. For example, on the feast of St. Nicholas a private Mass for the doge and the Collegio was held in the chapel of St. Nicholas, adjacent to St. Mark's in the ducal palace, with the doge's *piffari* standing outside the chapel to fulfill the role of the organ (document 44). However, a gloss on the document indicates that when this practice was discontinued, the singers of the *cappella* would sing a motet to St. Nicholas where the *piffari* formerly had played (document 45). Similarly, on Carnival Thursday Janequin's *Missa super la Bataille* was sung along with special motets *pro gratiarum actione* in honor of Venice's victory over Aquileia. However, if another feast fell on Carnival Thursday, the motets were not sung at all but were replaced by organ music (document 43). Moreover, we have the negative evidence of the document about Mass on Holy Saturday which warns the organists not to play for the missing liturgical items, which they might otherwise have done (document 28). Thus, there is a chain of evidence that the organs did play at the place of certain items of the Proper, although with what frequency, and on which occasions we really do not know.

What conclusions can one draw from this discussion, and in particular, what connections might one make between the material presented here and the liturgical compositions of Frescobaldi?

First of all, the documents from the *ceremoniali* of St. Mark's show that despite the efforts of Clement VIII to codify the use of the organ, there was not really a uniform practice in seventeenth-century Italy. Nearly fifteen years ago, Stephen Bonta made a masterful compilation of the information in organists' manuals, and his tables showed that no two manuals gave precisely the same instructions.[46] Indeed, were the materials from St. Mark's to be inserted into his tables, still more variants would result. Interestingly enough, however, the scant materials on the use of the organ at Mass in St. Mark's do correspond with the contents of Frescobaldi's *Fiori musicali*—in particular, the idiosyncratic specification of *alternatim* performance of the Ordinary for the Kyrie only, and the principle of organ compositions (or music for instrumental ensemble, or motets) substituting for items of the Proper.[47]

Scholars have been puzzled by certain aspects of the *Fiori*, especially the absence of *alternatim* settings for the items of the Ordinary after the Kyrie, a practice that agrees with neither the Italian organ Masses of the sixteenth century nor the manuals of Banchieri, Fasolo, Bottazzi, or Diruta.[48] But the correspondence between the contents of the *Fiori* and the rubrics of St. Mark's suggests that we have perhaps been comparing Frescobaldi's print with the wrong sources. That is, the compositions in the *Fiori musicali* may not be strict organ Masses in the sense of the *alternatim* Masses of the sixteenth century or the instructions presented in manuals for small churches which would have used plainchant almost exclusively. In fact, the *Fiori musicali* may represent something quite different: material for use during Mass in larger churches with major musical establishments, where the Ordinary was performed in polyphony on most feasts and independent instrumental or vocal music was used liberally to substitute for items of the Proper.

Certainly northern Italy had many churches in the early seventeenth century whose *maestri* composed works in the *stile concertato* scarcely less elaborate than those composed for St. Mark's and who could muster forces that approached those of the ducal chapel on major feasts—or, dare we say at this point, on certain Sundays, feasts of the Apostles, or feasts of the Virgin.[49] Indeed, it is perhaps significant that the *Fiori musicali* is one of those collections of Frescobaldi which was printed only in Venice. One should note, moreover, that the basic liturgical genres that Frescobaldi treats outside the *Fiori*—the Magnificat *versetti*, the *alternatim* hymn settings, the independent Elevation toccatas—are all mentioned, albeit indirectly in some cases, in the materials from St. Mark's. Thus, they would certainly have been at home in a church with a large musical establishment, and the argument that these are simple works for parish churches only is certainly untenable.

The other implications of the rubrics of St. Mark's relate more exclusively to the basilica itself. First, the emphasis at St. Mark's on short versets for psalms, Magnificats, hymns, the Te Deum, as well as pieces for the *Deo gratias* or verses for the Alleluia suggests that the larger part of the repertoire for the basilica was improvised on the spot. It is certainly significant that the entire *prova* for the organists was a test of improvisation in various styles and genres.[50] Indeed, the three tests—improvising a four-voice fantasia or ricercar on a given melody, improvising around a cantus firmus placed successively in each of four voices, and improvising versets in response to the *cappella*—certainly would cover the situations mentioned in the *ceremoniali*.

Second, while the ubiquitous statements "organa pulsantur" and "sonano li organo" are frustrating in their vagueness, they may accurately convey the freedom the organists enjoyed to improvise what they wished within certain stylistic limits.[51] There is no direct evidence that the stylistic recommendations that Banchieri provides—ricercars, *capricci*, and *canzoni francesi* all at specific points in the Mass or the Office—were strictly followed at St. Mark's. Nor is there any evidence of a functional differentiation among ricercars, *canzoni*, and toccatas, the three principal genres cultivated by the organists of the sixteenth century at the basilica.[52] Indeed, the documents seem to portray a looser and perhaps more varied tradition; and it is all the more a shame that much of the Venetian repertoire of the seventeenth century has ultimately been reduced to a series of fascinating but musically sterile entries in the ceremonial books.

Appendix: Documents

CHRISTMAS, AT MATINS

1. Venice, Biblioteca nazionale marciana, Cod. lat. III-172 (= 2276), fol. 21v

    Sed redeamus ad Officium Vigiliae Nativitatis Domini, unde digressi sumus. Post Salve Regina, Dominus Vicarius, finito Completorio, incohat Matutinum; Invitatorium cantant duo Ministri cum Pluvialibus induti; Organa pulsantur in fine cuiuslibet Psalmi, et similiter ad Responsoria.

2. Ibid., fol. 75v (cf. doc. 1)

    pollizza della vigilia de nadal à vespero . compieta . et matin . . . le tre letion cantano li cantori in canto figurato . la prima à quatro . la secunda à cinque . la terza à sej . le antiphone, et Responsorij tutti cantano li cantori . à tutti li psalmi, et à tutti li Responsorij sonano li organi.

3. Ibid., fol. 21v (after the Mass on Christmas Eve)

    . . . quo finito statim Diaconus et subdiaconus intonant Te Deum laudamus hoc fiebat quando cantores canebant Te Deum alternatim cum organis . sed posteaquam Magister capellae D. D. Adrianus composuit omnes versus ipsius Te Deum . cantores intonant, ut comodiorem sibi vocem accipiant . quo expleto per cantores alternatim . Diaconus et Subdiaconus cantant . V. Verbum caro factum est alleluia . longum .R. Et habitavit in nobis alleluia . Deinde celebrans versus ad altare cantat orationem ut in Vesperis praemisso Dominus vobiscum . et expleto oratione . et replicato Dominus vobiscum . organista sonant . pro benedicamus domino . cantores vero cantant Deo gratias.

4. Ibid., fol. 75v (cf. doc. 3)

   . . . canta l'orazion della natività . la qual finitta et replicato dominus vobiscum
   . l'organo sona benedicamus domino et li cantori cantano Deo gratias.

CORPUS CHRISTI, AT MATINS

5. Ibid, fol. 35v

   In Vigilia Sacratissimi Corporis Christi . . . Post completorium cantatur matutinum,
   organa pulsantur in fine cuiuslibet psalmi, et similiter ad responsoria. Cantores cantant
   tantum Te Deum . . . à capitulo in antea, omnia cantantur in cantu plano, et organa
   pulsantur, videlicet ad hymnum . ad benedictus . post benedictus . et ad benedicamus
   Domino.

SS. PETER AND PAUL, AT MATINS

6. Milan, Biblioteca ambrosiana, Ms. A. 328 inf., fol. 52v

   La Vigilia di San Pietro. Finito il Vespro li Titolati cantano l'Invitatorio del Matutino.
   Le prime lettioni le dicono li soddiaconi, le seconde li Diaconi, e le 3.e li sotto
   Canonici, Li Capi di Coro cantano li primi Responsorij, li secondi l'Organo, id est la
   replica di tutti tre li Notturni.

BLESSING OF THE WATER, EVE OF EPIPHANY

7. Venice, Biblioteca nazionale marciana, Cod. lat. III-172 (= 2276), fol. 22r

   . . . quo finito canonicus intonat Antiphonam Vox Domini dej qua completo a
   choro . ministri intonant psalmum. Afferte . sexti toni . (marginal addition, same
   hand: et organa pulsantur aut pulsare debent ut finito quolibet psalmo).

8. Ibid., fol. 23r (end of the Blessing of the Waters)

   . . . quo finito Diaconus et subdiaconus statim intonant Te Deum laudamus . et
   pulsantur campane . quo finito, vel à choris, vel alternatim à choro et organis. . . .
   (later in description:) . . . et finita oratione, repetitur Dominus vobiscum . postea
   cantatur benedicamus domino . magnum . et respondetur a choro . Deo gratias
   (addition, same hand: vel organa ipsum benedicamus sonant).

9. Ibid., fol. 76r

   polizza della vigilia della epiphania al baptizar la croce . . . li ministri intonano li
   psalmi . da poi ciascuno sona l'organo . finiti li psalmi . et sonato l'organo . el prette
   intona Exaudi nos domine con gloria patri . el diacono et subdiacono cantano le
   letanie. . . . Dapoi l'Epistola sona l'Organo; il Choro: Alleluia. . . . Finito l'Evangelo
   . . . el Diacono et suddiacono incontinente intonano. Te Deum laudamus . . . et si
   dice il Te Deum con l'Organo à un verso per uno; et un Zago leza el Verso dell'Organo
   in choro.

10.   Venice, Archivio della Curia Patriarcale, item 37, pp. 1, 4

Incipit ordo sive offitium ad benedicendum aquam in nocte Epiphaniae. . . . (latter part of ceremony:) Sequitur Graduale: Ultimo festivitatis die: quod cantatur à Choro cum suo V. et alleluia, et cum Organi pulsatione.

11.   Ibid, p. 13

Hic Canonicus benedicens pausam facit. Interim Organum pulsatur usque quo, processio cum cruce ad altarum aquae perveniat.

12.   Ibid., p. 15

Hic cantatur Sanctus à Choro cum organi pulsatione.

13.   Ibid., p. 20

Finito Evangelio statim campanae pulsantur; postea Ministri intonant Hymnum Ss. Ambrosij, et Augustini scilicet. Te Deum laudamus: qui quidem à Choro cum organi pulsatione alternatim cantatur.

14.   Ibid., p. 21 (end of service)

V. Dominus vobiscum. R. Et cum spiritu tuo. Postea ab Organo pulsatur. V. Benedicamus Domino: et Chorus in tono maiori. R. Deo gratias.

VESPERS

15.   Venice, Archivio di Stato, San Marco, Procuratia de Supra, Registro 142

Adi 18 Ottobre 1624
L'Illustrissimi Signori Procuratori tutti tre in numero hanno terminato che sij intimato il presente loro ordine à Messer Carlo Fillago, et Giovanni Pietro Berti tutti due organisti in San Marco che debbano conforme all'uso antico di chiesa di San Marco ritrovarsi tutte le Domeniche et le feste commandate tutti doi sopra li organi di chiesa et sonar alle Messe et Vespri rispondendosi un verso per uno à tutti li salmi.

VESPERS, EVE OF EPIPHANY

16.   Venice, Biblioteca nazionale marciana, Cod. lat. III-172 (= 2276), fol. 22r

In vigilia epiphaniae. . . . In primis vesperis . (texts for service given) . . . Et Dicta oratione . Dum pulsatur organum . et cantores cantant motetum pro Deo gratias.

VESPERS, HOLY SATURDAY

17.   Ibid., fol. 81r

Communicado el prete . l'intona vespere autem sabbatj. et li cantori seguitano tutte le cinque antiphone. poi diacono et subdiacono intonano Laudate dominum omnes gentes octavo ton. finitto dal choro. sonna l'organo. poi el prette intona la antifona ad

Magnificat Respondens autem angelus. et li cantori la compie. poi se dice el Magnificat col organo et cantori ut moris est. et se incensa l'altar solum. finitto. sonna l'organo. poi el prette se volta et dice dominus vobiscum. et compie la Messa. et se dice benedicamus domino alleluia alleluia dal diacono et subdiacono solenne . et l'organo sonna deo gratias.

18. *Officium hebdomadae sanctae, secundum consuetudinem ducalis ecclesiae S. Marci venetiarum* (Venice, 1678), fol. 277v

    5 antiphons sung before the psalm *Laudate Dominum omnes gentes*; then: Completo a Choris Psalmo: et ab organo reiteratis supradictis quinque Antiphonis, Canonicus celebrans intonet ad Magnificat. Antiph. Respondens autem Angelus . . . quam Cantores complent, et per organi pulsationem inchoatur Cantic. Magnificat . . . et alternatim à Cantoribus cantatur, et ab Organo (ut moris est) pulsatur. Quo finito, et ab organo reiterata Antiph. Canonicus celebrans dicit. V. Dominus vobiscum. . . . Et Ministri cantant. V. Benedicamus Domino. Alleluia, alleluia. Et organa pulsantur R. Deo gratias. Alleluia, alleluia.

VESPERS, EASTER SUNDAY

19. Venice, Biblioteca nazionale marciana, Cod. lat. III-172 (=2276), fol. 31r–v

    Cantatis tribus psalmis, et in fine unius cuiusque pulsato organo. . . . finito Magnificat, pulsato organo, et cantata oratione cum Dominus vobiscum.

20. *Officium hebdomadae sanctae, secundum consuetudinem ducalis ecclesiae S. Marci venetiarum* (Venice, 1678), fol. 195v

    Et Vesperae inchoantur sic V. Kyrie eleison. R. Christe eleison. V. Kyrie eleis. Antiphona. Vespere autem Sabbathi. . . . Psalm. Dixit Dominus. . . . Confitebor. . . . et Psalm. Beatus vir . . . cantantur cum Organi pulsatione quibus finitis, repetitur Antiph. Vespere autem Sabbathi.

    (later in service:) Postea reliqui duo Psalmi in cantu plano à choro cantantur alternatum [sic] videlicet Psalmus. Laudate pueri Dominum . . . et Psalmus In exitu Israel ex Ægypto.

21. Ibid., fol. 199r (service for Easter Sunday Vespers if the doge stays in St. Mark's and does not go to San Zaccaria)

    Kyrie eleison. Antiph. Vespere autem Sabbath. Psalm. Dixit Dominus. Confitebor. Beatus vir. Laudate pueri. et In exitu. . . . Et cantantur in canto figurato à duobus Choris Cantorum, cum organi pulsatione ad quemlibet Psalmum.

    end of service:
    V. Dominus vobiscum. R. Et cum spiritu tuo. V. Benedicamus Domino. Alleluia. R. Deo gratias, alleluia. Et decantato post Organum à Cantoribus. Deo gratias, alleluia. Celebrans dicit. . . .

MASS, HOLY SATURDAY

22.   Venice, Biblioteca nazionale marciana, Cod. lat. III-172 (= 2276), fol. 30v

. . . ut perventum est ad Altare Missa incohatur à Kyrie eleison per organa primum.

23.   Ibid., fol. 81r (cf. doc. 22)

Zonti al'altar. l'organo sonna li Kyrie della Messa senza altro introito.

24.   *Officium hebdomadae sanctae, secundum consuetudinem ducalis ecclesiae S. Marci venetiarum* (Venice, 1678), fol. 184r

Sabbato Sancto Ad Missam. . . . Et facta per dictum celebrantem, et Sereniss. Principem (ut moris est) coram Altare confessione: Per organi pulsationem incipiatur missa, et Cantores prosequentur. Kyrie eleis.

25.   Venice, Biblioteca nazionale marciana, Cod. lat. III-172 (= 2276), fol. 30

. . . cantata epistola in medio chori sacerdos immediate intonat Alleluya . et cantores replicant Alleluya . et ita faciunt ter alternatim . postea pulsatur organum breviter . Deinde cantores cantant tractum.

26.   Ibid., fol. 81r (cf. doc. 25)

. . . et da poi la Epistola el prette immediatte intona alleluia. tre volte alzando sempre la voce et li cantori tutti tre volte li rispondeno quel medesimo. poi sonna l'organo el verso confitemini . poi dui cantori cantano el tratto Laudate dominum et tutti quoniam confirmata est.

27.   *Officium hebdomadae sanctae, secundum consuetudinem ducalis ecclesiae S. Marci venetiarum* (Venice, 1678), fol. 184v

Finita Epistola Canonicum celebrans Missam decantat Allel. ter gradatim exaltando vocem. Et Cantores post quamlibet vicem in eadem voce repetunt illud idem. Postea pulsatur organum loco V. Confitemini Domino quoniam bonus. . . . Deinde Cantores cantant tractum.

28.   Venice, Biblioteca nazionale marciana, Cod. lat. III-172 (= 2276), fol. 81r

non se dice offertorio . ne si sonna l'organo per conto del offertorio. . . . non se dice Agnus dej . ne se sonna l'organo per conto del Agnus dej. non se dice communion . ne se sonna l'organo per ditta communion.

MASS, VIGIL OF PENTECOST

29.   Ibid., fol. 34v

Kyrie eleison pro Missa solemniter incohatur per organistas (added in same hand: et cantores ut moris est).

30.   Ibid., fol. 82r (cf. doc. 28)

Pollizza della vigilia delle penthecoste alla Messa. . . . et l'organo sona li Kyrie della Messa . et li cantori li rispondeno in canto figuratto.

31. Ibid., fol. 34v

Post Epistolam immediate à duobus cantoribus cantatur alleluia, et reiteratur ab omnibus cantoribus, postea pulsatur organum loco versi confitemini. pulsato organo, dicitur à duobus cantoribus tractus .vz. laudate dominum omnes gentes . postea ab omnibus cantoribus dicitur . quoniam confirmata est.

32. Ibid., fol. 82r (cf. doc. 30)

. . . da poi la Epistola duj cantori dicanno lo alleluia . poi tutti lo replicano tutto un altra volta poi sonna l'organo el verso confitemini. poj duj cantano el tratto Laudate Dominum . poi tutti quoniam confirmata est.

LITANIES

33. Ibid., fol. 44v

In vigilia Sanctj Marcj. . . . Et fit processio cum lethanijs maioribus à duobus choris cantorum. . . . (later in document:) . . . quia cantores cantant, et organa pulsantur.

LOW SUNDAY

34. Ibid., fol. 32v (ceremonies at San Geminiano; then all return to the door of St. Mark's)

. . . et Chorus distenditur praecedentibus Cruce, et Cereis, usque extra Portam Ecclesiae. et ibi se firmat facto choro donec pulsato Organo decantetur Deo gratias cum dupplicj alleluia.

TRANSLATION OF THE BODY OF ST. ISIDORE

35. Ibid., fol. 44r

De festo translationis corporis sanctj ysidori Martyris. Missa canitur in eius saccello in quo est corpus. . . . Cantores vero cantant Missam in pulpito magno . et similiter organistae sonant ad signum Magister chori.

36. Ibid.

Dum transeunt scholae sine cantu . organa pulsantur. . . . (later in procession:) Capitulum Sancti Marci in principio transitus octavae congregationis intonat: Exaudi nos Domine . . . et in Processione cantantur Litaniae à duobus Choris Cantorum.

CORONATIONS AND INVESTITURES: PRIMICERIO, DOGARESSA, DOGE

37. Venice, Biblioteca Correr, Codice Cicogna 2768, fol. 85v

Polizza della Creation et Possesso del Reverendissimo Primicerio di San Marco. . . . et li Cantori in pergolo grando cantano Te deum laudamus a dui chori, finito sonano li organi per fino che tutti vanno a tocharli la man et allegrarsi.

38. Venice, Archivio di Stato, Collegio, Ceremoniali, II, fols. 7r–8r (ceremony of the entrance of the dogaressa into the ducal palace, 19 September 1557)

Quando l'Illustrissima Madonna Zia . . . moglie del Serenissimo Principe Lorenzo di Prioli sontuosissimente entrò nel Palazzo . . . l'ordine, et la pompa fù tale, cioè. . . .

La onde il rimanente de nobeli sedetero nel mezo della chiesa fuori di esso choro. Ivi alquanto si dimorò mentre sonando gli organi la Serenissima Principessa sentando si ripossò.

39. Venice, Biblioteca nazionale marciana, Cod. lat. III-172 (= 2276), fol. 89v

pollizza della creation del ser.mo principe. . . . Et se li canta una bella Messa della Trinità . . . e li Sonatori sonano li Piffari, dapoi l'Epistola dietro l'Altar Grando, et all'Elevazion sonano cornetti, over altri Instrumenti.

. . . Poi ogn'anno el di del suo Annual el vien in Chiesa a Messa Grande etc. Se li canta la soprascritta Messa della Trinità . . . con Instrumenti, con li Cantori; et in Organo all'Epistola, et Elevatione.

LENGTH OF ORGAN MUSIC

40. Venice, Archivio di Stato, Procuratia de Supra, Registro 128, fol. 49r

Die 8. Maj 1556
I Clarissimi Signori Procuratori tutti in numero . . . hanno à bossoli et ballote terminato ut infra videlicet che attesa la inobedientia de ser Hannibal organista, et confessata per lui nel sonar l'organo al tempo che fu detto la messa della Serenissima Regina de Polonia per la qual merita condegno castigo, che detto ser Hannibal sia casso per messi sei.

41. Ibid., fol. 33v

In vigilia Ascensionis Domini post prandium. . . . Vespere hodie . . . dicuntur solemnissime. Organistae tamen potius tendant ad mediocritatem quam ad prolixitatem propter indulgentias.

CARNIVAL THURSDAY

42. Milan, Biblioteca ambrosiana, Ms. A. 328 inf., fol. 20v

Il Giovedi Grasso si canta la Messa Grande à hora di Terza composta da un Todesco sopra le ricercate dell'organo molto allegra, e si chiama la Messa della Battaglia, se bene de presente la chiamano la Messa della Cazza. Questa fu composta per la Vittoria del Rè di Francia contro l'elvetij.

43. Venice, Biblioteca nazionale marciana, Cod. lat. III-172 (= 2276), fol. 76r

El Zorno della Zuobba grassa . si canta la Messa della bataglia da li cantori . con li mottettj soliti . salvo sel non fusse festa che sonasse l'organo . perche non se dissa li motteti, ma in loco da quelli sonasse l'organo, come è accaduto el di di s.to mathia venir in tal di.

FEAST OF ST. NICHOLAS

44. Venice, Archivio della Curia Patriarcale, item 53, fol. 63v

   De Sancto Nicolao Episcopo Confessore. 6 Decembris
   . . . Et sic cantatur Missa post Adventum Domini Ducis cum Colleggio in Sacello, sine Organis, cum Sonatoribus Dominij, qui supplentur pro Organo quando opus fuerit. Et Cantores cantant in Sacello praedicto, Sonatores ante Ianuam extra Sacellum.

45. Ibid., fol. 307r

   Nell'annotazione circa la festa di S. Nicolò . . . apparisce, che li Suonatori debbano essere à sonare in supplimento dell'Organo, mà ciò non si prattica, perche li Cantori cantano un Mottetto proprio di S. Nicolò nel tempo, che quelli doverebbono suonare.

FUNERAL, ELECTION OF POPE

46. Venice, Biblioteca nazionale marciana, Cod. lat. III-172 (=2276), fol. 97r

   l'ordine della morte et creation del papa. . . . (Mass is sung:) in canto fermo se ben li sonno li cantori in chiesia . ma li ditti cantano l'offertorio . et la communione.

Notes

Research for this study was supported by the National Endowment for the Humanities, the American Council of Learned Societies, and the Gladys Krieble Delmas Foundation.

1. W. Gurlitt, "Ein Briefwechsel zwischen Paul Hainlein und L. Friedrich Behaim aus den Jahren 1647–48," *Sammelbände der internationalen Musikgesellschaft* 4 (1912–13): 497: "Was Organisten betrifft, wirtt des *Frescobaldi* gleichen nit mehr anzutreffen sein, und lest sich der jenige, so ein gutter *practicus*, nit allezeit hören, so wohl alß hier *Sig: Cavalli* in *S: Marco*."

2. See Giovanni Stringa, *Venetia città nobilissima . . . da M. Francesco Sansovino* (Venice: Salicato, 1604), fols. 28v–29r and fol. 31r–31v. On the instruments themselves, see also Adriano Banchieri, *Conclusioni nel suono dell'organo* (Bologna: Rossi, 1609), 12; Johann Mattheson, *Der vollkommene Capellmeister* (Hamburg: C. Herold, 1739), 466; Giovanni Meschinello, *La chiesa ducale di S. Marco* (Venice: Bartolomeo Baronchelli, 1753), 2:94 and 3:34–35. The most important modern studies are Francesco Caffi, *Storia della musica sacra nella già cappella ducale di San Marco in Venezia dal 1318 al 1797* (Venice: Antonelli, 1854), passim, especially 2:5–22; Giacomo Benvenuti, *Andrea e Giovanni Gabrieli e la musica strumentale in San Marco. Istituzioni e monumenti dell'arte musicale italiana* (Milan: Ricordi, 1931–32), 1 and 2, passim; Sandro dalla Libera, *L'arte degli organi a Venezia* (Venice: Istituto

per la collaborazione culturale, 1962), 17–50; Renato Lunelli, *Studi e documenti di storia organaria veneta* (Florence: Olschki, 1973), passim; Eleanor Selfridge-Field, *Venetian Instrumental Music from Gabrieli to Vivaldi* (New York: Praeger, 1974), 8–13; and idem, "Gabrieli and the Organ," *The Organ Yearbook*, 8 (1977): 2–19.

3. See James H. Moore, *Vespers at St. Mark's: Music of Alessandro Grandi, Giovanni Rovetta and Francesco Cavalli* (Ann Arbor: UMI Research Press, 1981), 1:103–10; idem, "The *Vespero delli Cinque Laudate* and the Role of *Salmi Spezzati* at St. Mark's," *Journal of the American Musicological Society* 34 (1981): 275–77; and David Bryant, "The *Cori Spezzati* of St. Mark's: Myth and Reality," *Early Music History 1: Studies in Medieval and Early Modern Music*, ed. Iain Fenlon (Cambridge: Cambridge University Press, 1981), 165–86.

4. See *Fiori musicali* in the "Bibliography of Frescobaldi's Printed Collections," this volume.

5. These items were published in a single print; see *Toccate II* in the "Bibliography of Frescobaldi's Printed Collections," this volume.

6. See Moore, *Vespers* 1:97–103, and Selfridge-Field, "Gabrieli and the Organ," 2–3, 12.

7. The major manuals printed before 1650 include the following prints: Adriano Banchieri, *L'Organo suonarino* (Venice: Amadino, 1605; 2d ed., Venice: Amadino, 1611 and 1620; 3d ed., Venice: Alessandro Vincenti, 1622, 1627, and 1638); idem, *Conclusioni nel suono dell'organo* (Bologna: Heredi di Gio. Rossi, 1609); Girolamo Diruta, *Il Transilvano: Dialogo sopra il vero modo di sonar organi, et istromenti da penna* (Venice: Giacomo Vincenti, 1593, 1597, 1612; Alessandro Vincenti, 1625), and *Seconda parte del Transilvano* (Venice: Giacomo Vincenti, 1609; Alessandro Vincenti, 1622); Bernardo Bottazzi, *Choro et organo* (Venice: Giacomo Vincenti, 1614); Antonio Croci, *Frutti musicali* (Venice: Alessandro Vincenti, 1642); Giovanni Battista Fasolo, *Annuale che contiene tutto quello, che deve far un organista, per risponder al choro tutto l'anno* (Venice: Alessandro Vincenti, 1645). General principles on the use of the organ are also included in the *Caeremoniale episcoporum iussu Clementis VIII* (Rome: Ex typographia linguarum externarum, 1600). The information in these manuals and in certain other sources is summarized and correlated in Stephen Bonta, "The Uses of the *Sonata da Chiesa*," *Journal of the American Musicological Society* 22 (1969): 54–84. For a list of the most important manuals published before ca. 1650, see ibid., 56 n. 7; for a comparative table of the information on the use of the organ at Mass, see 72–75; for a parallel table on the use of the organ at Vespers, see 81–82.

8. The most complete discussion of the complex of manuscripts spawned by Bonifacio's *ceremoniale* is found in James H. Moore, "Bartolomeo Bonifacio's *Rituum ecclesiasticorum ceremoniale:* Continuity of Tradition in the Ceremonial of St. Mark's, Venice," forthcoming in *Music and Ceremony: Proceedings of the 13th Congress of the International Musicological Society, Strasbourg, 1982*. For an earlier attempt to construct a stemma of the manuscripts, see idem, *Vespers* 1:71–73.

9. The principal manuscript of Pace's text is preserved as *I-Ma* Ms. A. 328 inf. On Pace's *ceremoniale*, see Moore, *Vespers* 1:68–71, and idem, "Bartolomeo Bonifacio's *Rituum.*"

10. *Officium in nocte nativitatis domini ad matutinum, secundum consuetudinem ducalis ecclesiae Sancti Marci Venetiarum* (Venice: Poleti, 1722; Pinelli, 1759); *Benedictio aquae quae fit in nocte Epiphaniae, juxta consuetudinem ecclesiae ducalis Sancti Marci Venetiarum* (Venice: Poleti, 1722; Pinelli, 1759).

11. Documents recording the printing of the special Holy Week office of St. Mark's are found nearly every year during the first half of the seventeenth century; see Venice, Archivio di Stato (hereafter ASV), San Marco, Procuratia de Supra, Giornali Cassier. In *I-Vmc*, item I. 5176, printed volumes of the Holy Week office survive from the following years: 1597, 1653, 1678, 1695, 1703, 1716, 1722, 1736, 1746, 1755, 1767, 1791.

12. These manuscripts are primarily in the Biblioteca Correr and in Venice, Archivio della Curia Patriarcale; for the present study, the most important source is Archivio della Curia Patriarcale, Archivio capitolare di Venezia, item 37, a manuscript which contains the ceremony for the Blessing of the Water.

13. See *I-Ma* Ms. A. 328 inf., fol. 168r: "Ogni volta che vengono cantori sono obligati ancò li Organisti come segue." Bonifacio heads his list of duties "Tabula descriptionis Dierum totius Anni in quibus Cantores et Organistae tenentur ad nostram Ecclesiam Sanctj Marcj convenire pro suis officijs" (*I-Vnm* Cod. lat. III-172 [= 2276], fol. 63v), but he adds the following qualification at the end (fol. 65v): "Organistae semper veniunt et sonant . in omnibus suprascriptis diebus . exceptis simplicibus diebus et Dominicis Adventus . et a Dominica Septuagesimae usque ad Dominicam palmarum inclusive . Dum modo in talibus Diebus festum aliquod de supra scriptis non occurrat . Excepta etiam feria secunda . tercia . quarta . et sexta majoris hebdomadae . ut moris est."

These exceptional dates are spelled out in more detail in two *tariffe* of the eighteenth century. The first, from 1752 (ASV, San Marco, Procuratia de Supra, Registro 99, fol. 412v) is reproduced in Moore, *Vespers* 1:301 (document 142; see the section "Circa gl'Organisti"). The second, printed in 1761, reverts to a document of 1515 which was revised in 1661 and 1694; the entire table is reproduced in ibid., 1:301–7 (document 143; see the section "Obblighi degli Organisti"). The passage dealing with the organists' duties is also printed in Selfridge-Field, "Gabrieli and the Organ," 17.

14. *I-Vnm* Cod. lat. III-172 (= 2276), passim. See, inter alia, fol. 22r: "In Die Nativitatis Dominj in Aurora cantant illi de canonica tantum Missam in Aurora in cantu plano sine organis."; fol. 40v (feast of St. Anianus): "Olim fiebat cum cantoribus et organis . hodie vero in cantu plano sine organis."; fol. 51r (dedication of the Church of Ss. Peter and Paul): "Duplex, omnia fiant, ut in Dedicatione Ecclesiae Sanctj Marcj, cum suis psalmis, in cantu plano, sine organis, nisi venerit in Domenica . tunc fit cum cantoribus, et organis, cum commemoratione Dominicae."

15. See Selfridge-Field, "Gabrieli and the Organ," 17, and Moore, *Vespers* 1:301.

16. In the appendix, I have grouped together those documents on a particular service and for a particular feast. Since the discussion proceeds according to more generalized topics, the documents are not discussed in numerical order. Nonetheless, all of them can be located by the numbers cited in the text.

17. On the *alternatim* performance of psalms, see Banchieri, *L'Organo suonarino* (1605), 45–59; Diruta, *Seconda parte del Transilvano* 4:19–20; and Bottazzi, *Choro et organo*, 136. On the performance of the Magnificat, see Banchieri, *L'Organo suonarino* (1605), 42–44, 90–105; Diruta, *Seconda parte del Transilvano* 4:7–16, 18–19; Fasolo, *Annuale*, 120–56. The *alternatim* performance of office hymns is discussed in Banchieri, *L'Organo suonarino* (1605), 71–86; Diruta, *Seconda parte del Transilvano* 4:1–7; Bottazzi, *Choro et organo*, 84–127; and

Fasolo, *Annuale*, 10–63. On the Te Deum, see Banchieri, *L'Organo suonarino* (1605), 87; Diruta, *Seconda parte del Transilvano*, 4:21; Fasolo, *Annuale*, 4–9.

18. On the *alternatim* performance of Marian antiphons, see Banchieri, *L'Organo suonarino* (1605), 113–17; Diruta, *Seconda parte del Transilvano* 4:20; Bottazzi, *Choro et organo*, 128–35; Fasolo, *Annuale*, 157–60.

19. It is certain that the *alternatim* performance described in the document involves polyphony rather than plainchant, for the singers of the *cappella* were required to be present in church on all Sundays, and we know from an inquest of 1600 that the professional singers' primary duty was to sing *canto figurato*. Psalmody in *falsobordone* was considered beneath the dignity of the ducal chapel, and psalmody in plainchant was relegated to ferial days and the plainchant choir. (See Moore, *Vespers* 1:172, and 1:361 n. 345). The phrase "un verso per uno" at the end of the document is somewhat ambiguous. It may mean merely that the organists played at the place of alternate psalm verses; however, it might also imply that the two organists alternated between themselves and that the "missing" verses were supplied now by the first organist, now by the second.

20. Walter Gerstenberg, foreword to Adrian Willaert, *Opera omnia* (Corpus mensurabilis musicae 3), vol. 8, ed. H. Zenck and W. Gerstenberg: American Institute of Musicology, 1972), x.

21. The structure of this unusual service is described in Moore, *Vespers* 1:127, 180.

22. Banchieri, *L'Organo suonarino* (1605), 38.

23. On the manner in which the organists Giovanni Gabrieli and Paolo Giusti transposed the Magnificat tones in St. Mark's, see Banchieri, *L'Organo suonarino* (1605), 43–44. The entire document is reproduced in Moore, *Vespers* 1:280 (document 130).

The three sets of Magnificat versets published by Frescobaldi in the second book of toccatas show no such transpositions; the settings use the Magnificat tones as given by Banchieri, i.e., Tone 1 with its finalis on D, Tone 2 on G, and Tone 6 on F. See Banchieri, *L'Organo suonarino* (1605), 90–93 and 100–101.

24. Frescobaldi set four of the principal hymns of the church year: *Iste confessor, Ave maris stella*, the "Hinno della Domenica" (*Lucis creator optime*) and the "Hinno dell'Apostoli" (*Exultet celum laudibus*, before Urban VIII's reform of the hymnal).

25. The annotated copy of the liturgy for Matins of Christmas is found in *I-Vmc* Codice Cicogna 1151. It is the edition printed by Pinelli in 1759, cited in n. 10 above. Since the annotations within the volume seem to have been written before the *aggiunte* at the end, and the first of the latter is dated 1798, I would suggest that the marginalia were added sometime during the last four decades of the eighteenth century.

26. While the one example from the *ceremoniale* cites a performance between the organ and the plainchant choir, organ versets were surely used for performances in polyphony as well. The most specific piece of evidence is the rubric that follows the musical setting of *Ave maris stella* in Giovanni Rovetta's first book of *Motetti concertati* (Venice: Alessandro Vincenti, 1635): "Qui si suona un poco con l'Organo, et serve per l'aversetto che segue, poi si ripiglia da capo, principiando dalla proportione, et così l'altre volte." See also Moore, *Vespers* 1:362 n. 359.

Presumably those extant hymn settings of Willaert written for St. Mark's were also performed in this manner, that is, those in *I sacri e santi salmi* . . . (Venice: Gardane, 1555), in manuscripts in Piacenza and Treviso, and possibly some of the settings in the *Hymnorum musica secundum ordinem romanae ecclesiae excellentissimi Adriani Wilart ac aliorum authorum* (Venice: G. Scotto, 1542). On the Piacenza and Treviso cycles, see Jane Weidensaul, *The Polyphonic Hymns of Adrian Willaert* (Ph.D. diss., Rutgers University, 1978), 42–74.

27. *I-Vmc* Codice Cicogna 1151, *Officium in nocte nativitatis domini* . . . , 7, 8, 10, 14, 20, 21, 22, 31, 32.

28. See *Caeremoniale episcoporum iussu Clementis VIII*, 151–52. On the purchase of Clement VIII's *ceremoniale* by the Procurators of St. Mark's, see Moore, *Vespers* 1:74 and 246 (document 44).

29. *I-Vmc* Codice Cicogna 1151, *Benedictio aquae quae fit in nocte Epiphaniae* . . . , 15, 16, 18, 19, 20, 22, 26, 27, 29.

30. See Banchieri, *L'Organo suonarino* (1605), 110–11.

31. Ibid., 38.

32. Frederick Hammond, *Girolamo Frescobaldi* (Cambridge, Mass.: Harvard University Press, 1983), 62.

33. "Missa feriae quintae sexagesimae." See Archivio della Curia Patriarcale, Libroni corali, Registro 3. For a more detailed discussion of the manuscript, see Moore, "Bartolomeo Bonifacio's *Rituum*," n. 25.

34. I am indebted to Anthony Newcomb for the suggestion that the *ricercate dell'organo* might be keyboard *battaglie*. Banchieri also cites the use of a keyboard *battaglia* during Mass although in a different context entirely: that of Easter Sunday, on which the *battaglia* symbolizes the battle between Life and Death described in the Easter sequence *Victimae paschali laudes* ("Mors et vita duello conflixere mirando: dux vitae mortuus, regnat vivus"). See Bonta, "The Uses of the *Sonata da Chiesa*," 84 n. 62.

35. Diruta, *Il Transilvano*, fol. 36r. It is possible, however, that the performance heard by Diruta took place on Carnival Thursday during the *Messa della battaglia* or on Easter Sunday; see above, n. 34.

36. Act of the Procurators of St. Mark's, 28 November 1564, cited in Caffi, *Storia della musica sacra* 1:31.

37. *Messe d'intavolatura d'organo di Claudio Merulo da Correggio organista dell'illustriss. Signoria di Vinetia nella chiesa di San Marco* . . . *Libro Quarto* [sic] (Venice, 1568).

38. There are three organ Masses of Andrea Gabrieli in volume 3 of the Giordano collection in Turin. See Willi Apel, *The History of Keyboard Music to 1700*, trans. Hans Tischler (Bloomington: Indiana University Press, 1972), 121.

39. See above, n. 14.

40. See Denis Arnold, *Monteverdi*, rev. ed. (London, 1975), 29; for the complete document, see Moore, *Vespers* 1:261–62 (document 67).

41. *I-Vmc* Ms. P.D. 183–c, II, fascicolo 21, fol. [2r]: "Li Musici, che sopra gl'organi erano accomodati, cantorono, e suonorono un motetto, mentre processionalmente s'andò in Choro tutti alli loro luoghi."

42. Ibid., fol. [2v]: "finito, Monsignor . . . disse la Messa dello Spirito Santo, leggendo, se bene li Cantori, et Instrumentisti degl'Organi dall'Offertorio in poi fecero Musica."

43. Ignazio Donati, *avvertimenti* to the *Salmi boscarecci* (Venice: Alessandro Vincenti, 1623): "Il Sanctus, et l'Agnus Dei si sono posti così semplici, et brevi alla Venetiana, per sbrigarsi presto, et dar loco al Concerto per l'Elevatione; et a qualche Sinfonia alla Communione." Reproduced in Gaetano Gaspari, *Catalogo della Biblioteca del Liceo Musicale di Bologna* (Bologna: Romagnoli, 1892), 2:216.

44. Grandi had a three-movement Mass published in the *Raccolta terza di Leonardo Simonetti . . . de messa et salmi del Sig. Alessandro Grandi et Gio. [Croce] Chiozotto* (Venice: Magni, 1630). Rovetta's three-movement Masses were published in his *Messa e salmi* (Venice: Alessandro Vincenti, 1639) and his *Salmi a tre, et quattro voci . . . et nel fine un Kyrie, Gloria, et Credo pur à tre voci* (Venice: Alessandro Vincenti, 1642).

45. See Selfridge-Field, *Venetian Instrumental Music*, 18 n. 56.

46. Bonta, "The Uses of the *Sonata da Chiesa*"; see n. 7 above.

47. On the organization of the *Fiori musicali* and the liturgical significance of its contents, see Apel, *The History of Keyboard Music*, 477–83; Hammond, *Frescobaldi*, 203–12, 285–87; Anthony Newcomb, "Girolamo Frescobaldi," *The New Grove Dictionary of Music and Musicians* (London: Macmillan, 1980), 6:832–33; Bonta, "The Uses of the *Sonata da Chiesa*," 72–75, 78. The places at which Frescobaldi directs independent organ compositions to be inserted into the Mass—*avanti la Messa, dopo l'Epistola, dopo il Credo, per l'Elevazione,* and *post il Comunio*—correspond quite closely with the points at which the rubrics of St. Mark's sanctioned motets (or other para-liturgical music): before the Mass, at the Gradual, the Offertory, the Elevation, the Communion, and at the very end of Mass.

48. See Banchieri, *L'Organo suonarino* (1605), 7–21; Fasolo, *Annuale*, 64–119; Bottazzi, *Choro et organo*, 14–82; Diruta, *Seconda parte del Transilvano* 4:16–17. See also the organ Masses in Croci's *Frutti musicali*, 2–20, 45–86. While Frescobaldi states that his Kyrie versets can be used in other contexts, it is doubtful that they could serve for all five items of the Ordinary.

49. The most complete survey of the repertoire of Masses in the *stile concertato* published in Italy during the first half of the seventeenth century is found in Jerome Roche, "North Italian Liturgical Music in the Early Seventeenth Century" (Ph.D. diss., Cambridge University, 1967), 233–48, and in idem, "Liturgical Music in Italy, 1610–60," *New Oxford History of Music*, 5 (London: Oxford University Press, 1975): 350–70. On the size of musical establishments outside of Venice, see Roche, "Music at Santa Maria Maggiore in Bergamo, 1614–43," *Music and Letters* 47 (1966): 296–312, and Anne [Mary Nicole] Schnoebelen, "The Concerted Mass at San Petronio in Bologna, ca. 1660–1730: A Documentary and Analytical Study" (Ph.D. diss., University of Illinois, 1966). A more detailed study of the *cappella* in Bergamo over a limited period is found in John Westcott, "Music at Santa Maria Maggiore under Alessandro Grandi, 1627–1630: An Archival Study" (unpublished typescript), which shows that elaborate polychoral works employing the full resources of the *stile concertato* were by no means beyond the reach of major provincial churches.

50. The explanation of the three trials for the organists of St. Mark's is reproduced in Moore, *Vespers* 1:237 (document 21), and it was printed earlier in Caffi, *Storia della musica sacra* 1:28. See also James Haar, "The *Fantasie et recerchari* of Giuliano Tiburtino," *Musical*

Quarterly 59 (1973): 235–36 for an attempt to correlate the types of compositions to be improvised with surviving prints.

51. I do not think there is any significance in the language that refers to the organs of the basilica now in the singular, now in the plural. To be sure, both organs were used on major feasts and only one on minor feasts; however, there seems to be no consistency in the use of singular and plural forms. In fact, within a single source, both forms may be used to describe the same liturgical item.

52. Perhaps the most frustrating lacuna is the absence of an explanation of the function of the *intonazioni* of Andrea and Giovanni Gabrieli. Murray Bradshaw's theory that the Venetian toccata developed from the *intonazione* which, in turn, had stemmed from keyboard *falsobordoni* would theoretically link all three genres with the performance of Vespers psalms; however, the ceremonial documents are silent on the topic. See Bradshaw, *The Origin of the Toccata* (n.p.: American Institute of Musicology, 1972), 19–41 and 93–129; and idem, *The Falsobordone* (Neuhausen-Stuttgart: American Institute of Musicology, 1978), 73–81. [Bradshaw's theory has been disputed; see Alexander Silbiger, *Italian Manuscript Sources of Seventeenth-Century Keyboard Music* (Ann Arbor: UMI Research Press, 1980), 191 n. 1, 192 n. 4.—*Ed.*]

Bibliography of Frescobaldi's Printed Collections, with Key to Short Titles

THIS BIBLIOGRAPHY is limited to seventeenth-century printed collections containing exclusively works by Frescobaldi. The publishing history of the printed collections is rather complex, since some collections appeared in several successive editions, in some cases merely with a revised title page, but in other cases with substantial changes of the contents. The collections are listed in alphabetical order by short title, and for each collection according to the chronological order of the editions. The short titles used in this volume occasionally include more of the original title than given below, in order to highlight a specific feature of a collection. References to short titles without dates apply to all editions of a collection, as listed in the generic entries.

The following information is provided in the entries:

Original title. The parts of the title that are descriptive of the contents, intended performance medium, and format (e.g., *intavolatura*, *partitura*) have been included, but those that refer to the composer, editor, dedicatee, and publisher have been omitted. Original spellings have been preserved, but capitalization follows modern bibliographic practice and some punctuation has been added for clarification. Line breaks and other typographic features are not shown. Complete transcriptions of the text of title pages and typographical features are given in Hammond and Mischiati (see below); Mischiati also provides full texts of the dedications and prefaces. A remark on the relation of the edition to an earlier edition sometimes follows the titles, or, when the title is identical, takes its place.

Facts of publication. Place, publisher, and year of publication.

Format. Open score refers to four-stave score intended primarily for keyboard performance (*partitura*); keyboard score refers to two-stave score, ordinarily with six lines in the upper staff and eight lines in the lower staff (*intavolatura*).

Dedication. Name of dedicatee, and title or office as given in the dedication (common titles are anglicized). The last name of the dedicator is given in parentheses, and is followed by the place and date of the dedication when provided.

Modern editions. Only the most comprehensive and reliable scholarly editions are listed; for additional modern editions, see Hammond and Newcomb. An asterisk indicates that an edition does not include the complete musical content of the collection.

Sigla or entry numbers in work catalogues and bibliographies. The final line of each entry provides the sigla or entry numbers (if available) in Hammond, Mischiati, RISM, Sartori, and Vogel. These reference works provide information on the location of surviving copies (the listings in Hammond and Mischiati are the most current and comprehensive).

Work Catalogues and Bibliographies

Hammond, Frederick. "Catalogue of Works," in *Girolamo Frescobaldi*, 274–325. Cambridge, Mass.: Harvard University Press, 1983.

Mischiati, Oscar. "Catalogo delle edizioni originali delle opere di Girolamo Frescobaldi." In *Frescobaldi e il suo tempo*, 44–75. Venice: Marsilio Editore, 1983.

Newcomb, Anthony. "Girolamo Frescobaldi." In *The New Grove Italian Baroque Masters*, 125–27. New York: Norton, 1984.

(RISM) *Répertoire international des sources musicales. A/I/3*, Einzeldrücke vor 1800, ed. Karlheinz Schlager. Kassel: Bärenreiter, 1971–81.

Sartori, Claudio. *Bibliografia della musica strumentale italiana stampata in Italia fino al 1700*. 2 vols. Florence: Olschki, 1952–68.

Vogel, Emil, et al. *Bibliografia della musica italiana vocale profane pubblicata dal 1500 al 1700*. Pomezia: Minkoff, 1977.

Modern Editions

Darbellay, Etienne, ed. *Girolamo Frescobaldi: Opere complete*, vols. 2–4. Milan: Suvini Zerboni, 1977–84.

Harper, John. "The Instrumental Canzonas of Girolamo Frescobaldi: A Comparative Edition and Introductory Study." Ph.D. dissertation, University of Birmingham, 1975.

Jacobs, Charles. *Frescobaldi's Il primo libro de madrigali a cinque voci*. University Park: Pennsylvania State University Press, 1983.

Pidoux, Pierre, ed. *Girolamo Frescobaldi: Orgel- und Klavierwerke*, 5 vols. Kassel: Bärenreiter, 1949–54.

Shindle, W. Richard, ed. *Girolamo Frescobaldi: Keyboard Compositions Preserved in Manuscript*. 3 vols. American Institute of Musicology, 1966.

Spohr, Helga, ed. *Girolamo Frescobaldi: Arie musicali (Florence 1630)*, Musikalische Denkmäler, vol. 4. Mainz: Schott, 1960.

Thomas, Bernard, ed. *The Ensemble Canzonas of Frescobaldi*. 10 vols. London: London Pro Musica, 1975–77.

Frescobaldi's Printed Collections

Arie = Arie musicali I and Arie musicale II

Arie musicali I (1630): *Primo libro d'arie musicali per cantarsi nel gravicembalo, e tiorba, a una, a dua, e a tre voci*. Florence: Gio. Battista Landini, 1630.
Format: Score.

Dedication: Ferdinando II, Grand Duke of Tuscany (Frescobaldi).

Modern edition: Spohr.

Hammond: III.A.5. Mischiati: 11. RISM F 1854. Vogel: 1021.

Arie musicali II (1630): *Secondo libro d'arie musicali per cantarsi nel gravicembalo, e tiorba, a una, a dua, e a tre voci.* Florence: Gio. Battista Landini, 1630.

Dedication: Marchese Roberto Obizzi, Cavallerizzo Maggiore to the Grand Duke of Tuscany (Frescobaldi).

Format: Score.

Modern edition: Spohr.

Hammond: III.A.6. Mischiati: 12. RISM F 1854. Vogel: 1022.

Canzoni (score, 1628): *In partitura: Il primo libro delle canzoni a una, due, tre, e quattro voci, per sonare con ogni sorte di stromenti; con dui toccate in fine: una per sonare con spinettina sola, overo liuto, l'altra spinettina è violino, overo liuto, e violino.* Ed. Bartolomeo Grassi. Rome: Paolo Masotti, 1628.

Dedication: Mons. Girolamo Bonvisi, chierico di camera (Grassi), Rome, 1628.

Format: Score.

Modern editions: Harper, Shindle 3*, Thomas*.

Hammond: II.2. Mischiati: 8a. RISM: F 1869. Sartori: 1628i.

Canzoni (partbooks, 1628): *Il primo libro delle canzoni a una, due, trè, e quattro voci, accomodate per sonare ogni sorte de stromenti.* Rome: Gio. Battista Robletti, 1628.

Format: Five partbooks.

Dedication: Ferdinando II, Grand Duke of Tuscany (Frescobaldi).

Modern editions: Harper, Thomas*.

Hammond: II.2a. Mischiati: 8b. RISM: F 1868. Sartori: 1628j.

Canzoni (1634): *Canzoni da sonare a una, due, tre, et quattro, con il basso continuo.* Venice: Alessandro Vincenti, 1634.

Format: Five partbooks.

Dedication: Desiderio Scaglia, Cardinal of Cremona (Frescobaldi), Venice, 10 January 1635.

Modern editions: Harper, Thomas*.

Hammond: II.3. Mischiati: 8c. RISM: F 1870. Sartori: 1634.

Canzoni (1645): *Canzoni alla francese in partitura.* Ed. Alessandro Vincenti. Venice: Alessandro Vincenti, 1634.

Format: Open score.

Dedication: Giovanni Pozzo, Abbot of S. Salvatore di Venezia (Vincenti), 15 December 1644.

Modern edition: Pidoux 1.

Hammond: I.A.8. Mischiati: 7. RISM: F 1872. Sartori: 1645a.

Capricci = Capricci (1624), (1626), (1628), (1642).

Capricci (1624): *Il primo libro di capricci fatti sopra diversi sogetti, et arie, in partitura.* Rome: Luca Antonio Soldi, 1624.

Format: Open score.

Dedication: Alfonso d'Este, Prince of Modena (Frescobaldi), Rome, 12 April 1624.

Modern editions: Darbellay 3, Pidoux 2.

Hammond: I.A.5. Mischiati: 5a. RISM: F 1862. Sartori: 1624b.

Capricci (1626): *Il primo libro di capricci, canzon francese, e recercari, fatti sopra diversi soggetti, et arie, in partitura.* Combines the content of *Recercari* (1615) with that of *Capricci* (1624), with some revisions. Venice: Alessandro Vincenti, 1626.

Format: Open score.

Dedication: None.

Modern editions: See *Capricci* (1624).

Hammond: I.A.5a. Mischiati: 5b. RISM: F 1863. Sartori: 1626i.

Capricci (1628): Reprint of *Capricci* (1626). Venice: Alessandro Vincenti, 1628.

Hammond: I.A.5b. Mischiati: 5c. RISM: F 1864. Sartori: 1628l.

Capricci (1642): Revised reprint of *Capricci* (1626). Venice: Alessandro Vincenti, 1642.

Hammond: I.A.5c. Mischiati: 5d. RISM: F 1865. Sartori: 1642h.

Fantasie (1608): *Il primo libro delle fantasie a quattro.* Milan: Herede di Simon Tini, & Filippo Lomazzo, 1608.

Format: Open score.

Dedication: Francesco Borghese, Duke of Regnano and General of the Holy Church (Frescobaldi), Milan, 8 November 1608.

Modern edition: Pidoux 1.

Hammond: I.A.1. Mischiati: 3. RISM F 1855. Sartori 1608.

Fiori musicali (1635): *Fiori musicali di diverse compositioni, toccate, kirie, canzoni, capricci, e recercari, in partitura a quattro, utili per sonatori.* Venice: Alessandro Vincenti, 1635.

Format: Open score.

Dedication: Cardinal Antonio Barberini (Frescobaldi), Venice, 20 August 1635.

Modern edition: Pidoux 5.

Hammond: I.A.7. Mischiati: 6. RISM: F 1871. Sartori: 1635a.

Liber secundus diversarum modulationum: *Liber secundus diversarum modulationum singulis, binis, ternis, quaternisque vocibus.* Rome: Andrea Fei, 1627.

Format: Five partbooks (only four are extant).

Dedication: Cardinal Scipione Borghese (Frescobaldi), Rome, 1 June 1627.

Modern edition: none.

Hammond: III.B.5. Mischiati: 10. RISM: F 1853.

Madrigali (1608): *Il primo libro di madrigali a cique voci.* Antwerp: Pierre Phalèse, 1608.

Format: Five partbooks.

Dedication: Guido Bentivoglio, Archbishop of Rhodes and Papal Nuntio in Flanders (Frescobaldi), Antwerp, 13 June 1608.

Modern edition: Jacobs.

Hammond: III.A.1. Mischiati: 10. RISM: F 1852. Vogel: 1023.

Recercari = Recercari, et canzoni; Recercari (1615), (1618).

Recercari (1615): *Recercari, et canzoni franzese fatte sopra diversi obligghi. Libro primo.* Rome: Bartolomeo Zanetti, 1615.
> *Format*: Open score.
> *Dedication*: Cardinal [Pietro] Aldobrandini (Frescobaldi).
> *Modern edition*: Pidoux 2.
> Hammond: I.A.4. Mischiati: 4a. RISM: F 1860. Sartori: 1615g.

Recercari (1618): Reprint of *Recercari* (1615). Rome: Bartolomeo Zanetti, 1618.
> Hammond: I.A.4a. Mischiati: 4b. RISM: F 1861. Sartori: 1618g.

Toccate I = Toccate I (1615), (1615–16), (1616–?), (1628), (1637).

Toccate I (1615): *Toccate e partite d'involatura di cimbalo.* Rome: Nicolò Borboni, 1615.
> *Format*: Keyboard score.
> *Dedication*: Dedicatee not named, but coat of arms of Cardinal Duke Ferdinando Gonzaga of Mantua (see *Toccate I* [1615–16]) (Frescobaldi), Rome, 22 December 1614.
> *Modern editions*: Darbellay 2, Pidoux 3*, Shindle 3*.
> Hammond: I.A.2. Mischiati: 1a. RISM: F 1856. Sartori: 1615a.

Toccate I (1615–16): *Toccate e partite d'intavolatura di cimbalo.* Rome: Nicolò Borboni, 1615.
> Revised edition of *Toccate I* (1615) with some additions and substitutions. On p. [v]: Christophorus Blancus sculpsit 1616.
> *Format*: Keyboard score.
> *Dedication*: Cardinal-Duke [Ferdinando Gonzaga] of Mantua and Monferrato (Frescobaldi), Rome, 22 December 1614.
> *Modern editions*: Darbellay 2, Pidoux 3.
> Hammond: I.A.3. Mischiati: 1b. RISM: F 1586/1587. Sartori 1615–1616b.

Toccate I (1616–?): Reprint of *Toccate I* (1615–16) with a revised title page and no date of publication (but must have been issued in 1616 or later). Rome: Nicolò Borboni.
> Hammond: I.A.3a. Mischiati: 1c. RISM: F 1587. Sartori: 1616f.

Toccate I (1628): *Il primo libro d'intavolatura di toccate di cimbalo et organo, partite sopra l'aria di romanesca, ruggiero, monica, follie, e correnti.* Rome: Nicolò Borbone, 1628. Reprint of *Toccate I* (1615–16) with revised title page and added page with portrait of the composer.
> Hammond: I.A.3b. Mischiati: 1d. RISM: F 1858. Sartori: 1628k.

Toccate I (1637): *Toccate d'intavolatura di cimbalo et organo, partite di diversi arie e corrente, balletti, ciaccone, passachagli.* Rome: Nicolò Borbone, 1637. Reprint of *Toccate I* (1615–16) with revised title page (including coat of arms of Cardinal Francesco Barberini), revised preface, no dedication, and an addition of twenty-six pages of new compositions, headed "Aggiunta."
> *Format*: Keyboard score.
> *Modern edition*: Darbellay 2, Pidoux 3.
> Hammond: I.A.8. Mischiati: 1e. RISM: F 1859. Sartori: 1637f.

Toccate II = Toccate II (1627), (1637).

Toccate II (1627): *Il secondo libro di toccate, canzone, versi d'hinni, magnificat, gagliarde, correnti et altre partite d'intavolatura di cimbalo et organo.* [Rome: Nicolò Borbone, 1627?]

Format: Keyboard score.

Dedication: Luigi Gallo, Bishop of Ancona and Nuntio of Savoy (Frescobaldi), Rome, 15 January 1627.

Modern editions: Darbellay 3, Pidoux 4*, Shindle 3*.

Hammond: I.A.6. Mischiati: 2a. RISM: F 1866. Sartori: 1627b.

Toccate II (1637): Reprint of *Toccate II* (1627) with revised title page and omission of the last two compositions. Rome: Nicolò Borbone, 1637.

Modern editions: Darbellay 3, Pidoux 4.

Hammond: I.A.6a. Mischiati: 2b. RISM: F 1867. Sartori: 1637b.

Index

Contributors

Alexander Silbiger teaches at Duke University. His publications include *Seventeenth-Century Manuscript Sources of Italian Keyboard Music* and Matthias Weckmann, *Sacred Concertos*.

Claudio Annibaldi teaches at the Conservatorio di Musica S. Cecilia in Rome. His publications include *Bibliografia e catalogo delle opere di Goffredo Petrassi*.

Victor Coelho teaches at the University of Calgary. His publications include *Chitarrone Music Preserved in Manuscript Sources*.

Etienne Darbellay teaches at the University of Geneva. He is editor of several volumes of the *Opere Complete* of Frescobaldi and of C. P. E. Bach, *Sechs Sonaten mit veränderten Reprisen*.

Sergio Durante is a doctoral candidate at Harvard University. He is editor of *Nuovissimi studi Corelliani* and *Catalogo dei manoscritti del Conservatorio Cesare Pollini di Padova*.

Emilia Fadini teaches at the Conservatorio di Musica Giuseppe Verdi in Milan. She is editor of the *Opere Complete* of Domenico Scarlatti published by Ricordi.

Frederick Hammond teaches at the University of California at Los Angeles. His publications include *Girolamo Frescobaldi* and *Ralph Kirkpatrick: Early Years*.

John Harper is on the faculty of Magdalen College, Oxford University. His publications include *The Instrumental Canzonas of Girolamo Frescobaldi* and Orlando Gibbons, *Consort Music* (Musica Brittanica, vol. 48).

John Walter Hill teaches at the University of Illinois in Champaign/Urbana and is former general editor of the *Journal of the American Musicological Society*. His publications include *The Life and Works of Francesco Maria Veraccini* and *Studies in Musicology in Honor of Otto E. Albrecht*.

James Ladewig teaches at the University of Rhode Island. His publications include *Frescobaldi's "Recercari et canzoni franzese"* and *Italian Instrumental Music of the 16th and Early 17th Centuries*.

Margaret Murata teaches at the University of California at Irvine. Her publications include *Operas at the Papal Court, 1631–1668*, and *Cantatas by Marc'Antonio Pasqualini*.

Anthony Newcomb teaches at the University of California at Berkeley and is general editor of the *Journal of the Musicological Society of America*. His publications include *The Madrigal at*

Ferrara and *Girolamo Frescobaldi* in *The New Grove Italian Baroque Masters*.

Susan Parisi is a doctoral candidate at the University of Illinois at Champaign/Urbana.

Friedrich Wilhelm Riedel teaches at the Johannes Gutenberg Universität in Mainz. His publications include *Quellenkundliche Beiträge zur Geschichte der Musik fur Tasteninstrumente* and *Kirchenmusik am Hofe Karls VI*.

W. Richard Shindle teaches at Kent State University. His publications include Girolamo Frescobaldi, *Keyboard Compositions Preserved in Manuscripts*.